Communications in Computer and Information Science 933

Commenced Publication in 2007
Founding and Former Series Editors:
Phoebe Chen, Alfredo Cuzzocrea, Xiaoyong Du, Orhun Kara, Ting Liu, Dominik Ślęzak, and Xiaokang Yang

More information about this series at http://www.springer.com/series/7899

Kirstin Krauss · Marita Turpin
Filistea Naude (Eds.)

Locally Relevant ICT Research

10th International Development Informatics Association Conference, IDIA 2018
Tshwane, South Africa, August 23–24, 2018
Revised Selected Papers

Springer

Editors
Kirstin Krauss
University of South Africa
Johannesburg, South Africa

Filistea Naude
University of South Africa
Johannesburg, South Africa

Marita Turpin
University of Pretoria
Pretoria, South Africa

ISSN 1865-0929 ISSN 1865-0937 (electronic)
Communications in Computer and Information Science
ISBN 978-3-030-11234-9 ISBN 978-3-030-11235-6 (eBook)
https://doi.org/10.1007/978-3-030-11235-6

Library of Congress Control Number: 2018966825

This Springer imprint is published by the registered company Springer Nature Switzerland AG
The registered company address is: Gewerbestrasse 11, 6330 Cham, Switzerland

Preface

There is still little consensus among scholars on what development means, who and what needs to be developed, and for what purpose. This raises fundamental questions for future directions in development informatics research and brings to mind Professor Geoff Walsham's question, "Are we making a better world with technology?" (Walsham, 2012). A predominant perspective is that ICTs can support the development, promotion and realization of a model of development that is holistic, inclusive, just, and sustainable, which will lead to an appropriate quality of life for each individual on the planet. However, ICTs have not delivered on the promise of making a better world for all; and there is evidence that technology has increased inequality in many cases (Toyama, 2015).

As such, the goal of the IDIA conferences is to provide delegates with an opportunity to share ideas and research on the use of ICT for developing economies and societies, where different constraints impact on the use of ICT compared to highly developed regions. IDIA aims to balance the need for a high level of academic input from all involved with the need to develop emerging researchers. The 10th IDIA conference offered the opportunity to look back, take stock, and debate the way ahead. Accepted papers reflect local and international discourses in ICT4D, in keeping with the 10th IDIA conference theme of "Making ICT Research Locally Relevant." Given the interdisciplinary focus of our conference theme, we recognized that the debate would not be complete without industry and government representation or without a renewed emphasis on quality research education. Inevitably, we also asked questions about how to better understand these problems and challenges.

In a keynote at the third IDIA conference, Professor Ron Weber reflected on how our discourse is sustained by the research findings we present: "Is the field of ICT4D research still driven too much by rhetoric and not enough by rigor and have we been able to gain reasonable levels of consensus about the realities we face?" (Weber, 2009). We believe that our review processes should not be divorced from what we seek to interrogate with our conference theme. We therefore invited papers that reflect on the local relevance of the research undertaken. Full research papers that considered novel designs, new technologies, project assessments, policy analyses, impact studies, theoretical contributions, and social issues around ICT and development were considered. Manuscripts were evaluated according to their novel research contribution, methodological soundness, theoretical framing and reference to related work, quality of analysis, and quality of writing and presentation. Authors were encouraged to address the diversity of approaches in their research by providing context, implications, and actionable guidance to researchers and practitioners beyond the researchers' primary domains.

This year we were fortunate to have Professor Geoff Walsham from Judge Business School, University of Cambridge, as keynote speaker. We also co-hosted an IFIP 9.4 Masters and Doctoral Symposium for Sub-Saharan Africa (Southern and Eastern). This was chaired by Professor Caroline Khene and Ms. Gugu Baduza with Professor Walsham and the IFIP 9.4 Chair, Professor Robert Davison from the City University of Hong Kong, as invited speakers. Our international Program Committee of 66 members contributed hugely to the quality of the papers. A total of 61 papers were submitted. Each paper was reviewed by at least three Program Committee members in a rigorous double-blind peer review process. Authors had to submit corrected versions of the papers before final decisions were made about the papers' acceptance. The review process concluded with 20 papers and an acceptance rate of 33% for the Springer CCIS volume.

Thank you again to our Program Committee and authors for making this conference a success, and a great thanks to Ms. Cecile Koopman and her team, who so diligently managed paper submissions and Springer template compliance checks.

October 2018

Kirstin Krauss
Marita Turpin
Filistea Naude

References

Walsham, G. (2012). Are we making a better world with ICTs? Reflections on a future agenda for the IS field. Journal of Information Technology, 27(2), 87–93. https://doi.org/10.1057/jit.2012.4

Kentaro Toyama, (2015). Special for USA TODAY, May 29, Can technology offer solutions to inequality?, Available online at: https://www.usatoday.com/story/tech/2015/05/29/kentaro-toyama-guest-column-inequality-zuckerberg-braff-clinton/28034093/

Weber, R. (2009). Research on ICT for development: some reflections on rhetoric, rigor, reality and relevance. In: Proceedings of the 3rd International IDIA development informatics conference. 28–30 October 2009.

Organization

Steering Committee

Conference Chair

Judy van Biljon	University of South Africa, South Africa

Proceedings Chairs

Kirstin Krauss	University of South Africa, South Africa
Marita Turpin	University of Pretoria, South Africa
Filistea Naudé	University of South Africa, South Africa

Postgraduate Symposium Chairs

Caroline Khene	Rhodes University, South Africa
Gugulethu Baduza	Rhodes University, South Africa

Program Chairs

Marlien Herselman	CSIR, MERAKA, South Africa
Adele Botha	CSIR, MERAKA, South Africa

Marketing, Liaison, and Sponsorships

Adele Botha	CSIR, MERAKA, South Africa
Wallace Chigona	University of Cape Town, South Africa
Hossana Twinomurinzi	University of South Africa, South Africa

Conference Administrator

Cecile Koopman	University of South Africa, South Africa

Program Committee

Hanifa Abdullah	University of South Africa, South Africa
Millicent Agangiba	University of Mines and Technology, Ghana
Hans Akkermans	Vrije Universiteit Amsterdam, The Netherlands
Antonio Diaz Andrade	Auckland University of Technology, New Zealand
Farshad Badie	Aalborg University, Denmark
Gugulethu Baduza	Rhodes University, South Africa
Jacqueline Batchelor	University of Johannesburg, South Africa
Anna Bon	Vrije Universiteit Amsterdam, The Netherlands
Adele Botha	CSIR, MERAKA, South Africa
Wallace Chigona	University of Cape Town, South Africa
Baldreck Chipangura	University of South Africa, South Africa

Marijke Coetzee	University of Johannesburg, South Africa
David Salomão Cumbula	Instituto Nacional das Comunicações de Moçambique, Mozambique
Robert M. Davidson	City University of Hong Kong, SAR China
Carina de Villiers	University of Pretoria, South Africa
Andrew M. Dearden	Sheffield Hallam University, UK
Melissa Densmore	University of Cape Town, South Africa
Godwin Dzvapatsva	University of the Western Cape, South Africa
Sunet Eybers	University of Pretoria, South Africa
Wernher Friedrich	University of South Africa, South Africa
Malcolm Garbutt	University of Cape Town, South Africa
Aurona Gerber	University of Pretoria, South Africa
Apostolos Giannakopoulos	University of South Africa, South Africa
Marie Hattingh	University of Pretoria, South Africa
Richard Heeks	University of Manchester, UK
Marlien Herselman	CSIR, MERAKA, South Africa
Marlene Holmer	University of Pretoria, South Africa
Grant Howard	University of South Africa, South Africa
Gloria Iyawa	University of Namibia, Namibia
Lynette Jacobs	University of the Free State, South Africa
Leandra Jordaan	Central University of Technology, South Africa
Caroline Khene	Rhodes University, South Africa
Sim Lau	University of Wollongong, Australia
Awie Leonard	University of Pretoria, South Africa
Carmen Leong	University of New South Wales, Australia Business School, Australia
Oláñrewájú O Lewis	Rhodes University, South Africa
Maria Barbosa Lima Toivanen	VTT Technical Research Centre of Finland, Finland
Hugo Lotriet	University of South Africa, South Africa
Mario Marais	CSIR, MERAKA, South Africa
Nita Mennega	University of Pretoria, South Africa
Jan Mentz	University of South Africa, South Africa
Mvurya Mgala	University of Cape Town, South Africa
Bojelo Esther Mooketsi	University of Botswana, Botswana
Yusuf Motara	Rhodes University, South Africa
Hafeni Mthoko	Rhodes University, South Africa
Selina Mudavanhu	University of Johannesburg, South Africa
Samwel Mwapwele	University of Cape Town, South Africa
Joshua Rumo A. Ndiege	United States International University-Africa, Kenya
Tembisa Ngqondi	University of Mpumalanga, South Africa
Petter Nielsen	University of Oslo, Norway
Melanie Platz	University of Koblenz-Landau, Germany
Tania Prinsloo	University of Pretoria, South Africa
Karen Renaud	Abertay University, UK
Jaco Renken	University of Manchester, UK

Hanlie Smuts	University of Pretoria, South Africa
Riana Steyn	University of Pretoria, South Africa
Bobby Tait	University of South Africa, South Africa
Hannah Thinyane	United Nations University, Macau, SAR China
Mamello Thinyane	United Nations University, Macau, SAR China
Pitso Tsibolane	University of Cape Town, South Africa
Hossana Twinomurinzi	University of South Africa, South Africa
Jean-Paul Van Belle	University of Cape Town, South Africa
Ronell Van der Merwe	University of South Africa, South Africa
Alta Van der Merwe	University of Pretoria, South Africa
Izak Van Zyl	Cape Peninsula University of Technology, South Africa
Gamel Wiredu	Ghana Institute of Management and Public Administration, Ghana

Sponsor

Unisa, College of Science, Engineering and Technology

UNISA college of science, engineering and technology

Contents

ICT Adoption and Impact

An Investigation of the Government-Related Factors that Inhibit Small to Medium Enterprises' Adoption and Effective Use of Information and Communication Technology in Developing Countries: The Case of Zimbabwe

Peter Makiwa(✉) and Riana Steyn

Department of Informatics, University of Pretoria, Pretoria, South Africa
pmakiwa@gmail.com, riana.steyn@up.ac.za

Abstract. The utilisation and adoption of information and communication technologies (ICTs) in small to medium enterprises (SMEs) around the world has had a significant effect on most economies, and has resulted in sustainable growth and prosperity. This has led most global governments to develop an interest in the development of SMEs; however, most SMEs in developing countries, including Zimbabwe, are still ages behind their counterparts in developed countries with regard to the application of ICTs in business processes. The reviewed literature for this study indicates that the Zimbabwean government has failed to stimulate the adoption of ICT and its use in Zimbabwean SMEs in recent decades. This paper seeks to reveal key government-related factors and strategies that can lead to the effective adoption of ICTs in the SME sector. A case study and qualitative methodology was employed for this investigation. This facilitated an all-encompassing view of the phenomenon under study. The approach utilised semi-structured interviews to collect data, and employed a thematic analysis method. The research findings revealed that key factors that impact on ICT adoption in Zimbabwean SMEs include a lack of government support, poor policy formulation, implementation and awareness, a lack of finances, and inadequate infrastructure. Key strategies outlined in this paper include the introduction of ICT import subsidies, tax rebates for SMEs, the formulation of SME-friendly policies, the expansion of electricity and Internet infrastructure to marginalised areas, and the establishment of government ICT centres to stimulate the adoption of ICT and its use in SMEs.

Keywords: Small to medium enterprise
Information and communication technology · Government policies

1 Introduction

According to Abor and Quartey [1], small to medium enterprises (SMEs) account for more than 70% of new jobs in both developing and developed countries, and play a critical role in enhancing gross domestic product (GDP). Globally, the adoption of

K. Krauss et al. (Eds.): IDIA 2018, CCIS 933, pp. 3–16, 2019.
https://doi.org/10.1007/978-3-030-11235-6_1

information and communication technology (ICT) in most SMEs has transformed the business landscape, resulting in critical social and economic developments that have stimulated every aspect of human life [2]. Meso, Musa and Mbarika [3] also point out that the integration of ICT tools in SME business processes will enhance their competitive edge in any economy.

Most SMEs in Zimbabwe still lack the means and knowledge to apply ICT effectively in their business operations, resulting in a lack of innovation, poor and inferior products and services, and an insignificant contribution to GDP [4]. Tsarwe [5] believes that the key driver of the adoption of ICT in Zimbabwean SMEs is the effective implementation of government policies and support. National policies have the potential to affect the adoption of ICT in organisations either positively or negatively, as policy-makers can coin policies that create an enabling environment that supports and encourages ICT use [6]. The Zimbabwean government's initiatives and subsidies have not had the desired effect on SMEs' adoption of ICT, and have lacked the appropriate support that could have positively influenced SMEs' use of ICT, hence the need for an effective guideline that supports implementation [7].

The adoption and integration of ICT in Zimbabwean SMEs continue to face severe setbacks that undermine all the government's efforts [5]. Martinsons [8] points out that the government is not aware of the reasons why SMEs are failing to effectively adopt ICT. Information on the challenges that SMEs face in adopting ICT is critical, and can facilitate the development of a guideline that can assist government in stimulating SMEs' adoption of ICT. Despite failing to realise policy goals, the government has not initiated an investigation into how it can play a role in curbing the barriers to SMEs' adoption of ICT.

The next section outlines the research question for the study, followed by a presentation of the study objectives and their significance. This is followed by a literature review which elaborates on the research context – which is the Zimbabwean SME environment and government involvement. The review also outlines ICT in Zimbabwe and ICT adoption factors. Section 2.5 outlines the study's theoretical framework, which consists of the Diffusion of Innovation (DOI) model, the Technology, Organisation and Environment (TOE) model, and the Unified Theory of Acceptance and Use of Technology (UTAUT) model. Section 3 discusses the study's methodology, and Sects. 4 and 5 present the study's results, analysis, discussion and contribution.

1.1 Research Question

What government-related factors inhibit SMEs' adoption and effective use of ICT in Zimbabwe?

1.2 Objective and Significance

This paper highlights the need for an investigation that reveals the government-related challenges that SMEs are facing in adopting ICT. It also recommends key strategies that can help the Zimbabwean government to effectively support SMEs in the adoption of ICT. The paper also reveals key guidelines that the Zimbabwean government can employ to equip SME owners to leverage sophisticated ICT tools and features which facilitate staff training and development, in order to close the technological skills gap in most SMEs.

The significance of the paper lies in presenting evidence and findings that ensure that the government is better positioned to implement ICT policies and initiatives in Zimbabwean SMEs. It is also critical to mention that this paper's findings have a substantial effect on the information systems (IS) discipline that will equip the Ministry of Information and Communication Technology and Cyber Security (MICTCS), as well as the Ministry of Small and Medium Enterprises and Cooperative Development (MSMECD), and give them a deeper understanding of the adoption of ICT.

2 Literature Review

2.1 SMEs in Zimbabwe

The main governing authority of SMEs in Zimbabwe is the MSMECD. This Ministry insists that an organisation should meet certain criteria that relate to the legal structure, the number of employees, and the asset base, for the organisation to be defined as an SME in Zimbabwe [9]. Most SMEs in Zimbabwe are not legally registered under the Companies or Factory and Works Act; hence, these informal entities do not pay corporate tax, and their revenues are not part of the country's economic statistics [9]. The main criterion for SMEs' participation in this study was registration.

With over 300 000 graduates being churned out of the country's colleges and universities every year, SMEs have been earmarked to ease the potentially disastrous unemployment rate; however, only 28% of SMEs in Zimbabwe have more than one employee [10]. The contribution of SMEs to the country's GDP is assessed at 50% [11]. According to Mugozhi and Hlabiso [12], SMEs in Zimbabwe play a focal part in the nation's social and economic advancement. Nyoni and Bonga [13] add that Zimbabwean SMEs are the drivers of economic empowerment and development in the country's formal and informal sectors. Nyoni [9] ascertains that a more grounded SME sector in Zimbabwe can enhance the flexibility of the national economy by expanding and widening economic activity, and subsequently diminishing its weakness during intermittent shocks.

2.2 Zimbabwean Government Support for SMEs

The Government of Zimbabwe developed a small, micro- and medium enterprises (SMMEs) policy document that was affirmed by Cabinet in July 2002. This policy had the mandate to provide a mutual vision for all stakeholders in propelling the SME cause, and empowering them to attain their maximum capacity; however, the policies and initiatives proposed to enhance the growth and sustainability of Zimbabwean SMEs have had poor success, despite the government's effort to promote the SME sector, and the invaluable contributions of SMEs to Zimbabwe's economic development [9]. According to Ndlovu [14], this is mainly due to a plethora of issues that have beset the development of SMEs in Zimbabwe.

The key challenges that have seen the implementation failure of these initiatives are corruption in key government rankings, the lack of decisive leadership, a lack of infrastructure, SMEs' continued constrained access to credit, and, most importantly, the insincerity of purpose caused by senior government officials, and the beneficiaries' abuse of the various initiatives [14]. According to Naicker and Saungweme [15], huge amounts of money obtained from various institutions for the purpose of implementing these policies and programmes, have been diverted and spent elsewhere, which has resulted in these initiatives yielding poor results.

2.3 The Adoption of Information and Communication Technology in Zimbabwe

In recent years, Zimbabwe has seen the liberalisation of various ICT sectors [16]. Over the last decade, ICT in Zimbabwe has been characterised by an assortment of players who have been fighting to remain vibrant in offering efficient Internet, broadcasting and telecommunication services [17]. The government has set up regulatory bodies, such as the Postal and Telecommunications Authority of Zimbabwe (POTRAZ), as a way of acknowledging the critical value of ICT to the economic turnaround of the country [18]; however, the integration of ICT through online business operational platforms is still an unfulfilled dream, with most organisations still relying on traditional means of gaining a competitive edge [5].

2.4 Information and Communication Technology Adoption Factors

Margherita and Petti [19] point out key factors that affect the adoption of ICT, and reveal that effective ICT adoption requires the serious consideration of strategy, people, systems, procedures and culture. Margherita and Petti [19] also add that a systematic view of these elements is imperative in streamlining ICT adoption and process redesign.

Individual Context Factors: Literature recognises owners or managers as critical elements of the ICT adoption process in SMEs [4, 6, 20]. Factors that relate to the owner or manager are mainly concerned with executive decisions, including financial and resource commitments that are made to shape the organisation's direction.

The level of ICT knowledge is another fundamental factor that affects SMEs' adoption of ICT. If SME managers and other organisational members have an acceptable level of ICT knowledge, they can encourage the SME to embrace the appropriate ICT activities in its business [3, 10].

Organisation Context Factors: The support and attitude of SMEs' top management play a vital role in the adoption and use of ICT in the organisation. SME owners and managers are responsible for establishing an appropriate vision, culture and policy for the SME [21].

Among the difficulties that prevent the advancement in SMEs' adoption of ICT is the issue of financial capacity, as it identifies with the measure of resources a firm can utilise to acquire ICT assets for business execution, marketing and the delivery of products and services [22].

According to Zhelyazkov [23], one of the key factors that affect SMEs' adoption of ICT in developing countries, is the lack of proper guidance. Kabanda [24] highlights that most SMEs in developing countries lack the time, energy and ability to migrate to new technologies, mainly because of a lack of expertise, support and guidance.

The adaptability of the training system in an organisation will also affect the adoption of ICT, since this will determine ICT training policies, and how an organisation copes with technological changes, in most cases [24].

Environmental Factors: The government's role in providing different types of mediation has been referred to as a catalyst for the advancement of SMEs' adoption of ICT [2, 25]. Government support can come through policies that facilitate SMEs' operations in the country, institutional support for technological assistance and finance provision, and the sanctioning of well-articulated ICT business laws [26].

Researchers [8, 27] highlight that the capacity of developed nations to receive and utilise ICT at cutting-edge levels has been significantly improved by the proactive role their governments play in providing an enabling infrastructure to enhance the adoption of ICT. Tharayi and Wesley [28] and Alshmrany and Wilkinson [29] have also identified the culture of the business environment in the SME sector as a critical factor that affects the adoption of ICT. Kapurubandara [30] ascertains that an accessible and effective infrastructure is critical to the ICT adoption level of organisations. This relates to the cost and availability of Internet connectivity, electricity supply and the country's telecommunication infrastructure.

2.5 Theoretical Framework

This study utilised three theoretical frameworks: the DOI model, the TOE model and the UTAUT model to facilitate the identification and classification of government-related factors that affect SMEs' adoption of ICT in Zimbabwe.

The DOI model reveals that organisational innovation is directly linked to three elements. These are the external factors of an organisation, internal organisational characteristics, and individual characteristics [31]. The diffusion framework offers an all-encompassing guideline to study SMEs' adoption of ICT, as it contains relational perspectives, and the adoption of decision-making processes that conceptualise the adoption of ICT by SMEs in Zimbabwe.

The TOE framework that was developed by Tornatzky and Fleischer [32] ascertains that three elements (technology, the organisation and the environment) affect how an organisation adopts technology. These elements facilitate the identification of key ICT adoption factors in the framework. The drivers of the adoption of the TOE model are consistent with those in the DOI model, emphasising internal, external and individual characteristics.

The UTAUT model of Venkatesh, Morris, Davis and Davis [33] is the most popular model in the technology acceptance field, as it synthesises perspectives from top technology acceptance models. The model is built on four key constructs: effort expectancy, social influence, performance expectancy, and facilitating conditions. The UTAUT model facilitated the study, as it facilitated the identification of relationships between different variables and government-related ICT adoption factors in Zimbabwean SMEs.

3 Research Method

The research employed a case study strategy with semi-structured interviews, as the main data collection tool. The case study strategy was selected, because it is an ideal approach for an in-depth and holistic analysis and investigation of participants' views, thoughts, and behaviour in organisations [34]. Semi-structured interviews were conducted with three members of 12 SMEs in Zimbabwe. A total of 36 interviews were conducted with employees, managers, supervisors, owners, secretaries, functional officers and administrative personnel. This ensured a broader perspective of the study, as well as data triangulation.

The researcher used non-probability, purposeful sampling to select 12 cases from the population sample, which included the five major Zimbabwean cities of Harare, Masvingo, Bulawayo, Mutare, and Gweru. The University of Pretoria's ethics committee approved and authorised the study, and letters of consent were obtained from each of the participating organisations. The table below outlines the city of origin for the selected SMEs and the industries they represent (Table 1):

Table 1. SME's city of origin and industry

SME	Industry	Area of origin
A	Mining	Gweru
B	Retail	Harare
C	Hospitality	Bulawayo
D	Transport	Harare
E	Legal	Harare
F	Insurance	Mutare
G	Manufacturing	Bulawayo
H	Agricultural	Mutare
I	Manufacturing	Gweru
J	Education	Gweru
K	Retail	Masvingo
L	Technology	Harare

3.1 Data Analysis

The collected data was analysed using thematic analysis. The data was grouped into different themes based mainly on the literature review and repeated response pattern. The identified themes for this research included the following:

- Government's role in the adoption of ICT – This theme identified the role that government plays in facilitating SMEs' adoption of ICT.
- The significance of ICT in the selected SMEs – This theme identified how ICT was significant for the selected SMEs.
- The adoption of sophisticated ICTs – This theme highlighted the SMEs' level of inception of sophisticated ICT tools.

- Involvement of the owner or manager in ICT – This theme facilitated an understanding of SME owners and managers' level of involvement in ICT initiatives.
- ICT barriers – This theme incorporated all factors limiting ICT adoption.
- ICT success factors – This theme included all factors that encouraged SMEs' adoption of ICT.

4 Research Findings

Twelve SMEs participated in this research and 36 members of SMEs were interviewed. Four of the SMEs were based in rural areas, one was based in a semi-urban area, and seven were located in urban areas.

4.1 Government ICT Policy Awareness

With regard to the awareness of government ICT policies, some SMEs highlighted that they had some knowledge of the policies, but they could not elaborate on the critical elements of the policies.

SME A – "*I am not aware of any ICT-related policies that government has put in place. If the policy is there, then no one has brought it to our attention*".

SMEs outlined that government has not made any efforts to make the relevant stakeholders aware of policies that affect SMEs, clearly highlighting that the mandates of the policies have not affected SMEs. Stockdale and Standing [6] point out that national policies could affect the adoption of ICT in organisations negatively or positively, as policy-makers can develop policies to create an enabling environment that supports and encourages ICT use.

4.2 Government Financial Subsidies

SME C – "*Government has neglected to inform the key stakeholders how to access subsidies because if you ask any small business in this area, there are none who know about the subsidies or know how to access them*".

SMEs D and E highlighted that banks still charge them 30% interest, which is equivalent to the charge for large corporates. SMEs I, J, K and L also indicated that they had no access to government financial subsidies, and relied on unconventional means of obtaining funding for their business, including borrowing from friends and family. The other key point SMEs raised was the inaccessibility of cash from banks, which has made it nearly impossible to continue with business operations.

According to Mutula and Van Brakel [22], one of the key challenges that prevent advancement in SMEs' adoption of ICT is the issue of financial capacity, as it allows SMEs to acquire ICT assets for business execution, marketing, and the delivery of products and services.

4.3 Government Support for SME ICT Adoption

When asked how they perceive the importance of government support in the adoption of ICT and its use in their organisations, participants made the following comments:

SME C – "*Government support would be very useful to our efforts to use and adopt ICT. The support should, however, be relevant and add value to small businesses*".

SME G: "I do not think government cares enough to assist marginalised small businesses like ours and the issue is that we do not even know where to go for help with issues related to ICT".

SME I – *"I think government support for small businesses like ours should be through the provision of infrastructure that facilitates ICT use. Government should facilitate the provision of affordable Internet and reliable electricity supply, which are key to the adoption of ICT".*

The above comments confirm the environmental context that Tornatzky and Fleischer [32] highlight in the TOE model, which emphasises that SMEs' adoption of ICT relies heavily on a supportive external environment. This includes government support in various forms, including regulations and financial subsidies that facilitate SMEs' adoption of ICT.

According to Martinsons [8], SMEs in any economy require government support to realise their organisational goals and make a significant contribution to the nation's economy.

4.4 Government Laws, Policies and Regulations

When asked if the current national laws, policies and economic regulations encouraged their business to adopt ICT, the interviewed participants presented the following responses:

SME A – "*The current government regulations actually bring constraints for small businesses, especially in the mining sector*".

Participants from SMEs C and D also pointed out that the current national laws do not protect SMEs from exploitation and abuse by various institutions. The SMEs feel that, for their part in creating employment and alleviating poverty, government has failed to formulate regulations and policies that tackle SMEs' challenges in a systematic manner. According to the participants, this will encourage SMEs to turn their attention from surviving the day-to-day challenges to adopting ICT.

A participant from SME G added that government policies and regulations should be developed in such a way that SMEs can also contend for government tenders. Obtaining tender documents to supply government departments should be decentralised, as the only place one can currently obtain the documents is in Harare.

SME L – "*The problem is that it is not so much government regulations, but the absence of social assistance and the lack of clarity and coordination that exists between government SME agencies and departments that wear small businesses down. The system is now characterised by frustrating bureaucratic procedures and penalties that discourage small business operation*".

The above comments confirm the point raised by Teo and Ranganathan [10]. They state that the current regulatory environment in Zimbabwe is not designed to enhance

SME operations. According to Scupola [26], government SME support should come through practical and implementable policies that facilitate SME operations in the country, institutional support for technological assistance and finance provision, and the sanctioning of well-articulated ICT business laws.

4.5 Lack of Finances

Members of all 12 SMEs indicated lack of finance as a barrier to effectively implementing ICT in their businesses.

SME A – *"It is an expensive endeavour that is quite limiting for us. The cost of running a generator to support ICT initiatives is very constraining. We cannot afford to even upgrade. It is also difficult for us to access bank loans to fund ICT initiatives mainly because we do not have collateral".*

SME L – *"Cost is key because, currently, state-of-the art graphic design software is beyond our reach. We would have to sell all our current hardware just to get our hands on that software".*

The above confirms the point raised by Teo and Ranganathan [10] that most SMEs in developing countries do not have access to bank loans, and will most often fail to obtain capital to enhance their ICT efforts.

4.6 Electricity and Internet Constraints

The issue of electricity and Internet constraints was also pointed out as a negative factor that impacted on the adoption and use of ICT.

SME A – *"We do not have any connection to the electricity grid and we totally rely on the generator. This is discouraging, especially when it comes to using ICT equipment. Despite our location, the electricity grid lines are not far away, but our application has been sitting there for months".*

SME D – *"Internet service is also very bad in that it frequently goes off. We have an asymmetric digital subscriber line (ADSL) connection that gives us problems almost every day. It does not help that it is also expensive".*

Kapurubandara [30] also highlights the negative effect of the lack of reliable infrastructure on SMEs' adoption of ICT.

4.7 Corruption

Eight of the participating SMEs pointed out that one of the major factors that limit their use and adoption of ICT, is rampant corruption in the departments that are linked to SMEs.

SME L – "Indirectly and directly, corruption plays a critical role in the advancement of ICT, not only in the SME sector, but in the country as a whole. These people are selfish and will not part with money to advance SME initiatives".

5 Discussion, Recommendations and Conclusion

5.1 The Zimbabwean Government's Role in SMEs' Adoption and Use of ICT

This section discusses the research findings that relate to the Zimbabwean government's role in the process of Zimbabwean SMEs' adoption of ICT and its use. The insights gained from the research findings indicate that government has a significant role to play in stimulating ICT adoption in Zimbabwean SMEs.

5.2 Government Financial Subsidies

The research findings show that the Zimbabwean government has not offered SMEs any financial subsidies that would facilitate the adoption of ICT. Government has not stepped in to ensure that SMEs have access to cheap loans that would give them an incentive to acquire ICT tools for their businesses. Interest rates are too high for SMEs, and options to import ICT equipment are beyond the reach of these organisations, as they lack the financial muscle to do so. Mutula and Van Brakel [22] confirm the abovementioned point by arguing that SMEs struggle to perform on the same platform as large organisations, without effective government subsidies.

5.3 Government Support for SMEs' Adoption of ICT

The research findings from both the reviewed literature and the interviews indicate that government support for SMEs' adoption of ICT is a critical variable. Insights from the study findings highlight that the Zimbabwean government should provide support for SMEs in their efforts to enhance ICT adoption in their businesses. The government has been called upon to provide support through infrastructure development and accessibility for SMEs, including the provision of electricity and Internet connection. Support through financial facilities that are tailormade for small businesses, was also indicated as being critical. A study by Martinsons [8] confirmed that various forms of government support can stimulate SMEs' adoption of ICT in any economy, which results in the realisation of organisational goals, and makes a significant contribution to the nation's economy. Nyoni [9] confirms the points mentioned above by pointing out that the assistance the Zimbabwean government has offered in recent years has been piecemeal, clumsy, and irrelevant to the critical needs of SMEs, including ICT adoption.

5.4 Government Laws, Policies and Regulations

Insights from the research findings indicate that the current Zimbabwean government regulations, policies and laws that relate to SMEs are actually a major constraint to the operation of small businesses. It is evidently quite difficult for SMEs to even consider the adoption of basic ICT, let alone that of advanced ICT in an environment where policies and laws are constantly squeezing the life out of them. Various studies also emphasise the constraining nature of the regulatory environment in Zimbabwe, highlighting the absence of incentivised policies and schemes that have the potential to drive and stimulate ICT adoption by Zimbabwean SMEs [5, 9].

5.5 Corruption

The officials' diversion of funds meant for ICT policy implementation has become common knowledge in business circles, and is indicated in the research findings. The UTAUT model of Venkatesh et al. [33] also highlights the importance of facilitating conditions that support the effective and efficient adoption of ICT in organisations. These facilitating conditions include a supportive and friendly business environment, in which government plays a key role.

5.6 SME-Friendly Policies and Subsidies

Another key driver of effective and successful ICT adoption highlighted in the research findings is the presence of SME-friendly policies and subsidies. Insights from the research show that well-formulated and relevant policies could change the ICT landscape for a country's business environment. The empirical findings point out that there is limited knowledge and awareness of government policies that relate to SMEs. There is no in-depth understanding of what the policy entails. The abovementioned statement aligns with the views of Kapurubandara [30], who noted in a study in developing nations, that government policies play a critical part in the advancement of SMEs' adoption of ICT.

5.7 Recommendations and Success Strategies

See Table 2.

Table 2. Success strategies

Factor	Success strategy
Enhance government support and initiatives	• Include an extensive consultative process with SMEs when formulating and reviewing policies, regulations and laws that affect the welfare of these organisations
	• Invest in a policy implementation framework that is measurable and quantifiable
	• Formulate SME-friendly policies that assist SMEs in the area of equity finance, and simplify loan acquisition processes for SMEs
	• Embark on policy awareness initiatives that ensure that all SME stakeholders are aware of the current portfolio of policies that affect their welfare

(*continued*)

Table 2. (*continued*)

Factor	Success strategy
	• Set up government ICT centres in marginalised areas to facilitate the coaching and training of SME owners, and the employees on the value of ICT in business, as well as the identification of relevant ICT tools
	• Introduce tax rebates for SMEs that reduce the tax burden on SMEs
	• Introduce import duty subsidies for ICT equipment for SMEs
	• Implement active legislation against corruption, including the tracking and punishment of corrupt government officials
	• Enhance the relationship between SMEs and financial institutions, and suggest workable funding programmes
	• Include mandatory ICT training in the curricula of education and training institutions
Reduce electricity and Internet constraints	• Expand the electricity infrastructure to marginalised areas
	• Implement financial subsidies for SMEs for equipment that supplies alternative energy
	• Improve the quality of service by Internet service providers
	• Subsidise the cost of services for SMEs
Enhance SMEs' finance capacity	• Reduce interest for SME loans
	• Enable easy access to capital for SMEs
	• Enhance relationships between SMEs and financial institutions
	• Enable SMEs to diversify their product and service offerings in order to increase revenue streams

5.8 Research Contributions

This study has contributed considerably to the existing body of literature and the IS field, through the identification of the shortfalls of past studies with regard to the adoption and utilisation of ICT in developing countries, with specific emphasis on Zimbabwe. Empirical evidence from the study identified key constructs that have the potential to stimulate the effective adoption of ICT and its use by Zimbabwean SMEs. The study has also made a considerable contribution by identifying the role of government in a developing country in stimulating the adoption of ICT in the SME sector. This study has made a novel contribution through the identification of key stakeholders that hold the responsibility of enhancing ICT adoption in Zimbabwean SMEs.

This study has also contributed towards practice and policy, through the provision of a rich insight into the experiences of Zimbabwean SMEs in light of the adoption of ICT and its use. The experiences are outlined by the individual responses of the research participants. The analysis of the respondents' perceptions revealed critical areas where the Zimbabwean government needs to take responsibility, and be accountable for SMEs' adoption of ICT. The findings will benefit SMEs in Zimbabwe, as they have exposed key entities and stakeholders that need to play their part to enhance the adoption of ICT.

5.9 Conclusion

Insights from this study revealed key government-related factors that affect the adoption of ICT and its use in Zimbabwean SMEs. Key factors identified included government support, policy formulation and implementation, infrastructure constraints, and access to finance. Significant research contributions from the study were highlighted. These included the identification of key government-related ICT adoption factors in Zimbabwean SMEs, as well as the identification of key practical strategies that government can utilise to stimulate the adoption of ICT by Zimbabwean SMEs.

References

1. Abor, J., Quartey, P.: Issues in SME development in Ghana and South Africa. Int. Res. J. Finance Econ. **39**, 218–228 (2010)
2. Sarosa, S., Zowghi, D.: Strategy for adopting information technology for SMEs: experience in adopting email within an Indonesian furniture company. Electron. J. Inf. Syst. Eval. **6**(2), 165–176 (2003)
3. Meso, P., Musa, P., Mbarika, V.: Moderating information and communication technologies' influences on socioeconomic development with good governance: a study of the developing countries. J. Am. Soc. Inform. Sci. Technol. **57**(2), 186–197 (2006)
4. Caldeira, M.M., Ward, J.M.: Understanding the successful adoption and us of IS/IT in SMEs: an explanation from Portuguese manufacturing industries. Inf. Syst. J. **1**(2), 79–85 (2002)
5. The Herald Business. http://www.herald.co.zw/is-there-value-out-of-the-informal-sector. Accessed 01 June 2016
6. Stockdale, R., Standing, C.: A classification model to support SME e-commerce adoption initiatives. J. Small Bus. Enterp. Dev. **13**(3), 381–394 (2015)
7. Baro, E.E.: A critical examination of information and communication technology policies: effects on library services in Nigeria. Libr. Philos. Pract. **3**(1), 464 (2011)
8. Martinsons, M.G.: Relationship-based e-commerce: theory and evidence from China. Inf. Syst. J. **18**, 331–356 (2008)
9. Nyoni, S.: Small, micro and medium enterprises (SMMEs). Policy and strategy framework. Republic of Zimbabwe (2012)
10. Teo, T.S.H., Ranganathan, C.: Adopters and non-adopters of business-to-business electronic commerce in Singapore. J. Inf. Manage. **42**(1), 89–102 (2004)
11. Republic of Zimbabwe: The Development Framework of Small and Medium Scale Enterprises in Zimbabwe. Government Printers, Harare (2002)
12. Mugozhi, F., Hlabiso, G.: Determinants of small to medium enterprises' success or failure: an ex-post appraisal of startup business by young entrepreneurs in Zimbabwe. Int. J. Humanit. Soc. Stud. **5**(3), 39–46 (2017)
13. Nyoni, T., Bonga, W.G.: Anatomy of the small and medium enterprises (SMEs) critical success factors in Zimbabwe: introducing the 3E Model. J. Bus. Manage. **1**(2), 1–18 (2018)
14. Ndlovu, E.: The performance of microfinance institutions in Zimbabwe. Dev. South. Afr. **20**(1), 129–142 (2013)

15. Naicker, V., Saungweme, P.: Strategic alliances governance in Zimbabwe policy and strategy. Afr. J. Bus. Manage. **3**(8), 325–332 (2014)
16. Zindiye, S., Roberts-Lombard, M.: The influence of human investment on the performance of small and medium enterprises (SMEs) in the manufacturing sector of Harare, Zimbabwe. Afr. J. Bus. Manage. **6**(33), 9431–9436 (2012)
17. Ruhode, E.: E-government for development: a thematic analysis of Zimbabwe's information and communication technology policy documents. Electron. J. Inf. Syst. Dev. Countries **73**(7), 1–15 (2016)
18. Zanamwe, N., Bere, M., Zungura, C., Nyamakura, S.A., Muchangani, B.: E-commerce usage in the pharmaceutical sector in Zimbabwe. J. Internet Bank. Commer. **17**(1), 1–15 (2012)
19. Margherita, A., Petti, C.: ICT-enabled and process-based change: an integrative roadmap. Bus. Process Manage. J. **16**(3), 473–491 (2010)
20. Cragg, P.B., King, M.: Small-firm computing: motivators and inhibitors. MIS Q. **17**(1), 47–60 (2013)
21. Singh, S.: The South African information society: problems with policy, legislation, rhetoric and implementation. J. South. Afr. Stud. **36**(1), 209–227 (2010)
22. Mutula, S.M., Van Brakel, P.V.: ICT skills readiness for the emerging global digital economy among the SMEs in developing economies: case study of Botswana. Libr. Hi Tech News **25**, 231–245 (2007)
23. Zhelyazkov, G.I.: The Impact of ICT Systems on Road Transport SMEs in Australia. Strathclyde University Glasgow, Glasgow (2012)
24. Kabanda, G.: The impact of information and communication technologies (ICTs) on millennium development goals (MDGs): context for diffusion and adoption of ICT innovations in east and Southern Africa. J. Afr. Stud. Dev. **3**(8), 154–170 (2014)
25. Southern, A., Tilley, F.: Small firms and information and communication technologies (ICT): toward a typology of ICT usage. New Technol. Work Employ. **15**(2), 138–154 (2000)
26. Scupola, A.: SMEs' e-commerce adoption: perspectives from Denmark and Australia. J. Enterp. Inf. Manage. **22**(1/2), 152–166 (2010)
27. Dunt, E.S., Harper, I.R.: E-commerce and the Australian economy. Econ. Record **78**(242), 327–342 (2002)
28. Tharayi, S.R., Wesley, R.: Factors affecting students' adoption of ICT tools in higher education institutions: an Indian context. Int. J. Inf. Commun. Technol. Educ.: Official Publication Inf. Resour. Manage. Assoc. **13**(2), 82–94 (2017)
29. Alshmrany, S., Wilkinson, B.: Factors influencing the adoption of ICT by teachers in primary schools in Saudi Arabia. Int. J. Adv. Comput. Sci. Appl. **8**(12), 143–156 (2017)
30. Kapurubandara, M.: A framework to e-transformation SMES in developing countries. Electron. J. Inf. Syst. Dev. Countries **39**(3), 1–24 (2009)
31. Rogers, E.M.: Diffusion of Innovations, 4th edn. The Free Press, New York (1995)
32. Tornatzky, L.G., Fleischer, M.: The Processes of Technological Innovation. Lexington Books, Idaho Falls (1990)
33. Venkatesh, V., Morris, M., Davis, G., Davis, F.: User acceptance of information technology: towards a unified view. MIS Q. **27**(3), 425–478 (2003)
34. The Qualitative Report. https://nsuworks.nova.edu/tqr/vol3/iss3/1. Accessed 27 May 2016

It Should Be There, but It Is Hard to Find: Economic Impact of ICT in Sub-Saharan Economies

Sergey Samoilenko[1(✉)] and Kweku-Muata Osei-Bryson[2]

[1] Averett University, Danville, VA, USA
ssamoilenko@averett.edu
[2] Virginia Commonwealth University, Richmond, VA, USA
kmosei@vcu.edu

Abstract. This study relies on a modified framework of the Networked Readiness Index (NRI) to investigate the presence of relationships between the impact of ICT on innovation and productivity and on micro- and macroeconomic outcomes. The context of the study is a 3-cluster sample of sub-Saharan (SSA) economies, and the time frame is 2012–2015. The results indicate that SSA economies, as a whole, are efficient in translating ICT capabilities into ICT impacts; however, the evidence of efficient translation of ICT impacts into micro- and macroeconomic impacts remains inconclusive. Furthermore, there is no evidence to suggest that higher levels of relative wealth of SSA economies are associated with higher levels of ICT capabilities. The results of the data analysis suggest that the framework of NRI should be supplemented by other constructs if an investigation targets micro- and macroeconomic impacts of ICT capabilities.

Keywords: Sub-Saharan economies · Networked readiness index · Microeconomic outcomes · Macroeconomic outcomes · DEA · Decision trees · Clustering

1 Introduction

Investments in Information and Communication Technologies (ICT) are common to all economies of the world, and they are allocated to pursue common goals of positively impacting context-specific socio-economic targets. ICT is considered to be a backbone of the Fourth Industrial Revolution and new levels of economic growth and social impact [12]. Among the various groups of economies of the world, those of sub-Saharan Africa (SSA) could greatly benefit from the positive socio-economic impact of ICT [1].

The *Networked Readiness Index* (NRI) serves as an established measure of the ICT capabilities, or *drivers*, of socio-economic development [12]. The framework of NRI is reflected by a single composite index comprised of four sub-indexes – three *drivers* (*Environment*, *Readiness*, and *Usage* sub-indexes) and one *Impact* sub-index. An increase in the value of NRI for a given economy is indicative of the increase of the *impact* of ICT on innovation and productivity [4].

K. Krauss et al. (Eds.): IDIA 2018, CCIS 933, pp. 17–34, 2019.
https://doi.org/10.1007/978-3-030-11235-6_2

One of the underlying principles of the framework is that "NRI should provide clear policy guidance" [13] (p. xi) to its users. This is not an easy undertaking to implement, because within the framework "…the complex relationships between ICTs and socio-economic performance are not fully understood and their causality not fully established" [3] (p. 4). Simply put, *drivers* of the framework are not directly associated with *impact*. The presence of the causal association is not essential to the framework, for the basic structure of "if (capabilities), then (impact)" reflects the statement of presence, and not causality. Nevertheless, it is intuitively expected that the higher levels of ICT capabilities would be associated with higher levels of socio-economic impacts.

Conceptually, an impact of any capability on an economy could be perceived from two vantage points – from macroeconomic and microeconomic perspectives. Given the legitimacy and a wide acceptance of the framework of NRI, it may be of benefit to expand it in order to investigate if, in fact, the level of ICT capabilities is associated with the level of the impact of the capabilities, and then, in turn, associated with the levels of the micro- and macroeconomic impact.

Furthermore, the origins, or sources, of ICT capabilities must also be investigated, for capabilities do not appear from nowhere, but, instead, must be crafted. Fundamentally, a capability could be defined as *an ability to utilize a resource for a given purpose.* ICT capability, then, could be defined as an ability of human resources (e.g. labor force) to utilize ICT resources to obtain socio-economic outcomes. As a result, ICT capabilities require investments to be allocated to create resources, and a labor force to utilize them.

Our definition of ICT capabilities is not in discord with the definition of drivers of NRI; instead, it aims to explain why ICT capabilities do not automatically result in the ICT impacts, and why drivers of NRI do not have a direct causal relationship with the impact of NRI. Simply put, we point out the importance of the context (e.g. social, political, geographical, religious, etc.) to the presence of capabilities, and the crucial role that it plays in translating capabilities into impacts.

A simple linear model of the type "*ICT Capabilities → Impacts*" is not sufficient to investigate a sustainability of the process of development, for neither does it explain the sources of capabilities, nor does it elaborate on the outcomes of the impacts. We suggest, instead, that a feedback loop-type of model is preferable, where the various impacts of ICT make their ways to "give back" and contribute towards developing increasingly higher levels of ICT capabilities. Thus, the more appropriate model is "*ICT Capabilities → Impacts → Contribution to ICT Capabilities*". The conceptual model of this investigation is presented in Fig. 1.

It is worth noting that the framework presented above is sufficient to investigate micro- and macroeconomic outcomes of the impact of ICT capabilities, and minimal enough to allow doing so in the most efficient manner. Furthermore, this framework is consistent with a grand economic theory – the framework of Neoclassical Growth Accounting [11]. According to the Neoclassical model, long-term economic growth is a product of capital investment, labor and technological progress. To reconcile the framework of Fig. 1 with the Neoclassical model, we only need to accept the fact that ICT capabilities (e.g. *drivers*) of NRI are not given, but a result of appropriate investments in ICT. The resultant framework is depicted in Fig. 2.

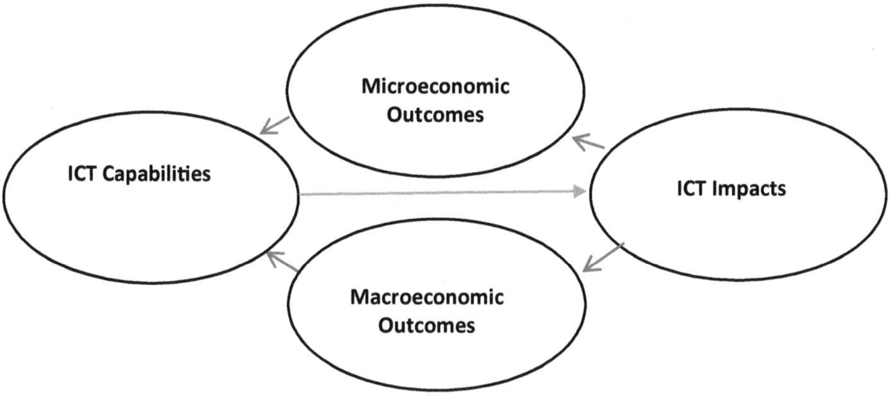

Fig. 1. Conceptual framework of the inquiry

The general question of this investigation, conducted in the context of 26 SSA economies, is that of efficiency and effectiveness of a feedback loop between ICT capabilities and impacts.

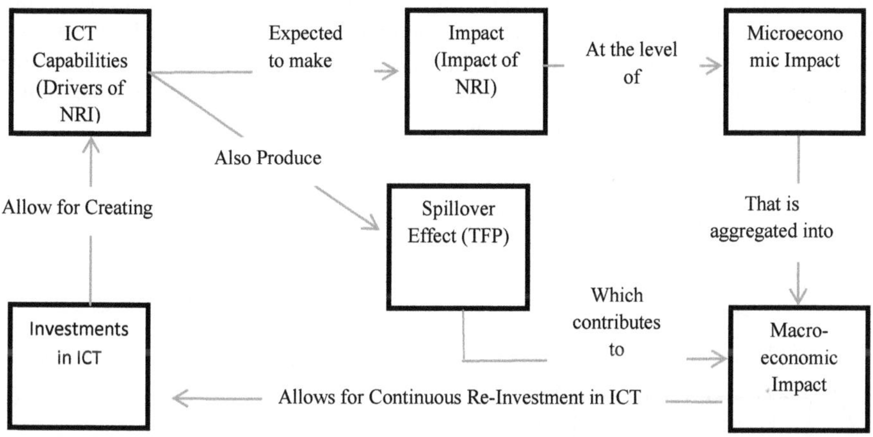

Fig. 2. Integrating framework of NRI with the framework of neoclassical growth accounting

Fundamentally, we are interested in investigating a *presence of a level-based feedback loop "ICT Capabilities → ICT Impacts → ICT Capabilities"*. As a result, the main research goal of this investigation is to find out –

Whether SSA economies that have a high level of ICT Capabilities also have a high level of ICT Impact, and also have high levels of Micro- and Macroeconomic Outcomes that allow for contributing to ICT Capabilities.

In order to accomplish our research goal, we are interested in investigating three general questions:

1. *Whether SSA economies translate, efficiently, ICT capabilities into ICT impacts.*
2. *Whether SSA economies translate, efficiently, impacts of ICT capabilities into macroeconomic and microeconomic targets.*
3. *Whether the macroeconomic and microeconomic targets are efficiently translated into ICT capabilities.*

The proposed conceptual framework serves as a foundation of the research model of our investigation, which is presented next.

2 Research Framework of the Study

In our investigation, we rely on the framework of Networked Readiness [5], the adapted version of which is depicted below in Fig. 3. While the framework allows for a good representation of the state of ICT capabilities and socio-economic impacts, it does not, in its original form, allow for investigating the sustainability of the ICT capabilities (represented by NRI *drivers*). Previous investigations linked investments in ICT to ICT capabilities, as well as ICT capabilities to microeconomic and macroeconomic outcomes [8]. However, in order to reconcile the link "*ICT Capabilities → Microeconomic Outcomes → Macroeconomic Outcomes*" with the framework of NRI, we have to incorporate the *impact* subindex within our research framework. As a result, we arrive at the framework that allows us to investigate relative efficiencies of various links – those associated with the conversion of –

- ICT capabilities into impacts
- impacts into macroeconomic outcomes

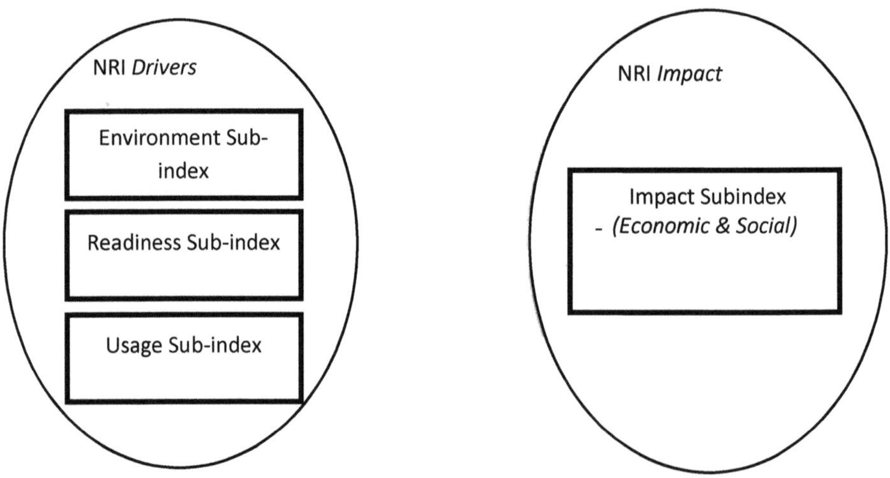

Fig. 3. Framework of NRI

- impacts into microeconomic outcomes
- macroeconomic outcomes into ICT capabilities
- microeconomic outcomes into ICT capabilities

One of the basic premises of this study is that *efficiency of conversion of inputs into outputs contributes to sustainability*. This premise implies that two SSA economies that differ in the scores of the relative efficiencies of conversion of inputs into outputs, will differ, *ceteris paribus*, in the level of sustainability of impacts of inputs on outputs, where a more efficient economy will have a more sustainable mechanism, and a less efficient economy, wasting more resources during the process of conversion, will have a less sustainable mechanism.

Specifically, we are interested in uncovering the presence of any association-type relationship between the levels of inputs and outputs and the relative efficiency of the conversion process (e.g. a high-level economy is more efficient, and a low-level economy is less efficient). In order to proceed with our inquiry, we constructed a research framework depicted in Fig. 4. The proposed framework will allow us to put forward a set of general research questions, as follows:

RQ1: Is there an association between the levels of NRI Drivers and NRI Impact and the relative efficiency of the link "*NRI Drivers → NRI Impact*"?

RQ2: Is there an association between the level of NRI Impact, the values of the macroeconomic outcomes and the relative efficiency of the link "*NRI Impact → Macroeconomic Outcomes*"?

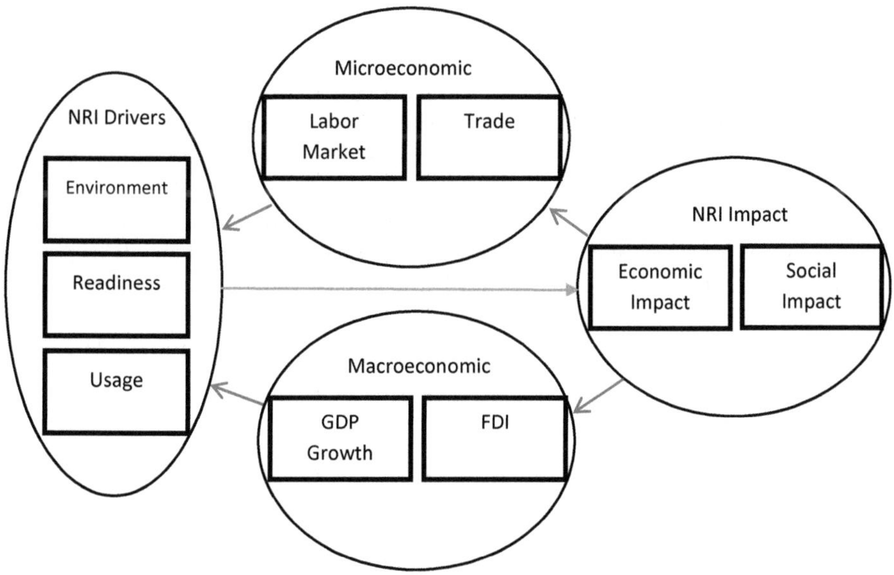

Fig. 4. Research model of the investigation

RQ3: Is there an association between the level of the impact of NRI, the values of the Microeconomic outcomes and the relative efficiency of the link "*Impact → Microeconomic Outcomes*"?
RQ4: Is there an association between the values of the Microeconomic outcomes, the level of NRI Drivers and the relative efficiency of the link "*Microeconomic Outcomes → NRI Drivers*"?
RQ5: Is there an association between the values of the Macroeconomic outcomes, the level of NRI Drivers and the relative efficiency of the link "*Macroeconomic Outcomes → NRI Drivers*"?

Next, we need to operationalize the four constructs of the research model.

3 Description of the Data and Operationalization of the Constructs

In the case of *drivers* and *impact* of NRI, we use the representation provided by the World Economic Forum's Global Information Technology Report, where values of the NRI Index, the NRI sub-indexes, as well as the individual pillars, could be found (latest version is available at www3.weforum.org/docs/GITR2016/WEF_GITR_Full_Report.pdf). The representation of microeconomic outcomes via such proxies as 'state of labor market' and 'state of trade' have been previously utilized (e.g. recently, by [9]).

We obtained the data from three publicly available and highly reputable sources. NRI data was downloaded from the World Economic Forum's Networked Readiness Index page [13], the values of *FDI* and *GDP Growth* were obtained from the Africa Development Indicators of the World Bank [12], and the values of *Labor Market* and *Trade* were obtained from the Millennium Development Goals data set of the World Bank [12].

In 2012, the number and representation of the *pillars* of three sub-indexes, the *drivers*, of NRI, have changed, and it was also the year when the *impact* sub-index was introduced. Given the changes that took place between 2011 and 2012, we decided to concentrate on the new version of NRI, and collect the data for the period between 2012 and 2015 (data for later years were not yet available) (Table 1).

Overall, we were able to compile the data set representing 26 economies of sub-Saharan Africa (the classification of the International Monetary Fund (IMF) as of October 2014). The sample consists of 13 low-income economies, nine low-middle economies, and four upper-middle economies (the classification of the World Bank as of July 2014). Membership of each group of the sample is provided in Table 2.

Table 1. Representation of the constructs

Construct	Measure	Metadata	Source
NRI drivers	Environment	Environment sub-index of NRI	Global information technology report, world economic forum
	Readiness	Readiness sub-index of NRI	
	Usage	Usage sub-index of NRI	
NRI impact	Economic impact	Economic Impacts pillar of *Impact* sub-index	
	Social impact	Social Impacts pillar of *Impact* sub-index	
Macroeconomic outcomes	FDI	Foreign direct investment, net inflows (% of GDP)	Africa development indicators, the world bank
	GDP growth	GDP per capita growth (annual %)	
Microeconomic outcomes	Labor market	Employment to population ratio, ages 15–24, total (%) (modeled ILO estimate)	Millennium development goals, the world bank
	Trade	Trade (% of GDP)	

Table 2. Sample of Sub-Saharan economies, by income level

Income level	Sub-Saharan economies
Low	Burundi, Chad, Ethiopia, Gambia, Kenya, Madagascar, Malawi, Mali, Mozambique, Rwanda, Tanzania, Uganda, Zimbabwe
Low-Middle	Cameroon, Cape Verde, Côte d'Ivoire, Ghana, Lesotho, Nigeria, Senegal, Swaziland, Zambia
Upper-Middle	Botswana, Mauritius, Namibia, South Africa

4 Methodology of the Study

The aim of this part of the paper is to describe the purpose and the expected outcome of each of the four steps of the methodology. For a more comprehensive introduction to the methods and techniques used in the methodology, we refer our readers to [10].

4.1 Step 1: Cluster Analysis (CA)

The purpose of CA is to identify naturally occurring subsets, or groupings, that may exist in the data set, while in our case SSA economies are categorized by the level of income; that categorization is based on the external criteria, and is not NRI specific. By performing CA, we can determine whether SSA economies are alike in terms of NRI-specific criteria, or whether the sample is heterogeneous and consists of multiple subgroups. The outcome of Step 1 is N-cluster solution. It is worth noting that partitioning of the sample into subgroups is logical in nature, where no physical division of the sample takes place.

4.2 Step 2: Data Envelopment Analysis (DEA)

During the second step, we rely on DEA to evaluate the scores of relative efficiencies of the five paths for each of N clusters in the sample. The purpose of using DEA in this investigation is to evaluate the level of efficiency with which inputs of the DEA model are transformed into outputs. DEA is a commonly used application in the area of ICT and productivity research [7]. The outcome of this step is a set of averaged scores for each of the N clusters, which would allow us to identify the benchmark group in the sample of SSA economies (Table 3).

Table 3. DEA models of the investigation

DEA model	DEA inputs	DEA outputs
NRI Drivers → NRI Impact	Environment, Usage, Readiness	Economic Impact, Social Impact
NRI Impact → Macroeconomic Outcomes	Economic Impact, Social Impact	FDI, GDP Growth
NRI Impact → Microeconomic Outcomes	Economic Impact, Social Impact	Labor Market, Trade
Macroeconomic Outcomes → NRI Drivers	FDI, GDP Growth	Environment, Usage, Readiness
Microeconomic Outcomes → NRI Drivers	Labor Market, Trade	Environment, Usage, Readiness

4.3 Step 3: Comparison of the Values of Inputs and Outputs with the Results of DEA

The third phase of the methodology serves the purpose of comparing the values of all the measures of the four constructs of the research models among the N clusters of the data set. Specifically, we want to find out, by means of comparison, the following:

- *Is there is an association between the level of values of NRI Drivers and the level of values of NRI Impact*? It is reasonable to expect that SSA economies with the higher values of NRI Drivers also have higher levels of NRI Impact.
- *Is there is an association between the level of values of NRI and the levels of values of macroeconomic and microeconomic impacts*? Similarly, it is only reasonable to expect that SSA economies with higher levels of NRI impact also have better micro- and macroeconomic indicators.
- *Is there is an association between the levels of values of macroeconomic and microeconomic outcomes and the level of NRI Drivers*? The expectation is that those SSA economies that are better off, micro- and macroeconomically, would direct more resources than the poorer economies to creating a greater level of ICT capabilities.

The outcome of this step is a relative ranking of the N-clusters of the data set in terms of the relative values (percentages) of the measures representing each of the four constructs in our research model.

Additionally, we use DEA to calculate the values of the Malmquist Index (MI) – this allows us to assess the changes in relative efficiency of SSA economies that took place over time. Such results would not only identify the economies and clusters that exhibited growth in productivity (under assumption of constant return to scale), but to also identify the sources of growth (EC-change in efficiency vs. TC-change in technology). Calculation of MI allows for answering two important questions:

- *Did SSA exhibit growth in productivity of conversion of NRI Impacts into NRI Drivers over the period of time?* We would expect that over the period of time SSA became better (e.g. more productive) at converting ICT capabilities into socio-economic impacts.
- *What was the driving force behind the growth in productivity?* If the growth in productivity took place, then we would like to see that the growth was balanced – driven by improvements in efficiency and technology.

4.4 Step 4: Decision Tree Induction (DTI)

If the results of Phase 1 yield a multi-cluster solution, then we create a variable *target*, with its domain of values being the number of identified clusters (e.g. 3-cluster solution will yield *target* {1, 2, 3}). By performing DTI, we will be able to identify, based on the top-level splits, the variable(s) that differentiate the clusters the most. The pool of variables used in DTI will be based on pillars of NRI – the variables used to represent sub-indexes of NRI (see Table 4).

Table 4. Variables used in DTI to identify sources of heterogeneity of the clusters

Main index	Sub-index-Component of NRI	Pillar-representation of sub-index
NRI	Environment sub-index	Political and regulatory environment
		Business and innovation environment
	Readiness sub-index	Infrastructure
		Affordability
		Skills
	Usage sub-index	Individual usage
		Business usage
		Government usage
	Impact sub-index	Economic impacts
		Social impacts

The outcome of Step 4 is a set of variables differentiating N-clusters comprising the sample.

5 Results of the Data Analysis

5.1 Step 1: CA

While performing CA on the NRI data set, we have followed a rule of thumb for the relative size of any single cluster being greater than 10% of the overall size of the sample [7].

By performing hybrid hierarchical clustering (there seems to be a consensus that this approach combines the advantages of other methods [2, 6] without having any unique disadvantages), we arrived at a 3-cluster solution. Results are summarized in Table 5.

Table 5. Results of CA: membership, income composition, and size of a cluster

Cluster #	Composition	Cluster membership
Cluster 1	LI 21.88% LM 43.75% UM 34.38%	Mauritius, South Africa, Cape Verde, Ghana, Uganda, Zimbabwe (2013-2015), Botswana (2012), Kenya (2014–2015)
Cluster 2	LI 69.35% LM 30.65% UM 0.00%	Burundi, Chad, Ethiopia, Madagascar, Malawi, Mali, Mozambique, Tanzania, Swaziland, Lesotho, Côte d'Ivoire (2012–2014), Nigeria (2013–2015), Zimbabwe (2012)
Cluster 3	LI 27.78% LM 47.22% UM 25.00%	Cameroon, Senegal, Zambia, Gambia, Rwanda, Namibia, Kenya (2012–2013), Côte d'Ivoire (2015), Nigeria (2012–2013), Botswana (2013–2015)

Based on the original solution, 21 SSA economies are "permanent residents" of a given cluster, while 5 SSA economies are "migrants." This indicates that 84% of the economies are stable with regard to their membership. Furthermore, if we consider three out of four years to be the indicator of stability, then over 92% of the clusters' membership is stable.

5.2 Step 2: DEA

During the third phase, we rely on DEA to evaluate the relative efficiency of various paths for each of the three clusters. We used the *input-oriented* model and the variable *return to scale* (VRS) DEA model to conduct the analysis, for it is reasonable to argue that SSA economies have not yet reached the point of developing a level of ICT infrastructure allowing for accruing the benefits yielded by capitalizing on economies of scale. The results of DEA are presented in Table 6a, and the results of the calculations of MI are presented in Table 6b.

Table 6a. Results of DEA

DEA model (Input-Oriented)	Average relative efficiency scores		
	Cluster 1	Cluster 2	Cluster 3
NRI Drivers → NRI Impact	0.97	0.94	0.98
NRI Impact → Macroeconomic Outcomes	0.88	0.85	0.86
NRI Impact → Microeconomic Outcomes	0.93	0.90	0.91
Macroeconomic Outcomes → NRI Drivers	0.66	0.37	0.75
Microeconomic Outcomes → NRI Drivers	0.81	0.90	0.91
Average Scores of Relative Efficiency	**0.85**	**0.79**	**0.88**

Table 6b. Results of MI analysis

Growth in productivity (*NRI Drivers → NRI Impact*, 2012–2015)	Cluster		
	Cluster 1	Cluster 2	Cluster 3
MI (Growth in Productivity)	0.989	**1.009**	**1.005**
Overall Growth?	No	Yes	Yes
EC (Growth via Change in Efficiency)	0.993	**1.010**	**1.006**
Growth via EC?	No	Yes	Yes
TC (Growth via Change in Technology)	0.997	0.999	**1.000**
Growth via TC?	No	No	Yes

5.3 Step 3: Comparison of the Values of the Measures of the Constructs and the Results of DEA

During this phase, we compare the values and calculate relative magnitudes, in percentages, of the measures representing various constructs of the research model, for each of the clusters in the sample of SSA economies. We present the actual values is Table 7, while the relative values, in percentages, are presented in Table 8. This relative comparison allows us to find out whether there appears to be a relationship between the relative efficiency of each path and the relative "state" of the involved constructs.

The DEA scores were reported in percentages so the percentages of the scores could be compared to the percentages in the values of the measures for the constructs of the model.

While comparison of the values allows us to gain some insight into the differences between the values of the measures of the constructs of our research model, it is their relative representation, provided in Table 8, that offers a richer picture regarding the differences between the three clusters of SSA economies.

Table 7. Average scores of relative efficiency and the values of the measures

Criterion		Average measure value		
Construct	Measure	Cluster 1	Cluster 2	Cluster 3
NRI Drivers	Environment	4.03	3.27	4.00
	Readiness	4.20	2.75	3.23
	Usage	3.27	2.62	3.19
NRI Impact	Economic Impact	3.02	2.54	3.11
	Social Impact	3.27	2.67	3.38
Macroeconomic Outcomes	FDI	3.42	5.69	4.47
	GDP Growth	2.83	3.33	1.87
Microeconomic Outcomes	Labor Market	44.65	51.70	38.57
	Trade	80.70	74.45	72.07

DEA Model	Average relative efficiency score		
	Cluster 1	Cluster 2	Cluster 3
NRI Drivers → NRI Impact	0.97	0.94	0.98
NRI Impact → Macroeconomic Outcomes	0.88	0.85	0.86
NRI Impact → Microeconomic Outcomes	0.93	0.90	0.91
Macroeconomic Outcomes → NRI Drivers	0.66	0.37	0.75
Microeconomic Outcomes → NRI Drivers	0.81	0.90	0.91

Table 8. Scores of efficiency and measures of the constructs, relative within the sample

Criterion	Cluster 1	Cluster 2	Cluster 3
NRI Drivers → NRI Impact	98.98%	95.92%	100.00%
NRI Impact → Macroeconomic Outcomes	100.00%	96.59%	97.73%
NRI Impact → Microeconomic Outcomes	100.00%	96.77%	97.85%
Macroeconomic Outcomes → NRI Drivers	87.58%	50.07%	100.00%
Microeconomic Outcomes → NRI Drivers	88.95%	99.03%	100.00%
Averaged Scores of Relative Efficiency	***95.10%***	***87.68%***	***99.12%***
Environment	100.00%	81.14%	99.26%
Readiness	100.00%	65.48%	76.90%
Usage	100.00%	80.12%	97.55%
Averaged, NRI Drivers	***100.00%***	***75.58%***	***91.24%***
Economic Impact	97.11%	81.67%	100.00%
Social Impact	96.75%	78.99%	100.00%
Averaged, NRI Impact	***96.93%***	***80.33%***	***100.00%***
FDI	60.11%	100.00%	78.56%
GDP Growth	84.98%	100.00%	56.16%
Averaged, Macroeconomic Outcomes	***72.55%***	***100.00%***	***67.36%***
Labor Market	86.36%	100.00%	74.60%
Trade	100.00%	92.26%	89.31%
Averaged, Microeconomic Outcomes	***93.18%***	***96.13%***	***81.95%***

5.4 Step 4: DTI to Identify Sources of Heterogeneity of the Sample

By performing DTI, we were able to identify sub-indexes and pillars that differentiate the three clusters of SSA economies in our sample. During this phase, we generated various decision trees based on different variables (e.g. sub-indexes, pillars, NRI). We were able to determine, for example, that the three clusters cannot be clearly differentiated based on the value of NRI, or based on the *impact* sub-index of NRI; however, we obtained evidence that the clusters do differ based on the values of the associated pillars. We present a summary of the most relevant results of DTI, in Table 9.

Table 9. Results of DTI: English rules, split variables and split criteria

English Rules	Split Variables
Pillars-based DT	
B04 > 3.880	B04 – Readiness sub-index: Affordability
| B05 > 2.815: One {three=0, **one=32 (100%)**, two=0}	B05 – Readiness sub-index: Skills
| B05 ≤ 2.815: two {three=1, one=0, two=10}	
B04 ≤ 3.880	A01 – Environment sub-index: Political and regulatory environment
| C07 > 3.220	C07 – Usage sub-index: Business usage
| | A01 > 3.005: three {**three=35 (97%)**, one=0, two=5}	
| | A01 ≤ 3.005: two {three=0, one=0, two=4}	
| C07 ≤ 3.220: two {three=0, one=0, **two=43 (69.35%)**}	

6 Discussion of the Results

Results of CA indicated that the sample of SSA economies is not homogeneous in terms of the values of NRI sub-indexes. Furthermore, the composition of each of the three clusters indicated that the levels of values of NRI for each cluster are not indicative of the wealth of its members. Consequently, the first insight of our inquiry is the following:

The values of NRI sub-indexes do not serve as a reliable indicator of the wealth of an economy as measured by FDI and growth in GDP.

Meaning, even if the values of NRI drivers indicate that economy A has a higher level of ICT capabilities and impacts than economy B, this does not mean that economy A is, in fact, wealthier than economy B (recall results in Table 8).

Analysis of the results of DEA suggests that, overall, those SSA economies that have higher scores of ICT capabilities and impacts also receive higher scores of the relative efficiency of conversion of inputs into outputs (recall results in Table 7), and this insight is along the lines of what is expected; as economies become more capable, they become more efficient.

Examination of the calculation of MI demonstrates, surprisingly, that there is no association between the levels of relative efficiency of conversion of ICT capabilities into impacts, and growth in productivity (recall results in Tables 6a and 6b). Meaning, the most relatively efficient SSA economies (e.g. Cluster 3) do not exhibit the highest growth in productivity; furthermore, even if the economies are ranked in the middle, in terms of their levels of relative efficiency, overall, those economies still can demonstrate a decline in productivity. With regard to the economies that exhibited growth in productivity, their growth was balanced and driven by positive technological changes (i.e. *TC*) and positive changes in efficiency of utilization of technology (i.e. *EC*).

The comparison of relative magnitudes of values of the measures of the constructs of the research model yields a surprising find: there is no direct association between NRI and economic well-being of SSA economies (see results in Table 8). Meaning, those SSA economies that have higher values of ICT capabilities and impact have the lower values of micro- and macroeconomic outcomes, and vice versa. Specifically, Cluster 2 has by far the lowest averaged values of NRI drivers and impacts, but it has the highest averaged values of micro- and macroeconomic outcomes. A similar discrepancy holds true for clusters 1 and 2, where the scores of NRI drivers and impact are high, but micro- and macroeconomic outcomes are relatively low.

The results of CA offer some insights into differentiating the clusters' factors, where the major sources of heterogeneity are associated with ICT-related affordability and skills, as well as the levels of business usage of ICT. None of the insights can, however, conclusively account for the observed discrepancies between NRI impact and micro- and macroeconomic outcomes.

At this point we are well positioned to answer the five research questions of the study; the answer to a corresponding question is preceded by the original question.

RQ1: Is there an association between the levels of *NRI Drivers* and *NRI Impact* and the relative efficiency of the link "*NRI Drivers → NRI Impact*"?

Answer to RQ1: *There seems to be an association between the level of NRI Drivers and Impact and the relative efficiency of the link, so SSA economies with higher levels of NRI Drivers and Impact are relatively more efficient than the economies with lower levels of NRI Drivers and Impact.*

RQ2: Is there an association between the level of *NRI Impact*, the values of the macroeconomic outcomes and the relative efficiency of the link "*NRI Impact → Macroeconomic Outcomes*"?

Answer to RQ2: *There is no discernable association between the level of NRI Impact, the values of the macroeconomic outcomes and the relative efficiency of the link "NRI Impact → Macroeconomic Outcomes".*

RQ3: Is there an association between the level of the impact of NRI, the values of the microeconomic outcomes and the relative efficiency of the link "*Impact → Microeconomic Outcomes*"?

Answer to RQ3: *There is no discernable association between the level of NRI Impact, the values of the microeconomic outcomes and the relative efficiency of the link "NRI Impact → Microeconomic Outcomes".*

RQ4: Is there an association between the values of the microeconomic outcomes, the level of *NRI Drivers* and the relative efficiency of the link "*Microeconomic Outcomes → NRI Drivers*"?

Answer to RQ4: *There is no discernable association between the values of the microeconomic outcomes, the level of NRI Drivers and the relative efficiency of the link "Microeconomic Outcomes → NRI Drivers".*

RQ5: Is there an association between the values of the macroeconomic outcomes, the level of *NRI Drivers* and the relative efficiency of the link "*Macroeconomic Outcomes → NRI Drivers*"?

Answer to RQ5: *There is no discernable association between the values of the macroeconomic outcomes, the level of NRI Drivers and the relative efficiency of the link "Macroeconomic Outcomes → NRI Drivers".*

Overall, the evidence seems to indicate that there is no discernable relationship between the levels of the measures of the constructs of our research model and the relative efficiency of the paths between the constructs, and we are justified to state that *the level of relative efficiency of conversion of inputs into outputs appears to be level-independent.*

The insights obtained during the investigation also allow us to answer the three general questions that were stated earlier in this paper. We provide the answers to the general questions next, where every answer is preceded by the original question.

1. *Whether SSA economies translate, efficiently, ICT capabilities into ICT impacts.* Answer: *In general, SSA economies appear to be efficient in translating ICT capabilities into ICT Impacts, for economies with higher levels of ICT capabilities also have higher levels of ICT Impacts, and economies with lower levels of ICT capabilities have lower levels of ICT impacts.*
2. *Whether SSA economies translate, efficiently, ICT impacts into macroeconomic and microeconomic targets.* Answer: *In general, there is no conclusive evidence that SSA economies efficiently translate ICT impacts into macroeconomic and microeconomic targets, for some SSA economies with higher levels of ICT impacts have lower levels of macroeconomic and microeconomic targets than the SSA economies with lower levels of ICT impacts.*
3. *Whether the macroeconomic and microeconomic targets are efficiently translated into ICT capabilities.* Answer: *There is no conclusive evidence that SSA economies efficiently translate macroeconomic and microeconomic targets into ICT capabilities, for some SSA economies with lower levels of micro- and macroeconomic targets have higher levels of ICT capabilities than SSA economies with higher levels of micro- and macroeconomic targets.*

Table 10. Overall comparison of the clusters of SSA economies

Criterion	Cluster 1	Cluster 2	Cluster 3
NRI	Higher ICT Affordability and Higher Skills	Lower ICT Affordability and Lower Business Usage	Lower ICT Affordability and Higher Business Usage
Efficiency & productivity	Good efficiency, but decline in productivity	Inefficient but Productive, growth balanced	Efficient and Productive, growth balanced
Economic Outcomes	Good – relative conversion of NRI Impacts into economic outcomes is 85%	Excellent – relative conversion of NRI Impacts into economic outcomes is 122%	Poor – relative conversion of NRI Impacts into economic outcomes is 77%
Impact of outcomes on capabilities	Excellent – relative conversion of outcomes into NRI capabilities is 121%	Poor – relative conversion of outcomes into NRI capabilities is 77%	Excellent – relative conversion of outcomes into NRI capabilities is 122%

At this point we can accomplish the main research goal of this investigation by answering the following question:

Whether SSA economies that have a high level of ICT Capabilities also have a high level of ICT Impact, and also have high levels of Micro- and Macroeconomic Outcomes that allow for contributing to ICT Capabilities.

The answer is as follows:

In the context of SSA economies, the level of ICT capabilities and impacts seems to have no association with levels of Micro- and Macroeconomic outcomes, and vice versa.

7 Conclusion

In conclusion, we would like to offer a brief, simplified summary of the findings in Table 10. Our results, unfortunately, do not offer any clear indications regarding what needs to be done in order to sustain a virtuous circle of "investments in ICT -> impact of investments -> re-investments in ICT". Our findings are in line with the other studies regarding the "ICT Capabilities -> Impact of ICT Capabilities" within the framework of NRI, that showed, basically, that a higher level of capabilities results in a higher level of impact.

If we step "outside" the framework of NRI, however, then our findings disappoint. For example, if SSA economies do translate NRI impacts into economic outcomes relatively well (e.g. Cluster 2), then those economies do not show that economic outcomes are associated with a higher level of ICT capabilities. On the other hand, if some SSA economies (e.g. Cluster 3) do not translate NRI impacts well into economic outcomes, then those economies really do show their relatively higher level of NRI capabilities.

The general sense that we get is that the framework of NRI has to be expanded to include some micro- and macroeconomic targets that will allow for better assessment of the impact of the investments in ICT and the impact of ICT capabilities.

In practical terms, this means that investments in ICT must be made with the clear picture of the chain of impacts in mind, of the type of "if this, then that, if that, then …". We are not sure that this clear picture exists at this point.

Thus, the biggest contribution of this study, unfortunately, is the suggestion that researchers and practitioners alike should have a clear path according to which investments in ICT should contribute to the macro- and microeconomic bottom lines. Also, this clear path has to be made efficient and effective. Some of the "lessons learned" from our investigation are the following:

- While the framework of NRI could provide valuable information regarding cross-country comparison, it paints the picture with too broad a brush, not allowing for discerning the reasons for inter-economy differences. The first take-away is that *in the cases of investigating the economic impact of ICT, the framework of NRI should be supplemented by the inclusion of the additional constructs.*
- An investigation relying on the framework of NRI, and dealing with the economic impact of ICT, should have a specific target in its cross-hairs that will allow for scrutinizing the effectiveness and efficiency of the path of the impact. We cannot explain, for example, why Cluster 2 has the lowest relative score of NRI impact, but the highest relative values of micro- and macroeconomic outcomes, while Cluster 3 has the highest score of the impacts and the lowest scores of the outcomes. The second take-away, therefore, is that *ICT capabilities and impacts must be target traceable,* meaning that an investigator should be able to, in an almost algorithmic fashion, elucidate the chain of the links leading from ICT capabilities to their economic targets.
- From a practical perspective, policy-makers should monitor the multi-year performance of *ICT drivers -> ICT* impact path, to assess any changes in productivity. As our results show, a group of economies could be relatively efficient, yet exhibit a decline in productivity. Sources of growth in productivity should also be analyzed, so that the appropriate investment decisions could be made. Simply put, *productivity growth and efficiency of conversion of inputs into outputs should not be made into proxies for economic development.*

Overall, this investigation raises more questions than it answers. Failure to obtain evidence linking the impact of ICT and economic outcomes could be due to the short period of time – it could be argued that four years is not a sufficiently long period to obtain reliable evidence. Another limitation of this study is associated with the chosen representation of the constructs: it is possible that other measures of micro- and macroeconomic outcomes could have been preferable. Availability of the data remains a constant struggle to overcome. We attribute some of the shortcomings of this investigation to data-related issues; nevertheless, we hope that our peers and readers will find our work worthy of consideration – if not providing evidence, then raising additional questions possibly leading to it.

References

1. Bankole, F.O., Osei-Bryson, K.M., Brown, I.: The impacts of telecommunications infrastructure and institutional quality on trade efficiency in Africa. Inf. Technol. Dev. **21** (1), 29–43 (2015)
2. Chipman, H., Tibshirani, R.: Hybrid hierarchical clustering with applications to microarray data. Biostat. Adv. Access **7**(2), 286–301 (2006)
3. Di Battista, A., Dutta, S., Geiger, T., Lanvin, B.: The networked readiness index 2015: taking the pulse of the ICT revolution. Glob. Inf. Technol. Rep. **2015**, 3–28 (2015)
4. Dutta, S., Jain, A.: The Networked Readiness Index 2003–2004: Overview and Analysis Framework: 3–22. Oxford University Press, New York (2004)
5. Kirkman, S.G., Osorio, A.C., Sachs, D.J.: The Networked readiness index: measuring the preparedness of nations for the networked world. In: Kirkman, S.G. (ed.) The Global Information Technology Report 2001–2002 Readiness for the Networked World, pp. 10–29. Oxford University Press, New York (2002)
6. Laan, M., Pollard, K.: A new algorithm for hybrid hierarchical clustering with visualization and the bootstrap. J. Stat. Planning Infer. **117**(2), 275–303 (2002)
7. Samoilenko, S., Osei-Bryson, K.M.: Using Data Envelopment Analysis (DEA) for monitoring efficiency-based performance of productivity-driven organizations: design and implementation of a decision support system. Omega **41**(1), 131–142 (2013)
8. Samoilenko, S., Osei-Bryson, K.M.: An analytical framework for exploring context-specific microeconomic impacts of ICT capabilities. Inf. Technol. Dev. 1–25 (2017). https://doi.org/10.1080/02681102.2017.1336072
9. Samoilenko, S., Osei-Bryson, K.M.: A methodology for identifying sources of disparities in the socio-economic impacts of ICT capabilities in Sub-Saharan economies. In: Proceedings of the 2017 International Conference on Information Resource Management. Santiago, Chile (2017)
10. Samoilenko, S., Osei-Bryson, K.-M.: Creating Theoretical Research Frameworks using Multiple Methods: Insight from ICT4D Investigations, 1st edn. Auerbach Publications, Boca Raton (2017)
11. Solow, R.: Technical change and the aggregate production function. Rev. Econ. Stat. **39**(3), 312–320 (1957)
12. The World Bank Data Bank. World Development Indicators. http://databank.worldbank.org/data/reports.aspx?source=world-development-indicators. Accessed 21 Feb 2018
13. WEF_GITR. Networked Readiness Dataset, http://reports.weforum.org/global-information-technology-report-2016/networked-readiness-index. Accessed 21 Feb 2018

Domestication of ICTs in Community Savings and Credit Associations (Stokvels) in the Western Cape, South Africa

Nokwazi Biyela, Pitso Tsibolane(✉), and Jean-Paul Van Belle

University of Cape Town, Cape Town, South Africa
BYLNOK004@myuct.ac.za,
{Pitso.Tsibolane,jean-paul.vanbelle}@uct.ac.za

Abstract. The stokvel economy is estimated to be worth R49 billion in South Africa, with more than 810 000 groups consisting of about 11.5 million members. This study aimed to discover how stokvel members domesticate information communication technologies (ICTs). Domestication theory was used as a theoretical lens for this study. The study used semi-structured interviews to collect data from a sample of 20 stokvel members from 20 different groups of stokvels in Cape Town. The qualitative data was analysed using thematic analysis. The findings revealed that stokvel members use ICTs such as mobile phones, spreadsheet applications (Excel), mobile banking, social media communications (mostly WhatsApp) and e-mail (for those who are employed) in the running of their operations. The members indicated that the use of WhatsApp enables them to reduce the amount of times they have to meet on a face-to-face basis as they did before. They also use technology to send money through mobile money transfer services and banks. Age influenced the adoption of ICTs among stokvel members – i.e. older members seem resistant to the use of technology. This study makes a contribution to the discourse on digital financial inclusion, as well as a contribution to practice by providing empirically grounded insights regarding ICT use behaviour patterns among members of informal savings and credit associations.

Keywords: ICT4D · Savings and credit associations · Stokvel
Domestication

1 Introduction

South Africa is faced with the challenges of high levels of inequality, poverty and unemployment [1]. Most affected are the poverty-stricken communities, which are unable to meet their basic needs [2], as well as women, who are noted to rely on their spouses and/or the governmental child support grant (CSG) for a living [3].

Informal savings schemes such as rotating savings and credit associations (ROSCAs), well known as stokvels in South Africa [4], have emerged as a way of addressing these challenges. A stokvel can be defined as “a type of credit union, or communal buying group, in which a group of people enter into an agreement to contribute a fixed amount of money to a common pool weekly, fortnightly or monthly, to be drawn in

K. Krauss et al. (Eds.): IDIA 2018, CCIS 933, pp. 35–47, 2019.
https://doi.org/10.1007/978-3-030-11235-6_3

rotation according to the rules of the particular stokvel" [5, p. 5]. Globally, a number of informal saving schemes are known; these include the microcredit self-help groups (MSHGs) [6] and accumulating savings and credit associations (ASCAs) [7]. Through these saving schemes, people have been able to save and/or invest money and, ultimately, improve their standard of living [2]; furthermore, these schemes reinforce teamwork, moral support and financial management skills [2].

The study seeks to understand the role of ICTs in the way in which stokvels are being operated in the South African context. The study focuses on the types of ICTs that are being domesticated by the stokvel members; however, the use of ICTs by members of stokvels in South Africa is not adequately researched. A better understanding of this phenomenon will enable practitioners in this field to make ICT design decisions to digitally transform stokvels. The digital transformation of stokvels and other savings and credit associations worldwide can potentially contribute to the digital and financial inclusion of the millions involved in such practices in the developing world. The three main questions explored for this research are the following:

- What types of ICTs are stokvel members using?
- How are these ICTs being used, integrated and adapted by stokvel members?
- What are the benefits and challenges of using ICTs in stokvels?

The study adopted domestication theory [8] as a lens to understand the adoption, incorporation and use of ICTs in stokvels. The study employed a qualitative approach, where stokvel members were interviewed on their adoption and use of ICTs.

2 Background

2.1 What Are Stokvels?

According to the National Stokvel Association of South Africa (NASASA), a self-regulatory body authorised by the government to work with stokvels for regulatory compliance, there are 11.5 million individuals who are members of different groups of stokvels, who are contributing approximately R50bn every year [9]. There are eight recognised types of stokvels in South Africa. One of these is the high budget stokvel, where members contribute, in savings and investment, a substantial amount to buy household goods and other necessary resources [10]. The burial stokvel is specifically for moral support to family members in times of death. The money is strictly for funeral expenses such as the coffin, food and undertaker [2]. The third type is the grocery stokvel. Members contribute money specifically to buy food or coupons (stamps) so that they can buy food at the end of the year, or members simply distribute money at the end of the year, and each member buys their own choice of food [11]. In the family stokvel, members contribute money to buy things, depending on the needs of the family, such as a car, land and business investments [12]. Investment stokvels, on the other hand, are done in a form of generating interest. The investment interest is split among members. In other cases, the interest is re-invested, or used to invest in other businesses [2]. The sixth type of stokvel is the party stokvel among a group of friends wishing to donate money for gifts, or to give the cash to celebrate [13]. They are informally also called "birthday" stokvels [3]. Borrowing stokvels are the seventh type, in which members contribute a fixed amount once, and then get a chance to borrow money so they can pay it back with interest. The interest is usually charged from 20% to 50% [10]. Last is the rotational stokvel. In this type of stokvel, members contribute a fixed amount of money monthly, and the money is handed to one member. This rotates until all members have had the opportunity to receive the money [13]. A constitution between members ensures a good working environment, and serves as a binding contract between members [2].

These schemes are utilised largely by domestic workers and owners of survivalist enterprises such as street trading, spaza (corner) shops, shebeens, daycare centres and hairdressers [2]. While recent surveys show that South Africa represents a fairly inclusive financial sector for a developing country, with 77% of the adult population having a bank account, 10% of those banked adults still report saving and accessing credit through stokvels, and not through the mainstream banks [14]. This suggests that the level of being underbanked is still prevalent. Stokvels are still channels through which quality access to finance (financial inclusion) still takes place. This research will also contribute to the discourse of quality financial inclusion with the help of ICTs.

2.2 Benefits of Stokvel Membership

The following are said to be benefits of joining a stokvel [2].

- Ability to meet basic needs – Helps people to save so they can meet their basic needs, such as helping them to buy groceries. Individuals who participate in stokvels are able to meet their basic needs and fight the poverty that they were previously facing.
- Ability to save and invest – Gives people the chance to save money and helps them to do big things that they could not do with their basic income. It helps when one wants to buy household property; furthermore, individuals are able to save and invest their money to aid in other projects.
- Easy access to credit and mini-loans – Charges interest to borrowers which increases the savings; moreover, the money received from stokvels helps individuals in securing credit and loans from larger institutions. Individuals use the money received from stokvels as a down payment.
- Moral support – Helps members to support each other, including for events such marriages and parties but not funerals; however, for individuals to reap these benefits, they need to ensure that there is mutual trust and honesty with the stokvel group, to ensure that funds are not mismanaged.
- Creation of social capital – Begins friendships and social networks where members teach each other things not related to stokvels [2].

2.3 Use of ICTs for Stokvels and Challenges

The challenges of using ICTs in informal financial groups such as stokvels in developing countries, are the limit of Internet access, and the lack of credit card diffusion, which are also challenges to the individuals accessing Internet banking services [15].

There are few IT businesses, and that results in the slow distribution of Internet, as there is also a shortage of electricity in some rural areas [15]. Stokvels were built from trust or from "Ubuntu", which is the culture of collectivism, or the spirit of unity. As time goes by, participants will become unreliable within stokvels, and they will take advantage of the fact that there were no contracts which may possibly hold them responsible [13]. This increase has resulted in ICTs being enablers for societies in developing communities for economic growth with projects such as stokvels [15]. Social networks are also a driver in individuals joining stokvels, as they are used as a platform to motivate individuals to join a stokvel [2].

To make these schemes more convenient, innovative methods are a necessity. Information communication technology (ICTs) assists with coordinating communication, learning, time management as well as overall interaction in the workplace and beyond [16]. This has resultantly brought about economic development globally. At the community level, the most effective and powerful tool has been mobile devices, because of the different features they provide to the user [17]. This study therefore seeks to understand the role of ICTs in the way in which stokvels are being operated in the South African context; furthermore, it focuses on the types of ICTs that are being domesticated by the stokvel members. For these reasons, domestication theory [8] was adopted as a lens to understand the adoption and use of ICTs in stokvels. A qualitative approach was undertaken, where stokvel members were interviewed on their adoption and use of ICTs.

3 Theoretical Framework: Domestication Theory

Domestication theory describes how people adopt ICTs into their world: "The framework looks beyond the adoption and use of ICTs (as well as gratifications or benefits) to ask what the technologies and services mean to people, how they experience them and the roles that these technologies can come to play in their lives" [18]. This theory will be used for this study, to explore and investigate the ways in which ICTs are adopted, incorporated and used in the daily routines of community savings and credit associations (stokvels). Due to the exploratory nature of this study, as well as the interpretive stance adopted where meaning will be derived through interaction with members of stokvels to gain insights into how they have adopted and incorporated ICTs, the choice of domestication theory provides the study with a rich lens through which to analyse the taming of ICTs.

Commodification is considered the first phase of the framework; it is also known as imagination. This is when the technology is introduced to its users, and the users have sufficient information about the technology through advertisements. At this phase, the information received about the technology drives the decision to accept or decline the technology [17]. At this stage, symbolic artefacts and material are created, and the user can be driven to adopt (or not to adopt), which leads to the user purchasing the technology. This phase analyses the user's domestic needs and potential benefits of using the technology or gadget before it is adopted [18].

The appropriation process is a domestication phase whereby the technology product or gadget is possessed or controlled by the user [19]. The phase further describes how the product is not only about buying the gadget or technology, but also looks at what the user does with the gadget, or how the technology finds a space in the user's environment; however, this phase does not necessarily mean that the technology has been accepted by the user. The appropriation process can be divided further into objectification and incorporation [19].

Incorporation focuses on the way the product is being incorporated into the user's daily life [18]. For the ICTs to be incorporated, they must be keenly used to perform certain tasks [19]. Mobile phones are the best form of communication to check the well-being of relatives, but they are also useful in the work environment. The incorporation is simply the integration of new activities and social practices, with and around the new product, in the user's life [18].

The objectification phase is concerned with configurations and how the physical objects is being placed [21]. Objectification is when the participants think through the location of the technology in daily routines [22]. Objectification considers the way technology is physically included in the user's environment [21]. The technology might be in the possession of the user, but that does not mean the technology is being accepted by the user, as it might not be suitable to the intentions or daily routines of the user [19]. This phase focuses on the way people give space to the technology in their households.

Conversion focuses on the relationship between the use of the technology and the community field [20]. This is where we see the demonstration of ownership of the technology, or how "these technologies become part of the user's identity and how users present the technology as part of themselves, in the sense that they talk about and display their usage to the public" [20]. It is how people share the technology with other people outside their space. This can be assumed as the stage when ICT is shared or used among the stokvel group members.

The domestication framework will help us understand how stokvel individuals have adopted and use the technology. This framework will also serve as a tool when grouping and analysing data. This framework is appropriate for this study, since the study aims to find the way in which stokvel members use technology to facilitate their stokvels.

4 Research Methodology

A qualitative, interpretivist approach was chosen for this research, given its exploratory nature. Interviews were deemed to be the most productive way to proceed, and a cross-sectional time frame was selected, in order to complete the research within a relatively short time period.

The population targeted for this study focused on individual members of different types of traditional stokvels in Cape Town. The size of the population was 20 stokvel members from 20 different groups of stokvels. Semi-structured face-to-face or telephonic interviews were conducted. The data was analysed using thematic analysis to organise, identify and interpret themes. Flexibility, accessibility, imaginary choice and the accepting participants' responses are the advantages of thematic analysis, which analytically defines data and interpretations. NVivo software was used to analyse the data. The participants' right to decline to answer questions and withdraw from the interview was reiterated, and emphasis was laid on ensuring that the data was retained as private. The study was approved by the UCT ethics committee, and the personal details of the participants or stokvel members were kept confidential.

5 Findings

5.1 Sample Demographics

Twenty (20) semi-structured interviews with 20 different individuals from 20 different stokvels were undertaken. Two-thirds of the interviewees were female. All participants were based in Cape Town. Interviews were done until saturation was reached.

5.2 Purpose of Stokvels

The main purpose of the stokvel was to assist people to uplift their standard of living. Some authors said it was for friends, to keep their relationship. According to the findings for this research, the members joined stokvels to save money so that they could buy things that they are unable to buy with their monthly income, and that it teaches them to save money. The membership is usually a group of friends, colleagues, family members, etc.: "*…we are all working together*" (X1, X2, X7 and X16); "*Stokvel taught me to save money*" (X5 and X9); "*We save money for the festive season…*" (X10).

Other members join stokvels so that they can gain interest and buy things for their homes and families. *"With us…ours is money…it is just saving money and after 12 months we split it… so that's the type, but the members of the stokvels are allowed to borrow money and they will be charged interest"* (X8).

5.3 Uses of Stokvel Funds

The spending of the stokvel funds depends on the stokvel type. If the stokvel is a burial stokvel, the funding is specifically for burial expenses such as the coffin, food, tents and other burial concerns. If it's a grocery stokvel, the money is used for buying food, usually at the end of the year; the stokvel members buy food in bulk and then divide it equally among themselves. With the most common stokvel type, the rotational stokvel, the money has no restriction as to how it should be spent. Some are saving money to pay school or tuition fees for their kids, some save so they can buy cars, and some save just for the sake of not wasting money on unnecessary things. Members therefore buy what they were planning to buy, and if they change their minds, it is still OK. But most of the members that were on the rotational stokvel wanted to buy things like furniture. They seemed to be faithful to themselves; hence they bought what they were saving for. Sample comments are the following: "*…wanted to buy the fridge and a bed and I bought it…*" (X2); *"I don't want to buy anything, I am just saving money"* (X1); *"It helps me a lot on January because I pay for my child's school fees"* (X4).

Most of the stokvels prefer rotation or savings stokvels, because it makes their lives easy; they are not limited as to how and where to spend their money. It is actually their decision how they spend their money: *"It does happen, there was a time last year the money came and my car needed fixing; therefore, I didn't do the thing that I needed to do. I had to fix my car"* (X8).

5.4 Commodification

The commodification process deals with the observed adoption of ICTs after hearing about it and not yet adopted. This phase looks at the challenges that were faced by the stokvel members before they started to use the ICTs, and how the adoption of ICTs helped to overcome those challenges. The analysis of the results showed that 20 participants had commodified the use of ICTs through the use of WhatsApp, emails, etc. for their stokvel. The themes for the commodification phase looks at the types of ICTs owned by the stokvel members, the challenges before the use of ICTs, the ICTs perception before its use in stokvel, and lastly, the payment method and tools.

Types of ICTs Owned by Stokvel Members
Most of the stokvel members already had knowledge and own some ICTs such as smartphones, laptops, tablets, TV, radio, as well as desktops at work. Other stokvel members do not own the same type of ICTs, but they are able to use the features or the same social media to do their stokvels.

The dominant type of ICT owned by the stokvel individuals is the smartphone (49%), and the most popular social media that they use to facilitate their stokvels is WhatsApp, followed by email, and the least used is phone calls: *"I have a smartphone, a laptop, and at work we all have desktops that we also use for our own personal staff"* (X7); *"I have a smartphone and a desktop as you can see here, even though it is for work, but I use it a lot as I spend most of my time here"* (X1); "*I have a smartphone, and obviously a radio and TV, yeah*" (X6) (Fig. 1).

Challenges before the Use of ICTs
There were a few challenges that were faced by stokvel members before using ICTs. One of the main challenges was that other members were not attending meetings, and if they did, they were often late. It was stated by most of the members that the money would be stolen, since previously they were meeting in one place to distribute the money. Before that they would have set the date before, and then sometimes there would be a group of robbers who would come to rob them.

Another challenge was poor communication between members; as a result, they would have to go to the member's place to send a notification, which they can now do easily with ICTs.

Some of them they are scared to carry cash as the rate of theft is high: "*When we were going to the stokvel one day, a group of guys just came in the room and took all our money because some members of the community knew that we were playing stokvel, and they also knew that whenever we have meetings there will be money involved.*" (X5); *"We used to give people cash, but other members were scared to carry cash, then we decided to use bank"* (X2).

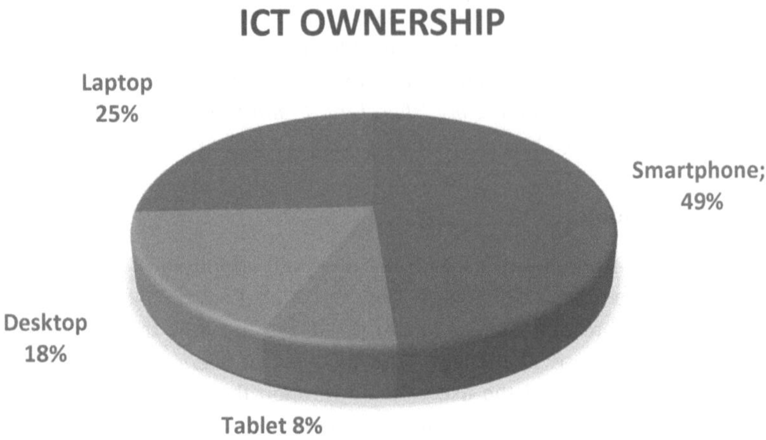

Fig. 1. Types of ICTs owned by individual stokvel members interviewed

ICT Perception before Use in Stokvels

They had a clear understanding of WhatsApp already, which helped them to use it for their stokvel: *"When I first started, I used WhatsApp for communicating with my friends and family, only for personal use"* (X19); *"I saw WhatsApp as best way for communicating with your family and loved ones, and as a way of saving time and money when you want to be in touch with people"* (X20).

Other stokvel participants had commodified the use of emails for their stokvel. In their minds, at first, they had that emails are for work purposes only, but after some time they realised that they could be helpful in their stokvel in terms of communication: *"We are all working together and therefore we all have emails. The emails are specifically for work purposes, but we saw it as a platform that we can use in our stokvel since all of us have access to it…"* (X1); *"I had never thought that we could use emails as form of communication for our stokvel"* (X4).

Other members owned ICTs but they did not have enough knowledge about them; therefore, they were being assisted by other stokvel members or family members: *"He does so many things, he changes the profile picture, the ringtone, sometimes he downloads the things that he thinks they are useful, and tells me there is no space so he deleted some photos, and he does whatever. He teaches me a lot…he's the one who taught me more about the phone. I remember when we started this WhatsApp group, he is the one who created it for me because now I am the administrator and told me this is how we do this…"* (X8).

Even though most of the stokvel members own smartphones and have knowledge of social media such as WhatsApp, email, etc., there are still those few who claim not to have smartphones. The ones that do not have smartphones allow other members to use social media when communicating stokvel matters, but they only make calls: *"For an example, I for one do not have a smartphone, therefore, they will call me whenever we have something to do or if we are meeting somewhere, they would call just to give directions and all that. But for other members, they use WhatsApp"* (X2).

Payment Method and Tools.
As for money, the members used to sit down and give cash to that one person, but now, things are different, as members are using banks to pay money for the stokvel. Even though some of the members still prefer to be given money in their hands, most prefer banks: *"I knew that banks are used to send money to people, but I never thought that it might be useful to our stokvel, since before, we used to withdraw cash and give it to the respective person"* (X15); *"I had bank account before I joined the stokvel, since we have different banks I wasn't sure that we could be able to use the banks to transfer money until they told me about the mobile application..."* (X6).

Members who did not have enough knowledge of the electronic money transfer got assistance from members in their group who had a better understanding of electronic money transfer, which encouraged them to use it. As a result, they all started to use the mobile money transfer and they made it one of their rules to use electronic money transfer: *"We are all using Capitec bank, but not of all us were aware of mobile application; therefore, the members that knew about it asked if do we all have a Capitec bank account and surprisingly, we all use the same bank. Then we all installed the mobile banking app. Then we taught each other how to use it, and from there life was easy for all of us"* (X7).

Most of the groups seemed to prefer banks, but other groups felt that banks were not beneficial for them; instead they were losing some money every time they make transactions: *"It is a better option, the bank created this thing so we can be dependent on them...there's no other they charge you, you put money you get charged, you withdraw money you get charged, so there is no way of escaping it. My wish is that we grow in such a way that as a stokvel we don't flat use money at the end of the year...we grow in such a way that we end up buying shares doing things that are more...like property doing those things, because keeping cash does not bring much value"* (X8).

5.5 Appropriation

The appropriation phase has two stages: objectification and incorporation. This phase's findings are divided and discussed below as the objectification phase, which looks at the reaction of stokvel members towards ICTs and the benefits of ICTs in the stokvel processes, and the incorporation phase, which looks at the trust issues between the stokvel members. The appropriation phase has two important themes: challenges and benefits.

Objectification
The objectification phase comes first in the appropriation phase, and it focuses on the physical space where technology is being acquired. At this stage, the users, or stokvel members, already own and use the ICTs, but they haven't necessarily adopted it. They use the ICTs just to create a better environment for themselves. Most of the stokvels had started before the adoption of ICTs: *"Ten years ago, that's when we started this group of informal savings. What was happening, no one had any cell phones or any other type of ICTs at that time, except radio which we could not use for our stokvel?"*

(X5); *"Not all of us had smartphones when we started tour stokvel, then we did not use ICTs before, but after sometime we realised that we all have phones, why not use them for our stokvel?"*(X20); *"Our stokvel started this year, whereby we all had smartphones, but at the beginning we didn't really think of using social media for our stokvel, we just adopted it after some time but really it does makes life easy"* (X2).

Most of the stokvel members seem to have at least one type of ICT, even though they did not use all the ICTs for their stokvel, but they were using others for other interests. Some of the members owned more than one type of ICT, and they only used one for their stokvel; for other members, they have ICTs which they could not use for their stokvels, since some of the members do not own any type of ICT which might be useful for the stokvel. Members seemed to have a good understanding of the ICTs that they have adopted for their stokvel: *"We all deposit the money into the group bank account…"* (X3 and X8); *"We use WhatsApp which is makes our lives easy and a lot more flexible, because we don't have to meet physically to do the stokvel stuff, it's easy, we just do everything using cell phones"* (X7).

Members had many challenges, mentioned above, in the commodification process, which they faced before adopting ICTs. Now that they have specific types of ICTs and/or social media that they use to facilitate the stokvels, they are then able to mitigate and overcome some of the challenges they were facing. One of the biggest challenges was the loss of money through theft or robbery. ICTs also help to improve the recording of payments, since, previously, members had to have a book that could be lost any time, so the use of ICTs helps them by giving them a platform where they can just type the records and send to anyone such as via WhatsApp, emails or Excel.

"If we want to discuss something like, who is getting the money? This money, or maybe one member has an emergency, as a result, he/she needs money next month and it's not his/her turn to get the money. Instead of calling all of us, they just state the matter on the group and the person who was supposed to be getting money for that month then will be one taking the decision" (X7).

"Some of the members would come late for the meetings or not pitch up at all; therefore, they would need to be informed on what was being discussed…so WhatsApp made it easy for everyone because then no one would to update anyone. Even if the person could not be online on the time we were discussing something, but at least then we are sure that he/she will see the messages once she opens WhatsApp…" (X13).

"We all have emails…" (X1 and X4).

"I use Excel spreadsheet to record all the payments made for the month, everyone has to confirm that she has received the money so I can update it, and it becomes easy for us to see who had not paid yet, but then we don't really go that far since we work together, and all get paid on the same day" (X4).

"We don't have a book where we write down the payments because we just use Capitec application to transfer money, our records are just the messages we get after sending money" (X7).

Incorporation

This stage of domestication deals with the integration of ICTs in the daily life of the stokvel members. It shows how long they use ICTs and how they manage their time, as well as how well the members trust each other. The phase also looks at the things that can to be done to improve the operations of the stokvel.

The stokvels are created on the bases of trust; as a result, most of the members of the stokvel are most likely to be specific to colleagues, family members, friends, etc. It is very rare to find a stokvel with people who do not know each other well. *"We trust each other, even if we don't; we are working together so everyone has to pay when it's time to pay"* (X7).

Even though most of the stokvel members seemed to trust other members, there was one individual from a family stokvel who said that for them, it is not that easy to guarantee that people will pay money when they have to. The member mentioned that "you must never trust family members", emphasising the fact that because people are your family, they just know that you will always understand because you know them better. *"We do trust each, but you know family members"* (X3).

5.6 Conversion

This stage refers to the process where members who have already adopted ICTs show off or promote the technology to other members. The sub-theme for this phase is the effect of ICTs on member relationships.

Effect of ICTs on Member's Relationship
The use of ICTs has a positive effect on the relationships of the stokvel members, and it creates good and continuous relationships. Even though members do not have to meet in person, as before, the use of ICTs provides continuous connectedness. They do not only communicate to each other simply because they are discussing stokvel matters, but they also have general talks. It actually builds a relationship, and WhatsApp group members get to know each other better. They often share things that are outside the main goal of the group, including inviting each other for birthdays, other celebrations, job opportunities, etc. The use of ICTs has allowed most of the stokvel members to become like family members, because they communicate any time, which is unlike before the adoption of ICTs where they usually only met once a month. The use of ICTs in stokvel groups is increasing, since members encourage other members to use the same type of ICTs which they feel makes the running of the stokvel more efficient and effective. Members seem to really appreciate the adoption of ICTs in their stokvels: *"We are just like family"* (X6).

6 Summary and Conclusion

The findings of this research revealed some interesting information regarding domestication of ICTs in stokvel groups in Cape Town. Before the domestication, the findings identified a new stokvel type, meat stokvel, which was not discussed in the literature. It then identified all the types of ICTs owned by different stokvel members, and also explained how they use those technologies inside and outside the stokvel context. Social media is also adopted by the stokvels, especially WhatsApp, followed by email and, lastly, calls. Age influenced the adoption of ICTs amongst stokvel groups. A few of the groups were resistant to other types of ICTs and, for others, it was due to age. Overall, stokvel groups had adopted the use of ICTs to facilitate the matters of the stokvels such as for communication and payment methods.

Although stokvels have adopted the use of ICTs, it appears that their members do not have enough knowledge of, or information on, the other financial platforms or applications that they could use to facilitate their stokvels, since the findings showed that they have only adopted WhatsApp, email, and a few other things such as Excel. Most of the traditional stokvels are not registered with the NASASA; as a result, they are missing more benefits and knowledge about stokvels. Most of the participants did not even know about NASASA. We recommend that NASASA embarks on a publicity campaign to inform the community about the services and information they can provide. A final recommendation is for banks to do the same, given that few of the stokvels are using bank club accounts, based on the findings. Banks should explore innovative means to encourage stokvel groups to have specific accounts for their stokvels. One innovative mechanism could be extending credit to stokvels groups; for example, if a burial stokvel does not have enough money for a burial, the bank loans the group an amount to cover all necessary expenses, since the members are likely to be contributing every month.

References

1. Statistics South Africa - P0310 - Living Conditions of Households in South Africa - 2014/2015. http://www.statssa.gov.za/?page_id=1866&PPN=P0310. Accessed 03 Aug 2018
2. Mataku, S., Kaseke, E.: The role of Stokvels in improving people's lives: the case in Orange Farm, Johannesburg, South Africa (2014) Social Work **50**(4), 504–515 (2014)
3. Mashigo, M.: Informal finance for survivalist enterprise development in South Africa: A case study of Soshanguve Township. Thesis, Tshwane University of Technology (2015)
4. Verhoef, G.: Informal financial service institutions for survival: african women and stokvels in urban South Africa, 1930–1998. Enterp. Soc. **2**(2), 259–296 (2001)
5. Lukhele, A.K.: Stokvels in South Africa: Informal Savings Schemes by Blacks for the Black Community, 1st edn. Amagi Books, Johannesburg (1990)
6. Nithyanandhan, S.H.: Socio-economic Status of Women in Micro Credit Self Help Groups in Chennai, India. Ph.D. diss., Jabatan Statistik Gunaan, Fakulti Ekonomi dan Pentadbiran, Universiti Malaya (2014)
7. Ardener, S.: Credit unions and money clubs (ROSCAs). Anthropol. Today **30**(4), 3–6 (2014)
8. Lie, M., Sørensen, K.H.: Making technology our own? Domesticating Technology into Everyday Life. Scandinavian University Press North America, Boston (1996)
9. National Stokvel Association of South Africa: Introduction. http://nasasa.co.za/site/#intro. Accessed 03 May 2018
10. Mfekaye, Z.M.: An investigation of factors surrounding food insecurity in kwaMthethwa. University of Zululand, Department of Social Work (2013)
11. Motsoeneng, M.: Nine case Studies from the Social Protection and Local Economic Development (LED): Graduation Pilot Project (2015)
12. van Donk, M., Secretariat, G.G.: In Search of Community Resilience. Community Resilience and Vulnerability in South Africa **9**, 1–89 (2014)
13. Moloi, T.P.: An exploration of group dynamics in "stokvels" and its implications on the members' mental health and psychological well-being. Ph.D., University of Zululand (2011)

14. FinScope - South Africa Financial Inclusion Report. http://www.finmark.org.za/wp-content/uploads/2017/12/08Nov2016_FinScope_Consumer-survey-South-Africa-2016.pdf. Accessed 03 Aug 2018
15. Johnston, K.A., Jali, N., Kundaeli, F., Adeniran, T.: ICTs for the broader development of South Africa: an analysis of the literature. Electron. J. Inf. Syst. Dev. Countries **70**(3), 1–22 (2015)
16. Hart, T.G., Ramoroka, K.H., Jacobs, P.T., Letty, B.A.: Revealing the social face of innovation. S. Afr. J. Sci. **111**(9–10), 01–06 (2015)
17. Egbe, D.A., Mutanga, M.B.: Technical sustainability in rural ICT deployments in South Africa. In: IST-Africa Week Conference, pp. 1–9. IEEE (2016)
18. Chigona, A., Chigona, W., Kayongo, P., Kausa, M.: An empirical survey on domestication of ICT in schools in disadvantaged communities in South Africa. Int. J. Educ. Dev. Inf. Commun. Technol. (IJEDICT) **6**(2), 9–22 (2010)
19. Letsie, M., Kabanda, S., Chigona, W.: Economically disadvantaged families domesticating mobile devices: case of South African. In: Proceedings of the 9th IDIA Conference, pp. 72–83. Nungwi, Zanzibar (2015)
20. Vuojärvi, H., Isomäki, H., Hynes, D.: Domestication of a laptop on a wireless university campus: a case study. Australas. J. Educational Technol. **26**(2), 250–267 (2010)
21. Willett, R.: Domesticating online games for preteens–discursive fields, everyday gaming, and family life. Children's Geographies **15**(2), 146–159 (2017)
22. Rosales, A., Fernández-Ardèvol, M., Comunello, F., Mulargia, S., Ferran-Ferrer, N.: Older people and smartwatches, initial experiences. El profesional de la información **26**(3), 457–463 (2017)

Rethinking ICT4D Impact Assessments: Reflections from the Siyakhula Living Lab in South Africa

Hafeni Mthoko[1(✉)] and Caroline Khene[2]

[1] University of Cape Town, Cape Town, South Africa
hafeni.mthoko@uct.ac.za
[2] Rhodes University, Grahamstown, South Africa
c.khene@ru.ac.za

Abstract. The approach to outcome and impact assessments of ICTD has often relied solely on identifying project effects in relation to project baseline data; however, such an approach limits the potential learning that could be occurring throughout a project's lifecycle. Impact assessments should be conducted in a comprehensive manner, taking into account the evaluation data that has been captured from the initiation of the project through to its implementation, and beyond. This study sought to reflect on the implementation of an impact assessment framework that is based on a comprehensive approach to evaluation. The framework was implemented in the Siyakhula Living Lab to assess for its outcomes and impacts on the community. A pragmatic approach was applied through a reflective process, to assess the utility of the framework within this context. Semi-structured interviews with project stakeholders were conducted to further gain insight into the comprehensive approach to conducting impact assessments. It was found that a comprehensive approach to assessing impacts provided a meaningful way to understand the effects of the ICTD initiative, and provided an overview of project areas that required improvement. However, it was found that the proposed assessment framework required a customisation component in order to modify it to better suit the project context. The way in which future impact assessments are conducted can draw on the lessons gained from following a more comprehensive approach to evaluation, and thus improve learning over time.

Keywords: Impact assessment · Evaluation · Learning · Living lab
Sustainability

1 Introduction and Background

The field of ICTD has been evolving over the years, with changing trends influenced by shifting development paradigms [1, 2]. The effects of ICTs on socio-economic development in developing contexts continue to be an area of debate, and the need for the documentation of tangible evidence of such effects is growing.

As a response to this need, there have been various evaluation frameworks developed to demonstrate the effects of ICTD [3, 4]; furthermore, there has been a need

K. Krauss et al. (Eds.): IDIA 2018, CCIS 933, pp. 48–60, 2019.
https://doi.org/10.1007/978-3-030-11235-6_4

to glean more on development studies to demonstrate the 4D aspect of ICT4D. As a result, Sens Capability framework has been one of the popular frameworks utilised to aid in evaluating the 'impact' of ICTD initiatives.

Along with the shift in ICTD trends there has been the shift in the evaluation of such initiatives. Looking at the ICTD value chain developed by [1], focus has shifted from assessing readiness and adoption of ICTs in developmental contexts towards impact and demonstrating value for human development. However, despite the rise in impact assessment frameworks being developed, there still remains a disconnect between ICTD project lifecycles and the assessment of impact [5, 6]. This tends to result in assessments that are not informed by the various project activities and effects over time, limiting the potential learning and project improvement that could occur [7].

ICTD evaluations aid projects to not only demonstrate what has been occurring and whether project objectives have been met, but to also learn from the project in order to improve and grow [8, 9]. Learning is key in any ICTD project, to move from the challenges of pilotitis and the documented failures of ICTD. Evaluators and project teams need to be more conscious of learning through evaluations. The concern is not so much the failure of ICTD projects, but rather the failure to reflect on and learn from these failures [10]. One means to enhance learning is through a process of evaluating projects more holistically, and take into account the changes that evolved throughout a project's lifecycle; therefore, [11] proposed a comprehensive approach to ICT4D evaluation, comprising seven domains of evaluating ICT4D: Baseline Study, Needs Assessment, Programme Theory Assessment, Process Assessment, Outcome and Impact Assessment, Efficiency Assessment and Scalability Assessment [6]. They define a rural comprehensive evaluation as follows:

> *"The comprehensive application of all appropriate domains of evaluation throughout the life of a rural ICT project, in ways that are adapted to the social, political, cultural, and economic rural environment, and designed to inform ICT interventions to improve and support rural development."*

Their rationale, building from the work of programme evaluation [12], is that to gain a more holistic understanding of what is occurring, one needs to evaluate a project throughout its lifecycle. Each evaluation domain applies a different approach of analysis, and provides results that interdependently build on other domains of evaluation to create a more reflective iterative evaluation [11]. This research paper specifically focuses on the *Outcome and Impact Assessment* domain, as part of ongoing research on the Rural ICT Comprehensive Evaluation Framework (RICT-CEF) [11] which has been applied in the Siyakhula Living Lab ICT project. This paper builds on the initial theoretical analysis conducted by [7] who proposed an Outcome and Impact assessment framework that is informed by a comprehensive evaluation. They argue that to further aid in continuous learning, and gain a rich understanding of the effects of ICTD initiatives, impact assessments should form part of a comprehensive approach to evaluation, rather than assessing for impacts in isolation, disregarding the various processes throughout a project's lifecycle [7].

2 The Theoretical Framework

The Outcome and Impact Assessment framework was developed from a theoretical analysis, conducted by [7]. [13]'s theorising approach was used to develop the framework, based on an analysis of social development theories/frameworks, and Information Systems and Information Technology theories/frameworks. This paper builds on the analysis by [7], exploring the framework in an empirical setting. The Outcome and Impact assessment framework is illustrated in Fig. 1, comprising three components to guide evaluators: (i) the evaluation guidelines to take into consideration when assessing outcomes and impacts, (ii) the critical themes of rural ICT4D outcome and impact assessment, and (iii) the preceding domains of evaluation:

Evaluation Guidelines: These provide a basis for planning for the outcome and impact assessment process. The guidelines highlight the need to take into account preceding evaluation data from different stages of the project [6, 14], consider project stakeholders in the evaluation process [11, 12, 15], consider the external environment that provides the context in which the assessment results may be understood [9, 16–18], and consider the ethical implications surrounding the project [18–21].

Critical Outcome and Impact Themes: The Outcome and Impact themes represent the critical aspects that should be assessed in rural ICT4D projects. The framework highlights five key themes identified from literature as important for assessing for outcome and impact. The five themes demonstrate their interdependence through a progressive process towards sustainable development; however, this does not demonstrate a restrictive sequential process, but rather the overlapping relationship between them [7]. These include the following:

Strategic Value – Creating strategic advantage within ICT4D programmes entails enabling individuals and community members to equip themselves to achieve the developmental goals they desire. Strategic value assesses a project from a forward-looking perspective, to determine its value from the perspective of beneficiaries [17, 22, 23].

Most Significant Change: Identifies the beneficiaries' perspectives on significant changes that have occurred as a result of an ICTD intervention. Project recipients would openly reflect on their project experiences, with particular emphasis on the changes that have taken place within the community that they view as most important – this allows for unintended effects to emerge [17, 24].

Empowerment: Is seen as the ability to expand people's knowledge, enhancing people's confidence, enhancing their decision-making, and enhancing their access and management of resources [14, 25–28].

Livelihoods: Aims at understanding how ICTs have influenced the ways in which beneficiaries make a living and protect themselves against vulnerability [14, 29, 30].

Sustainability: Aims to understand the mechanisms in place that support the positive outputs, outcomes and impacts that have been identified as a result of the ICT4D project. This is to ensure that positive effects are indeed sustainable and not short lived; moreover, as an evaluator one would need to further determine what measures are being utilised to mitigate any negative outputs, outcomes and impacts that have been identified [24, 31–34].

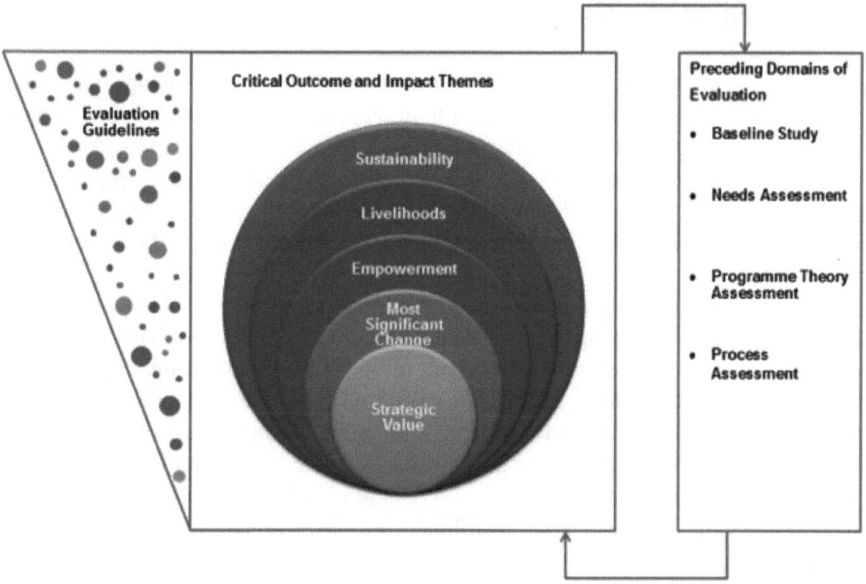

Fig. 1. Framework for the outcome and impact assessment of Rural ICT4D

Preceding Domains of Evaluation: The preceding domains of evaluation provide the comprehensive arena which the Outcome and Impact assessment themes form a part of – that is the Baseline Study, Needs Assessment, Programme Theory Assessment, and Process Assessment. The assessment of the abovementioned themes is not only informed by preceding evaluations, but also informs future project evaluations that are to be conducted. The preceding domains all evaluate a particular aspect of a project, which adds perspective to the results obtained from the outcome and impact assessment of rural ICTD projects [11, 12].

2.1 The Relationship Between Themes

The proposed themes interact in multiple ways in an iterative manner; they reinforce and build on each other to demonstrate change within communities [7]. Through a process of *strategic value,* ICTD initiatives should position communities and rural activities in such a manner that enables individuals and community members to better achieve their development goals. Furthermore, *strategic value* paves the way forward for *most significant change*, *empowerment*, *livelihoods* and *sustainability* to take effect. Through *empowerment* people's capabilities are enhanced, in order to make better life choices, achieve positive *livelihood* effects and positive *most significant change,* given the external environment and context in which people live. As much as ICTD programmes can facilitate positive change, empower people, and positively impact people's livelihood, they are not deemed a success unless such outcomes and impacts are *sustainable* [35]. The above processes further facilitate the expansion of ICTD initiatives and add new *strategic value*.

3 Research Methodology

The research study applies a pragmatic approach, enabling an interchangeable process of action and knowledge enquiry, in order to address a 'real life' problem in its context [36, 37]. In this particular research study, the Outcome and Impact Assessment framework is implemented to assist in evaluating the outcome and impact of the Siyakhula Living Lab, from 2013–2015. Here, the tool to conduct the evaluation is being assessed for its utility in the case study, and not necessarily the results of the evaluation.

A case study approach was applied to the study using the Siyakhula Living Lab (SLL). The research investigation aimed to explore the application of the proposed framework to assess the outcome and impact of the SLL as part of ongoing evaluation, and *why* particular evaluation approaches (based on theory and empirically emergent) were applied to the evaluation of the case study. The Siyakhula Living Lab (SLL) operates in the rural Dwesa area, in the Mbashe municipality along the Wild Coast of South Africa [38]. It began as a collaboration between multiple entities, "to co-create, develop and field test a distributed, multifunctional community communication platform, for marginalised and semi-marginalised communities in South Africa" [38]. The SLL formed part of continued research on a comprehensive approach to evaluation. All domains of evaluation prior to the Outcome and Impact assessment – the Baseline Study, the Needs Assessment, the Programme Theory Assessment, and Process Assessment – had been conducted.

Qualitative data was collected using participant observation, semi-structured interviews, and documentation

- *Participant Observation*: The researcher primarily observed the assessment of all outcome and impact themes in the case study as the framework was implemented. The researcher, as the evaluator, also reflected on her decisions and approaches used (how and why) to apply the proposed framework, based on the context circumstances and response of project participants.
- *Interviews*: Interviews were conducted in a focus group environment, or as one-on-one interviews with project stakeholders, at the end of the actual Outcome and Impact assessment application. The interview questions were directed towards the participants' experiences, the evaluation process, and the assessment themes applied. The project implementation team, rural project champions, teachers and community members were interviewed.
- *Document Analysis*: As this research is part of ongoing evaluation research, documentation from preceding evaluations in the Siyakhula Living Lab, such as the Baseline Study, Needs Assessment, Programme Theory Assessment, and the Process Assessment, were consulted. The lessons learned from preceding evaluation domains informed the reflective process and further informed the evaluator on what to expect and possibly apply within the field.

Data analysis was conducted using thematic analysis and the iterative explanation building technique suggested by [39] for case studies. These approaches are well suited to the abductive reasoning enquiry process that is characteristic of pragmatic research.

4 Findings and Discussion

The implementation of the Outcome and Impact Assessment framework in the Siyakhula Living Lab was an opportunity to demonstrate the use of the proposed evaluation framework within a rural ICT4D context. Questioning and observing the actual evaluation tool allowed lessons to emerge that reviewed the suitability and shortcoming of the evaluation framework in an ICT4D context. These lessons were framed around the different components that make up the Outcome and Impact Assessment framework.

4.1 Application of Evaluation Guidelines

Stakeholder Relationship: A lengthy engagement period within the project allowed the researcher the opportunity to develop and grow relationships with different stakeholders, specifically local community members. The evaluation process took on both a participatory and empowering role, engaging various stakeholders in the project. Moreover, involving stakeholders in the evaluation process created a sense of ownership and facilitated the overall process [40–42]. The following lessons were learned through the engagement process:

L.1. Engaging with stakeholders aided the refinement of data collection instruments. Involving teachers, project champions and community members in the evaluation planning process helped gain different perspectives on the evaluation process. The ICT champions assisted with identifying ways considered appropriate to conduct the evaluation; moreover, the input from the ICT champions and several teachers on the data collection instruments used, aided the researcher in revising the research instruments. For example, ICT champions provided suggestions on questions to explore during interviews; furthermore, the project leader and founder for the SLL reviewed the proposed evaluation instruments and provided their suggestions for improvement and changes. Such interactions with stakeholders facilitated the evaluation process. Successful engagement with development-related projects involves working closely with community members [43, 44].

L2. Engaging with stakeholders gave the researcher the opportunity to grasp the project. Through the engagement with the project leader and project champion, the researcher became familiar with the project. The engagement process further facilitated the transition from being a complete outsider to being someone the community became acquainted with; furthermore, assisting in the computer literacy training gave the researcher first-hand experience on some of the key project activities.

L3. Project recipients, particularly project champions, are key informants for planning an evaluation. Engaging with stakeholders during the evaluation planning process created an environment where stakeholders played an advisory role for the overall research process. Stakeholders, particularly project champions, were in the capacity to recommend key informants who could take part in the research, the appropriate channels to follow to successfully complete the research, and recommend methods for data collection. This speaks to the process of applying **ethical considerations** [21, 42].

L4. Collaborating with stakeholders creates an opportunity for empowerment evaluation to take place. Project champions highlighted that their involvement in the evaluation process was an opportunity to learn about research. For example, one project champion planned to pursue an Honours degree in education, and wished to take part in the evaluation process to gain exposure on the various techniques of conducting research. Her involvement in the outcome and impact assessment gave her the opportunity to gain first-hand experience of the different aspects involved in conducting research-related work. Through a collaborative evaluation approach, project stakeholders also gain the skills required to lead and conduct future evaluations. Evaluations can influence various change processes and outcomes. Evaluation goes beyond *use* to cover concepts such as evaluation influence (the consequence of evaluation) [45].

Application of the Comprehensive Evaluation Approach: Prior evaluation documentation aided the researcher in contextualising the Outcome and Impact Assessment framework to suit the Siyakhula Living Lab and provide meaning to the outcomes and impacts identified. All preceding evaluation reports – Baseline Study, 2009; Needs Assessment, 2009; Programme Theory Assessment, 2009; Process Assessment, 2012; and Impact assessment 2009, were made available to the researcher. The Outcome and Impact Assessment framework outlined generic questions to consider for the evaluation. It further provided guidelines on the types of questions to ask for assessing each theme; therefore, referring to the above reports, the researcher gained a holistic picture of the Siyakhula Living Lab context in which the Outcome and Impact Assessment would take place. This aided in particularising each Outcome and Impact theme to the specific project, and formulating appropriate questions. The following lesson was learned:

L5. Preceding evaluation data is relevant for contextualising the Outcome and Impact Assessment framework. Data from the other domains of evaluation was utilised as a means to contextualise the various data collection methods employed; moreover, preceding evaluation data aided the researcher in scoping findings from the Outcome and Impact assessment. Preceding evaluations also played a role of providing the evaluator with an understanding of the **external environment** that influences the project positively or negatively; for example, an ICT policy imposed by the Department of Education, required principals and teachers to submit electronic records of the school reports. As a result, teachers and principals from several schools felt the pressure to learn how to utilise ICTs in order to fulfil their job requirements. This, in turn, influenced their engagement in the SLL. Such data from previous evaluations supported the development of data collection tools, and analysis of data.

4.2 Application of Outcome and Impact Themes

Assessing Strategic Value: The assessment of Strategic Value revealed that project recipients also have a responsibility in positioning themselves to take advantage of the opportunities offered by an ICTD initiative; moreover, the researcher identified that the attitude and behaviour of the project recipients influenced the ways in which they were equipped to achieve the goals they desired. The key lessons learned were the following:

L6. Participant observations provide a relaxed environment to engage with community members and elicit their opinions about the services being offered by a project. During participant observation, one is accepted by the community, which opens doors for open engagement to occur and unexpected indigenous understanding to emerge [24, 26, 46]. From the data collection process, the participant observations were most fruitful. The researcher gained insight into what was occurring on the ground, and could interact with the different community members. The researcher could also observe that the type of services offered by the project did not reflect what was originally planned in the Programme Theory Assessment.

L7. The Strategic Value of a project should be clear and clearly communicated to community members. Community members have more confidence in a project when they see that the services offered by the project can be utilised in a practical manner; therefore, it is important for evaluators to be aware of the alignment between services offered and the goals of the community, and capture this information for the project's improvement. Understanding why particular services are offered will aid in determining if there is an actual need for that service, and provide a clearer understanding of where and how the project services will suit a particular context [47].

L8. An Outcome and Impact Assessment informs other domains of evaluation. Findings from the Outcome and Impact Assessment process can inform subsequent iterations of the RICT-CEF application; for example, outcome and impact findings highlighted emergent needs as a result of the SLL, which calls for a subsequent iteration of the Needs Assessment process to take place.

Assessing for Most Significant Change: The assessment of Most Significant Change was a fruitful exercise, as it gave project recipients the platform to freely express their views about the project. However, the assessment for Most Significant Change identified results that could be categorised as part of the other four Outcome and Impact themes; therefore, the researcher acknowledged that assessing Most Significant Change should instead be incorporated as an essential method to collect data within the other themes. The key lesson identified was the following:

L9. The assessment of Most Significant Change creates an environment for unintended outcomes/impacts to emerge. Assessing for Most Significant Change aided in exploring the hidden and intangible effects of the project on both users. It also gives recipients the opportunity to highlight the aspects of the project they value or would value if change were to occur; moreover, a key benefit of the method is the ability to identify unintended outcomes/impacts through storytelling [24, 46, 48].

Assessing for Empowerment: The assessment for Empowerment in the SLL was quite generic, as the project aims were broad, and the project was not tailored to meet one particular need, but rather a range of needs; therefore, the assessment of Empowerment had to cover a wide range of variables, from health, education, income generation, employment, communication, culture, etc. All ICTD projects should have a clear set of aims and goals they would like to achieve, and rather have a focused approach. For projects that have a wide range of goals and no specific direction they would like to follow, evaluators should also keep the evaluation process quite broad, so as not to miss any of the planned goals of the project. The key lessons identified were the following:

L10. Community members should be encouraged to complete surveys based on their own experiences. Researchers should ensure that research participants are aware of the purpose of the research and the importance of providing their views in a safe environment. Researchers should keep in mind that "if you ask someone to tell his or her life story, will what you get be in that person's authentic voice, or in a voice that he or she thinks you might be looking for?" [49]; moreover, the questionnaire should be personalised and phrased in the first person, to encourage an atmosphere of ownership of the questions. This minimises the need to provide "correct" answers.

L11. Outcomes and Impacts should not be presented in isolation from each other. Upon completion of an Outcome and Impact Assessment, the discussion of project impacts should be presented in relation to the outcomes they emanate from; the reason being that an attempt to have outcomes and impacts explicitly separate takes away from having a holistic picture of what happened.

Assessing for Livelihoods: Through the observations made and through the interview discussions, all project recipients focused on aspects related to Livelihoods (ways in which they lived their lives). From the data collected, the researcher observed that participants paid less attention to the processes that would lead to their end goals, but preferred to dwell on the achievement of end goals. For example, participants equated project success to the attainment of the desired end goal, and not necessarily the process that would lead to the attainment of such goals. The key lesson learned was the following:

L12. Understanding the alignment between project outputs and community goals is important for understanding the types of Livelihood outcomes and impacts experienced by community members. It was observed from the data analysis that, due to the poor alignment of project services with community goals, the Livelihood outcomes and impacts experienced were minimal.

Assessing for Sustainability: Through the assessment of Sustainability, the researcher acknowledged that a workshop was required to discuss the Outcome and Impact assessment findings in detail, with key stakeholders. It is important to follow up on the findings with users, and a workshop is one way to do so [42]. The aim would be to gain their insights on the results, and initiate discussions on ways in which the teams will sustain the positive Outcomes and Impacts, and also mitigate the negative effects identified. Assessing for Sustainability in this case also drew stakeholder attention to think about the long-term management of such a project. The key lessons learned were as follows:

L13. Low engagement of project recipients, such as project champions, in the management of the project, influences their engagement in the sustainability of project outcomes and impacts. Project champions who should be involved in the management of the project should be aware of the existing ways in which project outputs, outcomes and impacts are being sustained. A top-down approach to project management creates an atmosphere whereby project recipients feel they cannot contribute towards the sustainability of the project and subsequent improvements in the project [8, 50]. As a result, project ownership is minimised, and evaluation use limited [42].

L14. The assessment of Sustainability should be a continuous process that extends even after the Outcome and Impact Assessment is complete. Not all outcomes and impacts that are identified are intended by the project team. As a result, the project might not have any measures in place to ensure that unintended positive effects are sustained and negative effects dealt with. Through the outcomes and impacts identified, it would be best to present this information to the project team, and continue to elicit their views on ways to ensure that positive outcomes and impacts are sustained.

5 Limitations of the Study

The following study reflected on one iteration of the implementation of the Outcome and Impact Assessment framework; moreover, an account of feedback from SLL stakeholders on the utility of the framework would add a context-specific perspective on the framework itself. Continued implementation and reflection of the Outcome and Impact Assessment framework proposed by [7] would provide a wider data set to refine and modify the framework; moreover, application of the framework in case studies that have not followed a comprehensive approach to evaluation, would provide useful insights into the utility of the framework in different contexts.

6 Conclusion

There has been a continued shift in the evaluation focus of ICTD initiatives. As a result, several ICTD impact assessment frameworks have been developed over time, with the hope that we gain a better understanding of ICTD and the impact they have on development goals; however, despite the rise in impact assessment frameworks, there still remains a disconnect between ICTD project lifecycles and the assessment of impact [7]. This tends to result in assessments that are not informed by the various project activities and effects over time, limiting the potential learning and project improvement that could take place.

This paper aimed to provide an account of the implementation and application of the Outcome and Impact Assessment framework within the SLL. It was found that the preceding domains of evaluation were essential in the overall assessment process. The assessment of the five themes – Strategic Value, Most Significant Change, Empowerment, Livelihoods, and Sustainability – aided in describing the effects of the SLL on the Dwesa community. All themes worked together to describe the project; furthermore, the assessment of Most Significant Change resulted in outcomes and impacts that could be categorised as part of Strategic Value, Empowerment, or Livelihoods. It was therefore suggested that the Most Significant Change theme should be collapsed as a distinct theme. It should rather be an essential method to be incorporated within Strategic Value, Empowerment and/or Livelihoods.

It is concluded that the iterative application of the framework in different case studies will result in continuous revision to the framework; moreover, the application of the framework in different cases acts as a basis on which different cases can learn from one another. The SLL project stakeholders acknowledged the importance of knowing how the ICTD initiative was performing in favour of facilitating positive change and development in accordance with project aims. Such a process of learning is enhanced when the assessment process is embedded within a comprehensive approach to evaluation; therefore, future ICTD outcome and impact assessments may need to reconsider the ways in which such assessments can yield a holistic overview of what is happening, beyond the traditional 'before and after' impact scenarios. The involvement of stakeholders in the entire evaluation process, and keeping an account of various project activities throughout its lifecycle, create a rich overview of project effects in the long term.

References

1. Heeks, R.: Information and Communication Technology for Development (ICT4D). Routledge, London (2018)
2. Walsham, G.: ICT4D research: reflections on history and future agenda. Inf. Technol. Dev. **23**(1), 1–24 (2017)
3. Gomez, R., Pather, S.: ICT evaluation: are we asking the right questions? Electron. J. Inf. Syst. Dev. Ctries. **50**, 1–14 (2012)
4. Heeks, R., Molla, A.: Impact Assessment of ICT-for-Development Projects: A Compendium of Approaches (2009)
5. Pade-Khene, C., Lannon, J.: Learning to be sustainable in ICT for development: a citizen engagement initiative in South Africa. In: Choudrie, J., Islam, M.S., Wahid, F., Bass, J.M., Priyatma, J.E. (eds.) ICT4D 2017. IAICT, vol. 504, pp. 475–486. Springer, Cham (2017). https://doi.org/10.1007/978-3-319-59111-7_39
6. Pade-Khene, C., Sewry, D.: Towards a Comprehensive Evaluation Framework for ICT for Development Evaluation – An Analysis of Evaluation Frameworks. Presented at the (2011)
7. Mthoko, H., Khene, C.: Building theory in ICT4D evaluation: a comprehensive approach to assessing outcome and impact. Inf. Technol. Dev. (2017). https://doi.org/10.1080/02681102.2017.1315359
8. Pade-Khene, C., Lannon, J.: Learning to be Sustainable in ICT for Development: A Citizen Engagement Initiative in South Africa. Presented at the (2017)
9. Toyama, K.: Geek Heresy: Rescuing Social Change from the Cult of Technology. Public Affairs, New York (2015)
10. Dodson, L., Sterling, S.R., Bennett, J.K.: Considering failure: eight years of ITID research. In: Proceedings of the Fifth International Conference on Information and Communication Technologies and Development, pp. 56–64. Georgia (2012)
11. Pade-Khene, C., Sewry, D.: Proposed stages of a rural ICT comprehensive evaluation framework in ICT for rural development projects. In: Proceedings of the South African Institute of Computer Scientists and Information Technologists Conference on Knowledge, Innovation and Leadership in a Diverse, Multidisciplinary Environment, SAICSIT 2011, p. 326 (2011). https://doi.org/10.1145/2072221.2072269

12. Rossi, P.H., Lipsey, M.W., Freeman, H.E.: Evaluation: A Systematic Approach. Sage Publications, London (2004)
13. Weick, K.E.: What theory is not, theorizing is. Adm. Sci. Q. **40**, 385–390 (1995)
14. Gigler, B.S.: Including the excluded: can ICTs empower poor communities? Towards an alternative evaluation framework based on the capability approach. Presented at the (2004)
15. Mansell, R.: Power and interests in information and communication and development: exogenous and endogenous discourses in contention. J. Int. Dev. **26**, 109–127 (2011)
16. Brydon, L.: Ethical practices in doing development research. In: Doing Development Research, pp. 25–33. Sage Publications, London (2006)
17. Grunfeld, H.: Framework for evaluating contributions of ICT to capabilities, empowerment and sustainability in disadvantaged communities. In: CPRSouth2 (Communication Policy Research) Conference, "Empowering Rural Communities Through ICT Policy and Research, Madras (2007)
18. Krauss, K.: Ethical research practice for community entry: using ICT4D in a deep rural context. In: 3rd International IDIA Development Informatics Conference, Kruger National Park (2009)
19. Brunet, P., Tiemtore, O., Vettraino-Soulard, M.C.: Ethics and the Internet in West Africa: Toward an Ethical Model of Integration. IDRC, Ottawa (2004)
20. McNamara, K.S.: Information and Communication Technologies, Poverty and Development: Learning from Experience. InfoDev, Geneva (2003)
21. Mthoko, H., Pade-Khene, C.: Towards a theoretical framework on ethical practice in ICT4D programmes. Inf. Dev. J. 1–18 (2012). https://doi.org/10.1177/0266666912449456
22. Hallikainen, P., Chen, L.: A holistic framework on information systems evaluation with a case analysis. Electron. J. Inf. Syst. Eval. **9**, 57–64 (2005)
23. Hamel, J.: ICT4D and the human development and capabilities approach: the potentials of information and communication technology. United Nations Development Programme, New York (2010)
24. Batchelor, S., Norrish, P.: Framework for Assessment of ICT Pilot Projects: Beyond Monitoring and Evaluation to Applied Research. InfoDev, The World Bank, Washington D.C (2006)
25. Rabaya, K.S.: Economic and social empowerment of women through information and communication technology: a case study of palestine. J. Commun. Inform. **5**
26. Wieman, A., Gast, L., Hagen, I., Van Der Krogt, S.: Monitoring and Evaluation at IICD: An Instrument to Assess Development Impact and Effectiveness. International Institute for Communication and Development (IICD), The Hague (2001)
27. The World Bank: ICT for Greater Development Impact-Information and Communication Technology. The World Bank, Washington D.C (2012)
28. Alsop, R., Bertelsen, M.F., Holland, J.: Empowerment in Practice: From Analysis to Implementation. The World Bank, Washington D.C (2006)
29. Parkinson, S., Ramirez, R.: Using a sustainable livelihoods approach to assessing the impact of ICTs in development. Commun. Inform. **2**, 116–127 (2006)
30. Duncombe, R.: Using the livelihoods framework to analyse ICT applications for poverty reduction through microenterprise. Inf. Technol. Int. Dev. **3**, 81–100 (2006)
31. Marais, M., Meyer, I.: Design for sustainability: countering the drivers of unsustainability in development projects. J. Commun. Inform. **11**, 1–13 (2015)
32. Souter, D.: ICTS, the Internet and Sustainability: A Discussion Paper. International Institute for Sustainable Development, Winnipeg (2012)
33. Hilty, L.M., Hercheui, M.D.: ICT and sustainable development. In: Berleur, J., Hercheui, M.D., Hilty, L.M. (eds.) CIP/HCC -2010. IAICT, vol. 328, pp. 227–235. Springer, Heidelberg (2010). https://doi.org/10.1007/978-3-642-15479-9_22

34. Ali, M., Bailur, S.: The Challenge of "Sustainability" in ICT4D - Is Bricolage the Answer? Presented at the (2007)
35. Unwin, T.: ICT4D: Information and Communication Technology for Development. Cambridge University Press, Cambridge (2009)
36. Goldkuhl, G.: Pragmatism vs interpretivism in qualitative information systems research. Eur. J. Inf. Syst. **21**, 135–146 (2012)
37. Feilzer, M.Y.: Doing mixed methods research pragmatically: implications for the rediscovery of pragmatism as a research paradigm. J. Mix. Methods Res. **4**, 6–16 (2010)
38. Pade-Khene, C., Palmer, R., Kavhai, M.: A baseline study of a dwesa rural community for the siyakhula information and communication technology for development project: understanding the reality on the ground. Inf. Dev. **26**, 265–288 (2010). https://doi.org/10.1177/0266666910385374
39. Yin, R.K.: Case Study Research: Design and Methods. SAGE Publications, Thousand Oaks (2009)
40. O'Neill, D.: Assessing community informatics: a review of methodological approaches for evaluating community networks and community technology centers. Internet Res. Electron. Netw. Appl. Policy **12**, 76–102 (2002)
41. Rogers, P., et al.: IE4D – Impact Evaluation for Development: Principles for Action (2011)
42. Patton, M.Q.: Utilization-Focused Evaluation Checklist (U-FE). SAGE Publications, London (2012)
43. Maxwell, S.: The Meaning and Measurement of Poverty. Overseas Development Institute (ODI), London (1999)
44. Markey, S., Connelly, S., Roseland, M.: Back of the envelope: pragmatic planning for sustainable rural community development. Plan. Pract. Res. **25**, 1–23 (2010)
45. Henry, G.T., Mark, M.M.: Beyond use: understanding evaluation's influence on attitudes and actions. Am. J. Eval. **24**, 293–314 (2003)
46. Myers, M.: Monitoring and Evaluating Information and Communication for Development (ICD) Programmes: Guidelines. Department for International Development (DFID), London (2005)
47. Pfeffer, J., Sutton, R.I.: The Knowing-Doing Gap. Harvard Business School Press, Boston (2000)
48. Tabassum, G., Yeo, A.W.: Measurement of tangible and intangible impacts of telecentres on rural communities. Presented at the (2015)
49. Atkinson, R.: The life story interview. In: Handbook of Interview Research: Context and Method, pp. 120–140. Thousand Oaks, CA (2001)
50. Hosman, L., Fife, E.: Improving the prospects for sustainable ICT projects in the developing world. Int. J. Media Cult. Polit. **4**, 51–69 (2008)

Supporting the Identification of Victims of Human Trafficking and Forced Labor in Thailand

Hannah Thinyane(✉)

United Nations University, Institute on Computing and Society, Macau SAR, China
hannah@unu.edu

Abstract. We present results from a mixed methods study, involving survey data collection and focus groups, to understand the current processes of identifying victims of human trafficking in Thailand. Participants represent a broad spectrum of inter-governmental organizations, regional and local NGOs, Thai government officials, translators, and previously exploited migrant workers. Across these different stakeholders, participants identified key problems of lack of trust, communication issues, and differences in understanding of the key indicators of human trafficking between parties. The study also highlighted participants' perceptions on the role that technology can play to address the problems they face in identifying victims. It identifies the use of a smart phone application on the NGO or frontline responder's own device as a potential facility to enable workers in vulnerable situations to self-identify and seek help, allowing them to bridge the communication and skills divide with the channels of help that already exist.

Keywords:: Mixed methods study · Labor exploitation and human trafficking Computer-supported communication

1 Introduction

The International Labor Organization (ILO) estimates that there are almost 21 million people in situations of human trafficking, with 68% of these occurring within supply chains of private sector industries, and 22% in situations of sexual exploitation [1]. In its 2017 Trafficking in Persons Report, the US State Department reported that, in 2016, 0.3% of the total estimated victims were identified (66,520 people) [2]. We use these figures, heeding the caution of researchers such as Weitzer, who note that "it is impossible to satisfactorily count (or even estimate) the number of persons involved or the magnitude of profits within an illicit, clandestine, underground economy at the macro level" [3]. Instead, we refer to them here to illustrate that there are large numbers of people, often migrant workers [4, 5], in situations of forced labor and human trafficking, and that a small fraction of them are being successfully identified and subsequently helped. This figure of 0.3% also indicates that current identification techniques are failing the vast proportion of victims of human trafficking.

K. Krauss et al. (Eds.): IDIA 2018, CCIS 933, pp. 61–74, 2019.
https://doi.org/10.1007/978-3-030-11235-6_5

This paper describes an investigation to understand how technology can be used to support frontline responders to identify victims of labor exploitation in Thailand. It begins by providing context for the process of identifying labor exploitation, and provides a definition of key terms and concepts. A review of current literature on the use of technology to identify victims of labor exploitation and human trafficking, is then presented. The paper then describes the findings of a survey and series of focus groups, aimed at understanding how frontline responders currently identify victims, the problems they face, how they currently use technology, and how they believe that technology can support them in identifying victims. This is followed by a discussion that brings together the comments made by the participants, highlighting how this broad group of stakeholders makes sense of the way in which ICTs can be used to improve the condition of migrant workers in situations of labor exploitation.

1.1 Labor Exploitation, Forced Labor, and Human Trafficking

In literature and popular media, the terms 'forced labor' and 'human trafficking' are often used interchangeably. The United Nations Protocol to Prevent, Suppress and Punish Trafficking in Persons, especially Women and Children (referred to as the Palermo Protocol) [6] provides the first international definition of human trafficking as follows: the *act* of recruitment, movement, harboring or receipt of a person; by *means* of force, fraud, or coercion; for the *purpose* of exploitation (referred to as the AMP model) [6 Article 3 (a)]. The definitions become more confused, as the *purpose* section of the protocol goes on to list a number of specific exploitations including sexual exploitation, slavery or slavery-like practices, servitude, forced organ removal and forced labor itself.

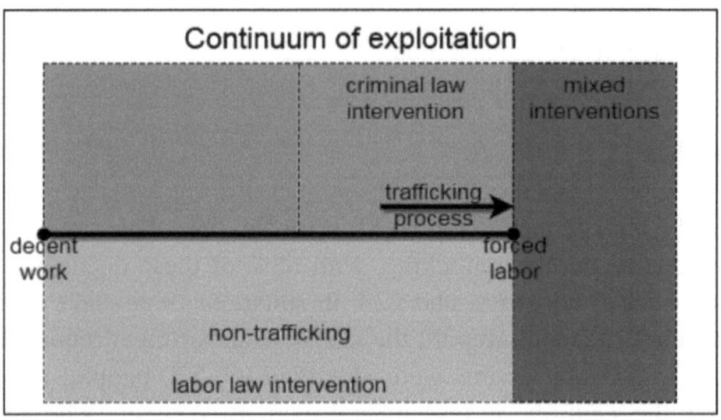

Fig. 1. Continuum of exploitation, adapted from [7].

In this paper we use Skřivánková's continuum of exploitation (Fig. 1) which ranges from 'decent work' (as defined by the International Labor Organization [8]) at one end to 'forced labor' at the other [7]. Between the two points are situations that do not comply with ILO's definition of decent work, and reveal labor law violations (to some degree or another). These range from on the left, more benign forms of labor violations such as discrimination and payment under minimum wage, to on the right, forced labor. As the arrow in Fig. 1 illustrates, the trafficking process is a series of exploitative acts that moves the worker towards a situation of forced labor.

1.2 Context

Thailand was selected as the site for this investigation, as it is a current hotspot of trafficking and exploitation in the Greater Mekong Sub-Region. Its rapid urbanization has generated a constant demand for cheap labor which is met by workers migrating to urban and semi-urban Thailand from its neighboring countries (Cambodia, Laos, Myanmar) or from rural Thailand. This imbalance in labor supply to demand gives rise to a conducive environment for exploitative working conditions [9].

In Thailand, local and federal police work with the Royal Thai Navy and inspectors from the Ministry of Labor, as well as other non-state partners including social workers, inter-governmental organizations, and non-governmental organizations, to assess working conditions, and to help potential victims become aware of, and gain access to, social services, complaint mechanisms and support (for example, emergency shelters, legal representation). In this paper, we refer to this broad cross-section of stakeholders as frontline responders.

Despite these mechanisms, labor exploitation and trafficking are widespread across Thailand. Over the last couple of years, Thailand has remained in the lowest rank (Tier 3) or watch list (Tier 2 watch list), signifying that the US State Department believes that the government does not meet the minimum standards of the Trafficking Victims Protection Acts, and are either making no effort or limited effort to do so. In a controversial move, Thailand was upgraded to the Tier 2 watch list in 2016, even though "… evidence from throughout 2016 shows that despite legal reforms made in 2015 and 2016, the reality on the ground has changed little for migrant workers, who are still vulnerable to trafficking" [10].

2 Related Work

This section presents a survey of the ways that ICTs are currently being used to identify victims in cases of labor exploitation and forced labor. It categorizes interventions as promoting access to information, reporting cases of abuse, and locating potential victims.

2.1 Access to Information

One of the first components that a number of interventions have in common is supporting access to information. Although based on the same premise of crowdsourcing information, the uses of technology differ based on the potential user: potential victims, consumers and businesses.

For potential victim-facing technologies, these tools enable interested parties to share information about practices of different recruiters and brokers, labor laws in different countries, and avenues for help in case of abuse of exploitation. Often governments, inter-governmental organizations and local NGOs work together to support both online and offline campaigns, in countries of origin as well as countries of destination. Some platforms such as Issara Institute's Golden Dreams provide a smart phone application for particular migrant groups, in this case Burmese workers, to learn and share information on their experience as migrant workers (recruitment information, ratings, comments, advice). This project is based on their finding that over 90% of the 3 million Burmese migrant workers in Thailand own smart phones with data packages [11]. The Philippines Overseas Employment Administration is an example of a government-run mobile app to allow potential migrant workers to check if recruiters were allowed to recruit Filipinos for jobs abroad, before they agree to work with them [12]. These examples show how individuals are using technology to access information about potential job opportunities, in order to prevent human trafficking. However, unscrupulous online recruiters have been found to use these same networks to exploit vulnerable and desperate workers [13].

Other platforms are consumer-facing, aimed at educating and building the awareness of the public to patterns of abuse that can be linked to their consumption behavior. Slavery Footprint[1] was one of the pioneers in this field, who used supply chain data to understand the working conditions in factories, and aggregate this information for consumers.

Business-facing tools, otherwise known as due diligence or supply chain monitoring tools, aim to provide information to businesses to reduce their risk of human trafficking within their supply chain. Labor Voices was the first to use an SMS polling framework to gather and aggregate information regarding working conditions within supply chains of businesses. A number of other platforms exist now, all differing in their use of primary data (such as information gathered from SMS, hotlines, mobile apps, and Facebook groups), and open source material (such as NGO and government reports, media articles) as a substitute to (or to complement) audits of factories within a supply chain. When used responsibly, a boycott of particular factories, due to their ranking by these tools, can encourage owners and managers to make changes to labor conditions for their employees.

While the consumer-facing and business-facing cases of access to information are less direct in their impact on workers in vulnerable situations, they are included here in order to give a holistic understanding of the field. Their aim is to address the economic benefits of using forced labor, by reducing demand for goods where there are cases of exploitation within the supply chain.

2.2 Reporting Cases of Abuse

There are a number of different types of technologies designed to help workers to report cases of abuse and exploitation, including those alluded to in the previous section discussing due diligence and supply chain monitoring tools. On top of these, governments often run their own hotlines, websites and mobile applications.

---

[1] www.slaveryfootprint.org.

A common problem with reporting cases of abuse is being able to prove the authenticity of the claim. Some tools allow photos or videos of abuse to be submitted, but, again, the legitimacy of these sources also comes into question. Systems such as eyeWitness to Atrocities stem from the difficulty of using data collected via mobile phones in courts, to prosecute criminals. This app is designed to allow witnesses to capture and send images and videos by creating a trusted chain of custody record, allowing collected information to be used within a court [14]. The app also has a 'panic button' that allows the witness to protect themselves and delete any information, as well as the app itself, from the phone in case it is examined by perpetrators or other hostile people.

2.3 Remote Sensing

Due to its hidden nature, it is often difficult for frontline responders to identify where instances of human trafficking occur. Remote sensing refers to the use of technology (most often satellites) to extract information about a location, where the sensor itself is not in direct contact with the area [15]. The use of satellite imagery to identify human rights violations is becoming more widely used across a number of different situations, including identifying situations of child slavery in Bangladesh [16], as a warning tool for conflict escalation in Aleppo, Syria [17], and in monitoring the development of political prisoner camps in North Korea [18]. The same technology has also been used to identify the location and number of boats used in fishing around Lake Volta [19]. This data is used by humanitarian groups to target interventions and support. Crowdsourcing projects such as Tomnod[2] provide a platform to engage people to view and tag a small section of a satellite image. As well as identifying victims in Lake Volta, this platform has been used across a wide range of situations, including finding wreckage of Malaysian Airlines Flight 370, identifying wildfires in Australia and South Africa, and identifying the preferred environments of Weddell seals in Antarctica.

Other remote sensing projects include Exchange Initiatives TraffickCam[3], which uses crowdsourced pictures of hotel rooms to help enforcement agencies to locate victims of sex trafficking. The system matches online adverts against the database of hotel room pictures, to try and identify the location where the potential victims have been. These types of tools can be used to collect evidence for further prosecution of traffickers, once they have been located and then apprehended.

3 Research Design

This research aims to understand how/if stakeholders believe that technology can help them to identify victims of labor exploitation and forced labor. To do so, it poses the following research questions:

---

[2] www.tomnod.com.

[3] https://traffickcam.com/.

- RQ1: How do frontline responders currently identify victims of labor exploitation and forced labor, and what problems do they believe there are in this method?
- RQ2: How do frontline responders and migrant workers in vulnerable situations currently use technology, and what factors enable and constrain their use?
- RQ3: What do frontline responders and migrant workers in vulnerable situations view the role of technology could be to alleviate these problems?

This research used a mixed method approach to understand how victims of labor exploitation and forced labor are currently identified. First, a quantitative survey was used to understand the current access and use of technology by NGOs and frontline responders, to provide more contextual information for RQ2. This survey consisted of two sections: basic demographic information (four questions), and current access to (and use of) technology, as well as any barriers to the use of technology (eight multiple choice questions, plus one long answer question). The survey was circulated via email to a contact person at each of the 8 NGOs and 1 inter-governmental organization that were invited to focus groups, one week prior to the research trip to Thailand. The survey was available for one week, and then responses were downloaded, translated and analyzed, and used to inform the focus group discussions. The survey was available in English and Thai, and was completed by 7 respondents. The government officials were not sent the survey, but instead were asked similar questions about their access to, and use of, technology in their focus group.

Qualitative methods allow the researcher to obtain a more nuanced understanding of the reasons behind an event. This research uses a focus group, which Powell and Single define as "a group of individuals selected and assembled by researchers to discuss and comment on, from personal experience, the topic that is the subject of the research" [20]. The focus group was used, because it allows respondents to discuss and draw out from each other a wide variety of views and processes, in an open and conversational manner. Due to the fact that these discussions happen in a group, rather than as individuals, a benefit of focus groups is that it allows participants to identify shared opinions, and points of contrasting views.

Recruitment of participants was undertaken on behalf of the researchers by the United Nations Action for Cooperation against Trafficking in Persons (UN-ACT), Bangkok Office. Using the terminology of Puri et al. [21], they acted as the mediating agency between the researchers and the local stakeholders. They had the local connections to be able to suggest a broad range of stakeholders to participate in the study.

Table 1 provides an overview of the number of participants in each group, basic demographic information, and the code used to refer to comments made by participants in the group. As this table shows, groups were formed with the social hierarchical structures within Thailand in mind, in order to support stakeholders to participate freely.

The research team was cognizant of the fact that only a few migrant workers who had previously been exploited, might want to participate in the sessions. Other research with vulnerable populations suggests the use of proxies to represent the hidden or difficult-to-reach populations, such as with the inclusion of care givers or family members [22], diasporas [23], or medical specialists [24]. In order to ensure that the migrant workers' voice was represented, we initially invited translators as a proxy for the migrant workers, as we believed that as their job was to act as the interface between migrant workers and other stakeholders, they would be able to represent them most accurately. We also ensured that a large number of local NGOs were interviewed, as they often hire previous victims of exploitation once they have been rehabilitated. After concluding the focus groups, we were told that three participants from one of the local NGOs that took part in the study had themselves been trafficked, rescued, and now were working to help others in the same situation as they had been in. In total, there were therefore five migrant workers who had been severely exploited or trafficked. On reflection, we believe that the exploited migrant workers' voice was therefore adequately represented.

Table 1. Composition of focus groups, indicating reference code, number of participants, participant background, and the language(s) that focus groups were carried out in.

Code	#	Participant background	Language
FG1	10	Inter-governmental organizations, Regional NGOs	English and Thai
FG2	7	Local NGO, previously exploited migrant workers	Thai
FG3	2	Previously exploited migrant workers	Thai
FG4	3	Local NGO, Translators	Thai
FG5	9	Local NGO, Translators	Thai and Burmese
FG6	3	Government officials	Thai

In order to support the discussions among participants, all sessions were undertaken with the help of a translator. The translator would first translate the researchers' comments to the participants, and would make notes of what was said. When there was a natural break in the discussion, she would then translate her notes into English, rather than simultaneously translating each phrase. This prioritized participation by stakeholders over the researcher/designer. We believed that this was acceptable, however, as it ensured that the flow and discussions that occurred within the sessions were not disrupted. To thank stakeholders for participating, as well as attempt to make sessions less formal, snacks and drinks were made available during each of the focus groups.

The focus group sessions were undertaken over a week-long period in April 2017. Although sessions were planned to take two hours to complete, they ranged in length from 1 h 54 min to 3 h 4 min, depending on the contributions of the participants. Once consent was given by participants, audio from sessions was recorded. After sessions were completed, a transcript was made by one of the researchers. These transcripts, as well as survey responses, were then coded by one of the researchers, using open coding techniques. The codes were then grouped according to emergent themes, and are presented in the remainder of this document. At some points in this document, illustrative quotes from the transcripts are included in the analysis section. Where identifiable, quotes are prefaced by a unique identifier representing the respondent. Focus groups are identified with the codes included in Table 1, concatenated with "Nx" where x is a unique number for each participant in the group. When a comment cannot be directly correlated back to a particular participant within a group, the end two characters take the form of "N?".

The findings of these questions are presented below, as they relate to each of the three research questions.

4 Current Identification Process

The first research question aimed to understand how stakeholders currently identified potential victims. Across the stakeholders, discussants described a consistent two-step process in identifying potential victims. In the initial screening phase, frontline responders come in contact with workers, often in person, but in some cases via a call to a hotline. In the case of inspectors, part of their work is to undertake inspections (pre-informed or unannounced) at workplaces, and within the fishing sector, pre-departure, on return and at sea. This initial screening phase is used to understand if there is a case that requires further investigation for labor exploitation. Some participants noted that initial screening may occur in front of employers, and showed concern that responses may be influenced by a fear of retribution from the worker's employer. If the initial screening indicates signs of vulnerability, participants said that they give workers the option of leaving their work environment. If they consent, the frontline responders then take the vulnerable worker out of their work environment to a safe place, and perform an in-depth interview.

To understand the problems that frontline responders face with identifying victims, we asked questions to indirectly probe what stakeholders value, and what they perceive is lacking in their current method of identifying victims. From these questions, all focus groups mentioned language barriers when communicating with migrant workers. They noted that due to the number of languages spoken by migrant workers, it is impossible to take enough translators with them to ensure that they can communicate with whomever they encounter. They also mentioned the importance of a deep understanding of the migrant's language, as "*with the language barrier they can't ask profound questions*" (FG5N8).

Secondly, participants highlighted a lack of training in understanding key indicators of human trafficking and forced labor. Participants mentioned that although some indicators of human trafficking and forced labor were in common across different sectors, there were key differences that needed to be understood as well. Government officials who were involved in the focus group described a list of "*over 200 questions*" (FG6N1) that they use to understand if workers were in situations of forced labor or human trafficking. They said that it takes two hours to go through all of the questions, assuming that there is a good translator and the worker is willing to cooperate. The official suggested that they need a more concise way of being able to identify victims.

Perhaps a more complicated problem highlighted was trust: between workers and NGOs, in officials and in translators. Participants noted that due to the mental and physical abuse that workers had often suffered, they were guarded in approaching frontline responders. At the same time, participants mentioned a lack of trust in the motives of migrant workers, some stating that they were "*wasting our time*" (FG1N5), and "*just not pleased with their boss*" (FG2N?) or "*just want to get off a boat*" (FG2N?). Participants mentioned cases of corruption that they had heard of or experienced, and a lack of trust in "*the system*". Finally, a number of participants mentioned a lack of trust in translators. Some referred to cases where "*the translator is someone from the trafficker's side*" (FG6N1), while others mentioned that translators may show racist or unsympathetic views towards other ethnic groups from their home country, which colors the accuracy of their translations.

One participant brought each of these three problems together, saying: "*There is an obvious language barrier when dealing with migrant workers. When we engage interpreter for victim identification, we need someone with language skills and someone who understands and is trustworthy*" (FG1N3).

5 Access to Technology

The second research question wanted to understand to what technology different stakeholders had access. When asked about migrant workers' access, most participants mentioned that migrant workers only have "*simple mobile phones*" (FG4N1), rather than smart phones, with shared, rather than individual, access across groups of workers. One participant expanded further, saying, *"[the workers] have to sneak out and call them. They can borrow a phone from a friend, or go to a store and ask the worker to lend a phone. Sometimes find someone who is willing to help them and lend them a phone*" (FG2N?). Some participants suggested that mobile phone access depends on the area that the worker is in, with comparatively higher access to mobile phones by "*workers inland*" (FG4N1) than on boats. When asked to expand further on this, the participant said that "*simple mobile phones ... are smaller and easier to be hidden*" (FG4N1). Other participants referred to the perceived durability of simple mobile phones, as compared to smart phones that are not appropriate due to the "*lifestyle of people on the boat*" (FG4N?).

Responses to the survey, as well as to focus group questions, showed that all NGO and government participants have access to a personal mobile phone, with all but one NGO worker stating that they had a smart phone during a focus group session. When asked what hindered their use of the Internet, the survey highlighted "*limited or patchy network connectivity*" when in the field, and "*lack of information in my preferred language*".

6 Role of Technology

When asked what role they believed digital technology could play in supporting the identification of victims of human trafficking and forced labor (RQ3), participants suggested three roles: to collect evidence of abuse, to locate potential victims, and to screen potential victims. Participants first suggested that they could use video recordings, as well as images, to collect evidence of physical abuse when they are first identified. Some participants suggested that they already do this when they first come into contact with potential victims. One participant noted that "*most [potential victims] have cheap phones with no cameras so can't. Others with smart phones that can take a photo don't know they can*" (FG5N1).

Other participants suggested that mobile technology could be used to locate victims, either using network or GPS facilities (if available on the mobile device), or using photographs taken by victims. Participants suggested that the ability to locate victims could serve two purposes. Firstly, participants suggested that by allowing them to locate a victim, it could help to determine the "… initial prognosis of cases" (FG1N4). As an example, the respondent stated that if the victim had stated they were being held on a farm, but the location details showed they were nowhere near farmlands, this could help to prioritize assistance. The second and more common suggestion was to determine whence to rescue them. They noted that potential victims often do not know where they are, and cannot recognize characters in foreign alphabets, so they cannot tell NGOs or frontline responders where to send help. If a worker has access to a mobile phone with a camera, they suggested that they could take photos of any signs around and send them to frontline responders to try and help locate them.

Some participants suggested that mobile phones could help frontline responders because of "*a lack of knowledge and understanding on human trafficking*" (FG6N1). When asked if they would see value in the use of a list of simple questions or indicators, participants were interested. We polled them further about why they were interested in this proposal, and one participant said that "*a machine is more reliable than the person*" (FG2N?). Drawing on the mental state of victims of human trafficking and forced labor, another participant noted that "*Trauma is traumatizing. They [the victims] need someone to help them think logically, especially when traffickers are feeding them the opposite*" (FG1N?). She expanded on this further, saying that "*a predefined and vetted list of simple questions could provide the logical reminder to the victim that may be missing in their situation*". A number of participants also noted that a list that is based on Thai anti-trafficking law would allow them to easily follow on to the second stage of their victim identification system, which was to register the cases with the government assistance framework.

7 Discussion

This section draws together the findings of the initial focus groups, highlighting how exploited migrant workers, NGOs, intergovernmental agencies and government officials suggested they could use ICTs to identify more workers in vulnerable situations. Once identified, these migrant workers would be given the option to leave their exploitative work environment, and seek shelter.

We begin by considering the suggestion of using technology to locate potential victims. In Sect. 2.3, we presented a number of other cases of the use of technology (predominately satellites, but also networks of webcams) for remote sensing of environments, and this suggestion can be seen to fall into this category of ICT usage. A problem with these remote sensing technologies is that they do not operate in real time, and therefore can only identify where potential victims have been, rather than where they currently are. While this data can be analyzed and used to highlight trafficking hotspots or pathways, it does not provide any direct assistance to the workers who are currently being exploited. For this reason, we decided we were not going to pursue this idea further.

The other two suggestions were to screen potential victims and to collect evidence of abuse. We can categorize the ways that frontline responders currently make initial contact with potential victims into two groups: via phone, or in person. If we begin by considering the possibility of supporting communication via phone (for example, using a hotline), this presents some initial opportunities and obstacles. Firstly, if successfully managed and advertised, a hotline would have a far greater reach and accessibility than a group (however large) of frontline responders. It could potentially be accessible from any location and at any time of the day. This in itself seems very alluring, and we considered taking this approach. However, when we considered the ethical implications of providing potential victims with information about the severity of their situation *without being able to provide a means of exiting that situation*, we decided that it was not in their best interest to do so (either with respect to their physical or emotional welfare).

Instead, we chose to focus on the use of technology to support frontline responders to screen potential victims in person, where there is an immediate channel to exit an exploitative work environment (should the potential victim so choose). From the responses to RQ2, we suggest that frontline responders almost all have a smart phone that could be used to run an application, to support them to bridge the communication and skills gaps that they themselves suggested. Drawing from the comment made in the first focus group, we suggest that a number of predefined lists of simple questions could be developed, based on key indicators of trafficking and exploitation. These lists could be targeted at different types of human trafficking and labor exploitation (such as exploitation within processing and manufacturing, sex trafficking, forced begging), based on the respective labor and human trafficking laws. If these questions were translated and available in audio format, they could be played to low-skilled (and possibly illiterate or low-literate) workers. By providing translations of the questions, problems with untrustworthy or unskilled translators in the field would be alleviated. When coupled with a set of headphones, questions could be played to the migrant worker, and offer them more privacy than they are currently permitted. After completing the questions, a simple vulnerability rating could be calculated to determine the likelihood that a case requires further investigation (using for example the ILO's Hard to See, Harder to Count methodology for identifying cases of human trafficking and forced labor [25]). If in a vulnerable situation, the application could also provide frontline responders with a way to collect digital evidence of the exploitative situation that the worker was in (for example, work conditions or any signs of physical violence). Due to the intermittent connectivity available in the field that respondents described in the survey, an application would require online and offline capabilities.

This process led us to define a new research question:

RQ4: How can migrant workers in vulnerable situations be supported to self-identify as potential victims of human trafficking through the use of digital technology?

When considering the use of technology to support communication with migrant workers in the initial screening phase of victim identification, a number of critical factors need to be considered. Firstly, the best practices for obtaining consent from migrant workers before beginning the interview, needs to be considered, particularly when dealing with semi-literate or illiterate workers who could be in a traumatic situation. There has been ongoing discussion about this topic in the health field, which has pointed to problems with current consent mechanisms that do not take into account "poverty, limited or no education, and the complexity of the information provided" [26]. When considering the time-sensitive nature of some initial screening sessions, where migrant workers may only have a few minutes before their absence is noticed by their exploiters, we can also draw from emergency medicine research, where researchers suggest that "if independent decision-making is to be encouraged, informed consents should be adapted according to the targeted population" [27].

The second critical factor in designing a system to be used for initial screening of migrant workers, is privacy. Although this factor is important in most systems, when considering the immediate threats of retribution and retaliation from exploiters, the severity of this danger must be recognized. A value-sensitive design approach could be used with the privacy of migrant workers in mind, to support an "… ethical reflection in the state of design of architectures, requirements, specifications, standards, protocols, incentive structures and institutional arrangements" [28].

8 Conclusion and Future Work

This paper has presented the results of a mixed methods study, involving a broad range of stakeholders within the anti-trafficking and labor exploitation fields in Thailand. It has discussed the suggestions made by government officials, NGOs and previously exploited migrant workers, to make sense of how ICTs can be used to bridge the communication and skills divide between frontline responders and workers. Drawing from this, we discussed the importance of informed consent and privacy when designing a system for this context and user group, and suggested that a value-sensitive design approach could be used to support the informed and pro-active design of such a system.

Although initially conceptualized as focusing on labor exploitation and forced labor, we are cognizant of the fact that this kind of technology could be useful in the initial screening phase for any frontline responder who comes in contact with victims of exploitation. We are currently exploring the use of the same technology for initial screening of mental health issues in trafficking and exploitation survivors.

Acknowledgements. We thank our colleagues from The Mekong Club, in particular Silvia Mera, who helped to organize and conduct the field research that formed the basis of this research.

References

1. ILO: ILO global estimate of forced labour: results and methodology. International Labour Office, Special Action Programme to Combat Forced Labour (SAP-FL), Geneva, Switzerland (2012)
2. US State Department: Trafficking in Persons Report June 2017. US State Department (2017)
3. Weitzer, R.: New directions in research on human trafficking. Ann. Am. Acad. Pol. Soc. Sci. **653**, 6–24 (2014)

4. Schenker, M.B.: A global perspective of migration and occupational health. Am. J. Ind. Med. **53**, 329–337 (2010). https://doi.org/10.1002/ajim.20834
5. Ahonen, E.Q., Benavides, F.G., Benach, J.: Immigrant populations, work and health–a systematic literature review. Scand. J. Work. Environ. Health. **33**, 96–104 (2007)
6. UNODC: Protocol to Prevent, Suppress and Punish Trafficking in Persons. United Nations Human Rights Office of the High Commissioner, Palermo (2000)
7. Skrivankova, K.: Between decent work and forced labour: examining the continuum of exploitation. Joseph Rowntree Foundation, York (2010)
8. ILO: Decent work. http://www.ilo.org/global/topics/decent-work/lang–en/index.htm. Accessed 03 Sept 2018
9. Rouse, C., Darin, S.: Child trafficking in the Mekong Sub-Region. Safe Child Thailand. https://www.safechildthailand.org/sites/default/files/Child-Trafficking-in-the-Sub-Mekong-Region-Safe-Child-Thailand-web.pdf. Accessed 03 Sept 2018
10. Mcgill, A.: The highs and lows of the 2017 TIP Report | International Labor Rights Forum. International Labor Rights Forum, Washingtion, DC. https://laborrights.org/blog/201707/highs-and-lows-2017-tip-report. Accessed 03 Sept 2018
11. Issara Institute: Technological Innovation to Empower Workers and Eliminate Human Trafficking in Global Supply Chains. Issara Institute, Bangkok, Thailand. https://www.issarainstitute.org/reports-and-publications. Accessed 03 Sept 2018
12. Rie, T.: POEA launches mobile app vs. illegal recruiters. http://www.gmanetwork.com/news/story/353281/scitech/technology/poea-launches-mobile-app-vs-illegal-recruiters. Accessed 03 Sept 2018
13. Latonero, M., Wex, B., Dank, M.: Technology and Labor Trafficking in a Network Society: General Overview, Emerging Innovations, and Philippines Case Study (2015). https://doi.org/10.2139/ssrn.2574676
14. Weiss, J.: How eyeWitness to Atrocities empowers journalists to record evidence of international crimes, International Journalists' Network. https://ijnet.org/en/blog/how-eyewitness-atrocities-empowers-journalists-record-evidence-international-crimes. Accessed 03 Sept 2018
15. UN General Assembly: Principles relating to remote sensing of the earth from space (1986)
16. Rashid, C.M.M.: Satellites reveal "child slave camps" in UNESCO-protected park in Bangladesh. http://www.telegraph.co.uk/technology/2016/10/23/satellites-reveal-child-slave-camps-in-unesco-protected-park-in/. Accessed 03 Sept 2018
17. Syria crisis: Amnesty alarm at Aleppo "bombing" images. http://www.bbc.com/news/world-middle-east-19174257. Accessed 03 Sept 2018
18. Amnesty International: North Korea: New satellite images show continued investment in the infrastructure of repression. Amnesty International USA, London, UK. https://www.amnestyusa.org/reports/north-korea-new-satellite-images-show-continued-investment-in-the-infrastructure-of-repression/. Accessed 03 Sept 2018
19. Milton, C.: Ending Slavery on Lake Volta. http://blog.tomnod.com/ending-slavery-on-lake-volta. Accessed 03 Sept 2018
20. Powell, R.A., Single, H.M.: Focus groups. Int. J. Qual. Health Care **8**, 499–504 (1996). https://doi.org/10.1093/intqhc/8.5.499
21. Puri, S.K., Byrne, E., Nhampossa, J.L., Quraishi, Z.B.: Contextuality of participation in IS design: a developing country perspective. In: Presented at the Eighth Conference on Participatory Design: Artful Integration: Interweaving Media, Materials and Practices (2004). https://doi.org/10.1145/1011870.1011876

22. Cohene, T., Baecker, R., Marziali, E.: Designing interactive life story multimedia for a family affected by alzheimer's disease: a case study. In: CHI 2005 Extended Abstracts on Human Factors in Computing Systems, pp. 1300–1303. ACM, New York (2005). https://doi.org/10.1145/1056808.1056901
23. Best, M.L., Smyth, T.N., Serrano-Baquero, D., Etherton, J.: Designing for and with diaspora: a case study of work for the truth and reconciliation commission of Liberia. In: CHI 2009 Extended Abstracts on Human Factors in Computing Systems, pp. 2903–2918. ACM (2009). https://doi.org/10.1145/1520340.1520418
24. Boyd-Graber, J.L., et al.: Participatory design with proxies: developing a desktop-PDA system to support people with aphasia. In: Proceedings of the SIGCHI Conference on Human Factors in Computing Systems, pp. 151–160. ACM (2006). https://doi.org/10.1145/1124772.1124797
25. International Labour Office, Special Action Programme to Combat Forced Labour, Hard to see, harder to count: survey guidelines to estimate forced labour of adults and children. http://www.ilo.org/global/topics/forced-labour/publications/WCMS_182096/lang–en/index.htm. Accessed 03 Sept 2018
26. Verástegui, E.L.: Consenting of the vulnerable: the informed consent procedure in advanced cancer patients in Mexico. BMC Med. Ethics. **7**, 13 (2006). https://doi.org/10.1186/1472-6939-7-13
27. Schmidt, T.A., et al.: Confronting the ethical challenges to informed consent in emergency medicine research. Acad. Emerg. Med. **11**, 1082–1089 (2004). https://doi.org/10.1197/j.aem.2004.05.028
28. Van den Hoven, J.: ICT and value sensitive design. In: Goujon, P., Lavelle, S., Duquenoy, P., Kimppa, K., Laurent, V. (eds.) The Information Society: Innovation, Legitimacy, Ethics and Democracy In honor of Professor Jacques Berleur s.j. IIFIP, vol. 233, pp. 67–72. Springer, Boston, MA (2007). https://doi.org/10.1007/978-0-387-72381-5_8

Mobile Education

Youth Unemployment in South Africa and the Socio-economic Capabilities from Mobile Phones

Hossana Twinomurinzi(✉) and Joshua Magundini

School of Computing, University of South Africa, Roodepoort, South Africa
twinoh@unisa.ac.za

Abstract. Unemployment is a significant global challenge with major social and economic implications. Unemployment has however not prevented the youth from owning and using mobile devices nor other Information and Communication Technologies (ICT). This exploratory paper investigated the mobile usage patterns among 104 participants in an effort to contextualize mobile and ICT strategies that target unemployed youth. The exploratory findings suggest that contrary to the assumption of most ICT for development literature to target youth in rural areas, ICT strategies targeting youth unemployment may be more effective when targeted at youth in urban areas. The strategies may also need to be adjusted as the youth tend towards the age of 35 where they become apathetic about job opportunities. Two capabilities, 'individual' and 'interpersonal', emerged uniquely as the job related economic capabilities of ICT. The paper contributes to practice and theory in suggesting recommendations for further research for ICT skills development programmes targeted at youth.

Keywords: ICT4D · ICT skills · Mobile usage · Youth · Youth unemployment South Africa

1 Introduction

There is an acknowledged massive adoption of mobile phones in developing countries [1]. While most people use their mobile phones for social networking purposes [2], the phones can also be used for other benefits such as income generation. In this paper, we argue that an intentional effort may be required to take advantage of the characteristics and capabilities of mobile devices in order to alleviate unemployment, especially among youth. We refer to the intentional effort as part of a wider discourse on ICT skills and the role of ICT in social and economic development, more popularly regarded as ICT4D and Development Informatics. The paper argues that understanding how the unemployed use their phones could result in the better productive usage of mobile phones and the possible creation of income generating opportunities.

Unemployment, particularly youth unemployment, is not a new problem in a global perspective, nor in South Africa. In South Africa, a youth is defined as being between the age of 16 and 35. The unemployment figures indicate that youth unemployment in

K. Krauss et al. (Eds.): IDIA 2018, CCIS 933, pp. 77–93, 2019.
https://doi.org/10.1007/978-3-030-11235-6_6

South Africa was at 50.9% in the fourth quarter of 2016 down from 54.2% in the third quarter of 2016 [3]. The average rate between 2013 and 2017 was 51.54%.

The objective of this study was therefore to identify some essential capabilities of phones that could assist in alleviating unemployment especially among South African youth. In particular, the paper sought to answer the following primary research question, "*What are the essential characteristics and capabilities required to take advantage of mobile phones as a means to alleviate unemployment in South Africa?*"

The remainder of the paper is structured as follows: The next section explores literature on youth unemployment and ICT/mobile usage characteristics. It is followed by the research design section. The analysis and findings are discussed in the proceeding section. The paper then makes inferences in the conclusions section.

2 Literature Review

2.1 Unemployment and Job Searching Behaviour

One of the reasons for the growing challenge of unemployment is the evolving nature of labour markets, and the misalignment between the evolved labour market and the education systems especially in the digital age of today [4]. In South Africa, the education situation is worsened by the historically uneven quality of the public schooling system [5]. The apartheid heritage of spatial disintegration of populations adds to the unemployment complexity, especially in rural areas and areas where black workers lived [6]. There is limited economic growth, and therefore less jobs, in rural areas compared with the urban and metropolitan areas [7]. Further, the employment in urban and metropolitan areas often requires higher skill competences. Nonetheless, there are job opportunities in the rural areas and previously marginalised areas.

Wilkinson et al. [7] reported that whereas the unemployed claimed there were no resources for job opportunities in their local communities, the local authorities noted that there were several employment resources, especially entrepreneurship, in the local communities. The differing reports point to one of the many behavioural factors that influence employment through job searching. Some of these behavioural factors include social capital, gender and educational certification. Social capital also plays quite a strong role as individuals with relatives and friends who already have jobs tend to have an advantage [4, 7]. Men in urban areas appear to have an advantage for employment compared to those in rural areas [6]. Individuals with certified skills are more likely to find employment, as the certificates offer a form of evidence of concrete skills [7]. Despite the importance of educational certification, there is also a growing challenge of graduate unemployment.

2.2 Graduate Unemployment

Studies in human capital and economics have long drawn a direct and linear relationship between education and socioeconomic development [8]. The challenge of graduate unemployment in South Africa is even more pressing since the country concedes there is a critical gap for certain specialist skills. Unemployed graduates moreover present a bigger political challenge as seen in the 'Arab spring' where the collective actions of the majority unemployed graduates in Egypt managed to unseat the government [9, 10]. The causes of graduate unemployment have been placed on a number of factors but mainly on the lower quality of students coming out of educational institutions [11–13]. However, most publicly funded educational institutions concede that they are under intense pressure to increase the student output while receiving less subsidy and resources from the government [14, 15].

Employers prefer graduates for their 'soft skills' over and above the technical skills learnt at the educational institutions, and are therefore frustrated when they have to re-train the graduates to fit in with their organizational culture [16, 17]. Criticism has also been placed on educational institutions for their apparent unwillingness to engage and understand their local communities [11]. It is consequently cheaper and easier for employers to find an individual with the experience and necessary soft-skills set rather than take the risk of hiring a recent graduate, offer re-training and lose him/her to the next competitor [13]. There is therefore a higher demand for employees who are able to quickly adjust and use aspects of ICT and mobile devices as part of their job roles over and above their educational proficiency, soft-skills and experience. The research therefore sought to answer the following hypothesis:

H_1: *There is a difference in educational levels between the unemployed compared with the employed*

2.3 ICT Usage Characteristics

Initially, mobile devices were designed primarily with voice and text functionality. However, the convergence of media that occurred on the computer was soon adopted on the mobile device. The mobile device now has productivity software, voice, video, text and internet capabilities. There has been a significant growth of ownership and usage of mobile phone devices in developing countries [1]. The usage is however differentiated between in the different income groups [18, 19]. Studies suggest that lower income groups tend to have a more sophisticated usage of social media, internet telephony and multiple devices [20] as a price sensitivity strategy [21]. It has been reported that there is a resistance to using mobile devices for online activities such as chatting, collaboration and searching for information in some rural areas [22]. The assumption is that people living in rural areas lack the necessary literacy skills and understanding of how to operate such technology devices compared with people in urban areas [22, 23]. As may be expected, there are fewer to no job referral programs in remote and rural areas [24] yet with access to mobile devices, job referral programs and career advice could be made available through internet based job portals and even on social media. The paper therefore hypothesized that there is a difference between how the employed and the unemployed access the internet, as well as how they access job opportunities.

H_2: *The unemployed access the internet differently from the employed.*

H_3: *The unemployed receive job opportunities differently from the employed*

2.4 ICT Capabilities that Are Associated with Social and Economic Benefit

The role of ICT in enabling or driving social and economic growth has received growing attention among scholars, often under the label of ICT for Development (ICT4D) and Development Informatics. The arguments about the role of ICT remain contested yet the fundamental principle remains that ICT could be used to lift people (particularly women, youth and children) out of conditions of deprivation. Such deprivation is more commonly found in developing countries, and manifests mainly in economic and social forms. Sen's approach to development known as the Capabilities Approach (CA) departs from the linear approach to development [25, 26] in emphasizing individual well-being and social arrangements based on what the individual is able to do and to be, that is, the capabilities of the individual. In the CA, it is not enough to provide the opportunities for development as linear economic theory of demand and supply suggests, it is equally necessary to enable individuals and societies to draw upon those opportunities. For ICT, the real value to development would be in the capabilities of individuals to access and take advantage of economic opportunities such as jobs through ICT. There is however, no agreement on what skills make for general 'employability skills' [27]. For this study we hypothesize that the ICT/mobile capabilities that are associated with economic opportunities are related to the following employment process: finding a job vacancy, applying for the job, receiving communication about the status of the application, and attending an interview. The following ICT/mobile capabilities are therefore hypothesized:

1. Search: The ability to search for information on jobs using a search engine
2. Communicate: The ability to communicate effectively using email
3. Digital literacy (type): The ability to type a CV on the computer (equivalent of read and write)
4. Collaborate (social media): The ability to collaborate with other professionals online through social media networks e.g. LinkedIn
5. Collaborate (video): The ability to initiate video conference calls over the internet through apps such as Skype

In the next section, the means of inquiry to investigate the hypotheses is presented.

3 Research Approach and Findings

The study adopted the deductive positivist research method to investigate the capabilities and characteristics necessary for employment. Ethical clearance was given by the host university in which the study was taken. Data was collected using the online survey capability in Google® Forms with a non-probabilistic convenient sample of 106 unemployed and employed people in South Africa. All participants gave informed consent online. Two (2) responses were unusable and therefore discarded leaving 104 usable responses. SPSS® was used for the statistical analyses.

3.1 Descriptive Findings

There were 68 males and 46 female respondents (Table 1) which therefore called for non-parametric statistical methods [28]. 83.6% of the respondents were youth with 23.1% of them unemployed. 88.4% of the respondents had a smartphone. 24% of the respondents who had smartphones were unemployed. Only two unemployed respondents did not have a smartphone.

Table 1. Demographic data

		Employed		Unemployed	
Gender	Male	42	40.4%	16	15.4%
	Female	35	33.7%	11	10.6%
Residential area	Urban	61	58.7%	20	19.2%
	Township	10	9.6%	2	1.9%
	Rural area	6	5.8%	5	4.8%
Age bracket	Between 16 and 35 years	63	60.6%	24	23.1%
	Over 35 years	14	13.5%	3	2.9%
Education	Matric	20	19.2%	10	9.6%
	National diploma	26	25.0%	5	4.8%
	Bachelors degree	20	19.2%	9	8.7%
	Honours degree	2	1.9%	0	0.0%
	Masters degree	2	1.9%	0	0.0%
	PhD	0	0.0%	0	0.0%
	Postgraduate diploma	3	2.9%	1	1.0%
	Other	4	3.8%	2	1.9%
Own a smartphone	Yes	67	64.4%	25	24.0%
	No	10	9.6%	2	1.9%
Job hunting	Yes	46	44.2%	22	21.2%
	No	31	29.8%	5	4.8%

3.2 Residential Area and Unemployment

The respondents were mainly from urban areas (77.9%) with the township and rural areas at 11.5% and 10.6% respectively. While it is not possible to have conclusive inferences based on this convenient sample, there is a reality of rural to urban migration on the increase in most African and Asian countries [29] including South Africa [30] and it is more likely that youth will consider migrating to urban areas as a viable economic option. The p-value of 0.162 (>0.05) suggests that there is no association between youth unemployment and residential area (Appendix: Table 14) Unemployment, as expected, affects individuals in both urban and non-urban areas.

3.3 Job Search

A large group (18.5%) of the unemployed (4.8% of the total sample) are not actively looking for a job indicating a measure of apathy (Table 1). It is therefore worth considering means that engage with apathy within the ICT strategies.

Table 2. Job hunting by age by employment status

			Employed	Unemployed
Between 16 and 35 years	Job hunting	Yes	42	19
		No	21	5
	Total		63	24
Over 35 years	Job hunting	Yes	4	3
		No	10	0
	Total		14	3
Total	Job hunting	Yes	46	22
		No	31	5
	Total		77	27

On further bivariate analysis (Table 2 and Appendix: Table 15) the analysis suggests that it is those above 35 who are apathetic about jobs ($p = 0.023 < 0.05$). It does indicate that as youth get older and tend to the age of 35, and are still without a job, they become despondent and stop the active search. The finding therefore suggests that the emphasis needs to be placed on youth when they still have the will and hope that they will find jobs, or that the strategies need to include social support mechanisms that will encourage the youth not to give up even as they tend to 35 year of age. Similarly, the finding ($p = 0.041 < 0.05$) suggests that there is a significant difference between youth and non-youth in searching for jobs.

The finding ($p = 0.255 > 0.05$) for the youth suggests that there is no difference between unemployed and employed youth in terms of actively searching for a job. Youth actively seek for jobs whether or not they are employed.

3.4 Education and Unemployment

The education groups who responded highest were those with a national diploma (30%) matric (29%), and bachelor's degrees (28%). The ones who were highest unemployed had a matric (37%) and a bachelor's degree (33.3%). The finding does concur with the growing trend of unemployed graduates [31, 32].

A further inferential bivariate analysis (Appendix: Table 18) shows that there is no association between education and unemployment ($p = 0.85 > 0.05$). The finding suggests that there is no difference in education levels in terms of unemployment whether for the youth ($p = 0.85 > 0.05$) or the non-youth ($p = 0.58$). Hypothesis H_1 was therefore rejected; there is no significant difference in educational levels between the unemployed compared with the employed. The finding further highlights the growing increase of youth with a formal education but without employment.

3.5 ICT Usage Characteristics

Table 18 (Appendix) suggests that both employed and unemployed youth do not consider basic ICT skills as being important. The p-value of 0.934 (>0.05) confirms that there is no association between unemployed and employed youth in their perception of the importance of basic ICT skills. Also, non-youth do not consider basic ICT skills as being important. The finding points to both the unemployed and employed preferring more job-specific skills as carrying greater value than basic ICT skills.

3.6 Frequency of Accessing the Internet and Using the Phone for Social Purposes rather than Productivity Purposes

Table 19 (Appendix) suggests that both unemployed and employed youth actively use the internet on a daily basis. The p-value of 0.87 (>0.05) confirms there is no significant association between the groups in accessing the internet.

In considering the usage of the internet for social or productivity purposes, Table 3 suggests a varied usage. The p-value of 0.756 (>0.05) (Appendix: Table 20) shows there is no association between the groups' preferences. H_2 is therefore rejected. Both youth and non-youth, regardless of employment status, access the internet for social and productivity purposes in much the same way.

Table 3. Preference for using of phone for social or productivity purposes

			Employed	Unemployed
Between 16 and 35 years	Preference to use phone for social purposes rather than productivity purposes	Strongly agree	18	8
		Agree	8	2
		Neutral	16	6
		Disagree	11	3
		Strongly disagree	10	5
	Total		63	24
Over 35 years	Preference to use phone for social purposes rather than productivity purposes	Strongly agree	4	2
		Neutral	6	0
		Disagree	2	0
		Strongly disagree	2	1
	Total		14	3

3.7 ICT Means of Finding Employment

Job Application Method. Table 4 indicates that the majority of both groups apply for jobs mainly through non-ICT means such as the postal services. The p-value of 0.601 (>0.05) (Appendix: Table 21) however suggests that there is no association between the groups. Both the employed and unemployed have a preference for non-internet means when applying for jobs.

Table 4. Job application method

			Employed	Unemployed
Between 16 and 35 years	Job application method	Internet	16	5
		Postal services	47	19
	Total		63	24
Over 35 years	Job application method	Internet	2	0
		Postal services	12	3
	Total		14	3
Total	Job application method	Internet	18	5
		Postal services	59	22
	Total		77	27

3.8 Receive Job Opportunities Through Job Portals and Social Media

Table 5 indicates that if job portals were used, the employed youth (and non-youth) find the portals to have more value than the unemployed youth. The p-value of 0.03 (<0.05) (Appendix: Table 22) indicates an association between the two groups. There is a significant difference in the way employed youth receive job opportunities through internet based job portals with employed youth showing a higher preference to receive job opportunities through job portals. Non-youth ($p = 0.87 > 0.05$) however indicate the no preference in using internet-based job portals for applications whether employed or unemployed. The finding suggests that applications through job portals need to be included as part of the training for unemployed.

Table 5. Job portal applications

			Employed	Unemployed
Between 16 and 35 years	Receive job opportunities through job portals	Yes	49	13
		No	14	11
Over 35 years	Receive job opportunities through job portals	Yes	10	2
		No	4	1
Total	Receive job opportunities through job portals	Yes	59	15
		No	18	12

Table 6 suggests that both groups receive job referrals through social media and non-social media similarly. The p-value of 0.589 (>0.05) (Appendix: Table 17) indicates there is no association between the groups. Both unemployed and unemployed receive job referrals through social media and other avenues.

Table 6. Job referrals using social media

			Employed	Unemployed
Between 16 and 35 years	Receive job referrals from social networks e.g. Facebook, Twitter	Yes	33	14
		No	30	10
Over 35 years	Receive job referrals from social networks e.g. Facebook, Twitter	Yes	8	2
		No	6	1
Total	Receive job referrals from social networks e.g. Facebook, Twitter	Yes	41	16
		No	36	11

3.9 ICT Economic-Benefit Capabilities

Respondents answered to five ICT skills related questions which tested the level of e-skills of the respondents using the Likert scale with the following rating: 1 = strongly disagree, 2 = Disagree, 3 = neither agree nor disagree, 4 = Agree, 5 = strongly agree. The paper employed exploratory factor analysis (EFA) based on the Principal Components Analysis (PCA) extraction method with Varimax rotation to identify the underlying factor structure of the ICT economic-benefit capabilities construct. Exploratory factor analysis (EFA) is a statistical method that is recommended for identifying patterns in phenomenon where there are no pre-existing theories. EFA enables a reduction of factors to those that account better for the underlying causal impact in a measured phenomenon [33].

The 104 responses were analysed using SPSS® giving a response-to-item ratio of 20.8:1. Hair et al. [33] offers a rule-of-thumb recommendation for a minimum of 100 responses, and a corresponding response-to-item ratio greater than 10:1. The choice of factor selection was based on the Kaiser-Guttman K1 rule and Cattell's [34] scree plot breakpoints for items with eigenvalues greater than 1 and factors before the scree plot (Fig. 1) declines [34–36]. Factor loadings greater than 0.6 (Table 11) were considered sufficient considering the exploratory nature of the research [37]. The overall Cronbach α for internal consistency was 0.701 (Table 7). All items in the construct were considered substantially reliable with Cronbach α values (Table 9) greater than 0.61 [38]. The Kaiser–Meyer–Olkin coefficient was 0.710 and the Bartlett test of Sphericity was statistically significant ($\chi2 = 108.847$, df = 10, $p < 0.0001$) (Table 8) indicating that properties of the correlation matrix (Table 10) justified using EFA.

Table 7. Reliability statistics

Cronbach's alpha	Cronbach's alpha based on standardized items	N of items
.701	.724	5

The two factors identified (Table 13) consisted of the five items and accounted for 68.8% of the total variance explained. None of the items was removed. Factor 1 with eigenvalue of 2.39, Cronbach α of 0.711 accounted for 47.8% of the total variance and

Table 8. KMO and Bartlett's test

Kaiser-Meyer-Olkin measure of sampling adequacy		.710
Bartlett's test of sphericity	Approx. Chi-Square	108.847
	df	10
	Sig.	.000

Table 9. ICT economic-benefit capabilities

	Mean	N	SD	Cronbach's α
Search	4.13	104	1.124	0.665
Email communication	4.42	104	1.002	0.655
Digital literacy	4.51	104	1.070	0.624
Collaborate (social media)	3.48	104	1.428	0.616
Collaborate (video)	2.87	104	1.643	0.704

Table 10. Correlation matrix

		Search	Communicate (email)	Digital literacy	Collaborate (social media)	Collaborate (video)
Search	Pearson correlation	1	.501**	.362**	.268**	.194*
	Sig. (2-tailed)		.000	.000	.006	.049
Email (communicate)	Pearson correlation	.501**	1	.503**	.304**	.135
	Sig. (2-tailed)	.000		.000	.002	.171
Digital literacy	Pearson correlation	.362**	.503**	1	.423**	.288**
	Sig. (2-tailed)	.000	.000		.000	.003
Collaborate (social media)	Pearson correlation	.268**	.304**	.423**	1	.458**
	Sig. (2-tailed)	.006	.002	.000		.000
Collaborate (video)	Pearson correlation	.194*	.135	.288**	.458**	1
	Sig. (2-tailed)	.049	.171	.003	.000	

**Correlation is significant at the 0.01 level (2-tailed).
*Correlation is significant at the 0.05 level (2-tailed).

consisted of three items: Search, Email communication and Digital literacy. Factor 1 was identified as *Individual ICT/Mobile Skills*. Factor 2 with eigenvalue of 1.05, Cronbach α of 0.624 accounted for 20.96% of the total variance and consisted of two items: collaborate (social media) and collaborate (video). Factor 2 was identified as

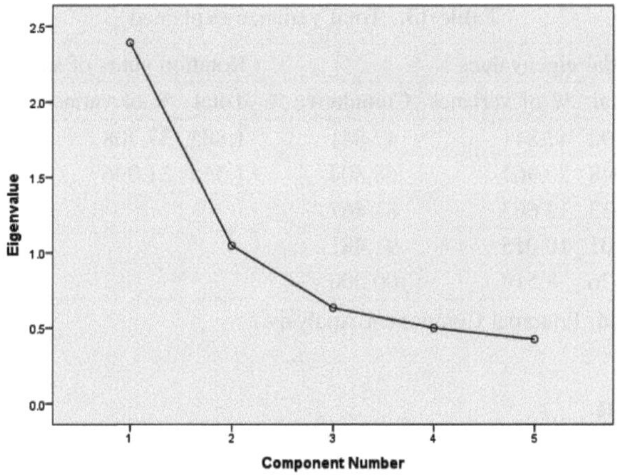

Fig. 1. Scree plot

Table 11. Factor structure matrix[a]

	Factor loading	
	1	2
Search	.783	.095
Email communication	.866	.076
Digital literacy	.662	.403
Collaborate (social media)	.289	.780
Collaborate (video)	.023	.878

Extraction Method: Principal Component Analysis.
Rotation Method: Varimax with Kaiser Normalization.
[a]Rotation converged in 3 iterations.

Table 12. Component Transformation Matrix

Component	1	2
1	.789	.614
2	–.614	.789

Extraction Method: Principal Component Analysis.
Rotation Method: Varimax with Kaiser Normalization.

Interpersonal ICT/Mobile Skills. The emergence of individual and interpersonal skills confirms recent literature that suggests that participation in the digital economy is not limited to technical capabilities alone, but that the technical capabilities need to relate to important personal and social skills [39, 40] (Tables 12, 16 and 17).

Table 13. Total variance explained

Component	Initial eigenvalues			Rotation sums of squared loadings		
	Total	% of variance	Cumulative %	Total	% of variance	Cumulative %
1	2.392	47.841	47.841	1.885	37.708	37.708
2	1.048	20.964	68.804	1.555	31.096	68.804
3	.633	12.663	81.467			
4	.501	10.015	91.481			
5	.426	8.519	100.000			

Extraction Method: Principal Component Analysis.

4 Conclusion

This study explored in the quantitative approach, the mobile usage patterns among 104 participants in an effort to contextualize mobile and ICT strategies targeted at unemployed youth. The purpose of the study was to identify the essential ICT and mobile phone capabilities and characteristics that may apply to the unemployed.

From the findings, it was evident that youth unemployment, particularly graduate youth unemployment, is on the rise. The youth form the predominant workforce in any economy and it is imperative to harness that vitality.

The finding that both unemployed and employed actively use their phones to download apps, and for social and productive purposes is not a surprise. Both groups appear to take for granted digital literacy as something that is within their fundamental capabilities, yet despite the presumption, the preferred method for job applications remains through postal services. Nonetheless, employed youth prefer internet-based job portals compared with the unemployed youth. Social media did not appear to be an option through which to receive job opportunities in any group.

A greater number of studies in ICT4D literature focus attention on rural areas and often assume that individuals in urban areas are covered. The finding of high youth unemployment in the rural areas and rural-urban migration means further research may need to be placed on creating effective strategies for youth unemployment in urban areas. Central Business Districts may need to consider ICT based training and interventions mechanisms that will cater for migration patterns of those from rural and township areas. The similar mobile phone access and usage patterns suggest that such interventions could ease the transition into urban areas that is often faced by unemployed migrants, or rather enable a better decision-making process before making the migration decision.

The two economic-benefit capabilities were individual and interpersonal ICT/mobile capabilities with a greater emphasis on the individual capabilities.

The paper was limited in its analysis of 104 individuals with a greater representation from urban areas. The individuals were taken from a convenient sample, and through the use of online survey forms. The sampling and online survey automatically disadvantages the unemployed who may not have such access. Further research needs to consider a more normal distribution of the groups as well as test the two economic-benefit ICT/mobile capabilities that emerged from the study.

Appendix

Table 14. Chi square results for residential area by employment status by age bracket

Age bracket		Value	df	Asymptotic significance (2-sided)
Between 16 and 35 years	Pearson Chi-Square	3.642b	2	.162
	N of valid cases	87		

Table 15. Chi-Square tests for job hunting by age by employment status

Age bracket		Value	df	Asymptotic significance (2-sided)
Between 16 and 35 years	Pearson Chi-Square	1.296c	1	.255
	N of valid cases	87		
Over 35 years	Pearson Chi-Square	5.204d	1	.023
	N of valid cases	17		
Total	Pearson Chi-Square	4.175a	1	.041
	N of valid cases	104		

Table 16. Chi-Square tests for education by employment status by age

Age bracket		Value	df	Asymptotic significance (2-sided)
Between 16 and 35 years	Pearson Chi-Square	2.662b	6	.850
	N of valid cases	87		
Over 35 years	Pearson Chi-Square	3.812c	5	.577
	N of valid cases	17		
Total	Pearson Chi-Square	4.370a	6	.627
	N of valid cases	104		

[a]8 cells (57.1%) have expected count less than 5. The minimum expected count is .52.
[b]8 cells (57.1%) have expected count less than 5. The minimum expected count is .28.
[c]12 cells (100.0%) have expected count less than 5. The minimum expected count is .18.

Table 17. Chi-Square tests for referrals through social media

Age bracket		Value	df	Asymptotic significance (2-sided)
Between 16 and 35 years	Pearson Chi-Square	.248c	1	.619
	N of valid cases	87		
Over 35 years	Pearson Chi-Square	.093d	1	.761
	N of valid cases	17		
Total	Pearson Chi-Square	.292a	1	.589
	N of valid cases	104		

Table 18. Importance of basic ICT skills by employment status by age bracket

Age bracket		Value	df	Asymptotic significance (2-sided)
Between 16 and 35 years	Pearson Chi-Square	.836b	4	.934
	N of valid cases	87		
Over 35 years	Pearson Chi-Square	.792c	3	.851
	N of valid cases	17		
Total	Pearson Chi-Square	1.160a	4	.885
	N of valid cases	104		

[a]6 cells (60.0%) have expected count less than 5. The minimum expected count is .78.
[b]7 cells (70.0%) have expected count less than 5. The minimum expected count is .83.
[c]7 cells (87.5%) have expected count less than 5. The minimum expected count is .18.

Table 19. Chi-square tests for the frequency of internet access

Age bracket		Value	df	Asymptotic significance (2-sided)
Between 16 and 35 years	Pearson Chi-Square	.107c	1	.744
	N of valid cases	87		
Over 35 years	Pearson Chi-Square	.228d	1	.633
	N of valid cases	17		
Total	Pearson Chi-Square	.027a	1	.870
	N of valid cases	104		

Table 20. Chi-square tests for preferences

Age bracket		Value	df	Asymptotic significance (2-sided)
Between 16 and 35 years	Pearson Chi-Square	.935b	4	.920
	N of valid cases	87		
Over 35 years	Pearson Chi-Square	3.238c	3	.356
	N of valid cases	17		
Total	Pearson Chi-Square	1.892a	4	.756
	N of valid cases	104		

[a]3 cells (30.0%) have expected count less than 5. The minimum expected count is 2.60.
[b]3 cells (30.0%) have expected count less than 5. The minimum expected count is 2.76.
[c]8 cells (100.0%) have expected count less than 5. The minimum expected count is .35.

Table 21. Chi-Square tests for job application methods

Agc brackct		Valuc	df	Asymptotic Significance (2-sided)
Between 16 and 35 years	Pearson Chi-Square	.198c	1	.657
	N of valid cases	87		
Over 35 years	Pearson Chi-Square	.486d	1	.486
	N of valid cases	17		
Total	Pearson Chi-Square	.274a	1	.601
	N of valid cases	104		

Table 22. Chi-Square tests for job portal applications

Age bracket		Value	df	Asymptotic Significance (2-sided)
Between 16 and 35 years	Pearson Chi-Square	4.731c	1	.030
	N of valid cases	87		
Over 35 years	Pearson Chi-Square	.027d	1	.870
	N of valid cases	17		
Total	Pearson Chi-Square	4.323a	1	.038
	N of valid cases	104		

References

1. ITU: ICT Facts and figures 2016 (2016)
2. Goldstruck, A.: Massive increase in SA smartphone purchases (2014)
3. TradingEconomics.com: South Africa Youth Unemployment Rate (2016)
4. Graham, L.: Youth unemployment: what can we do in the short run? (2016)
5. Graham, L., et al.: Youth assets for employability: An evaluation of youth employability interventions (Siyakha Youth Assets Baseline Report), Johannesburg, South Africa (2016)
6. Ardington, C., Bärnighausen, T., Case, A., Menendez, A.: Social protection and labor market outcomes of youth in South Africa. ILR Rev. **69**, 455–470 (2016)
7. Wilkinson, A., et al.: The employment environment for youth in rural South Africa: a mixed-methods study. Dev. South. Afr. **34**, 17–32 (2017)
8. Blaug, M.: Investment in human capital (book). J. Bus. **45**, 113 (1972)
9. Abou-Setta, A.: Towards more employable Egyptian HE graduates – a case study. Educ. Bus. Soc. Contemp. Middle East. Issues **7**, 229–244 (2014)
10. Lim, M.: Egypt. J. Commun. **62**, 231–248 (2012)
11. Mohamedbhai, G.: The challenge of graduate unemployment in Africa. Int. High. Educ. **80**, 12 (2015)
12. Oluwajodu, F., Blaauw, D., Greyling, L., Kleynhans, E.P.J.: Graduate unemployment in South Africa: perspectives from the banking sector. SA J. Hum. Resour. Manag. **13**, 1–9 (2015)

13. Gefen, D., Ragowsky, A., Miller, J., Licker, P., Stern, M.: The center cannot hold: how leading firms are managing the changing IT boundaries. Commun. Assoc. Inf. Syst. **36**, 655–667 (2015)
14. Universities South Africa: Universities Funding in South Africa. A Fact Sheet (2016)
15. Twinomurinzi, H., Schofield, A., Hagen, L., Ditsoane-Molefe, S., Tshidzumba, N.A.: Towards a shared worldview on e-skills: a discourse between government, industry and academia on the ICT skills paradox. South Afr. Comput. J. **29**, 215–237 (2017)
16. Schofield, A.: 2014 JCSE ICT Skills Survey (2014)
17. ITWeb: IT salaries 8% up, women closing the gap - Salary Survey 2015. http://www.itweb.co.za/index.php?option=com_content&view=article&id=143701
18. Rice, R.E., Katz, J.E.: Comparing internet and mobile phone usage: digital divides of usage, adoption, and dropouts. Telecommun. Policy **27**, 597–623 (2003)
19. Kongaut, C., Bohlin, E.: Investigating mobile broadband adoption and usage: a case of smartphones in Sweden. Telematics Inform. **33**, 742–752 (2016)
20. O'Neill, J., Toyama, K., Chen, J., Tate, B., Siddique, A.: The increasing sophistication of mobile media sharing in lower-middle-class Bangalore. In: Proceedings of the Eighth International Conference on Information and Communication Technologies and Development - ICTD 2016, pp. 1–11. ACM Press, New York (2016)
21. Ramachander, S.: The price sensitivity of mobile use among low income households in six countries of Asia. Telecommun. Policy **40**, 673–691 (2016)
22. Peyper, L.: Mobile phone usage in SA. http://finweek.co/2013.01/22/mobile-phone-usage-in-sa/
23. Kreutzer, T.: Generation Mobile: Online and Digital Media Usage on Mobile Phones among Low-Income Urban Youth in South Africa, pp. 0–13. Centre for Film and Media Studies, MA (2009)
24. Raftree, L.: Landscape Review: Mobiles for Youth Workforce Development, pp. 1–184 (2013)
25. Sen, A.K.: Development as Freedom. Oxford University Press, Oxford (2001)
26. O'Hearn, D.: Amartya Sen's development as freedom: ten years later. Policy Pract. Dev. Educ. Rev. **8**, 9–15 (2009)
27. Griffiths, D.A., Inman, M., Rojas, H., Williams, K.: Transitioning student identity and sense of place: future possibilities for assessment and development of student employability skills. Stud. High. Educ. **43**, 891–913 (2018)
28. Field, A.: Discovering Statistics Using SPSS. Sage Publications Ltd (2009)
29. United Nations: Policies on Spatial Distribution and Urbanization. Department of Economic and Social Affairs, UN (2016)
30. Pieterse, A.: The bright lights of city regions - Assumptions, realities and implications of changing population dynamics: Zooming in on the Gauteng city region (2014)
31. Caliendo, M., Künn, S., Schmidl, R.: Fighting youth unemployment : the effects of active labor market policies. IZA J. Labor Policy **54**, 1–51 (2011)
32. Twinomurinzi, H.: Social cognitive factors affecting career choice in mobile app development: comparing between employed and unemployed programming students. In: Proceedings of the Information Systems Education Conference, pp. 1–12. ISECON, Orlando (2015)
33. Hair, J.F., Black, W.C., Babin, B.Y., Anderson, R., Tatham, R.: Multivariate data analysis: a global perspective. Pearson, Upper Saddle River (2010)
34. Cattell, R.B.: The scree test for the number of factors. Multivar. Behav. Res. **1**, 245–276 (1966)

35. Kaiser, H.F.: The application of electronic computers to factor analysis. Educ. Psychol. Meas. **20**, 141–151 (1960)
36. Guttmann, L.: Some necessary conditions for common factor analysis. Psychometrika **19**, 149–162 (1954)
37. Hayton, J.C., Allen, D.G., Scarpello, V.: Factor retention decisions in exploratory factor analysis: a tutorial on parallel analysis. Organ. Res. Methods **7**, 191–205 (2004)
38. Landis, J.R., Koch, G.G.: The measurement of observer agreement for categorical data. Biometrics **33**, 159 (1977)
39. van Laar, E., van Deursen, A.J.A.M., van Dijk, J.A.G.M., de Haan, J.: The relation between 21st-century skills and digital skills: a systematic literature review. Comput. Hum. Behav. **72**, 577–588 (2017)
40. Alexander, P.M., Twinomurinzi, H.: Changing career choice factors as the economic environment changes. In: Kroeze, J. and De Villiers, R. (eds.) Proceedings of the South African Institute for Computer Scientists and Information Technologists Conference on – SAICSIT, pp. 1–11. SAICSIT, Pretoria (2012)

Smartphone Paradoxes in Working Mothers' Pursuit of Work-Life Balance

Karen Sowon(✉), Olga Sikhwari, Mphatso Nyemba-Mudenda, and Wallace Chigona

Department of Information Systems, University of Cape Town, Cape Town, South Africa
csowon@gmail.com, skholg001@gmail.com, mphatsonyemba@yahoo.com, wallace.chigona@uct.ac.za

Abstract. Technology has led to the intertwining of work and life, with persistent debates as to whether they facilitate better Work-Life Balance (WLB) practices or not. It is argued that while smartphones may provide capabilities that foster WLB, they may also contribute to negative outcomes that challenge the very pursuit and intention of WLB. The research adopts an interpretive, qualitative approach, using the paradoxes of technology to understand what conflicts the use of smartphones present to working mothers in their pursuit of WLB. A total of 15 participants were selected, through convenience sampling, to study a variety of experiences and views regarding smartphones, as experienced by working mothers. The sample differed in terms of age, marital status, type of employment, industry and income level. We used semi-structured interviews to collect data. The data were analysed using thematic analysis. The results indicate that though smartphones provide capabilities that potentially support WLB, their very use results in paradoxical experiences for mothers that challenge their very quest of WLB.

Keywords: Work-life balance · Working mothers · Technology paradox

1 Introduction

The mobile phone is the first truly mobile computing solution. Indeed, in its current iteration as a smartphone, the mobile phone (with its myriad capabilities) has evolved beyond its primary technology antecedents as just a communication device, into its current form as a lifestyle accessory and an extension of its owner's personality [1]. Smartphones have been defined as mobile communication devices that enable Internet-based services and other computer-like functions [2]. While there have been other mobile or handheld devices, what sets the smartphone apart is that it is rarely – if ever – far away from its owner [1].

The uptake of mobile phones on the African continent has seen the growth of the telecommunications sector by leaps and bounds. This growth has led to the development of mobile-centric applications that more and more people rely on for their day-to-day living – from mobile banking services to educational services, to mobile-based health insurance [3–5]. One area that has been significantly reshaped by mobile

K. Krauss et al. (Eds.): IDIA 2018, CCIS 933, pp. 94–106, 2019.
https://doi.org/10.1007/978-3-030-11235-6_7

technologies is work [6], leading to increasingly intertwined work and life domains [7, 8]. As such, debates exist as to whether the increasingly blurred boundaries between work and home spaces negatively or positively affect work-life balance [7]. It is evident that the pervasiveness of technology has invariably resulted in both positive and negative outcomes for the users; thus, it is this paradox of technological advancement that often influences individual and social lives.

The concept of paradoxes of technology is not new, having received more limelight in academia from the work of Mick and Fournier [9]. Since then, some studies have focused either directly or indirectly on these conflicts in more recent technologies. It is in light of this, that mobile technology paradoxes in various aspects of the users' lives, such as in organisational behavior contexts [8, 10, 11] and consumer behaviour [12], have been studied. Jarvenpaa and Lang [1] have presented a more detailed exposition on paradoxes presented by mobile technology; however, these studies on mobile technology paradoxes are still few in number. Variety in phenomena, as well as study sample, in research involving conflicts and paradoxes, offer great promise for advancing a more holistic understanding of the dialectical nature of technology [13]. Whereas mobile technology has greatly affected work-life balance, literature addressing technology paradoxes in this area is scarce. More specifically, studies on work-life balance among working mothers have not yet tackled the issue of paradoxes brought about by communication technologies like the smartphone. It is with this background that this study seeks to answer the following question: **What technology paradoxes do smartphones present in working mothers' pursuit of work-life balance?**

The insights thereof will yield a more holistic understanding on possible ambiguities and conflicts of communication technologies in the area of work-life balance. This would also translate into a broader outlook among stakeholders, governments and employers in designing and implementing policies relating to work and technology use that takes into account a complete view of technology experiences in users' lives. The insights will also be a step for researchers to seek solutions that minimise conflicts associated with mobile technology use in the area of WLB. Although this study is based on working mothers, we do not directly study the role of gender in the emergence of paradoxes. Instead, as ones who likely bear a heavier burden of domestic responsibilities, we seek to discover what paradoxes they accrue from their use of smartphones that may challenge their very pursuit of wellbeing. This work therefore only serves as a preliminary study to further research in this area.

The rest of this paper is structured as follows: Sect. 2 reviews the literature that situates this study; Sect. 3 presents the theoretical framework, while Sect. 4 elucidates the methodological aspects. In Sect. 5, we present the findings of the study. Finally, Sect. 6 presents a discussion, conclusion and further opportunities for research.

2 Literature Review

2.1 Work-Life Balance and Smartphone Technology

It is an undeniable fact that the development of smartphones has resulted in great progress; nevertheless, this same technology has also had a negative effect. One aspect of life affected by this is Work-Life Balance (WLB). WLB does not in actual fact connote an equal distribution of responsibilities in the two domains: home life and work, but rather to workers juggling home and work demands [14]. On one side, some hold to the notion that blurred boundaries created by mobile technology lead to negative outcomes for workers, because they encourage overwork and infringement on family life [15]. On the other side, it has been argued that technology has the potential to increase flexibility in attending to work and family responsibilities, thereby enhancing WLB. No matter the side of the debate taken, smartphone technology is not only here to stay, but is also advancing day by day; consequently, understanding how it affects lives, more so WLB, may hold the key to unravelling the root causes of some of the occupational and family problems faced today.

The pervasiveness of technology is linked to the greater blurring of work and family boundaries, and results in boundary permeability. Boundary permeability defines how easily a worker can switch between work and family roles. It is for this reason that the use of communications technology (like smartphones) is inextricably linked to increased spillover, compared to technologies like the personal computer. Due to how they so easily combine communication and personal computing capabilities with mobility and personality [6], mobile devices easily integrate into a person's life [15]. As a result, technologies like the smartphone present an interesting front to studying WLB, because of the various positive and negative experiences they could generate in the users' lives.

2.2 Working Mothers

There is a predominance of dual income families today [6], with women working for various reasons including self-fulfilment, financial independence, and supplementing the family's income pool [16]. As a result, balancing roles as a worker and a mother/wife is often necessary, because working mothers experience unique challenges in terms of successful careers, with higher demands of family obligations and childcare defined by socio-cultural norms and expectations [16]. These expectations sometimes define what being 'proper' is, hence informing a woman's decisions and behaviour consciously or unconsciously [17]. It is also evident that these socio-cultural definitions of gender roles have generally remained the same over time [16, 18].

In sub-Saharan Africa, working mothers are increasingly the bedrocks of not only the family, but the workplace as well [19, 20]. Nonetheless, as more mothers take to employment or business to support their families, they are still expected to perform the traditional family roles – taking care of children, coordinating the household, and, in a traditionally patriarchal society, supporting their husbands. The pull between family and work responsibilities often results in internal and external conflicts [21].

It is also true that juggling multiple roles often creates more family-work spillover for women than for men [15]. A sense of ambivalence is noted in that although women may appreciate the benefits of mobile technology, such as enabling them to be available for their families, the extended heightened sense of responsibility is reported as being potentially burdensome [22]. These sentiments are also corroborated by Lim and Soon [23], where mothers found the constant connectivity binding them to home responsibilities unnerving.

As mentioned earlier, two sides of the debate exist on how mobile technology affects WLB. Some researchers have shown that mobile technology has the potential to disrupt WLB [7], while others present the benefits that users could accrue [24]. Mobile technologies have been reported to offer workers opportunities like availability for their families [22], career commitment [25], and flexibility and autonomy [26]. For example, a study in Canada showed that by using their Blackberries to respond promptly to work emails and texts, younger Canadian working women portrayed an image of responsiveness and dependability with regard to their careers [25]. Technology affordances such as 'always-on' and ubiquity allowed these women to demonstrate accessibility and responsiveness, even when not physically present at their workplaces.

In summary, there is little consensus on how mobile technology affects WLB. Indeed, studies that explicate the relationship between mobile technology and women's 'double work' (home and paid labour) and social conditions, indicate that there are two 'camps' in literature around this issue [27]. This study seeks to find out the paradoxes of smartphones in the pursuit of WLB by working mothers.

3 Theoretical Framework

Jarvenpaa and Lang's [1] landmark paper on the paradoxes of mobile technology, highlight 8 key paradoxes that any user of this technology is likely to face. In their study of mobile phone use carried out across three countries, they developed a conceptual framework that demonstrates these 8 paradoxes, as seen in Fig. 1:

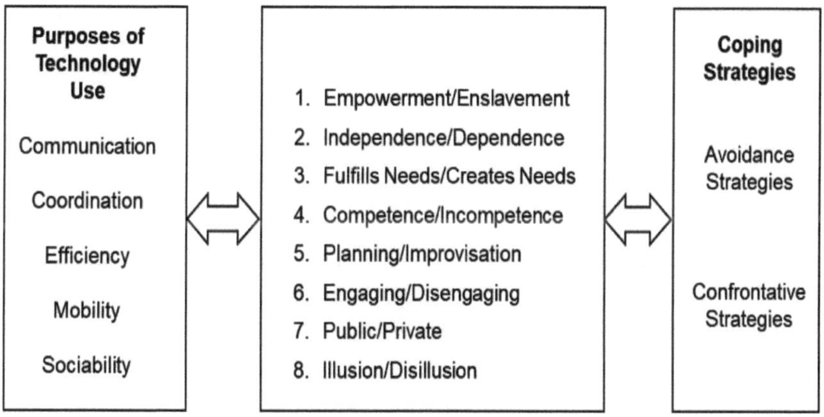

Fig. 1. Paradoxes of mobile technology use

According to this framework, mobile technology though useful, results in a series of conflict situations between the utility it provides and the disturbance it creates to social functioning. For example, while a smartphone may empower the user with continuous access to the latest information, news, or even new networks through social media, continual use may result in the user becoming addicted, or enslaved by the same technology. To achieve balance, there is a need for active corrective measures, which may mean disuse of the technology altogether (avoidance) or adjusting one's life to accommodate the disturbance brought about by the smartphone (confrontation).

Though the framework may not present a conclusive list of technology paradoxes, the list of eight applies more specifically to cell phone technology, rather than just technology in general, as detailed in the work of Mick and Fournier [9]. The framework also makes more explicit the mobile technology affordances, indicating that technology is not an end in itself, but, rather, it is adopted and used by its users as a means to an end. This makes it appropriate for our empirical scenario to discover what paradoxes may be accrued by working mothers as they use their smartphones for various purposes in the pursuit of work-life balance.

4 Methodology

4.1 Study Design

The study adopted a cross-sectional design to provide a snapshot of the paradoxes of smartphone use among working mothers in the pursuit of WLB. The design relied on qualitative methods to achieve the study objectives. An interpretivist approach was applied to understand arising smartphone conflicts from the users' perspectives.

4.2 Study Population and Sociodemographic Characteristics

The study population (Table 1) comprised working mothers in the age range of between 20 and 55 from various locations around the Western Cape province. This group of women included employees and entrepreneurs from different levels of education and different job roles. They also represented different work sectors, including finance, ICT, telecoms, education, and health and beauty, regardless of their marital status and race, as long as they owned a smartphone.

4.3 Sample Size and Sampling

Due to the limited amount of time allocated to complete this study, a convenience sample of 15 respondents was used. In order to minimise bias, efforts were made to ensure that there was as much variation as possible among the respondents, in terms of their sociodemographic characteristics.

4.4 Data Collection

Semi-structured interviews were used to explore the nuances of women's daily uses of smartphones. The questions were structured to reveal the opportunities and challenges of smartphone use for WLB in the lives of working mothers. The questions avoided the use of terms like "paradox", or "conflict" that might have influenced the participants to conjure up ambiguous experiences. The interviews, typically thirty minutes to an hour in length, were conducted on an individual basis. Interviews were audio-recorded with

Table 1. Sociodemographic characteristics of study respondents

#	Age	Race	Marital status	Children's ages	Job title
1	37	Black	Married	5, 7	Security Guard
2	26	Coloured	Single	5	Domestic worker
3	42	Coloured	Single	12, 18	Cleaner
4	36	Coloured	Single	4, 6	Legal Consultant
5	40	Coloured	Married	16	Switchboard operator
6	33	Coloured	Married	3, 10	Property Analyst
7	28	Black	Single	2, 9	IT Business Analyst
8	52	White	Single	12, 18, 22	Finance Director
9	25	Indian	Single	5	IT Manager
10	23	Indian	Single	3	Retail Sales assistant
11	28	Black	Single	1	Call centre operator
12	35	Coloured	Single	4, 6	Lecturer
13	51	Black	Married	17, 13, 22	Hair Dresser
14	38	Coloured	Married	8, 13, 17	IT Entrepreneur
15	26	White	Married	3, 4	Personal Assistant

the permission of the participants. Prior to each interview, informed consent was sought from each respondent.

4.5 Data Analysis

The collected data were analysed using thematic analysis. This involved transcription of data, identification of patterns, and coding similar words together to group arising conflicts. Arising conflicts were then grouped into higher-order themes. These themes were then compared against Jarvenpaa and Lang's [1] list of mobile technology paradoxes, and assigned to the best fitting paradox item. Excerpts were extracted to support the results.

4.6 Study Limitations

The selection of a small sample, as well as the use of convenience sampling, means that it may be difficult to generalise the study findings. This was necessitated by the short time frame within which the study was executed; however, the insights generated from the sample are useful in providing an understanding of how smartphone technology paradoxes play out in WLB. This study therefore serves as a starting point for further research in this area.

4.7 Ethical Considerations

This study complied with the rules of ethics, privacy and confidentiality, as stipulated by the University of Cape Town's Information Systems Department. All individuals selected for this study were formally approached, and invited to participate in the interview process, through emails, and they were also asked to sign a consent form. All participants were asked for permission to record the interviews. Information about individuals/participants collected during the process of research was not disclosed without permission. All findings are presented in a way that protects the individual's/participant's identity. Interviewees are referred to by a code (e.g. Candidate 1) and not by name, in all documentation.

5 Findings

5.1 Paradoxes of Smartphone Use Among Working Mothers

Empowerment/Enslavement: While the use of smartphones offered mothers the opportunity to feel empowered to juggle family and work responsibilities, mothers also felt enslaved by the expectations that owning a smartphone brought on them. For them, empowerment/enslavement demonstrated itself in the pull between *Family Availability and Time Infringement.*

For example, mothers reported that smartphones afforded them the opportunity to carry out tasks remotely that would otherwise require their physical presence. They were able to work from home –for example, when they had a sick child. Additionally, they were better able to manage their time, as the smartphones had the capability to coordinate and manage tasks. All these opportunities allowed them to be increasingly available for their families, something that most mothers reported as being important to them. In this way, they felt *empowered.*

> *"... Internet banking also helps instead of going to the bank. So, there's more time available for the children" (Candidate 3)*

> *"It's difficult, extremely difficult because you'd rather want to be at home with your kids. When your kids get sick, I am not sure if all mothers feel this way but sometimes you kind of .... I feel guilty that I have to be at work when my kids are sick and vice versa when my kids are sick I feel guilty that am not at work, so it's that kind of thing" (Candidate 4)*

In addition, smartphones provided mothers with the opportunity to work from home when they could not be physically present, like in cases of maternity leave.

> *"When I was on leave I felt like I was being left behind in the workplace, wanted to know what my colleagues were up to, and I must say that having a smartphone really helped because sometimes my boss would contact me to ask me about certain work project that I was involved in before I left and I could easily help him with all the information that I had on my smartphone. I even had access to see all the meetings which my colleagues were attending at work while I was still at home" (Candidate 11)*

Though mothers valued availability, whether for their families or for work responsibilities, they often found themselves having to deal with time infringement that technology characteristics such as "always on" brought with them. This infringement often caused a conflict within them, because instead of feeling empowered to be available for their families, they ended up feeling *enslaved.*

> *"Well having emails on my phone it's good, but I just cannot stand the expectation that when I am at home busy with my own life I must be expected to be answering work email. You know it's really irritating at times especially when you get those negative emails from your boss after hours, it really spoils your mood you know" (Candidate 4)*

Furthermore, respondents reported being unable to separate their private life from their work life, and vice versa, the end result of which was an imbalance in both spheres. While, on one side, the smartphone allowed them better time management, it also resulted in greater time demands from the responsibilities of one domain to another.

> *"...My challenge is keeping work, work and keeping my private life private..." (Candidate 3)*

Fulfils Needs/Creates Needs: To many mothers, having meaningful relationships with their children, spouses and friends, despite working away from the home, was important; therefore, conflict arose, as they felt that smartphones afforded them the opportunity to *Nurture Relationships,* but that their use was also responsible for *Ruining Relationships.*

Participants reported using smartphones for sociability and communication by connecting with their children, husbands, and friends while working away from home. They valued nurturing relationships, and the ubiquity and mobility of smartphones enabled them to *fulfil a need.* This was exemplified in these two responses: *"I have a friend of mine in UK that I haven't seen for two years, but since I got my smartphone we chat all the time on Facebook"* and *"my husband works evening shifts, it's important to stay in touch to keep our marriage going, I can't spend a day without talking to him either by calling or messaging him on WhatsApp."*

Though smartphones were offering capabilities to communicate on one end, hence helping to nurture relationships, participants also felt that their integration into life was to be blamed for habits that were not so relationship fostering. These were ruining the very thing they were pursuing – intimacy – by fostering habits and actions that were disengaging and, in fact, creating social isolation despite being in the same physical space with those they loved. In this way, smartphones created another need to be connected to a 'virtual community', to protect relationships, and to be 'socially aware'. The latter simply means that users were now forced to be more conscious of their phone habits when they were in social environments.

> *"My friends and I will go out for dinner and we will all be sitting on a table but we are all on our phones so what's the point for us going out and still be on our phone, we are not talking because we are all on our phones?" (Candidate 12).* This participant felt that smartphones were responsible for creating isolation. This was corroborated by *Candidate 3* who said, *"It (referring to smartphones) can be a complete conversation killer, you can be completely isolated, you can be withdrawn because you can live your life with just your phone and not interacting with other people".*
>
> *"At one stage I was on Facebook all the time. Now it's games. I could be seated with my husband but hardly speak to each other. At one point I told him that if we don't stop this, our marriage would head in the wrong direction. We had stopped talking..." (Candidate 14).* This participant felt the need to protect her relationship with her husband from the negative effect of smartphone use in her home. The need to connect with the 'virtual community' on social media was partly responsible for distracting their communication.

Apart from creating needs on the relationship front, the use of smartphones also created economic needs. For example, in an attempt to ensure that smartphone affordances were helping them to meet their work and family commitments, mothers indicated needing more airtime and more data. More often than not, they could not afford these extra costs, and this left them feeling perplexed.

Independence/Dependence: The respondents in this study indicated that their smartphones afforded them the ability to multitask between workplace and family demands during working hours, independent of space and time; thus, they were able to use their smartphones to support their various roles, and to coordinate tasks and activities both at home and in the workplace. This way, they felt more efficient in juggling home and work responsibilities.

> *"Say for instance I am in a meeting and I need my son to be picked up from school, I usually just send my brother or dad a WhatsApp message without walking out of the meeting to make a phone call to ask them to go pick him up. And they will also know that if I am in a meeting they can reach me through WhatsApp" (Candidate 9)*

When most participants were asked their general opinion regarding their use of smartphones, most of them described their smartphones as "something they love, something they can't live without", indicating their *dependence* on their smartphones. Some respondents reported always needing to check their smartphones, even in social settings, and more often than not, unconsciously.

> *"A smartphone can cause an imbalance because I have my phone with me all the time and when I go home it doesn't matter who is there am always checking my phone all the time and my parents complain" (Candidate 13)*

In addition to creating dependence in their social realms, smartphones also created dependence for some mothers in their work environments. An interesting scenario of this is demonstrated by *Candidate 15: "I find that I cannot do without my phone in meetings because they speak very quickly and for me to capture everything is difficult. So when I am compiling minutes, I simply check at what point I lost them, and I revisit my recording. I can do this at home which is great because I could also be watching over my kids while I am working."* This mother was dependent on her smartphone for the execution of her work responsibilities.

Another example of this work dependency was explained by *Candidate 4:*

> *"The minute I shut down and leave work without my phone I won't know what is happening at work while I am picking up my child or something. So my smartphone helps because most of the time I have to know when something goes wrong at work regardless of what time it is."*

In an attempt to cope with these conflicts, most mothers adopted avoidance strategies as demonstrated by Candidate 10, who said, *"When I am at home I don't check my email on my cell phone all the time purely because it takes too much data when the emails are downloading."* Unfortunately, the adoption of such strategies limited their very intention and purpose of using the smartphone in the first place.

Illusion/Disillusion: This paradox lends itself in the arising feeling of *Consonance or Dissonance* among mothers. Mothers expected that the Always-on affordance of smartphones would be a blessing to them in being able to keep in touch anytime, any-where.

Indeed, if a working mother needed to get in touch with her kids or family during the day, she was able to do so. Their smartphones enabled them to attain a level of agreement between the desire to check up on family, and the capability to do so; nonetheless, some of the respondents got disillusioned when they realized that the fine print in their 'anytime anywhere' expectation was 'so long as they had airtime and/or data', or if work policies allowed them to use their phones during work hours. One mother, whose experience epitomised this paradox, indicated that this ability to get in touch at any time during the day, also meant that the children or other family members would want to prolong the conversation. This knowledge resulted in internal conflict within the psyche of the working mother, because they had to consider the cost of communication.

> *"Sometimes I restrain myself from calling at home because I know my kids will want to go on and on talking because they miss me, so I will just send a message to their father and ask how the kids are doing, sometimes I feel like am robbing them of that interaction but calling is too much and sometimes I cannot afford it" (Candidate 14).* Once again, avoidance was the strategy adopted to deal with the conflict.

6 Discussion and Conclusion

This study found that smartphone use among working mothers in this subset of the population has resulted in four main paradoxical situations: (1) Empowerment/Enslavement lending itself to the conflict between family availability, and time infringement; (2) Fulfil needs/Create needs showing in the pull between nurturing relationships and ruining relationships; (3) Independence/Dependence; and (4) Illusion/Disillusion from the Consonance/Dissonance conflict that mothers often had to deal with. By taking advantage of technology characteristics such as mobility and ubiquity, smartphones permitted working mothers greater flexibility and convenience to manage multiple family and work demands competing for their time; however, their ability to cope with the accompanying paradoxes to a large extent determined how they interacted with their work and home domains and, hence, how they experienced work-life balance.

The working mothers were increasingly able to be available for their families, and even in some cases when they were not physically present, they were still able to communicate with, or coordinate, family or workplace matters from either work, or home, respectively. On the other hand, the constant connectedness of smartphones led to infringement on time with family and friends during their out-of-work hours, or infringed on time in home responsibilities while at work; hence, mothers viewed being 'always on' as more encumbering for them, and as likely to result in negative work-family spillover. This created social dilemmas [17] for mothers in determining when and when not to have their smartphones on; at the same time, however, being off was not always an option, because some of their responsibilities depended on them being accessible and reachable – or so they felt.

Smartphones either nurtured or ruined social relationships in the lives of working mothers in this study. These findings are in line with those of McDaniel and Coyne [28] who highlight a phenomenon known as "technoference". This is when technology gets in the way of family relationships – more so between couples. Indeed, for this study, respondents often found themselves in physical proximity to their family, yet socially distant. This also coincides with the findings of Lapierre [29], who also highlights the deleterious effect that excessive smartphone use has on social relationships.

It is not in doubt that smartphones have enabled and empowered working mothers to work from home, as well as perform remote-mothering from their places of work [30, 31]. Remote-mothering, as a phenomenon, was evident in this study. Working mothers relied on smartphones to check on their children, and meet/facilitate meeting their needs while at work; nevertheless, this constant reliance on the smartphone led to a feeling of dependence upon it, amplified by participants stating that they could not "live without my smartphone". Furthermore, some respondents indicated that they often found themselves using their smartphone unconsciously at inappropriate times and places. These findings correspond with Oulasvirta et al. [32], that smartphones are habit forming, and result in 'check-habits' which drive users to repetitively check their smartphone apps like emails, or social networking sites. This compulsive use of smartphones has been linked to stress [33, 34], sleep disturbances, and even depression symptoms [33], all of which do not promote healthy WLB. Dependence on the smartphone also created economic needs to keep up with cost of data in an environment where data costs are already very high. From the participants' experiences, cost of smartphone use – data and voice costs – was a major factor on how and when they used their smartphones in their pursuit of WLB.

Smartphones have helped working mothers to keep abreast of the happenings at home while at work, and vice versa; nonetheless, this Always-on connectedness (so-called smartphone intrusion) has resulted in an unnerving internal mental state [35]. There is dissonance between the working mother's need to keep in touch with the goings-on at home, and her desire not to get caught up with home issues for extended periods while at work. This has resulted in the avoidance of family while at work, in order to cope with this dissonance. This phenomenon was also noted by Pauleen et al. [36] who contend that smartphones – while integrating work and family life – have shifted the balance of time towards the workplace at the expense of the family.

In conclusion, smartphones allow working mothers greater flexibility and convenience to manage the multiple demands of family and work, but also create conflicts for them that may negate their very desires. Notably, however, although there were differences between smartphone usage, specifically related to the nature of work, responsibility, and affordability, for a working mother, there was not a satisfactory indication of smartphone use in any other work activities besides checking emails, calendar scheduling, and liaising with colleagues. It is no surprise therefore, that smartphone paradoxes mostly affected the 'life' domain of the 'work-life' equation.

Although most working mothers in this study didn't indicate active mechanisms to control the interference of their smartphones into their social lives, a few of them stated that setting boundaries and discipline on when and how to use their smartphones has helped them to manage the disruptions associated with smartphone use. More often than not, however, participants adopted avoidance strategies to cope with the conflicts. Further research will be necessary to determine why, when and how different coping strategies are adopted.

This research highlights the double-edged effects of smartphones, and shows how mobile technology paradoxes play out in the area of WLB for working mothers. From the findings of the study, there is a need for further research on mechanisms to actively or passively control the negative impacts of smartphones on WLB, and to provide potential solutions to the paradoxes. While this study focused on working mothers in general and not all women, its insights are still useful in shedding light on issues relating to mobile technology paradoxes and WLB.

References

1. Jarvenpaa, S.L., Lang, K.R.: Managing the paradoxes of mobile technology. Inf. Syst. Manag. **22**(4), 7–23 (2005)
2. Zainudeen, A., Galpaya, H.: Mobile Phones, Internet, and Gender in Myanmar. GSMA, London (2015)
3. Asongu, S.A.: Conditional determinants of mobile phones penetration and mobile banking in sub-Saharan Africa. J. Knowl. Econ. **9**(1), 81–135 (2018)
4. James, J.: Mobile phone use in Africa: implications for inequality and the digital divide. In: James, J. (ed.) The Impact of Mobile Phones on Poverty and Inequality in Developing Countries, pp. 89–93. Springer, Cham (2016). https://doi.org/10.1007/978-3-319-27368-6_7
5. Porter, G., et al.: Mobile phones and education in sub-Saharan Africa: from youth practice to public policy. J. Int. Dev. **28**(1), 22–39 (2016)
6. Wajcman, J., Bittman, M., Brown, J.E.: Intimate connections: the impact of the mobile phone on work/life boundaries (2009)
7. Duxbury, L., Higgins, C., Smart, R., Stevenson, M.: Mobile technology and boundary permeability. Br. J. Manag. **25**(3), 570–588 (2014)
8. Middleton, C.A., Cukier, W.: Is mobile email functional or dysfunctional? Two perspectives on mobile email usage. Eur. J. Inf. Syst. **15**(3), 252–260 (2006)
9. Mick, D.G., Fournier, S.: Paradoxes of technology: consumer cognizance, emotions, and coping strategies. J. Consum. Res. **25**(2), 123–143 (1998)
10. Hoeven, C.L.T., van Zoonen, W., Fonner, K.L.: The practical paradox of technology: the influence of communication technology use on employee burnout and engagement. Commun. Monogr. **83**(2), 239–263 (2016)
11. Mazmanian, M., Orlikowski, W.J., Yates, J.: The autonomy paradox: the implications of mobile email devices for knowledge professionals. Organ. Sci. **24**(5), 1337–1357 (2013)
12. Arnold, M.: On the phenomenology of technology: the "Janus-faces" of mobile phones. Inf. Organ. **13**(4), 231–256 (2003)
13. Smith, W., Erez, M., Jarvenpaa, S., Lewis, M., Tracey, P.: Adding complexity to theories of paradox, tensions, and dualities of innovation and change: introduction to organization studies special issue on paradox, tensions, and dualities of innovation and change. Organ. Stud. **38**, 303–317 (2017)
14. Guest, D.E.: Perspectives on the study of work-life balance. Soc. Sci. Inf. **41**(2), 255–279 (2002)
15. Chesley, N.: Blurring boundaries? Linking technology use, spillover, individual distress, and family satisfaction. J. Marriage Family **67**(5), 1237–1248 (2005)
16. Poduval, J., Poduval, M.: Working mothers: how much working, how much mothers, and where is the womanhood? Mens Sana Monogr. **7**(1), 63 (2009)
17. Mpazanje, F., Chigona, W.: How the mobile phone saved properness: the case of professional women in Malawi. In: 2012 e-Leadership Conference on Sustainable e-Government and e-Business Innovations (E-LEADERSHIP), pp. 1–7. IEEE (2012)

18. Lim, P.L., Yazdanifard, R.: Does gender play a role in online consumer behavior? Global J. Manag. Bus. Res. **14**, 7 (2014)
19. England, K.: Who Will Mind the Baby? Geographies of Child Care and Working Mothers. Psychology Press, London (1996)
20. Fapohunda, E.R.: The child-care dilemma of working mothers in African cities: the case of Lagos, Nigeria. Westview Special Studies on Africa, p. 277 (1982)
21. Patel, C.J., Govender, V., Paruk, Z., Ramgoon, S.: Working mothers: family-work conflict, job performance and family/work variables. SA J. Ind. Psychol. **32**(2), 39–45 (2006)
22. Rakow, L.F., Navarro, V.: Remote mothering and the parallel shift: women meet the cellular telephone. Crit. Stud. Media Commun. **10**(2), 144–157 (1993)
23. Lim, S.S., Soon, C.: The influence of social and cultural factors on mothers' domestication of household ICTs–Experiences of Chinese and Korean women. Telematics Inform. **27**(3), 205–216 (2010)
24. Towers, I., Duxbury, L., Higgins, C., Thomas, J.: Time thieves and space invaders: technology, work and the organization. J. Organ. Change Manag. **19**(5), 593–618 (2006)
25. Crowe, R., Middleton, C.: Women, smartphones and the workplace: pragmatic realities and performative identities. Fem. Media Stud. **12**(4), 560–569 (2012)
26. Gregory, A., Milner, S.: Work–life balance: a matter of choice? Gender Work Organ. **16**(1), 1–13 (2009)
27. Fortunati, L.: Gender and the mobile phone. In: Mobile Technologies, pp. 38–49. Routledge, London (2009)
28. McDaniel, B.T., Coyne, S.M.: Technoference": the interference of technology in couple relationships and implications for women's personal and relational well-being. Psychol. Popular Media Cult. **5**(1), 85 (2016)
29. Lapierre, M.A., Lewis, M.N.: Should it stay or should it go now? Smartphones and relational health. Psychol. Popul. Media Cult. **7**(3), 384–398 (2016)
30. Frizzo-Barker, J., Chow-White, P.A.: "There's an App for That" mediating mobile moms and connected careerists through smartphones and networked individualism. Fem. Media Stud. **12**(4), 580–589 (2012)
31. Madge, C., O'Connor, H.: Parenting gone wired: empowerment of new mothers on the internet? Soc. Cult. Geogr. **7**(2), 199–220 (2006)
32. Oulasvirta, A., Rattenbury, T., Ma, L., Raita, E.: Habits make smartphone use more pervasive. Pers. Ubiquit. Comput. **16**(1), 105–114 (2012)
33. Thomée, S., Härenstam, A., Hagberg, M.: Mobile phone use and stress, sleep disturbances, and symptoms of depression among young adults - a prospective cohort study. BMC Public Health **11**(1), 66 (2011)
34. Lee, Y.-K., Chang, C.-T., Lin, Y., Cheng, Z.-H.: The dark side of smartphone usage: psychological traits, compulsive behavior and technostress. Comput. Hum. Behav. **31**, 373–383 (2014)
35. Harris, T.R.: The Impact of Smartphones on Work-Life Balance. Middle Tennessee State University (2014)
36. Pauleen, D., Campbell, J., Harmer, B., Intezari, A.: Making sense of mobile technology: the integration of work and private life. SAGE Open **5**(2) (2015)

E-education

Development Outcomes of Training for Online Freelancing in the Philippines

Karsten Eskelund[1(✉)], Richard Heeks[2], and Brian Nicholson[1]

[1] Alliance Manchester Business School, University of Manchester, Manchester, UK
karsten.eskelund@postgrad.manchester.ac.uk
[2] Centre for Development Informatics, University of Manchester, Manchester, UK

Abstract. Impact sourcing focuses on training and hiring people who would otherwise not be able to land a job in the outsourcing business. The Philippine Government has initiated a training program to prepare people for online freelancing in socio-economically disadvantaged areas in the country.

We lack knowledge about the impact such training programs might have on marginalized individuals. Thus, this paper adds to previous research on impact sourcing by analyzing whether government-initiated training enables people in socio-economically disadvantaged areas to obtain online freelancing jobs. We analyze data from a survey and interviews with the Choice Framework.

We used an explanatory, mixed-methods approach. We used a survey to gather information from the trainees about their perception of the training. We also conducted interviews with trainees in selected locations.

The findings indicate that the trainees gained both technical and personal skills that enabled them to target jobs for which they were previously not qualified. However, structural challenges remained, such as a lack of a stable Internet connection in some areas.

This paper adds to previous research about impact sourcing, by examining how training can help marginalized people to obtain online freelancing jobs.

Keywords: Employability · Digital development · Choices · Training

1 Introduction

According to the latest report from the United Nations (UN), many individuals in developing countries lack employment, and thus also a sufficient income to support themselves and their families [26]. Policymakers in the Philippines, Pakistan, Malaysia, Kenya, and South Africa have responded to this challenge by creating training programs that teach people how to earn money from global online freelancing, a type of work in which clients contract professionals from third-party workers on platforms such as Upwork.com, Amazon MTurk, and others [16].

The Philippine Government, through its Department of Information and Communications Technology (DICT), has run the Rural Impact Sourcing (RIS) initiative since 2013. In addition to training individuals how to work in the global online freelancing

K. Krauss et al. (Eds.): IDIA 2018, CCIS 933, pp. 109–124, 2019.
https://doi.org/10.1007/978-3-030-11235-6_8

industry, the program aims to teach the individuals skills they can use to work for local enterprises and local government units [5]. The Philippine Government has identified this initiative as an "impact sourcing" program. Impact sourcing refers to "the practice of hiring and training marginalized individuals to provide information technology, business process, or other digitally-enabled services who would normally have few opportunities for good employment" [2: 401].

This paper responds to the call for more research about impact sourcing in general, and the impact that such initiatives have on individuals [2, 17]. By using the Choice Framework [13] as a sensitizing framework, we examine the following research question:

RQ: Does government-initiated training enable people in socio-economically disadvantaged areas to obtain online freelancing jobs?

We contribute to previous literature in three ways: (1) we reduce the knowledge gaps related to how this type of training initiatives can increase local ICT-enabled work; (2) we demonstrate how the Choice Framework can be used to analyze this type of government-supported learning initiatives; and (3) we offer guidance to practitioners and policymakers who wish to use ICT-enabled jobs as a development tool more.

The paper proceeds as follows: in Sect. 2, we review the literature on employability, and outline the Choice Framework that shaped our fieldwork and data-analysis process. In Sect. 3, we describe the case. In Sect. 4, we describe our research methodology. In Sect. 5, we present our findings, and, in Sect. 6, we conclude the paper.

2 Literature Review and Conceptual Framework

Two literature streams guide this research. First, we explore the literature on impact sourcing. Second, we review the literature on the capability approach—the foundation for the Choice Framework.

2.1 Impact Sourcing

Impact sourcing has emerged as a new theme in the wider outsourcing literature. It refers to "the practice of hiring and training marginalized people to provide technology, business process, or other digitally-enabled services who normally would have few opportunities for good employment" [2: 401]. Such people are often called impact workers, defined as "people hired into the organization who previously were long-term unemployed or living under the national poverty line" [8: 3]. Different models for impact sourcing have evolved over time. In the first phase of impact sourcing, the impact sourcing vendors were responsible for the training, as well as the hiring, of the impact workers [9]. A second model is where the vendor works together with an online platform. One example of this is the Malaysian initiative Digital Malaysia, where the government helps with the training and hiring of impact workers, while the jobs are sourced through platforms like eRezeki [11]. Today we see a third model, which we can call Impact Sourcing 3.0. In this model, the impact sourcing intermediary only takes responsibility for the training, while it is up to the individuals to land jobs. Often they choose online platforms like Facebook or UpWork to look for jobs [20]. Carmel et al. call for more research on the effect that impact sourcing has on marginalized populations, and raise the following research question: "How do marginalized people become engaged in impact sourcing?" (p. 419). In this paper, we respond to that question, and examine how training makes it possible for individuals to engage in impact sourcing 3.0 as what we define as freelance impact workers.

Studies of previous impact-sourcing initiatives indicate that not all such impact sourcing initiatives have been successful. While some initiatives have managed to uplift a marginalized population, there are other initiatives that failed to bring the desired results and were closed down within a short time. Some researchers, such as [24], discuss cases in which locals have strongly resisted a company that has initiated training. In initiatives that have focused on training individuals to obtain jobs through online freelancing, previous research indicates that not all trainees succeed in landing a job [20]. Other research, however, indicates that those who have participated in an impact-sourcing initiative have experienced positive changes in their life, like obtaining new skills, increasing their income, obtaining new physical assets or getting new contacts [9]. Yet other research has indicated that employees in impact sourcing companies have developed personally and financially [19]. Because of the mixed results identified by previous research, there is a gap in the knowledge of what particular factors enable successful impacts sourcing initiatives. Senior scholars have called for papers that can explain how the government may help in capacity building [22]. This paper is positioned to answer that call.

2.2 Capability Approach and the Choice Framework

Development research has widely used the capability approach, which Amartya Sen initially developed, for more than three decades [1]. The approach entails two main concepts: "functionings" (i.e. beings and doings, such as being educated or going travelling) and "capabilities" (i.e. the opportunity to achieve the beings and doings, such as the opportunity to learn or to travel) (Robeyns, 2005; Sen, 1999). As it concerns our study, governments provide training for individuals to gain these capabilities.

Some authors have criticised the capability approach for not having any specific, measurable capabilities [23]; however, Sen (1997) stated that each specific research has to draw up its own list of capabilities. One example of such a list is the Sustainable Livelihood Framework [4]. The Choice Framework, created by Dorothea Kleine, is another attempt to operationalise Sen's work [13]. She refines the list of what in the Sustainable Livelihood Framework is called "capitals," increases the list from 5 to 11, and renames "capitals" to "agency." Such agency is what Robeyns (2005, p. 99) calls "personal conversion factors": the individual attributes that impact whether a person is employable or not. All these frameworks suffer from the limitation that they are not particularly tailored for research on employability.

Structures are external factors that impact an individual's employability but that do not constitute attributes of individuals themselves. Uneven access to technology represents one example [7]: people would find it difficult to do online work if they cannot access the Internet. Institutions that individuals have some relation to, and other actors, can provide such structures [6].

We use the Choice Framework as the guiding framework for this paper [13–15]. In her research, Kleine focused on how telecentres in rural areas of Chile enabled inhabitants in these areas to make choices they otherwise probably could not have made and, hence, to live a life they valued.

Figure 1 illustrates the Choice Framework in more detail; specifically, it shows its four main pillars: structure, agency, empowerment, and development outcomes.

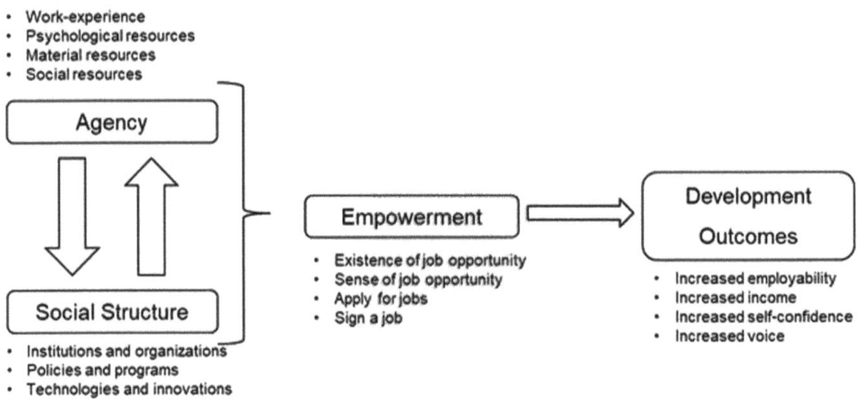

Fig. 1. The choice framework (Adapted from Kleine 2011)

Agency refers to individuals' capacity to act independently and to make their own free choices. The framework divides agency into two main groups: the simple, measurable attributes a person has, such as age, gender, ethnicity, and so on, and the different resources a person has. Resources refers to the capabilities that everyone has in some capacity, such as education, finance, information, health and psychological resources. Training will typically directly improve an individual's educational resources, but it may also, at least indirectly, affect other types of resources an individual has, such as psychological resources (e.g. increased self-confidence). If a person can obtain work online due to training, the training indirectly increases the financial resources.

There is a strong link between structures and agency. Educational resources are one example of this. In countries where the governments have policies that prevent girls from going to school, educational resources for girls will typically be fewer. On the other hand, such discrimination and lack of agency might get people to stand up and try to change the structure [29].

The dimension of choice (or degrees of empowerment, as Kleine defines it) is an important part of the framework. In other words, the possibility to choose something must exist before someone can choose it; however, to do so, people need also to understand that they have a choice, and that they can make it. This concerns our study: after having obtained new skills, individuals need to decide whether to apply for jobs relevant to those skills, to benefit from them.

Development outcomes, the final part of the Choice Framework, refers to what an individual has achieved. By using their agency to navigate the social structures, the outcome for an individual should achieve a life they have reason to value. According to Kleine [13], choice itself constitutes the principal outcome, while secondary outcomes differ from person to person.

The Choice Framework is a good fit for this research, for two reasons: firstly, the connection between agency and structure in the framework is relevant to how individual trainees' previous knowledge and the government-run program have an interlinked connection; secondly, development outcomes in the framework can aid in understanding how each trainee experiences their increased choices after the training.

While some previous literature discusses what impact getting a job has on individuals [9, 18, 20], we lack research on the training that enables individuals to join the impact-sourcing industry, which we address in this paper.

3 Case Description

From July 2017 to January 2018, the Philippine government conducted 25 rural empowerment, impact sourcing, technical training (RIS TT) projects across the Philippine archipelago [5]. The projects focused on the following: (1) increasing the ICT technical skills of people in the countryside; (2) increasing the hireability of the people to land a job in the ICT field; (3) empowering local talent and local businesses; (4) promoting micro-, small- and medium-sized enterprises (MSMEs); and (5) reducing the unemployment rate in the country.

Each location had around 25 trainees. Each training project comprised a 12-day face-to-face session over three weeks. The training included 12 different sessions on topics that ranged from branding, product photography, data privacy and business blogging to freelance-profile building and client negotiations. All trainers used the same training material created by Janette Toral, one of the pioneers of the Philippines' e-commerce business. In total, 14 different trainers provided training at one or more locations. Most of these trainers had conducted such training before, and some of them even ran small companies on their own, where they trained online workers. After the initial face-to-face sessions, there was a three-week online rollout in which the trainers monitored the trainees. The monitoring was done over the Internet. Each trainee had to complete online tasks, which were evaluated by the trainer. Trainer and trainees communicated primarily through Facebook chat during this period. The training ensured that each trainee worked with a dedicated MSME to promote their business. The trainees did so by creating a website for the MSME and various social media accounts (Facebook, Twitter, etc.). In addition to information about the MSME, the website contained a web-shop offering the MSME's products.

After the rollout period, the trainers made a final assessment of the work submitted by the trainees. The trainers judged the trainees based on the extent to which they completed tasks and how much revenue they generated for their dedicated MSME.

4 Methodology

The research is done as an interpretative case study [12, 27]. Interviews and surveys where individual trainees are asked about their perception of the training, are used to understand the impact of the training as a whole to represent the hermeneutic circle, in which the whole phenomenon being researched is understood by studying the different parts of it, and how they relate to one another. This means that to understand how the training initiative increases employability, we both explore individual agency, as well as structural implications by organisations like the government. We used an explanatory, sequential, mixed-methods approach to answer the research question [3].

The main informants were all trainees who participated in the technical training. To obtain baseline knowledge about the trainees, we distributed a survey. The main objective of this survey was to get some background information about the trainees, their age, education and so forth. DICT and the trainers helped to share the survey among the trainees.

Most of the trainees responded online via Google Forms. In some locations, there was a lack of Internet connection. To help gather data, DICT printed the form and handed it out to the trainees. The responses were later scanned and sent to the author who entered the answers directly in Google Forms. In total, we obtained 262 responses to the survey.

We collected qualitative data on a field trip to the Philippines between December 2017 and January 2018. In Masbate, Bicol, the first author participated in the last day of the technical training and the graduation session, and spent two days with DICT staff and the around 20 trainees. In two other locations (Cavite in Luzon and Bogo City in the Visayas), the first author conducted face-to-face interviews with seven and three informants, respectively. Bogo City was the first location that completed the training, while Masbate was the last. Both Bogo and Masbate are rural areas, while Cavite is a more urban area, close to Metro Manila. Due to the unstable situation in Mindanao, the first author conducted interviews with informants in Zamboanga City and Cabadbaran City, through Skype [25]. A total of 15 interviews were conducted that varied between 20 and 110 min. The first author also participated at the Philippine Impact Sourcing Conference in March 2018, where he conducted follow-up interviews with some of the trainees. Interviews were semi-structured in format and focused primarily on the perception the trainees had of the training and how they thought that the training could impact their future job situation. From conducting these interviews, we obtained a good spread of informants from across the Philippines, as seen in Fig. 2.

Through the implementation of the RIS TT program, DICT staff and trainers quite frequently used Facebook to publish stories about the progress. The first author created a Facebook page which was used to collect such stories [21]. In the period before and after the interviews, the first author also conducted several Facebook chats with DICT staff, trainers and trainees. Through these chats, we clarified answers to questions and obtained more information.

We recorded and transcribed the interviews. We uploaded the transcriptions and other field data, like notes and photos, to the computer-based qualitative analysis package NVivo, and coded it into theoretical themes based on the Choice Framework.

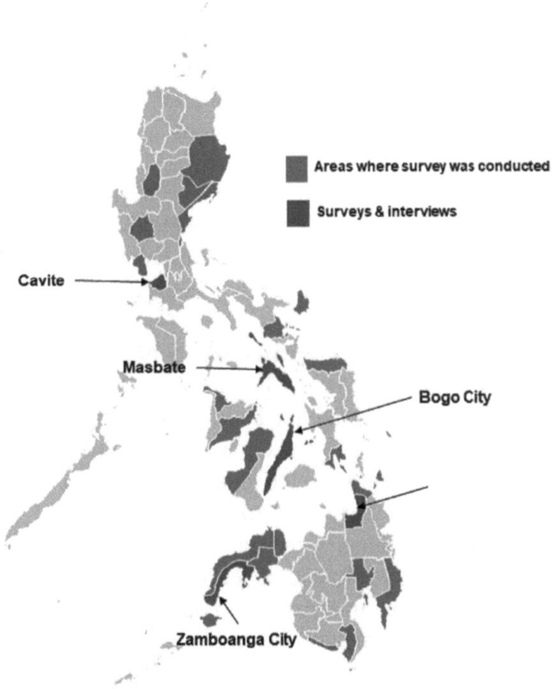

Fig. 2. Locations for the research

We also entered the Facebook chats and data collected through the Facebook page into NVivo, and analysed them in the same way as the interviews. Through constantly iterating between data and the literature, we defined and added new themes as separate nodes in NVivo [10].

The qualitative approach was chosen because we determined this to be the best approach to understand the meaning of people's lives – in this case, the meaning that the training had for the trainees [28].

5 Findings

In this section, we discuss the findings according to the different parts of the Choice Framework.

5.1 Outcomes

We found that the trainees thought they would be able to more easily find relevant ICT jobs given their training, which includes the potential to work as freelancers in the online outsourcing business, and to use the skill to get jobs for local customers. One trainee explained that she could obtain jobs through the online portal onlinejobs.ph. In

Cavite, the seven informants all helped to set up a new company, Digiworkz Carmona, to serve local customers in the area. One of the trainees in Bogo City explained that the local government approached him to train people at other locations close to Bogo—another example of a job the trainees could obtain after the training. Based on this, we can see that the training, at least in some locations, provided the trainees with **increased employability**.

People accept online jobs or create new companies to **increase their income.** Two of the employees of DigiWorkz posted photos on Facebook of check vouchers they had received from their customers to prove that they had received payment. Thus, we can see that at least some of the trainees successfully managed to increase their income due to the training.

The trainees also mentioned their **increased self-confidence.** One of the trainees in Masbate claimed that after the training she had gained a lot more knowledge and the confidence to choose whether she would like to work as a freelancer, a businesswoman, or a teacher. While increased self-confidence may not create any direct income, it can give trainees the boost they need to make the required choices of applying for work for which they would not previously have tried to apply.

Soon after finishing their training, some trainees started to use their knowledge to advocate for online freelancing work, and to teach people in their society, or nearby locations, about the opportunities that exist in online freelancing. For example, two trainees were part of starting a company, Narra Digital, in Zamboanga City, after the training. These two trainees also started a local group, Zamboanga Digital Professionals, which meet regularly, help each other and have an impact on other freelancers. These are examples of how these trainees **increased their voice** in society. The training has helped to foster an ecosystem of individuals who work as freelance impact workers.

5.2 Dimensions of Choice

The first level of empowerment is to see that there is an **existence of choice**. As we stated above, the training focused on enabling the trainees to obtain ICT-related jobs. However, a trainer from the Visayas stated:

> *...after the training, most trainees from Bogo went to look for offline office work, went to school, or managing the family business* (Female trainee, Visayas).

A trainee from Zamboanga expressed a similar sentiment.

> *We don't obtain enough relevant data to determine whether most people in other locations never tried to get any ICT-related job or not* (Female trainee, Mindanao).

Based on this, we cannot conclude whether there were some trainees who never experienced an existence of choice, but at least that there was someone who hardly tried to use the choice they might think existed.

The next level of empowerment is to **sense that there is a choice**. Other trainees stated that they had more opportunities in the job market, due to the training, and sensed that they have a choice. For example, a trainee from Bicol said:

> *Ah yes, I would say that through this training I gained more knowledge, so if God give me chance of becoming a businesswoman, very grateful if I can become a freelancer, a teacher, that is only about what my choices are as of now* (Female trainee, Bicol).

Other trainees used the opportunities that the training created, which is the next level of empowerment. Several chose to take up work as online virtual assistants and work from home. For example, one said:

> *The RIS made it possible for us to live decent lives and earn decent wages without having to leave our families behind. I no longer have to leave my kids with my parents or in-laws, so I can go to Manila to earn something above or at least twenty thousand pesos. I can do that within the comfort of my own home now* (Female trainee, Mindanao).

We can see that this individual was able to change careers, due to the learning she gained from training.

Achieving choice constitutes the final level one needs to achieve to be empowered. According to DICT, 124 of the trainees were able to land a job directly after the training. Some started to work in the online freelancing industry, while others focused more on local companies, such as DigiWorks and Narra Digital (see examples above).

5.3 Agency

In a group of more than 500 people, we found that the trainees had diverse backgrounds and agency attributes. Of our 262 responses, 52.6% were male, 45.7% were female, and 1.6% did not disclose their gender. The majority of the trainees (44.6%) were between 20–25 years old or 26–30 years old (18.9%). Most of the respondents (33.9%) lived with their parents, while 21.9% lived with their husband/children.

Before DICT selected them for the training, the applicants had to apply. The organisation reviewed the applications; in particular, they checked for English skills (oral and written). Also, DICT conducted interviews with prospective trainees in which they asked about why they wanted to complete the training. This process ensured that everyone who joined the training had a fair chance to complete it.

Educational Resources: Out of the 262 responses to the survey, 69.9% said that their highest level of education was that of college graduate. Another 16.7% said that their highest education level was that of college undergraduate. Some of the trainees had conducted most of their prior training in fields not relevant to ICT work, such as nursing, finance, and advertising; however, some trainees had previous experience with computers, such as via a bachelor's degree in IT.

The trainees' work experience varied considerably. Students most often did not have any relevant previous work experience at all. Among those who had previous experience, some had worked in the BPO business in larger cities, but now wanted to move back to their home town. Other trainees had previous experience in the freelancing business, and some had even worked as English teachers on different online portals. Some had experience from working as nurses or other similar jobs where they were used to working closely with other people. All the people with work experience as English teachers had better than average English skills, compared to the students and those individuals who had no relevant work experience. This difference in education and work experience indicates that some of the trainees had advantages compared with the other trainees both regarding their ability to successfully complete the training (which features mostly English material) and landing online jobs, which typically require English in order to communicate well with the clients.

Psychological Resources: Most of the trainees claimed to have quite high self-confidence. They stressed that they found this confidence important to be able to complete the training. One of the trainees explained that because she was so motivated to complete the training, she would stay until three o'clock in the morning to complete the tasks. Other trainees echoed this same attitude. Psychological resources are an important part of agency. Individuals with stronger psychological resources are more likely to take advantage of the opportunities they receive [15: 207]. In our case, trainees needed such resources to both choose to complete the training and to later pursue the career they wanted.

Some of the trainees also pointed to God as a reason for their success. When asked about who would decide whether they could reach their ambitions, one trainee in Masbate said that, in addition to herself, God would decide. Religious belief positively influences the agency, because it increases a person's confidence. When individuals believe they have God's support, they feel more confident in achieving their ambitions, which, as we stated above, makes it more likely that they will take advantage of opportunities.

Information: We divide the information that influences agency into three different categories: (1) information about the availability of the training; (2) information/ knowledge relevant for building the knowledge required to land jobs; and (3) information about available jobs. Information about the availability of the training was at least to some extent available for all the trainees; otherwise, they would not have been able to attend it. Our survey asked the trainees how they learned about the training. Most of them said that they obtained this information through social media and, in particular, Facebook. The other main source of information about the training was through friends and family.

The survey also asked the trainees what they would do to obtain the competence they needed to work as freelancers, and the survey allowed them to answer with more than one category. We found that 77% said that they would participate in government-supported training, 76% stated that they would Google for tips about freelancing, and 64% said that they would participate in online training. From the interviews, we realised that most of them were confident that they could find the information by using Google or YouTube, to learn more. Many trainees also stated that they would help each other. Some of them had created Facebook groups or Facebook Messenger groups where they shared information about what they learned during the training and tips on how to get jobs. Some of them even shared jobs with other trainees.

The trainees could easily access information about available jobs. They used online portals such as onlinejobs.ph and upwork.com to find jobs. They also used Facebook as a secondary source. The trainees were able to identify jobs in particular Facebook groups where customers would post relevant job information.

Financial Resources: The training was free for the trainees; hence, they did not need financial resources to attend (except for any fees associated with getting to the training location). When asked about their current income, 28.7% of the respondents preferred not to answer the question. A further 21.1% answered that their income was unpredictable and varied from month to month. Of those who answered, 27.4% said that their monthly income was below PHP10.000 (around US$193). For those who had a regular income, they mostly obtained it from working for the government (20.9%), and working as an independent in their own business (15.7%). The majority of the respondents (71.2%) said that they were not primarily responsible for their household's income (most of these individuals stated their parents were). Further, some respondents said that they depended on their husband or wife. Because most of the trainees were students and did not have a fixed monthly income, they did not suffer financially from participating in the training. Those who had a job made sure to complete all their tasks during the evenings/night, to ensure that they did not reduce their income.

Social Resources: Belonging to the right social group helped respondents to be selected for the training. While many trainees were selected through the application process, family members and political connections helped others access the training.

Material Resources: Two of the important material resources for anyone who wishes to do ICT-enabled work is a computer and an Internet connection. In the survey, we asked the respondents if they had access to a computer: 61.8% answered that they had their own computer, another 7.3% said that someone in their household had a computer they could use, 13% said that they used an Internet café within walking distance, and 9.8% said that they had to travel to gain access to a computer. In addition to the computer, the trainees used their phone extensively. As one trainee said:

> *I can work through phone; if I'm outside, then I receive e-mail that is a question like that I can search their tracking number through my phone, then screenshot, like that. Then like that, if I get a request to refund or they tell me that I want to cancel my order, I just log into Shopify to cancel their order, so I can work from my phone, although I prefer my laptop* (Female trainee, Mindanao).

Second, we asked about Internet access: 83.3% said that they had an Internet connection during the training, while a further 14.7% said that they had access to some of the training, but not all. During the interviews, it became clear that trainees in more remote locations found being able to connect to the Internet an issue. They frequently experienced periods in which they could not access the Internet, or it had a weak signal. In one location, the training was conducted in the local library, where DICT had provided sufficient connection. However, even at this location, there were days where the training had to be moved to a nearby hotel because of poor connectivity. When asked what they thought would be the biggest challenges working as a freelancer, as many as 69.3% of the trainees had a stable Internet connection at the top of their list.

After the training, the trainees would still require a good Internet connection to be able to look for jobs – and also when doing the jobs. Those who did not have a laptop and/or stable Internet connection at home, would have to go to other places to do the work. One trainee said that she could do her tasks at a local church:

> *Our church. I have a computer in the church. In the church, we have Wi-Fi and Internet access so that I can continue from there* (Female Trainee, Bicol).

Others continued to work from a public library:

> *...we can still use the library maybe I guess. They will help us with that the library because they have a strong Internet connection* (Female Trainee, Bicol).

Even those who had Internet connection at home sometimes experienced that there was a power failure and that the whole building got dark. They had invested in what they call a freelancer starter-kit—basically a LED lamp and a car battery. By using the car-battery and an inverter, they were able to have an Internet connection even if the building lacked power. With the LED lamp, the customers were still able to see them when they had Skype sessions or similar.

5.4 Structure

Institutions and Organisations: Various institutions are involved in the RISTT program, such as DICT, DTI and LGU.

One particular group of organisations that contributed to the RIS program is the MSMEs. They typically played the role of customer for the trainees. Each trainee got assigned one MSME, and during the training had to create an e-commerce portal for this MSME. To what extent the MSMEs contributed to the outcome of the training was disputed among the trainees and trainers. While some trainees established a good relationship with their MSME, others felt that the MSME took advantage of them for their own business, without contributing to their learning outcome. During the interviews, trainees agreed that the MSMEs hindered them in finishing their tasks by being slow to contribute with information. Some trainees stated that the MSMEs only wanted them to create a website for them for free.

On the other hand, it might be argued that working with local MSMEs helps the trainees in getting used to serving clients and in handling communication issues. As the MSMEs acted as customers for the trainees, it gave them some experience they can use when they target other customers after the training. The ability to handle challenging customers is important for anyone, and probably in particular for freelancers who work on their own, without a network around them to ask for help. Hence, the MSMEs were an important institution for the training, even if the trainees might not feel that they had a direct positive impact on the outcome of the training.

Discourses: Knowledge of the existence of the RISTT program is a prerequisite for attendance. How the organisers of the training shared this information had an impact on which people attended the training. In one location, information was shared through the

Facebook page of the city. By putting up this information, the information officer in the city got to know about the training and applied for it. Other trainees got to know about the training through word of mouth. Some of them were told about this by DICT-officers, while others got to know about it through friends in places like college or church. Informal communication was a mechanism for information sharing. Knowing someone who already knew about the training was an advantage to get the right information.

Formal and Informal Laws: In Masbate, there is a curfew in place from 10 pm. This means that for those who do not have a computer and Internet connection at home it is difficult to work online with customers that require you to work a night shift.

Technologies and Innovations: There were significant differences regarding both availability and affordability of ICT resources between the different trainees. Particularly in the most rural locations Internet connectivity was a problem. This led to trainees not being able to complete their tasks on time. There were numerous examples of this. The first author was supposed to travel to Allen in Northern Samar to conduct interviews. This had to be cancelled due to a typhoon in the area. This typhoon also impacted the training program, and the final sessions scheduled for December 2017 had to be postponed to January 2018. Likewise, in Masbate, there were times with no Internet connection at the training venue, which meant delay and that the training sessions had to be moved to a nearby hotel. On the other hand, some trainees had access to computers and a stable Internet connection at home. For example, in Cavite, we found no complaints about Internet connectivity.

One technology that in particular made the communication easier is Facebook Lite. This is a version of Facebook that allows the people to use some of the simpler parts of Facebook even without being online. This has been quite popular in the Philippines, and enables trainees to stay in touch with the trainer even when the trainer is not physically present at their location. Facebook Lite also enables trainees to have a dialogue with their customers – both the local MSME's and international customers.

The government of the Philippines has contributed to the availability of technology by setting up particular locations where the trainees could work. In two of the places where interviews were conducted, the government had invested in Internet connectivity in government offices, like the offices of DICT. In a third location, the local library had a decent Internet connection. Both a DICT-office and a local library could act as a place where the trainees could study, and also work, after they completed the training. Here, trainees had an environment where they could sit together with their peers, instead of always being by themselves.

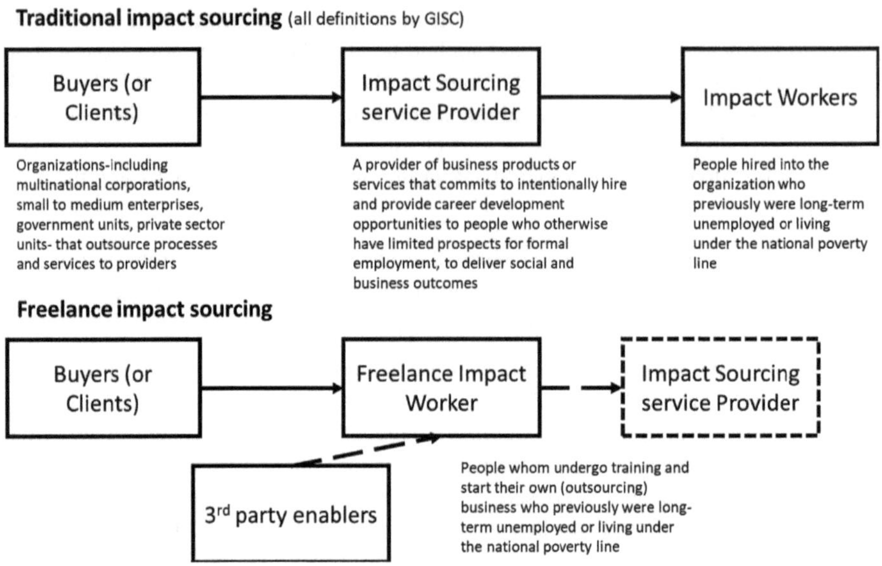

Fig. 3. Freelance impact sourcing

6 Conclusion

In this study, we address whether government-initiated training enables people in socio-economically disadvantaged areas to obtain online freelancing jobs. Our findings suggest that the training enables this in two main ways. Firstly, trainees obtain skills that make them more employable for online freelancing and other ICT-related jobs such as digital skills and computer communication skills. Secondly, trainees obtain more indirect personal skills, like increased self-confidence. Such skill helps them not just in targeting specific jobs, but it also helps trainees believe that they can achieve greater things. Examples of this include a new belief that they can start their own local business and serve the local market.

We argue that the traditional definition of impact sourcing is too narrow, and have added the term "freelance impact worker", as shown in Fig. 3. Instead of focusing on the impact sourcing service provider, this definition focuses more on the individual impact worker:

This figure, supported by the findings in the previous chapter, shows that people who undergo training and have the right support, can act as independent impact workers. Right support includes Internet connectivity and knowledge on how to use different online outsourcing platforms. As discussed above, like in the example of Narra Digital, some of these freelance impact workers even start their own impact sourcing companies.

Governments can contribute in various ways to enable freelance impact sourcing. Our finding is that the main contribution is Internet connectivity. Connectivity was an issue for a number of the trainees, and, in particular, those who live in rural areas. The government has already started the process of getting a third telco provider into the market, which could have a major impact for rural areas in particular. A second contribution is that the government will monitor the trainees over a period of 12 months. Such monitoring is vital for the trainees, to help them to continue their growth and help them build their confidence when they get rejections when applying for work on the different online portals. A third contribution is the government creating places where trainees can meet and work after the training is completed. For people who are about to start their career, such places have a significant impact. It means that trainees will have access to free Internet and a workplace where they do not pay regular rental fees.

This paper contributes knowledge to governments who plan to conduct similar training initiatives. We discovered several key areas that others can use, and also some areas that other initiatives can improve. So far, the majority of government-supported training initiatives for online freelancing have been in South-East Asia. Learnings from this paper can also be transferred to other developing countries in regions like Africa or South America. This paper adds to academic literature by focusing on the training, and how the training enables individuals to find employment in impact sourcing. It also enhances the Choice Framework, and demonstrates how this framework can be used in the area of impact sourcing. More research is needed, however, to examine the long-term impact of such training. Does it only create temporary jobs, or does it create a sustainable livelihood for individuals over the longer term?

References

1. Bass, J., Nicholson, B., Subhramanian, E.: A framework using institutional analysis and the capability approach in ICT4D. Inf. Technol. Int. Dev. **9**, 1 (2013)
2. Carmel, E., Lacity, M.C., Doty, A.: The impact of impact sourcing: framing a research agenda. In: Hirschheim, R., Heinzl, A., Dibbern, J. (eds.) Information Systems Outsourcing. PI, pp. 397–429. Springer, Heidelberg (2014). https://doi.org/10.1007/978-3-662-43820-6_16
3. Creswell, J.: Research Design. Sage, Thousand Oaks (2014)
4. DFID: Sustainable livelihoods guidance sheets. London (1999)
5. DICT: Rural Empowerment and Impact Sourcing Training Project. Manila (2017)
6. Duncombe, R.: Using the livelihoods framework to analyze ICT applications for poverty reduction through microenterprise. Inf. Technol. Int. Dev. **3**(3), 81–100 (2006)
7. Gerster, R., Zimmermann, S.: Information and communications technologies (ICTs) for poverty reduction? Bern (2003)
8. GISC: What is the Impact Sourcing Standard? (2018). https://gisc.bsr.org/impact-sourcing/impact-sourcing-standard. Accessed 28 Mar 2018
9. Heeks, R., Arun, S.: Social outsourcing as a development tool: the impact of outsourcing IT services to women's social enterprises in Kerala. J. Int. Dev. **22**(4), 441–454 (2010). https://doi.org/10.1002/jid.1580
10. Huberman, A.M., Miles, M.B., Saldana, J.: Qualitative Data Analysis: A Methods Sourcebook. Sage, Thousand Oaks (2013)
11. Ismail, S.A., Aman, A.: Impact Sourcing Initiatives in Malaysia: An Insight Through Porter's Diamond Framework BT - State-of-the-Art Theories and Empirical Evidence, pp. 197–214 (2018)

12. Klein, H.K., Myers, M.D.: A set of principles for conducting and evaluating interpretive field studies in information systems. MIS Q. **23**(1), 67–93 (1999). https://doi.org/10.2307/249410
13. Kleine, D.: ICT4What? - using the Choice Framework to operationalise the capability approach to development. In: 2009 International Conference on Information and Communication Technologies and Development (ICTD), pp. 108–117 (2009). https://doi.org/10.1109/ICTD.2009.5426717
14. Kleine, D.: The capability approach and the "medium of choice": steps towards conceptualising information and communication technologies for development. Ethics Inf. Technol. **13**(2), 119–130 (2011). https://doi.org/10.1007/s10676-010-9251-5
15. Kleine, D.: Technologies of Choice?. The MIT Press, Cambridge (2013)
16. Kuek, S.C., Paradi-Guilford, T., Fayomi, C.M., Imaizumi, S., Ipeirotis, P.: The Global Opportunity in Online Outsourcing, Washington, D.C. (2015). http://documents.worldbank.org/curated/en/138371468000900555/The-global-opportunity-in-online-outsourcing
17. Lacity, M.C., Khan, S.A., Yan, A.: Review of the empirical business services sourcing literature: an update and future directions. J. Inf. Technol. **31**(3), 269–328 (2016). https://doi.org/10.1057/jit.2016.2
18. Lacity, M.C., Rottman, J., Carmel, E.: Impact sourcing: employing prison inmates to perform digitally-enabled business services. Commun. Assoc. Inf. Syst. **34**(1), 913–932 (2014)
19. Madon, S., Sharanappa, S.: Social IT outsourcing and development: theorising the linkage. Inf. Syst. J. **23**(5), 381–399 (2013). https://doi.org/10.1111/isj.12013
20. Malik, F., Nicholson, B., Heeks, R.: Understanding the development implications of online outsourcing. In: Choudrie, J., Islam, M.S., Wahid, F., Bass, J.M., Priyatma, J.E. (eds.) ICT4D 2017. IAICT, vol. 504, pp. 425–436. Springer, Cham (2017). https://doi.org/10.1007/978-3-319-59111-7_35
21. McKenna, B., Myers, M.D., Newman, M.: Social media in qualitative research: challenges and recommendations. Inf. Org. **27**(2), 87–99 (2017). https://doi.org/10.1016/j.infoandorg.2017.03.001
22. Nicholson, B., Heeks, R., Sahay, S.: Information systems journal special issue on: global sourcing and development: new drivers, models and impacts. Inf. Syst. J. **25**(1), 61–63 (2015). https://doi.org/10.1111/isj.12049
23. Nussbaum, M.: Women and Human Development: The Capabilities Approach. Cambridge University Press, Cambridge (2000)
24. Sandeep, M.S., Ravishankar, M.N.: Impact sourcing ventures and local communities: a frame alignment perspective. Inf. Syst. J. **26**(2), 127–155 (2016). https://doi.org/10.1111/isj.12057
25. Searle, M.: Martial Law and Trust: Humanitarian Challenges in Marawi (2017). https://dr.ntu.edu.sg/handle/10220/43791?show=full#.WmnF4FK3ULU.mendeley. Accessed 25 Jan 2018
26. UNDP: Human Development Reports (2016). http://hdr.undp.org/en/2016-report. Accessed 4 Feb 2018
27. Walsham, G.: Doing interpretive research. Eur. J. Inf. Syst. **15**(3), 320–330 (2006). https://doi.org/10.1057/palgrave.ejis.3000589
28. Yin, R.: Qualitative Research from Start to Finish. The Guilford Press, New York (2016)
29. Yousafzai, M.: I am Malala: The Girl Who Stood Up for Education and was Shot by the Taliban. Little Brown, New York (2013)

A Qualitative Analysis of an E-education Initiative in Deep Rural Schools in South Africa: A Need to Build Resilience

Sifiso Dlamini[1(✉)] and Abraham van der Vyver[2]

[1] CSIR Meraka Institute, Meiring Naude Road, Pretoria, South Africa
sdlamini@csir.co.za
[2] Monash South Africa, 144 Peter Road, Roodepoort, South Africa
braam.vandervyver@monash.edu

Abstract. The Information Communication and Technology for Rural Education Development (ICT4RED) initiative in South Africa which was aimed at the introduction of ICTs into schools in disadvantaged communities, was coordinated by a government agency (the Meraka Institute). The initiative was supported by a number of government stakeholders, namely the Department of Science and Technology, the Department of Basic Education, the Department of Rural Development and Land Reform, and the Provincial Department of Education. Often, ICT4E projects fail once the implementation team and the funder withdraw, especially in rural schools where the only technological resources available at the school are those provided through the project or intervention. Although there are multiple reasons for this, the problem often lies with integration of the project into the day-to-day institutional arrangements of the education system. This puts pressure on the school environment, especially the teacher – who often receives little support from the District and Provincial departments. The researchers conducted semi-structured interviews with eleven teachers from five project schools that were selected for an evaluation at the time, in the Eastern Cape province of South Africa. Findings on the paper were generated by way of content analysis. The content of the interviews was finally analysed with Heeks's Resilience Assessment Benchmarking and Impact Toolkit (RABIT). The research showed that these schools are unable to sustain the change introduced, without support from their formal support system; therefore, this indicates that schools are required to be more resilient, in order to develop capacity to absorb the intervention, and to successfully implement it at the school level.

Keywords: ICT4E · Resilience · Sustainability · Implementation

1 Introduction

Recent developments in educational practices and new technologies have underscored the disparities between old and new models of schooling, thereby creating new demands upon teachers as agents of change. The integration of ICTs into the teaching and learning process is an innovation that requires radical change in the schooling

K. Krauss et al. (Eds.): IDIA 2018, CCIS 933, pp. 125–137, 2019.
https://doi.org/10.1007/978-3-030-11235-6_9

system [1]. At the centre of this change is the application of ICTs in teaching, learning and research. There is also a need to understand the complex education structure and the level of support for a teacher in the classroom. Evoh [2] pointed out that "(a)s a complex and challenging process, such innovation requires time and patience to produce sustained results". He added that "(t)he increasing role of ICTs in education and the complex nature of integrating technology in education, underscore a closer look at the factors that enhance the adoption and sustainability of such tools in education."

ICT4RED is a large-scale research, development and implementation pilot project of the South African government, that was developed and coordinated by the Meraka Institute, a government agency based at the CSIR in Pretoria. Its aim is to improve the quality of teaching and learning in a school district in the Eastern Cape province of South Africa. This research was conducted in a deep rural area of the Eastern Cape where resource scarcity is not only limited to the availability of ICTs and connectivity, but also transport, road infrastructure, stable electricity supply and water, among others. The lack of infrastructure, particularly roads, required researchers to get elevated vehicles to get to some of the schools. The communities are also characterised by child-headed households, with most of the families depending on government support or other resources. Unemployment among the youth is high, leading to some migrating to Cape Town, East London and Johannesburg, in order to seek employment opportunities.

The project was carried out over a period of three years, between 2012 and 2015. Its overall aim was to integrate technology into the teaching and learning processes, in order to establish sustainable improvement thereof, while dealing with very real logistical and infrastructural problems [3]. All the teachers in the project received training prior to implementation. This was done to ensure that the teachers not only know how to teach using technologies, but also how to use the technology when teaching.

The biggest lagging factor was that the education system was not geared up to provide the teacher with all the required support to make the intervention sustainable.

The ICT4RED had three main objectives:

- Explore and design systemic and sustainable approaches to providing access to digital content at resource-constrained rural schools in South Africa. This incorporated an investigation into new and evolving educational technologies, devices, platforms and processes that support the access to digital content for rural school environments.
- Explore and design approaches for Teacher Professional Development (TPD), towards the evolution of a more emerging teaching and learning engagement for the Information Age. This extends to the development of 21st century teaching practices of teachers and 21st century skills of learners.
- Use the evidence from the research within this context to inform policy in an integrated and coherent manner [3].

During follow-up visits to schools which implemented the technology, it came to light that there were problems with the implementation of the technology. A number of factors that hindered implementation were cited. The researchers took up this challenge, and explored these factors at schools level in a rural setting in South Africa.

The study took the form of a qualitative investigation. The reason for using the qualitative approach was to understand all the factors which hinder adoption and sustainability of ICT4E in a rural school, so that these findings could also indicate what elements are needed in building a resilient school. The researchers thus tried to find answers for the following two research questions:

- What are the factors that impact negatively on the adoption and/or the sustainable implementation of ICT4E in a rural school?
- What elements are needed to build a resilient school?

2 Methodology

The researchers designed the research in accordance with a deductivist model that holds that "there is no thing as 'all the relevant facts', there are only 'hypothesis-relevant facts', and that research must always start with a body of prior theory, if only to decide which set of 'collectable facts' should be collected or generated" [4]. The second author conducted semi-structured interviews with 11 teachers who work at five schools in the Cofimvaba region of South Africa's Eastern Cape. Ten of the interviews were in English, and the other in Xhosa. All the interviews were recorded in full. Only five schools were selected for the evaluation process. The purposefully selected sample comprised schools that albeit showing promise to champion technology integration, were struggling to deal with the challenges.

A pre-prepared set of questions are used to guide a semi-structured interview. The interviewer is, however, free to pursue topics that come up during the interview, or add questions to gain more clarity on the answers [4]. All persons interviewed could also put questions, and answer in a free-style manner. The digitally taped interviews were transcribed and analysed with qualitative content analysis. The aim of the interviews was to acquire school-specific information on the implementation and the sustainability of the tablets and the technology that were made available.

Respondents were purposively selected after consultation with the headmasters and/or the departmental heads. The authors then first listened to the recordings separately, and then, in discourse, analysed the data and the themes that were diluted from it. The first author featured as the independent researcher (he did not participate in data collection), and the second author, as the dependent researcher, provided analytical balance to the discussions. Kothari [5] describes qualitative content analysis as a set of techniques aimed at analysing and exploring the opinions, attitudes and behaviour of the respondents and other stakeholders. Lastly, the content of the interviews was analysed with Heeks's Resilience Assessment Benchmarking and Impact Toolkit (RABIT), in order to establish a resilience profile of the schools that were included in the study.

3 Literature Review

3.1 ICT in Education

Voogt et al. [7], in a call for action, make a strong case for comprehensive changes in a country's educational system, in order to "radically restructure schools to be able to use multiple technology-enhanced pedagogies to address individual needs of students." In the South African context, such changes would occur in an environment that is plagued by problems that include "ongoing changes to curricula, bureaucratic inefficiencies, teacher under-performance, lack of school leadership and management skills and the non-availability of learning and teaching materials such as textbooks, as highlighted by the recent textbook crisis in South Africa's rural provinces".

The Technological Pedagogical and Content Knowledge (TPACK) framework, which was developed by Mishra and Koehler, two of the world's leading experts in the field of development education, addresses the knowledge required by teachers' and education policy-makers' need for the constructive integration of ICTs in teaching [8]. The following constructs feature in the theory: technological capability, pedagogical skills/knowledge and content knowledge [9]. The authors warn that there is no single technological solution that accommodates every teacher, every course, or every teaching paradigm [9]. In the context of the ICT4RED project, the focus was to introduce 21st century learning into the classroom, and empower the teacher to be able to teach effectively, using the technologies. The training empowered the teacher to be able to teach with any technology available, hence the focus was on teaching with technology.

Christensen and Knezek [10] developed an empirically tested model to predict the adoption of technology in schooling systems. It makes use of three variables, namely teachers' attitudes, their skills levels, and their access to technology. These variables were all embedded in the qualitative investigation that the researchers conducted. The Dutch "Four in Balance model" is a conceptual benchmarking framework, as well as an implementation model, for the sustainable use of ICT in education. Four in Balance is intended to facilitate the use of ICTs in schools [11]. The model depicted in Fig. 1 consists of four building blocks, namely vision, expertise, digital content and infrastructure. Two mediating variables, namely leadership and collaboration, also feature in the model. These variables will all be brought into account when evaluating the Cofimvaba project.

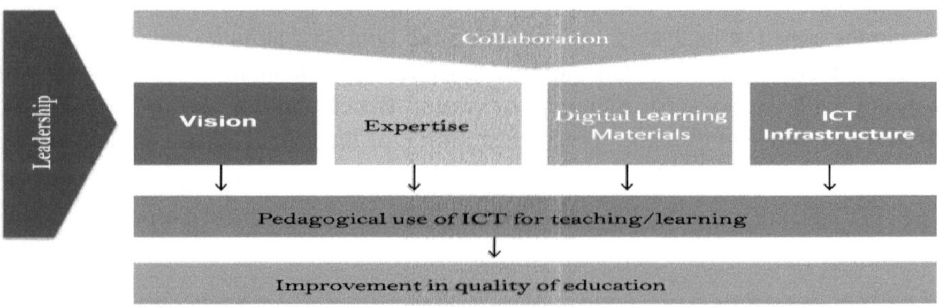

Fig. 1. The Dutch "Four-in-Balance model" [11].

3.2 Resilience

Systems are more and more exposed to shocks and trends [6]. "In today's fast-changing environment, IS have been placed in the forefront of new technological developments and these have been exposed to high levels of stress" [12]. In order to cope with this stress, Heeks postulated that resilience is required [13]. Norris et al. [14] pointed out that resilience has its roots in mathematics and physics, referring to "the capacity of a material or system to return to equilibrium after a displacement". Bonnano [15] expanded the meaning to include the adaptive capacity of individuals. Heeks and Ospina [6] define resilience as "the ability of vulnerable systems … to withstand, recover from, adapt to, and potentially transform amid change and uncertainty". Although there are exceptions, most discussions, if not the definitions themselves, distinguish resilience from resistance [14]. For them, "community resilience is a process linking a network of adaptive capacities (resources with dynamic attributes) to adaptation after a disturbance or adversity". They postulated that "(t)o build collective resilience, communities must reduce risk and resource inequities, engage local people in mitigation, create organizational linkages, boost and protect social supports, and plan for not having a plan, which requires flexibility, decision-making skills, and trusted sources of information that function in the face of unknowns" [14].

Heeks and his team at Manchester University developed the Resilience Assessment Benchmarking and Impact Toolkit (RABIT). Heeks [13] gave the following explanation: Nine attributes or sub-properties of resilience are embedded in RABIT: "Three are primary foundations of resilience: robustness, self-organisation, and learning. Six are secondary enablers of resilience: redundancy, rapidity, scale, diversity, flexibility, and equality. The stronger these are in a community, the more resilient it will be" [13].

Heeks and Ospina [16] concluded that "(t)he RABIT resilience framework in terms of attributes, definitions, and markers is generic and so should in theory be applicable to all types of system in all types of context." The descriptions of the attributes are as follows:

Robustness. The attribute of robustness is defined as the ability of the system to maintain its characteristics and performance in the face of external fluctuations, including shocks [17]. Heeks and Ospina [16] identified the following illustrative markers of robustness: Physical preparedness, institutional capacity, and multilevel governance. These markers can all be applied to an educational system.

Self-organisation. Self-organisation reflects the system's ability to self-correct in case of external disruption [18]. This is not only collectively illustrated by the internal workings of the system, but also by the enablers of those processes – such as social capital and trust [19]. Markers are collaboration and consensus, the use of social media, and the contribution of the system towards trust building [19].

Learning. The third attribute, which is learning, reflects a system component as well as a human dimension. In a system sense it is understood as the capacity of the system to generate feedback that can guide the designer to experiment and innovate [19]. It is important that a management information system provides feedback about its own efficiency and effectiveness. The reporting of its malfunctioning and transactions processing error rates is a simple example of this type of feedback. Statistics prepared by the system about who uses what system facility, as well as the frequency of use, are more sophisticated forms of feedback. Heeks and Ospina [16] listed capacity building, new and traditional knowledge, and reflective thinking, as markers. Apart from these three foundational attributes, Heeks and Ospina [16] also list six other attributes:

Redundancy. Redundancy is the extent to which components within a system are substitutable in the event of collapse or loss of quality [20]. This relates to interchangeability of such assets, as well as recoverability [21]. The following markers are listed by Heeks and Ospina [16]: functional overlaps and interdependency, and resource substitutability and sparseness.

Rapidity. Rapidity means how quickly the system can be activated in order to respond timeously to external challenges [14]. Veryard [21] emphasized that decision-makers should strive to achieve a careful balance between changing the technology to fit the organization, and changing the organization to cope with the technology. The markers identified by Heeks and Ospina [16] are rapid resource access, assessment/coordination and mobilisation.

Scale. Scale refers to the section of resources that a system can access within or outside the organisation to meet the challenges it may encounter [19]. Heeks and Ospina [16] suggested the following markers: multi-level networks, resource access and partnerships, and cross-level interactions.

Diversity and Flexibility. Diversity is the variety of institutional assets (including knowledge) that are available to deal with short- as well as long-term challenges [23]. The diversity of system elements can play an important part to retain continuity when the system is challenged. It can also serve as "the basis for innovation, learning and adaptation to slower, ongoing change" [24].

Flexibility forms part of this attribute. It refers to the ability of a system to undertake different sets of actions with the resources at its disposal, thereby not only offering fitting solutions to problems, but also capitalizing on opportunities arising from external changes [25].

The collective set of markers that define this complex construct include different actions/opportunities, adaptable decision-making and innovative backbone.

Equity. Finally, equity is the extent to which the system affords equal access to rights, resources and opportunities to its members [26]. Its markers are competency gap reduction, inclusiveness, and openness and accountability.

Alignment. Although alignment is not part of Heeks's RABIT model, it is clear that alignment plays an important role in a number of attributes. Alaveca and Rusu [27] found that low understanding of stakeholder environment, poor communication, unclear specifications, limited cooperation and lack of mutual commitment and support inhibit the achievement of alignment between business and IT domains in the social dimension.

4 Findings

4.1 Findings from the Interviews

The findings from the interviews indicated low levels of resilience from how the different schools struggled with the integration of technology in the classroom practices. The low levels of resilience are due to the following factors that impact on the sustainability of the project at the school level:

The Attitude of the Teachers. The responses regarding the attitudes of the teachers varied, as the teachers came from different schools with different adoption levels. Schools which had teachers and champions who were geared up to use technology for teaching and learning, had a different view of sustainability. The respondents were unanimous that teachers were all scared of the technology at the start of the project. One respondent initially refused to sign up for the project. She believed "it's for the kids and the young ones." A few others said they would resign if they couldn't cope; however, in the end they all overcame their fears once they were exposed to the training.

With the exception of one, all the teachers agreed that they and their colleagues were not making productive use of the tablets. One respondent indicated that "some teachers lost interest." Another reported that some teachers are reluctant to use it "It's a personal thing."

The tablets are not optimally used, because "it causes extra stress," a respondent stated. Another complained that the tablets take a lot of time. The teacher referred to lack of support – which they should be getting from ICT champions allocated to the schools to help the teachers with the technology in class. The champions would have to charge the tablets, take the tablets to class and attend to all the technological problems, while the teacher will primarily focus on teaching.

A respondent who seemed despondent confessed that he was struggling with the tablets. "I am always busy but I am trying". Another said there is not enough time in class to use the tablets.

When asked what the tablets mean to them the following responses were recorded:

"Interesting and challenging."
"A whole new world opened up before me."
"I want to share it with others."
"I learnt about the MS teaching tools."

The last word came from a respondent who felt that "sustainability was hindered by the attitude of some of the teachers".

Regular Use. Irregular usage seems to be a major lagging factor that prevents sustainable implementation of the technology in the school context. "It is not used every day," one respondent indicated. It was suggested that each teacher should use the tablet on a daily basis, so that both the learner and the teacher can be comfortable with using technology in class. "It should be compulsory", another teacher said. Another recurring complaint was that usage is not properly coordinated. The reason for this, another respondent expressed, is that "usage is not part of the teaching plan." He added: "(w)e can't use it all the time because of the workload." The absence of the ICT champions to help the teachers with the technology in class made them feel overloaded if they had to use the technology in class without being assisted or supported.

The Provincial Department of Education was also blamed for the unsatisfactory usage levels of the tablets: "It is not compulsory to use it and therefore not enough time is allocated for it." The problem with both the Provincial and District departments is that they were not successful in the institutionalisation of the project, and therefore the technology was not part of their curriculum planning.

Technological Support. Lack of technological/technical support was a recurring theme. The members of the National Rural Youth Service Corps (NARYSEC) that were meant to be stationed at every school, drew a lot of comments. The respondents indicated that the impression was created by the Department of Rural Development and Land Reform, on whose payroll they were, that two members of the Corps would be stationed at every school, but this was not the case. Some schools only had one. There was large-scale uncertainty about their duties and their working hours. Some respondents voiced their concern about their lack of technical skills.

All the respondents were dissatisfied with the lack of support they received from District officials and the Provincial Department. One respondent complained that his school was last visited in February 2015. He added that the researchers from the CSIR do come from time to time.

Integration of the Tablets into the Curricula. Many of the respondents voiced their concerns that the tablets were not incorporated in the curricula. One stated that "there is nothing in the workbook on tablets. It is not linked." Another respondent commented along the same lines and said that "the subject advisors don't integrate the tablets into the curriculum. We want the department to link this to the subjects." "I don't really implement what we have learnt in the ICT training." One of the biggest challenges with the content in South Africa was that most of the content used in the curriculum is not available in electronic format. This posed a challenge to the implanting team, as some teachers wanted to open the tablet and find the workbooks in it.

Some of the respondents pointed out that there is no content for some of the subjects. One respondent complained that none of the content is in Xhosa. As highlighted above, content for IsiXhosa was also not available on the tablets – which made other teachers reluctant to use the tablets when teaching vernacular.

Continuous Training. The respondents felt very strongly about the necessity for continuous training. For these teachers, sustainability heavily depended on continuous training. "Sustainability depends on continuous training", most teachers attested. One respondent asked for the training to be redone. Another suggested weekly training sessions. A number of respondents voiced their concerns about the training of new teachers.

The challenge with the notion of training was that because the initiative was not institutionalised into the structures of the Provincial and District departments, no continuous support and training was planned for the teachers at the schools. Continuous training was essential, especially since more than 90% of the teachers in the programme were using technology for the first time.

Community Involvement. The researchers were surprised that the communities of which the schools formed part, played an important role in securing the assets and the buildings of the schools. Most of the teachers mentioned the imminent risk of crime in their communities. Several respondents referred to the safekeeping of the tablets. In some cases, the community supplemented the services rendered by professional security companies.

A year later, after the study was conducted, 65% of the schools were broken into, with the technology, mainly the tablets, stolen. This created a huge challenge to the programme as most schools started removing the technology from the schools, resulting in non-use of technology for teaching and learning in these schools. Most of the tablets were "kept safe" at the teachers' houses in Queenstown and Cofimvaba town. The levels of crime, particularly the targeting of tablets in these communities, and the removal of the tablets from the school premises, affected the sustainability of the project at the school level.

A Design Template. One of the most creative suggestions that came from respondents was the request for a design template. Since it was required of the teachers to download content from the Internet, it made sense to create a design template in which this content can be embedded and shared. Such a template could be linked to the lesson plans and course content. One respondent indicated that "all tablets [of learners] are connected to my tablet. I can close learners' games when they play them." The program which allowed the teacher to close games on the learner tablets was only available at one school, as a pilot. The other schools did not have the program, and continuously had a challenge with learners playing game while the teacher was teaching. In the absence of the NARYSEC champion, this became a frustrating experience for the teachers.

A Policy Designed with and for All Stakeholders. The large number of uncertainties, discrepancies, misunderstandings and lack of support from the Provincial and District structures, confirmed the need for a comprehensive policy that describes the rights and responsibilities of all the stakeholders. Important aspects that need to be urgently addressed are the role of the District Office of the Provincial Education Department, the role and responsibilities of the local NARYSEC officials – aka Champions, the role and responsibilities of the local communities and its institutions and businesses, and last, but not least, the role and responsibilities of the teachers. The anecdotal evidence compiled during the data-gathering phase of this research project, underscores the need for such a policy.

4.2 Findings on the Four-in Balance Model

The model consists of four building blocks, namely vision, expertise, digital content, and infrastructure. Two mediating variables, namely leadership and collaboration, also feature in the model. Each variable was evaluated in terms of the feedback received in the interviews.

There seems to be discrepancies in terms of the vision of the project. The team leaders of Meraka, who acted as the implementation agency for the training, were mainly meant to empower the teachers with technology skills. Although it was about the people and not the technology, all the stakeholders didn't buy into the vision. Many of the teachers and some of the headmasters were not mentally ready to commit to the project. Leadership problems were detected in all spheres of government. The transfer of expertise and digital content to the teachers was done with mixed success. According to the feedback, collaboration between the teachers and the champions, and among themselves, were mostly dysfunctional.

4.3 Finding on Heeks's Model

The implementation of Heeks's model on the Cofimvaba case is presented in terms of the attributes and markers that were discussed under Sect. 3.2.

In terms of robustness, there seems to be limited constitutional capacity for continuous support and training. The trainers and advisors did provide ad hoc support, until the contract ran out. The respondents reported that preciously limited support was received from the departments at District as well as Provincial level.

With regard to the collaboration and consensus dimension of self-organisation, the so-called "champions" failed to deliver the services that were agreed on. Some of the communities supplemented the services rendered by the private security companies, with regard to the guarding of the assets of the schools. This initiative was in line with the definition of community resilience that Norris et al. [14] postulated of resilience. The reports in terms of personal resilience were mostly negative. Very little trust was built, and fears were exacerbated.

Learning was one of the variables that generated a number of positive results. Capacity building took the form of the transfer of new ICT skills to those who were not reluctant to learn. Unfortunately, there were no arrangements in place for the training of new appointees. The fact that the tablets were not incorporated in the new curricula, was a major problem. This meant that there were no rewards for reflective thinking. This problem was also the main cause for another variable, namely redundancy. Some of the tablets were not used at all. The limitations regarding the infrastructure contributed to the unwillingness of some of the teachers to remain involved with the initiative.

Rapidity and scale were not raised in the interviews. The lack of infrastructure or any multi-level networks were not conducive to involvement. Although there were a few positive signs in terms of diversity and flexibility, the lack of a general design template was a major lagging factor. According to Heeks's model there was thus no innovative backbone.

Teachers were able to download content from the Internet. Selection was limited and those who chose not to participate could not be forced to do so.

The reduction of the competency gap that was an important marker in terms of equality, rendered poor results. There were too many non-users. There were also no policies in place in which they could be forced to participate.

4.4 General Findings

At the start of the project, the respondents were all challenged by their lack of experience with technology. However, it did not take long before they took charge of the tablets. According to the respondents, they helped each other to cope, especially since they depended on each other to make things work, since the use of technology was a new thing for most of them. Once the training was completed and the badges and certificates handed out, the picture changed. Heavy workloads claimed its toll. Some of the teachers lost interest, while others could not find the time to experiment with the tablets. Although the learners were enjoying the new technology, not all the teachers shared their enthusiasm. Only a few managed to enrich the curricula by downloading new content.

The interim evaluation showed that some of the teething problems that were initially exposed, are now threatening the sustainability of the project. Although the MoU allowed for a design science research method, a more hands-on action research model, supported by a project management approach with a clearly defined critical path, may be needed to make similar projects work more effectively.

Technological interventions or ICT4E programmes will not work in such a context, unless the focus changes to creating resilient schools. The challenge of lack of support at schools is a nationwide problem, and the education system, as a whole, is not geared up for the implementation of ICTs for teaching and learning. It is mainly private and semi-private schools which have come close to championing the integration of technology for teaching and learning, by providing the required support to a teacher in the classroom. The study indicates further research on how to create resilient public schools as a prerequisite for introduction of technology for teaching and learning.

5 Conclusion

The first research question dealt with the factors that impact negatively on the adoption and/or the sustainable implementation of ICT4E in a rural school. This question was explored by way of in-depth interviews. The results have been discussed in Sect. 4.1. The second research question dealt with what elements are needed to build a resilient school. These questions were answered by using the Dutch "Four-in-Balance" framework for sustainable ICT use in schools, as well as Heeks's Resilience Framework. These analyses were discussed in Sects. 4.2 and 4.3, respectively.

Although the project generated a lot of enthusiasm when it was initiated, it lost momentum as implementation moved into the advanced stages. The 26 schools in the Nciba circuit were all non-fee-paying schools. As a result, all the schools depended on the financial supported allocated to them by the Province, and technical support provided to them by the District. The principals of these schools always attested that there is little that the schools can do on their own, as the budget from the Department is not enough to cover all the needs of the schools. With parents not paying fees, the school's financial budget is limited to the budget allocated to them.

For the school to effectively develop its capacity to absorb the change, some level of resilience is needed. To apply this definition to the context of the 26 Nciba circuit schools and community, will require the involvement of more than the Education Department alone to enable the schools to adapt and absorb technological intervention at the schools. The findings from the interviews with the eleven teachers in the selected schools indicate that the schools on their own are unable to absorb the introduction of technology into the schools and the change in teaching and learning practices. For the schools to be resilient, the community, public and private sector, businesses and other social structures would have to be involved in visioning the future of the education system in these communities.

References

1. Haddad, W.D. http://www.ictinedtoolkit.org/usere/pdfs/. Accessed 15 Oct 2017
2. Evoh, C.J.: The adoption and sustainability of technology-enhanced education in higher institutions of learning in Africa. Technol. Sustain. Rural Dev. Africa **2**(2), 19–39 (2013)
3. Herselman, M., Botha, A.: Designing and implementing an Information Communication Technology for Rural Education Development (ICT4RED) in a Resource Constrained Environment: Cofimvaba School District, Eastern Cape, South Africa. CSIR, Pretoria (2014)
4. Wengraf, T.: Qualitative Research Interviewing: Biographic Narrative and Semi-Structured Methods. Sage, Thousand Oaks (2001)
5. Kothari, C.R.: Research Methodology: Methods and Techniques. New Age, Delhi (2004)
6. Heeks, R., Ospina, A.V.: Analysing urban community informatics from a resilience perspective. J. Community Inform. **11**(1) (2014). http://ci-journal.org/index.php/ciej/article/view/1108
7. Voogt, J., Knezek, G., Cox, M., Knezek, D., ten Brummelhuis, A.: Under which conditions does ICT have a positive effect on teaching and learning? A call to action. Educ. Info. Technol. **3**(20), 641–654 (2011)
8. Evoh, C.J.: Emerging trajectories and sustainability of ICTs in educational reforms in Africa: exploring the prospects of the teacher laptop policy in South Africa. J. Educ. Int. Dev. **2**(4), 21–31 (2009)
9. Mishra, P., Koehler, M.J.: Introducing technological pedagogical content knowledge. Paper presented in the Annual Meeting of the American Educational Research Association New York City, 24–28 March (2008)
10. Christensen, R., Knezek, G.: Self-report measures and findings for information technology attitudes and competencies. In: Voogt, J., Knezek, G. (eds.) International Handbook of Information Technology in Primary and Secondary Education, vol. 4, no. 3, pp. 397–417 (2008)
11. Kennisnet: Four-in-balance Monitor (2013). https://www.kennisnet.nl/fileadmin/kennisnet/publicatie/vierinbalans/Four_in_balance_Monitor_2013.pdf. Accessed 15 June 2017
12. Azadeh, A., Salehi, V., Salehi, R.: A resilience-based model for performance evaluation of information systems: the case of a gas company. Enterp. Inf. Syst. **11**(9), 1337–1351 (2017)

13. Heeks, R.: RABIT: A New Toolkit for Measuring Resilience. Nexus for ICTs, climate change and Development. https://niccd.wordpress.com/2016/11/14/rabit-a-new-toolkit-for-measuring-resilience/. Accessed 04 Jan 2017
14. Norris, F.H., Stevens, S.P., Pfefferbaum, B., Wyche, K.F., Pfefferbaum, R.L.: Community resilience as a metaphor, theory, set of capacities and strategy for disaster readiness. Am. J. Community Psychol. **4**(1), 127–150 (2008)
15. Bonnano, G.: Loss, trauma, and human resilience. Am. Psychol. **59**(1), 20–28 (2004)
16. Heeks, R., Ospina, A.V.: Conceptualising the link between information systems and resilience: a developing country field study. Inf. Syst. J. **1**(1), 1–27 (2018)
17. Janssen, M.A., Anderies, J.M.: Robustness trade-offs in social-ecological systems. Int. J. Commons **1**(1), 43–65 (2007)
18. Carpenter, S., Walker, B., Anderies, J.M., Abel, N.: From metaphor to measurement: resilience of what to what? Ecosystems **4**(8), 765–781 (2001)
19. Folke, C., Carpenter, R.S., Walker, B., Scheffer, M., Chapin, T., Rockström, J.: Resilience thinking: integrating resilience, adaptability and transformability. Ecol. Soc. **15**(4), 20 (2010)
20. Folke, C.: Freshwater as shared between society and ecosystems: from divided approaches to integrated challenges. Philos. Trans. R. Soc. B **358**(1440), 2037–2049 (2003)
21. Rockefeller Foundation: Building Climate Change Resilience. http://www.rockefellerfoundation.org/uploads/files/c9725eb2-b76e-42eb-82db-c5672a43a097-climate.pdf. Accessed 19 Apr 2017
22. Veryard, R.: Technology Change Management. http://www.linkedin.com/in/richardveryard. Accessed 12 June 2017
23. Folke, C., Hahn, T., Olsson, T., Norberg, P.: Adaptive governance of social-ecological systems. Ann. Rev. Environ. Resour. **30**(1), 441–473 (2005)
24. Biggs, W.: TIM lecture series - 29 lessons learned in entrepreneurship. Technol. Innov. Manag. Rev. **2**(11), 46–48 (2012)
25. Folke, C.: Resilience: the emergence of a perspective for social–ecological systems analyses. Glob. Environ. Change **16**(1), 253–267 (2006)
26. Magis, K., Shinn, C.: Emergent principles of social sustainability. In: Dillard, J., Dujon, V., King, M. (eds.) Understanding the Social Dimension of Sustainability, pp. 15–44. Routledge, New York (2009)

Community Development

Global Standards and Local Development

Simon Pettersen Nguyen(✉), Petter Nielsen, and Johan Ivar Sæbø

Department of Informatics, University of Oslo, Oslo, Norway
{simonpn, pnielsen, johansa}@ifi.uio.no

Abstract. Substantial investments are made in ICTs to support socioeconomic growth in developing countries. As a side-effect of this, the public health sectors in developing countries are commonly challenged by the proliferation of multiple and parallel information systems. Investments are made, but not in a coordinated manner. Based on a case study of OpenHIE, a global community of practice supporting the development of ICT standards within health, and the implementation of these standards in Tanzania and The Philippines, we discuss the relation between global standards and local development. We do so by conceptualizing the global standards offered by OpenHIE as fluid standards and standards as composed of a package of the different components necessary to make them globally and locally relevant. Theoretically, we contribute to the standardization literature by applying and expanding the concept of fluid standards within this particular context of global initiatives to reduce fragmentation of health information systems locally in developing countries. We also contribute to the development literature by exemplifying and critically discussing how the fluid nature of standards, and the networked nature of standardization processes, promote local development.

Keywords: Standards · Standardization · Global standards · OpenHIE
Fluid standards · Health information exchange · Interoperability

1 Introduction

Governments and international agencies invest vast amounts of resources in projects aimed at boosting the adoption and diffusion of information and communication technologies (ICTs) in developing countries. These investments are based on the assumption that ICTs offer significant benefits for socioeconomic development [1, 2]; however, at the same time, the literature on ICTs in developing countries generally reports failure or partial failure of the application of ICTs [3–6]. ICTs are nevertheless acknowledged to have high potential value across all sectors – both public and private – at all levels in developing countries. Thus, the question is not whether, but how, ICTs can be made advantageous for developing countries [7].

ICTs have become ubiquitous, and most human activities involve a variety of technologies. The heterogeneity of these ICTs, and the networked nature of the services they offer, give standards an increasingly important role [8]. In a special issue of MIS Quarterly on Standard Making [8], the editors refer to the following definition of a standard: “A standard defines a uniform set of measures, agreements, conditions, or

K. Krauss et al. (Eds.): IDIA 2018, CCIS 933, pp. 141–155, 2019.
https://doi.org/10.1007/978-3-030-11235-6_10

specifications between parties" [9]. The literature on ICTs – and especially information systems – in developing countries has acknowledged the emerging complexity and challenges stemming from the multiplicity and common fragmentation of systems in private and public sectors. The literature has therefore focused on how to integrate information systems on a national scale [10, 11]; however, little attention is given to the role of standards and, in particular, global standardization in development. By development, we refer to Castells' definition: "as the self-defined process – self is important – by which humans, as a collective, enhance their wellbeing by creating the structural conditions for the expanded reproduction of the process of development itself, so enhancing their wellbeing and, at the same time, creating the structural conditions for this process to go on" [12].

To address the gap in the literature on the role of global standards in development, we attempt to answer the following research question: "What is the relation between global standards and local development?" By global standards, we refer to standards which are developed globally – by a variety of actors spread out throughout the world – to be generic and relevant at the national level across multiple countries. We discuss this question based on a case study of OpenHIE, a global community of practice "... dedicated to improve the health of the underserved through open and collaborative development, and support of country driven, large scale health information sharing architectures" [13]. This will give decision-makers – such as ministries of health, health programme leaders and clinicians – access to the data they need to support improved health outcomes. We explore the role of OpenHIE with reference to Tanzania and the Philippines, both of which have engaged with OpenHIE in their national efforts for consolidating fragmented information systems in the public health sector.

We show how global standards relate to development by building on the work of Castells [14, 15] and Escobar [16]. Castells argued that ICTs can be used to enable development, and Escobar posited that for such initiatives to be successful, they should be rooted in the local context. We argue that by fostering networks of both indigenous and exogenous actors, it is possible to address central development aims –such as better health – in a fashion that is cognizant of local conditions and needs, while at the same time drawing on global ICT developments and best practices.

We explore the role of global standards in promoting such networks, and show how OpenHIE enables a variety of actors – non-governmental organizations, research institutes, consultancy firms, and software firms – to use global standards as a coordinated approach for development. What makes this possible, we argue, is that the standards and standardization processes are not only and primarily concerned with standardization as the production of fixed, formal and written technical specifications. Rather, the standards are 'packages' [17] of components needed to make things work, including technical specifications, but also knowledge, techniques, business models and technologies. We argue that these 'fluid standards' [18] form networks and processes of negotiation between both complementary and competing actors, and they must have certain characteristics to become globally relevant in a sustainable way, including being flexible, scalable and robust. These characteristics, we argue, are central in allowing global standards to act as a common point of interest, allowing political, economic and technological forces to be joined for development [2].

The rest of the paper is structured as follows: we first describe Castells' and Escobar's view on ICT and development, and present literature on standards, followed by our research design and methodology. We then present our empirical material on the OpenHIE standardization initiative, and the relevance of this in Tanzania and the Philippines. In the following discussion, we look at the characteristics of standards, their fluidity, and how this enables different actors in different countries to work towards development. Finally, we conclude the paper by relating standards and development more closely.

2 Related Research

The objective of this study is to examine the relation between global standards and local development. In doing so, we draw on the work of Castells and Escobar; furthermore, we conceptualize the global standards promoted by OpenHIE as fluid standards. In this section, we present literature related to these objectives.

2.1 Castells and Escobar on ICTs and Development

The work of Castells and Escobar is essential for the argument we are building, as both call for local participation and ownership of the process, for development to succeed. Castells [14] posited that the architecture of the society of our new age is made up of 'informational' networks. He made a call for the use of ICTs as enablers for the network of society, and to reverse the downward spiral of exclusion. He argued that ICTs alone do not solve social problems, but that their existence is a prerequisite for economic and social development in our world. Castells [15] conceptualized the role of ICT in stimulating development, as a two-edged sword. On the upside, ICTs allow nations to leapfrog stages of economic growth by enabling the modernization of their production system, and creating an upward surge in their competitiveness. On the downside, for the economies which are unable to adapt to the new technological system, their retardation becomes worse.

Escobar [16] criticized the traditional concept of development as a mechanistic metaphor in which governments and international agencies spend huge amounts of money on ICTs and expect improved quality of life (which is seldom the outcome). He called for a reformulation of the concept of development, which considers the local discourses of progress and development, the prevailing power structures, and indigenous forms of knowledge in each country. Escobar asserts that if these aspects are not paid attention to, development initiatives are bound to fail.

2.2 Literature on Standards

The growing body of literature on standards reflects their increasing importance and variety. A change in requirements of standards caused by an increasingly rapidly-changing world has warranted research on the dynamics and flexibility of standards [19, 20]. Research studying standardization as dynamic processes shows how some standards are developed through linear stages – definition, implementation and use [21] – while others are based on more bottom-up and evolutionary approaches [22, 23].

The existing standardization literature has acknowledged standardization as a largely dynamic, flexible, socio-technical process, and researchers have discussed the need for standards to be open, negotiated and evolving [18]. Hanseth and Nielsen [18] argue that the literature is fragmented, and that these characteristics have been discussed across a range of different discourses. To bring these fragmented pieces together, they conceptualized *fluid standards*. A fluid standard is a software package with multiple key characteristics. These characteristics are adopted from characteristics of fluid technologies by De Laet and Mol [24] (described in Table 1).

Table 1. Characteristics of fluid technologies.

Characteristics of fluid technologies [24]	
No clear boundaries	Boundaries defined by all that is needed to make the technology work
Multiple identities	Attributed by different people, based on constituting or external elements, different boundaries, emergent and changing over time
Mixtures	Of different elements, elements that can be fluid themselves
Robustness	It is not clear when it stops acting, achieves its aims, and when it fails and falters from its multiple purposes and there being no single weak link that can make all the identities come apart. The strongest link may also dissolve and not be obvious
Continuity	Share characteristics with other technologies, a family resemblance, which forms continuity
Dissolving ownership	Fluid in itself, allowing the technology the flexibility to have unclear boundaries and multiple identities

Hanseth and Nielsen [18] point to how standards are traditionally understood as what is referred to as "immutable mobiles" – objects, knowledge, technology, practices – that diffuse across time and space without changing; however, as the world grows rapidly and unpredictably more complex, they argue that some standards must be "mutable mobile", or fluid – changing as they move across space and time. Seeing a standard as fluid is almost the exact opposite of the traditional view on standards (e.g. telecommunication), where a standard is viewed as an output of top-down, linear and stage-driven processes. Rather, it shows how a standard can be a product of non-linear and dynamic processes – which are more apt in a dynamic and changing world.

Standards are important in health, especially with the global ambition of Universal Health Coverage. This will require well-integrated information systems and the use of standards. From a health service point of view, the flow of information between integrated systems will make it easier for decision-makers to get a better picture of the health situation and the resource situation, and to choose the right priorities. While there are many studies on ICT standards in the health sector [10, 11, 21, 25, 26], little has been written about the relation between health ICT standards in development. This study is an attempt to fill that gap.

3 Methodology

The article reports from a qualitative, interpretive case study [27] of OpenHIE and its relation to Tanzania and the Philippines. Based on the interpretive case study tradition, qualitative data was collected from multiple sources, including interviews, documents and websites. A detailed description of the data source is listed in Table 2.

Table 2. Data sources.

Site	Data sources
OpenHIE	5 interviews with community members 2 interviews with a leader and founder of OpenHIE 11 online meetings
Tanzania	7 interviews with the coordinating and funding member, the project coordinator, the lead developer, and developers and implementers at Health Information Systems Programme (HISP) Tanzania, an organization responsible for the design, development and implementation of several health information systems for the government of Tanzania 1 interview with the head of the national integration efforts at the ICT unit of the Ministry of Health, Community Development, Gender, Elderly and Children (MoHCDGEC), hereafter referred to as the Ministry of Health) 9 governmental documents
The Philippines	1 interview with a central person in the national integration efforts of the Philippines 3 government documents

The interviews lasted between 30 min and 1 h, and were fully or partly transcribed for more detailed analysis. Overall, 15 people were interviewed, 16 interviews were conducted, 10 meetings were attended, and 12 governmental documents were collected and analyzed.

In line with the interpretive tradition, we conducted data analysis in parallel with data gathering [28]. The analysis was informed by theories of development by Castells and Escobar, and the fluid standards concept by Hanseth and Nielsen [18]. From the interpretive analysis perspective, theory was used as a sensitizing device to allow understanding to emerge from the data, and to analyze the data for potential analytical themes. In particular, the characteristics of fluid technologies by De Laet and Mol [24], as described by Hanseth and Nielsen [18], were used to analyze the fluidity of the OpenHIE standards.

We followed on the principle of the hermeneutic circle, which involves attempting to understand a complex whole "from the preconceptions about the meanings of its parts and their interrelationships" [29]. Concretely, this entails the consideration of all the various data sources in the interpretation process. When needed, we conducted follow-up interviews to verify emerging findings or pursue additional data.

4 The Case of OpenHIE

OpenHIE is a global community of practice "… dedicated to improve the health of the underserved through open and collaborative development and support of country driven, large scale health information sharing architectures" [13]. The community is an open and self-organizing collaborative of diverse organizations and people from governmental agencies, private sector companies, academia and non-governmental organizations. OpenHIE was established in 2013, following the establishment of the Rwanda Health Information Exchange (RHIE). According to OpenHIE [30], RHIE exemplified the potential of an integrated national health information architecture, and was therefore used as a reference example by other actors in the global health community for understanding how to achieve interoperability at scale, with technical, socio-political and capacity development challenges in mind. Following the launch of RHIE, there was a need for a more generalized approach, as multiple countries requested assistance in applying similar architectural tactics within their environments [30]. Out of this need, OpenHIE was established.

4.1 The OpenHIE Standards

The OpenHIE community promotes a stack of semantic, syntactic and information systems level standards. At the semantic level, it promotes the use of standards such as ICD-10 and SNOMED CT, which are used for classification of diseases, medical terms and medical laboratory observations. At the syntactic level, it offers a set of interoperability profiles to operationalize data exchange. Through its engagement with Integrating the Healthcare Enterprise, a non-profit organization working on interoperability profiles for health data exchange, the OpenHIE community continuously evaluates and implements already existing, consensus-based, international data exchange standards. An IHE profile is a precise definition of how standards such as DICOM, HL7 and W3C can be implemented to meet specific health data exchange needs. OpenHIE has implemented several IHE profiles in its framework, and is also developing future profiles through IHE. One of the leaders of OpenHIE community identified the development of IHE profiles on behalf of developing countries as one of the main purposes of OpenHIE:

> "I think one purpose of OpenHIE is to be advocating for developing countries in places like IHE, HL7 and others, where their voices are not well represented in the first place. So, I have been a delegate of [a country] to ISO at the technical committee on health informatics TC 215 for 10 years. Occasionally, you would see the South Africans there, and very occasionally there was a representative from Kenya. The Brazilians were quite active, but in terms of low- and middle-income countries, there was only the Kenyans and the South Africans. And, you know, as an observer, and the voices of the requirements side in low resource settings are not well represented. So, their specification wasn't attuned to what requirements are. I think OpenHIE provides a voice for those people who have not had their voices heard. That has been very much a role I myself, and others, even though we get supported by our countries to be attending, we speak on behalf of people that don't have their voices heard."

Currently, OpenHIE has 12 interoperability profiles in its portfolio, which are orchestrated in the framework to compose reusable workflows which support common care processes.

At the information systems level, OpenHIE offers an architectural framework. The framework is technology agnostic and service oriented, describing core components which collectively support national-level health information sharing activities. It includes seven components: a terminology service, a client registry, a shared health record, a health management information system, a facility registry, a health worker registry, and an interoperability layer coordinating the information flow among the components. The interoperability layer normalizes the context in which health information is created, based on who received health services, who provided them, where they were provided, and what specific health services were provided. By focusing on the four Ws of health care delivery – Whom For, Whom By, Where and What, OpenHIE aims at bringing relevant information directly to the point of care. The vision is that this should enhance the quality, safety and continuity of care, In addition, it should enable improved decision-making, and support the pertinent use of information to improve population health.

In addition to the seven core components, the framework allows external systems to be connected – such as point-of-service applications. These are applications used by clinicians and community health workers to record healthcare transactions and to access and update the person-centric shared health information of a patient. The framework is not restricted to the given components and interoperability profiles, and countries can adopt it as they want, either in whole or in parts. It facilitates flexible implementation on country level, making it possible to combine existing components through relatively simple and inexpensive interfaces, rather than implementing new ones. OpenHIE also offers reference applications for each of the components, which are various pieces of open-source software developed primarily by the community member organizations.

4.2 The OpenHIE Community Process

The OpenHIE community is primarily composed of health informatics experts. The OpenHIE community is divided into sub-communities which correlate with, and focus on, enhancing the design of each OpenHIE architectural component (e.g. Facility Registry Community, Terminology Service Community, and so forth). In addition, there are two overarching communities: one for architecture and one for leadership. These overarching communities are tasked with integrating all the other communities.

The community processes occur via community-specific channels and resources, which include a mix of regular community calls, email lists, wikis, community vision, mission and value statements, workflow design resources, IHE profiles and country implementation guides. The Regenstrief Institute, a U.S.-based research institute, provides operational support through these and other mechanisms, to the OpenHIE community. The Regenstrief Institute also cultivates leadership within the community and provides strategic guidance. The majority of the OpenHIE leadership is based in the Global North, except for a few representatives from Tanzania, Kenya and South Africa.

There are no governmental representatives from developing counties in the OpenHIE leadership; however, there is a clear link between the leadership and the organizations behind the OpenHIE reference applications, as they are all represented in the leadership. These applications are developed by disparate organizations, ranging from software companies to research institutes.

4.3 The Role of OpenHIE in Developing Countries

Today, OpenHIE's architecture, reference software, other resources and expertise are being leveraged or explored in multiple developing countries. In this section, we describe this in relation to Tanzania and the Philippines.

Tanzania: In 2009, the Tanzanian government, through the Ministry of Health, implemented the Health Sector Strategic Plan III (HSSP III) [31] to guide the prioritization and distribution of resources in the health sector. The purpose of HSSP III was to transform the health sector to deliver the Millennium Development Goals by their target year, 2015. The Tanzanian government acknowledged the potential of ICT in supporting the transformation, by enabling information access and supporting healthcare operations, management and decision-making. At the same time, the Tanzanian government recognized the development and implementation of an increasing number of nationally scaled health information systems without some form of national plan and coordination. While each health information system plays an important role in the health system, they have been driven by needs within particular domains. The Tanzanian health sector is hence characterized by a fragmented landscape of health information systems silos, where lack of shared services has resulted in duplication and redundancy of data. The fragmentation serves as a monumental barrier in achieving interoperability between systems to be scaled across the continuum of care. The Tanzanian government also acknowledged the absence of systems crucial for improved care delivery, and the lack of adequate definition of data and technical standards [32]. As a result, the Ministry of Health, in consultation with stakeholders, ranging from local health information systems managers to the United States Agency for International Development, decided to develop the Tanzanian National eHealth Strategy [32]. The purpose of the strategy is to guide the deployment of resources to facilitate the transformation towards ICT use in the health sector. To drive this transformation, the Ministry of Health and the health sector stakeholders agreed to incorporate the building of a nationwide health information exchange (HIE) as a pivotal segment of the strategy. The strategy emphasizes how nationwide HIE can help provide a better understanding of the overall delivery of health services within the health sector, in addition to reducing the risk of fragmentation and duplication of effort. On this, the head of the HIE efforts in Tanzania commented as follows in an interview:

> "We want our different systems to share information so it's easier to access information. We want to decrease the complexity. Different systems use different attributes, which makes it difficult to maintain the relevant information."

He further commented that, for creating their national HIE, they "…wanted to adopt standards that have already been adopted elsewhere". They therefore turned to OpenHIE as their standards were already adopted in a few other developing countries, such as Rwanda and South Africa. Members of the OpenHIE community therefore helped the country in writing and developing the strategy, and the implementation of OpenHIE components became central to the overall strategy.

The plan for implementing national HIE was finally established in 2015. In the process of determining its high-level requirement, the OpenHIE framework was used to analyze the current landscape of nationally-scaled information systems, with the intention to leverage what currently exists. It was discovered that several of the components of the OpenHIE framework did not exist in Tanzania, including shared health records, a client registry, terminology services, a facility registry and an interoperability layer. Most importantly, they found that the most critical missing component was an interoperability layer allowing the seamless exchange of information across the systems, and a national data warehouse where information from several sources could be merged and used for analysis.

As a pilot, an architecture supporting data exchange within a national immunization information system was built, using the OpenHIE architectural framework. This experience is now being used to construct the Tanzanian HIE, which will serve all health use cases. Currently, the efforts for creating the Tanzanian HIE have proceeded from planning into the implementation phase. As of now, the facility registry is rolled out nationally, using the OpenHIE reference application, and is made interoperable with the national health management information system (DHIS2, which is another OpenHIE reference application).

The Philippines: In 2011, the government of the Philippines released The Philippine Development Plan [33] to serve as a guide for formulating policies and implementing development programs. The vision of the plan was to enable the government to "work systematically to give the Filipino people a better chance of finally finding their way out of poverty, inequality, and the poor state of human development" [33]. Guided by the development plan, the Department of Health formulated the National Objectives for Health 2011–2016 [34], in which they emphasized the need for consolidation of fragmented national health information systems. Working towards the national objectives, the Department of Health later developed the Philippine eHealth Strategic Framework and Plan 2014–2020 [35]. In this document, they described their vision for standardizing and integrating the national information systems into the Philippine Health Information Exchange (PHIE). In setting up the project for the PHIE, the OpenHIE community provided consultancy on several aspects, including governance, architecture and financial sustainability. The project finally included a technical strategy focused on using the OpenHIE architectural model as a foundational framework.

Today, the construction of the PHIE has been approved by a government body, and 800 000 US dollars have been allocated to issue a tender for a private vendor to run the PHIE. So far, two biddings have failed. While waiting for the full PHIE, the Department of Health and Philhealtha, an agency attached to the Department of Health, agreed to develop a simpler PHIE Lite version which only supports the exchange of outpatient benefit claims, and is not scalable for any other use cases. As of June 2017, an average of 20,000 transactions occurred in the PHIE Lite on a daily basis. At the technical level, PHIE Lite is not using any of the standards promoted by OpenHIE. As put by one of the leaders of the efforts in the Philippines:

> "Technically speaking, I would not say that PHIE is an OpenHIE implementation. I would say that it is an OpenHIE inspired HIE. The reason is that it doesn't use any of the IHE profiles that OpenHIE recommends."

However, while the Philippines may not be strictly following the OpenHIE architectural framework, it is evident that OpenHIE has influenced the PHIE, and the agendas of the Department of Health, as further commented by the interviewee from the Philippines:

> "Even though there are no traces of OpenHIE interfaces in the PHIE, one might suggest that there is influence from OpenHIE. You can see that some things are very similar to the way in which OpenHIE labels things, like client registry, facility registry, provider registry, share health record and stuff like that [...] I think what OpenHIE introduced to the Department of Health is the need to have foundational registries [...] and that these registries should be connected to support HIE. That was not a thought that came to the Department of Health before OpenHIE [...] The Philippines is adopting some of its features it finds to be foundational and are exploring ways to adapt the interfaces for a HIE."

In other words, OpenHIE has introduced two central ideas to the Philippines: the idea of foundational registries, and the idea of HIE.

5 Discussion

In the following sections, we conceptualize the standards offered by OpenHIE as a fluid standard, and discuss how their fluid nature relates to local development.

5.1 The OpenHIE Standards a Fluid Standard

What OpenHIE offers is not just technical specifications, but, rather, a "standardized package" [17]. This standardized package contains a variety of necessary components of different types: an architectural framework, reference applications, implementation guides and interoperability profiles. In this section, we conceptualize the OpenHIE standardized package as a fluid standard, and discuss its characteristics.

No clear boundaries is possibly the most important and defining characteristic of a fluid standard [18]. Boundaries are defined by all that is needed to make the technology work. This leads to the closely related characteristic of *multiple identities*, and can be exemplified by asking the question, "What is OpenHIE?" It is a stack of standards, an architectural framework, a software stack, a community of practice and a consultancy service, among others. Each identity has its own boundaries that are defined by what is needed for the technology to work as that identity. The boundaries are different for each identity, and change over time. For example, the community promotes a set of open standards to countries, and not the enforcement of any particular requirements for implementation. The OpenHIE architectural framework is technology agnostic and flexible. This means that no matter how the countries choose to combine the OpenHIE standardized package with the local information systems profiles, it is still referred to as an OpenHIE implementation. This ability allows OpenHIE to exist as a standard, and also accommodate constraints in the context contributed to its transferability. The lack of boundaries makes it easy to extend the standard when new requirements have emerged [18]. The multiple identities of OpenHIE also show, as different aspects have been of prime importance for various groups of actors. For instance, in Tanzania it has been viewed as an architectural framework for HIE, and in the Philippines as a set of functional registries and interoperability profiles. What aided in terms of its internationalization, was that it carried the identity of allegedly being a success story from Rwanda (as RHIE), which other nations seek to emulate. The fact that a standard can accommodate different identities adds to its *robustness* in terms of satisfying more owners and encompassing different boundaries [18]. In addition, the fact that the OpenHIE can mean different things to different people enables it to be relevant for multiple actors and situations.

The *mixture* that composes the OpenHIE standardized package consists of an architectural framework, reference applications, implementation guides and interoperability profiles. Along with the boundaries, it is a mixture that is continuously composed and recomposed, with different parts having differing significance to different groups, and over time. For example, both the architectural framework and its components have changed over time. A continuously changing mixture also contributes to the *robustness* of the standard [18].

Continuity is an important characteristic, allowing the standards to be adopted and adapted while still being a part what existed previously. The OpenHIE standardized package is characterized by continuity, with its ability to be adapted to installed bases of the developing countries.

Dissolving ownership, an important characteristic of fluid standards, enables various actors to take ownership, make a contribution, and then release the ownership. This is very much in alignment with the mission of OpenHIE and the way in which they work: "Our mission is to improve the health of the underserved through the open collaborative development and support of *country driven*, large scale health information sharing architectures." [13]. For example, the work from Rwanda was released as a global standard for other countries to use. In this manner, dissolving membership allows the standard to move from one country to another.

We have summarized these characteristics of OpenHIE in Table 4, below.

Table 4. Summary of the fluid characteristics of OpenHIE sources.

Characteristics of OpenHIE as a fluid standard	
No clear boundaries	Open standards, no particular requirements for implementation, technology agnostic and flexible
Multiple identities	For some, a stack of standards; for others, an architectural framework, a set of functional registries or interoperability profiles
Mixtures	Architectural framework, reference applications, implementation guides and interoperability profiles
Robustness	Continuously composed and recomposed with different parts having different significance to different groups and over time
Continuity	Building on the installed base
Dissolving ownership	Continuously dissolving ownership by countries

By conceptualizing the OpenHIE standards as a fluid standard, we illustrate the usefulness of the concept in explaining the characteristics that make standards fit to an increasingly complex and dynamic global world [18]. Our empirical case shows how standards are used as a common point of interest [2], where a wide variety of actors are co-joined for standardization, for the purpose of development. This, we argue in the following section, is a specific way of doing standardization, made possible by the fluid nature of the standard.

5.2 Fluid Standards and Local Development

What is the relation between global standards and local development? In this section, this research question is addressed with reference to OpenHIE and the work of Castells and Escobar.

Central to the definition of development by Castells is the process "… by which humans, as a collective, enhance their wellbeing" [12]. Good health is essential for people's wellbeing, and the goal of OpenHIE is to support improved health outcomes; therefore, it can be viewed as a coordinated approach for development, where standards act as a common point of interest bringing together a wide range of actors – non-governmental organizations, research institutes, consultancy firms, software firms – for the purpose of development [2]. For the member organizations this is beneficial, as it provides a coordinated leeway into new markets, allowing them to seize a significant competitive advantage [8]. Related to this, one of the OpenHIE community members commented as follows:

> "It's also a way of marketing. You have highly profiled people going [to] the ministry of health saying: 'You need these components, you need a facility registry' and so forth, 'and the U.S. government will pay for it'. At the same time, the country might have an up-to-date de facto list of facilities in their national health management information systems, which is not labeled as a facility registry. All of a sudden, a need for development aid is created, and money from donors and new actors are invested into making a new facility registry".

Thus, while the purpose of OpenHIE might be to do coordinated development through global standards, it might also be used as a coordinated approach to development spending. Another OpenHIE member put it this way: "You can see a group of organizations coming together to produce something for the purpose of them gaining contracts". On the one hand, this might make developing countries dependent on the OpenHIE member organizations – i.e. for implementation, training and maintenance of ICTs. On the other hand, it is also beneficial for the developing countries. The lack of coordination between international actors usually makes the planning and coordination of ICT investments challenging, which in turn is often the root cause of fragmented information systems. OpenHIE has the potential to bring harmony to the often chaotic procurement processes in developing countries, by coordinating the efforts of the international actors. At the same time, it allows developing countries to draw on global ICT developments and best practices by leveraging on the OpenHIE software package. As such, our findings support the argument by Castells [15] that ICTs, and in our case global ICT standards in particular, has potentiality that allows developing countries to leapfrog stages of economic growth modernization; however, it does not necessarily cultivate innovation within the developing countries, as one of the OpenHIE community members put it: "They have to swallow something that has been created outside".

Escobar [16] advocated that knowledge should be created and disseminated from the bottom up. He called for a reformulation of the concept of development, which considers the local discourses of progress and development, the prevailing power structures, and indigenous forms of knowledge, in each country. If the local context is not considered, Escobar argued, investments aimed at development are bound to fail. The fluid nature of the OpenHIE standards, through their openness and flexibility, we argue, makes them better apt in considering the aspects of the local context than the traditional top-down driven standards. The flexibility allows the standards to have multiple identities, and to be used in many ways and contexts, and the openness allows them to have no clear boundaries. These characteristics are defining in contributing to local development, as called upon by Escobar. They allow the developing countries to adopt and adapt standards (as in done in Tanzania), or use them as inspiration (as done in the Philippines), and make them fit to the local context and their discourses, power structures and knowledge; however, this presupposes that there are local resources with the capacity and knowledge to do so.

The openness of the standards also means that anyone can participate in the standardization processes, and our empirical case shows that the developing countries themselves are not actively participating in the making of the standards. Rather, the OpenHIE community members, mostly residing in the Global North, develop the standards based on their experiences in working with the developing countries. The question then becomes how well the local contexts are reflected in the global standards, given that they are made by exogenous actors. Future research should therefore examine the contexts in greater detail, and try to further understand their relationship with global ICT standards.

6 Conclusion

By describing OpenHIE as a fluid standard, this paper attempts to bring new insights into how global standards are related to local development. We argue that our case gives evidence that global standards can be used as a common point of interest for coordinated development, where a wide variety of actors can work towards reducing fragmentation of health information systems in developing countries, with the ultimate goal of better health. Central to this, we argue, lies the fluid nature of OpenHIE, which allows it to be globally and locally relevant. As such, we contribute to the standardization literature by applying and expanding the concept of fluid standards, and contribute to the development literature by showing the relationship between global standards and development. We believe that our findings are relevant to deal with the issue of fragmentation of information systems in areas other than health, such as agriculture, education and related government services. We acknowledge that the study is limited in terms of scope, with the study being conducted in only two countries. A potential follow-up study should therefore involve collecting data from more countries.

References

1. Silva, L., Figueroa, B.E.: Institutional intervention and the expansion of ICTs in Latin America: the case of Chile. Inf. Technol. People **15**(1), 8–25 (2002)
2. El Sayed, H., Westrup, C.: Egypt and ICTs: how ICTs bring national initiatives, global organizations and local companies together. Inf. Technol. People **16**(1), 76–92 (2003)
3. Avgerou, C., Walsham, G.: Information Technology in Context: Studies from the Perspective of Developing Countries. Ashgate Publishing Company, Brookfield (2001)
4. Bhatnagar, S., Mayuri, O.: Social implications of computers in developing countries (1992)
5. Madon, S., Krishna, S.: The digital challenge: information technology in the development context. Ashgate (2003)
6. Odera-Straub, M.: Global Information Technology and Socio-Economic Development. Ivy League Pub, Nashua (1996)
7. Walsham, G., Sahay, S.: Research on information systems in developing countries: current landscape and future prospects. Inf. Technol. Dev. **12**(1), 7–24 (2006)
8. Lyytinen, K., King, J.L.: Standard making: a critical research frontier for information systems research. Mis Q. **30**, 405–411 (2006)
9. Spivak, S.M., Brenner, F.C.: Standardization Essentials: Principles and Practice. CRC Press, Boca Raton (2001)
10. Nielsen, P., Sæbø, J.I.: Three strategies for functional architecting: cases from the health systems of developing countries. Inf. Technol. Dev. **22**(1), 134–151 (2016)
11. Braa, J., Sahay, S.: Integrated Health Information Architecture: Power to the Users: Design. Development and Use. Matrix Publishers, New Delhi (2012)
12. Castells, M.: Rethinking Development in the Global Information Age. Higher Education and Development. African Minds, Cape Town (2014)
13. OpenHIE. https://ohie.org/. Accessed 19 Sept 2017
14. Castells, M.: The Rise of the Network Society, the Information Age: Economy, Society and Culture, vol. I. Blackwell Publishers, Malden (1996)
15. Castells, M.: Information technology, globalization and social development. United Nations Research Institute for Social Development Geneva (1999)
16. Escobar, A.: Encountering Development: The Making and Unmaking of the Third World. Princeton University Press, Princeton (2011)
17. Fujimura, J.H.: Crafting science: standardized packages, boundary objects, and "translation". Sci. Pract. Cult. **168**, 168–169 (1992)
18. Hanseth, O., Nielsen, P.: Fluid Standards: A Conceptualization of the Changing World of Standards Based on a Case Study of an m-Commerce platform (in review)
19. Brunsson, N., Rasche, A., Seidl, D.: The dynamics of standardization: three perspectives on standards in organization studies. Organ. Stud. **33**(5–6), 613–632 (2012)
20. West, J.: How open is open enough? Melding proprietary and open source platform strategies. Res. Policy **32**(7), 1259–1285 (2003)
21. Hanseth, O., Bygstad, B., Ellingsen, G., Johannessen, L.K., Larsen, E.: ICT standardization strategies and service innovation in health care (2012)
22. Hanseth, O., Monteiro, E., Hatling, M.: Developing information infrastructure: the tension between standardization and flexibility. Sci. Technol. Human Values **21**(4), 407–426 (1996)
23. Abbate, J.: Inventing the Internet. MIT Press, Cambridge (2000)
24. De Laet, M., Mol, A.: The Zimbabwe bush pump: mechanics of a fluid technology. Soc. Stud. Sci. **30**(2), 225–263 (2000)

25. Braa, J., Hanseth, O., Heywood, A., Mohammed, W., Shaw, V.: Developing health information systems in developing countries: the flexible standards strategy. Mis Q. **31**, 381–402 (2007)
26. Timmermans, S., Epstein, S.: A world of standards but not a standard world: toward a sociology of standards and standardization. Ann. Rev. Sociol. **36**, 69–89 (2010)
27. Walsham, G.: Interpretive case studies in IS research: nature and method. Eur. J. Inf. Syst. **4**(2), 74–81 (1995)
28. Walsham, G.: Doing interpretive research. Eur. J. Inf. Syst. **15**(3), 320–330 (2006)
29. Klein, H.K., Myers, M.D.: A set of principles for conducting and evaluating interpretive field studies in information systems. MIS Q. **23**, 67–93 (1999)
30. About OpenHIE. https://ohie.org/about/ - history. Accessed 23 Feb 2017
31. The United Republic of Tanzania Ministry of Health, C.D., Gender, Elderly and Children (MoHCDGEC): Health Sector Strategic Plan III July 2009–June 2015 (2009)
32. The United Republic of Tanzania Ministry of Health, C.D., Gender, Elderly and Children (MoHCDGEC): Tanzania National eHealth Strategy July 2015–June 2020 (2015)
33. Philippine Development Plan 2011–2016. http://www.neda.gov.ph/2013/10/21/philippine-development-plan-2011-2016. Accessed 26 Nov 2017
34. Department of Health Republic of the Philippines: National Objectives for Health 2011–2016 (2011)
35. Department of Health Republic of the Philippines: Philippines eHealth Strategic Framework and Plan 2014–2020 (2014)

Enablers of Egalitarian Participation: Case Studies in Underserved Communities in South Africa. Processes of Creativity "Not for the Sake of it"

Maria Rosa Lorini(✉), Wallace Chigona, and Malcolm Garbutt

University of Cape Town, Rondebosch, Cape Town 7701, South Africa
mariarosalorini@gmail.com

Abstract. Although ICT4D impacts peoples' lives, drivers for change are often from a self-serving perspective, and not sustainable, due to lack of buy-in in the affected communities. To overcome this, ICT4D must move from laboratory approaches and collaboration to grassroots innovation, with communities designing their use of ICT. This study presents three cases of ICT4D projects in underserved communities in Cape Town, South Africa, with the aim of determining enablers of egalitarian participation to support grassroots innovations. Egalitarian participation encourages acquiring self-confidence and empowerment, while remaining motivated to be part of the process. In the processes analysed, an emergent approach, characterised by openness, relaxed rules and flexibility, allowed participants to work on their skills to increase confidence in their capabilities, and to evaluate new opportunities. The primary outcome of an approach based on relationships, and not on design rules, promoted inclusive participation. Collectives engaged in processes, and developed self-determined behaviours and cohesion in supporting their communities. The social goal of the activities, where creativity developed 'not for the sake of it' backed the main aim of the egalitarian approach, involved the community and created ownership. Analysis of the cases highlighted methodological patterns that could potentially be replicated, and which are presented as enablers for egalitarian participation in underserved communities. In contrast to the approach of purely supplying solutions, a reflexive approach, permeated by the principles of mutual learning and solidarity, was observed, which evolved into grassroots innovations.

Keywords: Co-design · Community participation · Co-creation
Inclusive participation · Grassroots

1 Introduction

Information and communications technology (ICT) has been promoted in developing countries, for improving the well-being of underserved residents. The acknowledged term is ICT for development (ICT4D), and strives to improve lives through new communication means, access to knowledge and knowledge sharing. Paradoxically, the

K. Krauss et al. (Eds.): IDIA 2018, CCIS 933, pp. 156–170, 2019.
https://doi.org/10.1007/978-3-030-11235-6_11

neediest citizens are unable to afford the technology, while having limited information processing and knowledge sharing capabilities [1]. Although numerous organisations, especially from developed nations, propose to assist in ICT4D with the aim of making the world better [1], Heeks [2] indicates that their involvement is from self-serving interests, rather than concern for the recipients; nevertheless, Heeks [3] observes a move from talk to action in the literature.

To counteract the imposition of technology from outsiders, Walsham [1] proposes engaging with grassroots people and the creation of communities of practice. Similarly, Heeks [2] observes three levels of ICT4D involvement: (i) Laboratory activities, done on behalf of the community (they may not provide an appropriate solution for the community, however); (ii) Collaborative activities which involve collaboration between ICT4D practitioners and engaged community members (the engaged members may not be representative of the community, however, and the solution may not be suitable for the majority); (iii) Grassroots innovation (the approach is driven from within the community, who adopt, adapt or create technology suitable to their environment).

In this paper, three projects undertaken with inhabitants of underserved communities are discussed from an egalitarian participative perspective. The co-design methodology verified the potential for an egalitarian participation, and succeeded in generating grassroots innovations in cross-cultural environments fraught with inequalities. The aim of reporting on three studies is to illuminate enablers that may be helpful in similar underserved community projects where the roles of experts and non-experts are assumed, and where the sustainability of the projects is strictly connected with ownership by the communities [4]. Once the community participants emerged as designers and creators of the activities, the external participants could move aside in confidence that the positive outcomes of their engagement as active participant citizens would persist. At the same time, the researchers reached a better understanding of the world, with lower harm and improved benefit for the communities [5]. The initial collaborative approach ensured that the aims, processes and activities of the projects were not pre-determined, but emerged through the interaction between the research support team, the community participants and the technological artefacts.

When working in cross-cultural environments, where researchers and specialists belong to a culture different to the context, the reasons for participation and intentions of the local communities, in combination with their shared cultural values, need to be identified and evaluated before deploying an ICT approach [6]. Literature shows the importance of considering differences in skills, technical knowledge, cultures, value systems and power relations between all the participants [7]. This is particularly relevant when using participatory design approaches where researchers are not ethnographers, but actors who want to influence the process and transform reality [8]. The capacity of a professional to facilitate encounters, initiate processes and promote activities, is an example of representation of the balance of power. Finlay calls this 'essentially unequal relationships.' [9] (p. 220); nevertheless, 'the failure to acknowledge the positive or negative operations of researcher power in PAR [Participatory Action Research] does not mean it disappears, but that such recognition is sent underground' [10] (p. 97). Conscious of the power dynamics and the ethical stance to not harm but benefit the participants [11], the researchers and the practitioners involved in the project looked for ways to minimise possible adverse connotations linked with authority, positioning themselves as participants, the same as the local actors, with evolving roles. At the same time, they maximised the possibilities for inclusive involvement of the community members to move towards a grassroots approach, characterised by the role of the local actors – not only as users or co-designers, but as ideators, creators and owners of the projects.

The evolution from collaborative to grassroots resonates with the egalitarian approach informed by Blevins and colleagues [12], who sought to implement an egalitarian collaboration between stakeholders, and to shift the balance of power away from the researchers. The approach does not assume the elimination of differences amongst researcher and researched [13], but builds on the strengths of each participant. The enablers presented in this paper suggest ways to facilitate similar egalitarian and inclusive participation, at the same time transforming the role and position of the community members and the external professionals.

Through the analysis of the processes, this paper sought to answer the question:

"What factors enable egalitarian participation in ICT4D projects in underserved communities?"

In the next section, a background to the egalitarian participatory approach is provided, followed in Sect. 3 by a description of the research setting, and then of the methodology (Sect. 4). Section 5 provides an overview of the three projects from the initial collaborative approach. Section 6 explores the evolution of the projects from collaborative to grassroots, before a discussion of the observed enablers in the seventh section, and the conclusion.

2 Degrees of Participation – Towards Egalitarianism

The literature on participation has evolved over the years and, with it, its terminology; nevertheless, it remains possible to retrieve the essential differences connected with the degree of participation. Arnstein's ladder of citizen participation [14] indicates degrees of participation of users as subjects to be observed, informants, evaluators, partners in designing in a participatory approach, or as creators. The levels of involvement of stakeholders in a project are expressions of their '…power in determining the plan and program' [14] (p. 216).

In the User-Centred Design literature, participants are referred to as users, particularly in connection with an innovative methodology for implementing ICT projects [15]. The degree of participation resides in the users' initial involvement in disclosing their needs [16]. Users are evaluators of design which may be for the end-user, by the end-user, or for second-tier users (end-user of the user) [17]; nonetheless, the production and design solution phases rely on ICT professionals.

Participatory Design (PD) originated in the 1970s in the Scandinavian regions, from a political agenda connected to the computerisation of the workplaces [18]. In PD, the designer and the users are the foremost participants in the process of mutual learning and 'reflection-in-action' [19]. Distinct roles with a specific focus on ICT characterise this methodology, with participants gaining independence and becoming involved in the decision-making process [20]. The central ideas of PD are shared with those of co-design and the North American tradition of cooperative design [21].

Developed in the 1990s in the United States, the co-design approach sought the engagement of involved actors as joint problem solvers, and not merely as informants. As a design discipline, however, there are distinct differences between 'designers and people not trained in design' [22] (p. 6). A meta-design process may be followed to bridge the gap between PD and co-design, and to empower users as active designers [23]. Emergent co-creation literature aspires to reach the highest degree of participation, where every participant is a creator of the outcome [24]. Despite not being defined as egalitarian, the process starts to question the roles and definitions of the participants. Sanders and Stappers [22] underline an evolution of the role of the users who become co-designers in the creative process, where the roles of the stakeholders are reshaped. They illustrate the connection with Transformation Design and Service Design approaches [25, 26], in which people are involved in a creative and innovative learning environment, focused on changing processes and power relations [27].

The case studies in this paper were informed by co-design methodologies. Although the project started with an exploratory phase of focus groups, the design phases emerged from the encounters. The commitment of the groups to solve social issues, their openness to experimentation with ICTs, the use of their skills, and the desire to strengthen their networks for collective scope, let the process evolve into grassroots innovation (GI) (cf. the characteristic of GI highlighted by Hussain [28]). As expressed by Hussain, "GIs face difficulties to connect with skilled people, research institutes, and advisers' [28] (p. 977). For this reason, the researchers valued and enacted an egalitarian participatory approach, based on mutual learning, learning by doing, and peer-to-peer learning.

3 Context and Participants – Townships and Active Groups

The participants of the activities are from Philippi and Khayelitsha, two well-known underserved townships in South Africa. Both are part of metropolitan Cape Town, and are regulated by the housing policy of the city, with a shared history of being Former Black Authorities areas; they have more than half a million inhabitants and are growing. Most inhabitants live in the informal settlements, with only 44% living in formal dwellings in Philippi and 45% in Khayelitsha [29]. As of 2011, half the population live below the poverty line and depend on government grants [30].

The main researcher met and collaborated with people who have been part of some groups – in particular, women and youth. As the townships grow, groups of women form [31] around survival issues, such as the need to support the most vulnerable members of the community. Other groups form around traditional costumes which are significant in respect of culture, and predominant in events such as funeral planning [32]. Over the years, some of these groups connected through networks and social movements with lobbying and advocacy agendas [33].

Youth groups are also very common, but, unlike the women's groups, they are more flexible and less stable in formation and evolution, due to the extreme unemployment and limited mobility. National unemployment for South Africa is officially

26.7% [34], but noticeably higher in the more underserved communities. An informal survey, in 2011, of the socio-economic characteristics of youth groups aged between 15 and 25 years, revealed that the youth groups formed for diverse purposes, often for entertainment connected with sport, music or other performing arts.

Over the past decade, the main researcher has worked in the two communities and mapped 100 community groups, and collaborated with them in a series of social activities aimed at forming communities of belonging. The relationship of trust established helped her during formal and recreational gathering occasions. The initial research phase, based on ethnographic studies, minimised the risks associated with assumptions that the researcher may make based on previous experience and expectations of the community [35].

4 Methodology

With the support of local facilitators, a limited number of women's and youth groups were selected for the research project. The main researcher attended regular gatherings in the communities, and subsequently devoted time to analysing the interviews with focus groups [36] and triangulating the analysis with external stakeholders' views and approaches [37]. The triangulation was based on individual interviews done at the beginning of the project, and after the design activities. To maintain clarity of purpose, at each meeting everybody was reminded of the research approach, the limited facilities available, and the choice to work without a predetermined process. In particular, the main researcher had to differentiate the ongoing research from the past development activities guided by the logical framework approach 'that is underpinned by ideas of pre-planning, and predetermined what successful outcomes will look like' [38] (p. 2).

During February and March 2014, in-depth interviews and focus groups took place involving randomly selected active groups. A critical discourse analysis process [39] was followed to evaluate the relationships the groups had with technology, in particular with smartphones, computers and social media. To gain further insight into the groups' use of ICTs, a collective approach using digital storytelling technology (DST) was used [40]. This led to new ideas being generated by the community groups and collaboratively developed: members of a community radio station expressed their desire to have a website; young artists evaluated the opportunities offered by a digital platform; and, representatives of a women's network, from now on called the Mamas, expressed the desire to deepen their scarce ICT skills.

5 Co-creation Processes

The processes of co-creation are presented here as case studies. In Sect. 6 the evolving participation of the community members is explored, and in Sect. 7 the enablers are summarised as a contribution to the theoretical discussion.

5.1 Co-design Workshops for Computer Literacy with Mamas

The groups of Mamas belonged to a network of women sensitive to the social issues. The results of the initial exploratory discourse analysis showed similarities between the groups and the limited use of ICT. Rudimentary ICT was used to create a DST video with the active involvement of the main researcher as a method of giving voice to the groups; however, the Mamas were more interested in the opportunity of using the technology themselves and requested the main researcher to organise ICT training.

For the training, the main researcher contacted an organisation well established in the neighbouring communities: the RLab. Underlying the training methodology is the idea of an intergenerational exchange between mothers and younger trainers and peer-to-peer learning approaches.

The one-week basic computer training started with a hand- and nail-pampering session to put all the trainees at ease in front of a computer. The main researcher invited some of the youth from the same community as the Mamas to assist with the adaptation of the curriculum of the training to meet the requirements of the trainees, and to match their way of learning. In the beginning, the facilitators were considered by the trainers as trainees, interested in learning a replicable methodology. During the days of training, their role as translators, required as the community predominantly speaks an African language which is not spoken by the researchers or most of the RLabs trainers, evolved into that of mediators. The youth found ways to explain to the Mamas concepts that sounded too difficult for them, and showed the trainers ways to encourage the Mamas to express themselves publicly.

From the beginning, it was clear that the younger women were more familiar with working with ICT; nevertheless, all the Mamas persisted, and when asked to bring a smartphone for training, nine out of the ten Mamas arrived with one, mostly borrowed from other community members.

During 2016, the younger Mamas engaged in a series of follow-up training at the RLabs centre, after which some of them became facilitators, while the older women actively supported the training by enrolling new participants.

5.2 Co-design of the Youth Network Website

The Youth Network project commenced in 2014 with focus groups and interviews, and included groups active in street theatre, performing arts, sport and traditional music, sometimes with educational scopes. Specific interests in ICTs emerged, directly related to their current needs – such as the recording of their music. Similar to the Mama's project, the ethnographic study was deepened through the production of a DST video. The idea of a music video to solicit sponsorships for their art evolved into the production of a short documentary on social issues and youth collaborations.

The production gave the opportunity to the main researcher to facilitate, at the beginning of 2015, meetings between the leaders of several youth groups. Over time, the meetings saw the participation of groups' members and not only leaders. Two main ideas emerged: (i) the organisation of events in the community to perform and discuss social issues; and (ii) the creation of a website to showcase their artistic activities and promote events. During discussions, they exhibited a commitment to their community and the desire to continue their activities in their area, or, as they put it, they wanted to put ‘Philippi on the map’.

The process of organising a music event served to evaluate both the cohesion of the network and the commitment of the groups to take responsibilities, as well as to share resources. For the creation of a website, the participants worked in groups. A web designer helped the main researcher to facilitate the design process, and to train some youth in the maintenance and use of the website.

During 2016, the use of social media grew dramatically. The Youth Network Facebook page registered 400 followers, while one of the internal groups, ‘Poetics not for the sake of it’, reached 1 300 ‘likes’. Some of the leaders, meanwhile, registered for software developer training and started new projects, keeping alive their passions: organising events and creating music. The activities sensitised the communities around social issues and inclusive approaches, while developing the artistic passion of the youth.

5.3 Co-design of the Community Radio Station Website

In April 2014, one of the youth groups expressed a wish to create a community radio station; three months later the radio station was on air without a broadcast licence. To raise funds for their project, a DST video was created involving members of the community and volunteers, supported by the main researcher. To increase visibility and stable support while adding a professional look, the directors of the radio station expressed a desire to create a website. At the beginning of 2015, two professional journalists and a web designer joined the project. The professionals suggested including other members of the community, such as aspiring journalists, listeners and volunteers, to hear what the community valued. The co-design workshops with an extended group began in April 2015. To evaluate what could be included on the website, the professional journalists led a discussion on the types of radio stations (a commercial or service, or community) and around the ethics of journalism. After two months, a picture of a social design experience emerged. The discussions showed a level of consistency and coherence between the needs of the community, the desires of the journalists and the choices of the radio directors.

Subsequent workshops were organised to co-design the website. Working in groups, the participants presented their proposals and debated over administrative responsibilities, business opportunities, speed of the website, quality of the material and, most importantly, the possibility of online streaming. Two options were evaluated: either use podcasts, or have the radio live. Due to high connectivity costs and usability, this part of the design project evolved slowly, with trials and tests down over a period of months. In October 2015, a smartphone application that enabled broadcasting from outside the radio station via the website, was successfully tested. In 2016, the founding members of the radio applied for a broadcasting licence. To avoid problems as a pirate radio and reduce visibility, they chose to stop the analogue radio production, and communicate all the news via the social media. One year later, against the odds due to bandwidth restrictions, the radio station obtained their broadcasting licence.

6 Evolving Roles in the Three Community Social Processes

The roles of community participants, external professionals and researchers evolved and adapted over time. Exploring how the participation developed provides insight into the egalitarian approach beneficial for grassroots innovation, Table 1 summarises the activities undertaken, the role played by the different participants and their evolution.

Table 1. The roles of the participants in the three case-studies

Case-studies activities and roles	Mamas' groups	Youth network	Radio station
Co-design activities	ICTs training on: Keyboard exercises Gmail Search Netiquette Smartphones Blog Facebook	Co-design workshop on events organisation; Co-design workshop to create an interactive map website and digital platform	Co-design workshop on journalism, ethics and editorial board; Co-design workshop to create the radio website; Co-design workshop for the online radio and outside broadcasting
Role of community members	Mamas: initiator of the activity and learners; Youth: translator and facilitators	Leaders of the groups: initiator of the activity and decision-makers; Members of the groups: co-designers of the products	Funders of the radio: initiator and decision-makers; Local journalists: learners and co-designers; Local technicians: learners and co-designers
Role of external professionals	RLabs N.P.O.: trainers	Web-designer: workshop facilitator and trainer	Foreigner journalists: trainers; Web-designer: trainer
Role of the researcher	Organiser and Participant observant	Facilitator	Coordinator
Follow-up activities managed by the community members	Second training with another organisation to improve; Training for co-trainers at RLabs; Training in new ICT skills	Creation of the Philippi Music Project production (recording studio in a second-hand shipping container); Registration of the Bridge Experience (NPO devoted to organise cross-cultural events)	Licence request; Creation of an N.P.O. to keep on supporting the community; Collaboration with other radios for professionalisation
New role of the community members	Networkers (they found other stakeholders); Co-trainers; Developers of online activities; Facilitators and supporters for new members	Networkers (through crowdfunding and connections among more youth groups and with the University); Producers and event organisers for youth groups	Professional radio station producers; N.P.O. managers and event fundraisers

6.1 Training the Mamas

The idea of computer training among the Mamas was generated by them after limited exposure to new ICTs; the one-week training was designed by people external to the communities, and adapted to the needs of the participants.

Once the training started, the Mamas attended conscientiously. They showed engaged participation, being present on time every day despite lack of transport, and staying until late, despite their everyday household chores. Even though none of the Mamas possessed a computer, and, in most cases, even a smartphone on which to exercise and revise their new skills, they followed each step and tried every application and technology taught them; furthermore, their effort to overcome the linguistic barriers was evidence of their willingness to learn. As the interface programs were not written in their language, they had to memorise much of the content.

Being aware of their still limited skills and exposure to technologies, and needing to maintain the level of knowledge, the Mamas requested follow-up training. Some enrolled in new computer literacy training courses, and became facilitators to support other women in their community. This led to evolution of their role, and participation increased with the growth of their new skills.

The enthusiasm of the Mamas showed their engagement, and was commented on by all the non-community participants during the follow-up interviews. The organisers of the training were impressed by the participation of the Mamas, being on average older than their usual trainees, coming from deprived areas, and with limited literacy skills. The trainers maintained a flexible schedule, and provided more space for the translators to explain and integrate concepts, instead of merely translating.

The role of the main researcher was to identify the needs and to find a balance between community requests and resources. Over time, the role of the researcher decreased, with increasing involvement of the community, to the extent that the main researcher did not actively participate in the follow-up activities. Local facilitators supported the Mamas in searching for new opportunities, such as the creation of a WhatsApp group to coordinate their activities, and the request for subsequent training. In this way, the Mamas succeed in engaging more women and in developing new ideas to support their community better (e.g. learning online craft selling and children security online).

6.2 The Youth Network Website

The grassroots approach was evident in the Youth Network website creation, where the process was driven almost entirely by the youth themselves. The involvement of the main researcher started with focus groups and interviews with individual groups. The evolution of their idea to create a music video to the creation of a short motivational documentary and presentation of artists' collaborations was the occasion to meet and generate new brainstorming over possible activities, such as events and the creation of a website where to sponsor them.

When a digital interactive mapping idea emerged, the other phases for a website flowed naturally from this. At the same time, the roles of the participants changed. At first, only representatives of each group were present, but during later sessions additional members became involved. The roles of organiser, publisher, networker and fundraiser emerged; although the participation of additional members created problems in the time frame of the process, it also showed the general interest of the community, and supported the evolution of their ideas. The web designer and the researcher acted as facilitators during the workshops. Later, the web designer became the trainer for management and maintenance of the website.

The roles of the participants evolved with the increased use of social media; while the website required specialised skills, the Facebook pages enabled easier management and increased interaction with the community. The youth groups developed a process to connect with each other for events, while projecting a combined image for more significant proposals, showing their persistence to maintain the role of leaders, decision-makers and organisers of the youth at groups and network level.

6.3 The Radio Station Website

The founding members and the aspiring journalists of the radio station initiated the idea to create an analogue radio station in their community. They contacted the main researcher, who had interviewed those members months before, to assist with the creation of a DST video for fundraising for the radio station. This led to the idea of developing a website involving more members of the community. The driver for their involvement stemmed from a commitment to provide an excellent service to their community.

After the closure of the pirate activities, the members of the radio station kept the contact with involved stakeholders, and utilised their Facebook page to keep their followers updated on the status of the broadcasting licence application while doing live broadcasts through their website. With the high cost of the Internet, and limited possibilities for their community to listen to the radio via the web, they chose not to invest in that technology despite being aware of it and enthusiastic to learn about it.

Concerning the external participants' support, the professional journalists prepared their sessions in advance, and adapted these to the timing and requests of the local participants. Each workshop took longer than anticipated, and was guided by the requests of the radio station members. Working with volunteers, from both the radio station side and the professionals, supported this process of spontaneous evolution where nobody was pressurised by time, or by remuneration targets. The international journalists and the web designer recognised the commitment of the members of the radio station, the participation of the broader community, and perceived the possibilities of these activities to benefit the community. Consequently, they supported the project by dedicating more time than predicted – for instance, going over presentations several times, as the participants were not accustomed to taking notes, but listened and tried to remember and develop a shared knowledge as a group.

The main researcher moderated the workshops, organising the schedule and the optimisation of the procedures. She acted as a facilitator when needed, presenting examples connected with the local reality, and introducing the external stakeholders to the issues faced by the underserved community. The experts understood the priorities of the radio station, and supported the decisions of the founding members to dedicate time and resources to obtain the licence for an analogue radio station.

7 Enablers for Egalitarian Participation

The three case studies elaborated on the participation of the involved community members and of the external stakeholders, and the process of evolving of their roles to a grassroots approach. The evolution from collaborative (during the first phase of the activities) to grassroots (during and after the follow-up activities) is vital, as cross-cultural influences and power relations from external resources cannot be neutralised, and processes cannot rely on the same degree of participation [41]. To allow the roles to develop, the egalitarian participatory approach as a cross-cutting theme emerged as fundamental during all the processes.

The shift in power was possible due to the relaxed style and convivial approach of external participants, and it was enabled through supporting the improvement of self-confidence of the community participants in their capabilities. The participants made explicit choices to act in a manner that affected their surroundings and had an impact on the broader society. Shared decisions were then implemented as a collective of people in increasing independence from the researcher and awareness of the future options that could support their choices. This represented the climbing of the rungs of Arnstein's ladder of participation that can lead to active and motivated participation, where the imbalance of power is taken into account during decision-making [42].

The nine enablers of egalitarian participation, listed below, increased participants' awareness of available choices, and reduced their reliance on external stakeholders for decision-making. They can be classified as community enablers, methodological enablers and relational enablers.

I Community Enablers

Collective benefit focus appeared as the main enabler, which was a distinctive element of the three processes and which allowed the participants to engage in a transformative path. The persistence of the activities, at the time of writing, highlight the creativity 'not for the sake of it' that developed. The French student poster presented by Arnstein [14], 'I participate; you participate; … They profit' [14] (p. 216), shows how participation might not bring profit for those active and involved; thus, Arnstein highlights the need to redistribute power to gain real participation. The case studies show the top of the ladder 'citizen control' and evidence of the grassroots approach [2]. The focus on collective benefits acted like glue to maintain consistency, cohesion and an egalitarian approach on how to act and on sharing the results.

Collective Approaches: A multi-agent creation process with power-sharing enabled the community to collaboratively develop ICT solutions. The evolving processes revealed increasing potential after involvement from the larger community participating as another co-designer.

Grassroots Approach and Self-determination: Communities need to be involved in projects from the beginning, and they must attain and maintain decision-making capacities throughout the project. By building on the strengths of the participants, it is possible to realise the potential of the individuals in the community. The external participant cannot act as 'the designers'.

II Methodological Enablers

Cherishing the Process: The focus must remain on the process, as reducing focus to the outcome alone may shorten the time for the analysis, but allow essential elements or somebody's position to stay unnoticed and underestimated.

Alternative Methodologies and Flexibility: Methodologies studied for specific areas or groups require an ethnographic study and cultural sensitivity to address situations and needs. The flexible process presented here requires a longer time frame, but allows participants to follow their priorities, needs and desires. Flexibility implies the possibility to modify the procedures, and encourages the development of creativity. The apparent lack of structure and objectives allowed creativity to transpire and, while requiring more time to develop and evolve naturally, it showed the benefits of this investment and the possibility of sustainability due to the effective interest and ownership of projects by the people involved as creators and as beneficiaries. Such an approach may help the level of participation to be maintained – and even increase over time.

Minimise the Constraints: Participants with greater power must be ready to move out of their comfort zone to familiarise themselves and operate from the venues and in ways appropriate to the situation. In this study, each interview, meeting, training and workshop took place in the communities where the local participants live and were active.

III Relational Enablers

Long-term Relationship and Reciprocity: The establishment of a relationship of reciprocal knowledge and trust allowed the participants to externalise their thoughts, diminishing the embarrassment and shyness connected with the imbalance of technical expertise and professional skills.

Simplicity and Affordability: Effectiveness should be preferred over efficiency. Even if an interactive website or a digital radio station might appear easier to deploy, the needs of the participants and their intentions should take precedence.

Time is an essential enabler of the evolution of the processes. Time allows for the appropriation of the process, and remains a crucial factor for its concretisation. Each enabler requires time to concretise, to achieve its potential and to evolve and mature; for instance, the case studies were analysed over a period of three years.

The enablers present guidelines for community-driven participation in situated realities. The lofty aim of an egalitarian, democratic and inclusive participation evolves in distinct phases transforming the role and position of the community members and the external stakeholders throughout the process. The analysis of the case studies shows that processes guided by these enablers could spur initiative and impact on the sense of ownership of emerging creation in ICT4D. This is especially true when the desired outcome is to reinforce community agency and their control over their lives [14]. This will allow changing focus from a laboratory approach to a collaborative approach leading to grassroots initiatives [2].

8 Conclusion

In this study, three cases of ICT4D in underserved communities in Cape Town, South Africa are explored to determine enablers that supported their evolving into grassroots innovations. The research intended to empower participants to become independent creators of ICT-enabled processes [22] 'not for the sake of it', but to the benefit of the communities.

The activities developed [43] based on the intentions, desires, needs and dreams of the participants. The grassroots approach, combined with long-term knowledge of the communities, and an egalitarian approach, allowed the process to evolve, and for the participants to self-determine their roles. Considering the power imbalance and bias [44] of ICT4D, the concept of egalitarian participation resonates with the ideal proposed in co-creation literature of every person being a designer [45] (p. 31), and to move '…from highly hierarchical power relationships (e.g. researcher and participant) to more egalitarian relationships (e.g. co-researcher)' [27] (p. 281).

In the three cases, the participatory level of the community members evolved based on the skills, knowledge, roles and the desired outcomes of the groups in the community. The approach to creative activities [46] and participation in design and creation [47], is primarily afforded by the free, flexible and unconstrained nature of the evolving processes, and by the egalitarian nature of the relationships established. Analysis of the processes indicates that over time the participants gained self-confidence, were able to express and articulate their ideas, felt encouraged to set new goals, to move forward without the support of external participants, and to think of possibilities to work together for the benefit of their communities. From an initial stage of involvement in participatory design activities, the groups evolved to influencing their surroundings [48], thereby moving from collaborative to grassroots projects [2].

Acknowledgements. A sincere thank you to the community groups – Mamas, Youth and Community Radio, and the external professionals – the RLabs, the web designer and the journalists.

References

1. Walsham, G.: ICT4D research: reflections on history and future agenda. Inf. Technol. Dev. **23**(1), 18–41 (2017)
2. Heeks, R.: The ICT4D 2.0 Manifesto. University of Manchester. Institute for development policy and management. Development informatics group, Manchester, UK (2009)
3. Heeks, R.: Do information and communication technologies (ICTs) contribute to development? J. Int. Dev. **22**(5), 625–640 (2010)
4. Rey-Moreno, C., Sabiescu, A.G., Siya, M.J., Tucker, M.D.: Local ownership, exercise of ownership and moving from passive to active entitlement: a practice-led inquiry on a rural community network. J. Commun. Inform. **11**(2), 1–16 (2015)
5. Aluwihare-Samaranayake, D.: Ethics in qualitative research: A view of the participants' and researchers' world from a critical standpoint. Int. J. Qual. Methods **11**(2), 64–81 (2012)

6. Kapuire, G.K., Blake, E.: An attempt to merge local and technological paradigms in the digital representation of indigenous knowledge. In: Proceedings of the Indigenous Knowledge Technology Conference, pp. 28–72. IKTC, Windhoek, Namibia (2011)
7. Winschiers-Theophilus, H., Bidwell, N.J., Blake, E.: Community consensus: design beyond participation. Des. Issues **28**(3), 89–100 (2012)
8. Manzini, E., Rizzo, F.: Small projects/large changes: participatory design as an open participated process. CoDesign **7**(3–4), 199–215 (2011)
9. Finlay, L.: Negotiating the swamp: the opportunity and challenge of reflexivity in research practice. Qual. Res. **2**(2), 209–230 (2002)
10. Healy, K.: Participatory action research and social work: a critical appraisal. Int. Soc. Work **44**(1), 93–105 (2001)
11. Guillemin, M., Gillam, L.: Ethics, reflexivity, and "ethically important moments" in research. Qual. Inq. **10**(2), 261–280 (2004)
12. Blevins, D., Farmer, M.S., Edlund, C., Sullivan, G., Kirchner, J.E.: Collaborative research between clinicians and researchers: a multiple case study of implementation. Implementation Sci. **5**(76), 1–9 (2010)
13. Yost, M.R., Chmielewski, J.F.: Blurring the line between researcher and researched in interview studies: a feminist practice? Psychol. Women Q. **37**(2), 242–250 (2013)
14. Arnstein, S.R.: A ladder of citizen participation. J. Am. Inst. Planners **35**(4), 216–224 (1969)
15. Jokela, T., Iivari, N., Matero, J., Karukka, M.: The standard of user-centred design and the standard definition of usability: analyzing ISO 13407 against ISO 9241-11. In: Proceedings of the Latin American Conference on Human-Computer Interaction, pp. 53–60. ACM, New York (2003)
16. Maunder, A., Marsden, G., Tucker, W.D.: Evaluating the relevance of the "Real Access" criteria as a framework for rural HCI research. In: van Greunen, D. (ed.) 5th Conference on Human-Computer Interaction in Southern Africa. ACM, Cape Town (2006)
17. Eason, K.D.: User-centred design: for users or by users? Ergonomics **38**(8), 1667–1673 (1995)
18. Nygaard, K., Terje Bergo, O.: The trade unions-new users of research. Pers. Rev. **4**(2), 5–10 (1975)
19. Schön, D.A.: The Reflective Practitioner: How Professionals Think in Action. Basic Books, New York (1983)
20. Simonsen, J., Robertson, T.: Routledge International Handbook of Participatory Design. Routledgse, New York (2013)
21. Greenbaum, J., Hillsdale, N.J., Kying, M.: Design at Work: Cooperative Design of Computer Systems. Erlbaum Associates, Hillsdale (1991)
22. Sanders, E.B.N., Stappers, P.J.: Co-creation and the new landscapes of design. CoDesign **4**(1), 5–18 (2008)
23. Fischer, G., Giaccardi, E.: Meta-design: a framework for the future of end-user development. In: Lieberman, H., Paternò, F., Wulf,V. (eds.) End User Development. Human-Computer Interaction Series, vol. 9. Springer, Dordrecht (2006). https://doi.org/10.1007/1-4020-5386-X_19
24. Schumacher, J., Feurstein, K.: Living Labs-the user as co-creator. In: Proceedings 13th International Conference on Concurrent Enterprising (ICE 2007). The Free Press, Sophia-Antipolis (2007)
25. Burns, C., Cottam, H., Vanstone, C., Winhall, J.: RED paper 02: Transformation Design. Design Council, London (2006)
26. Sangiorgi, D.: Transformative services and transformation design. Int. J. Des. **5**(2), 29–40 (2011)

27. Karnieli-Miller, O., Strier, R., Pessach, L.: Power relations in qualitative research. Qual. Health Res. **19**(2), 279–289 (2009)
28. Hussain, M.: Grassroots innovation: a systematic review of two decades of research. J. Cleaner Prod. **137**, 973–981 (2016)
29. City of Cape Town City. https://www.capetown.gov.za/en/stats/Pages/-Census-Suburb-Profiles-land.aspx. Accessed 16 June 2016
30. Surender, R., Noble, M., Wright, G., Ntshongwana, P.: Social assistance and dependency in South Africa: an analysis of attitudes to paid work and social grants. J. Soc. Policy **39**(2), 203–221 (2010)
31. Bank, L.: Living together, moving apart: home-made agendas, identity politics and urban-rural linkages in the Eastern Cape, South Africa. J. Contemp. Afr. Stud. **19**(1), 129–147 (2001)
32. Roth, J.: Informal micro-finance schemes: the case of funeral insurance in South Africa. International Labour Office Geneva, Geneva, Switzerland (2000)
33. Robins, S.L.: From Revolution to Rights in South Africa: Social Movements NGOs & Popular Politics after Apartheid. Boydell & Brewer, Suffolk (2010)
34. Quarterly labour force survey: Quarter. http://www.statssa.gov.za/publications/P02111stQuarter2016.pdfst. Accessed 16 June 2016
35. Dearden, A.: See no evil?: ethics in an interventionist ICTD. In: Proceedings of the 5th International Conference on Information and Communication Technologies and Development, pp. 46–55. ACM, New York (2012)
36. Morgan, D.: The Focus Group Guidebook, vol. 1. Sage publications, London (1997)
37. Leech, N.L., Onwuegbuzie, A.J.: An array of qualitative data analysis tools: a call for data analysis triangulation. Sch. Psychol. Q. **22**(4), 557 (2007)
38. Lennie, J., Tacchi, J.: Evaluating Communication for Development: A Framework for Social Change. Routledge, New York (2013)
39. Lorini, M.R., van Zyl, I., Chigona, W.: ICTs for inclusive communities: a critical discourse analysis. In: Proceedings of the 8th International Development Informatics Association Conference, Port Elizabeth, South Africa, pp. 78–94 (2014)
40. Lorini, M.R., Sabiescu, A., Memarovic, N.: Collective digital storytelling in community-based co-design projects an emergent approach. J. Commun. Inform. **13**(1), 109–136 (2017)
41. Tritter, J.Q., McCallum, A.: The snakes and ladders of user involvement: moving beyond Arnstein. Health Policy **76**(2), 56–168 (2006)
42. Minkler, M.: Ethical challenges for the "outside" researcher in community-based participatory research. Health Educ. Behav. **31**(6), 684–697 (2004)
43. Dearden, A., Haider Rizvi, S.M.: ICT4D and participatory design. In: The International Encyclopedia of Digital Communication and Society, pp. 395–403. Wiley, Chichester (2015)
44. Dell, N., Vaidyanathan, V., Medhi, I., Cutrell, E., Thies, W.: Yours is better!: participant response bias in HCI. In: Proceedings of the SIGCHI Conference on Human Factors in Computing Systems, pp. 1321–1330. ACM, New York (2012)
45. Sanders, L., Stappers, P.J.: From designing to co-designing to collective dreaming: three slices in time. Interactions **21**(6), 24–33 (2014)
46. Alexiou, K.: Coordination and emergence in design. CoDesign **6**(2), 75–97 (2010)
47. Fischer, G.: Meta-design: beyond user-centered and participatory design. In: Proceedings of HCI International, pp. 99–92. Lawrence Erlbaum Associates, Mahwah (2003)
48. Cornwall, A.: Unpacking 'participation': models, meanings and practices. Commun. Develop. J. **43**(3), 269–283 (2008)

The Role of Local *Bricoleurs* in Sustaining Changing ICT4D Solutions

Elisabeth Fruijtier(✉) and Wilfred Senyoni

University of Oslo, Blindern, 0317 Oslo, Norway
fruijtie@tcd.ie, senyoni@gmail.com

Abstract. This paper problematizes the way ICT4D projects are rarely equipped to anticipate for the longitudinal and organic nature of ICT4D processes. As such, it aims to explore how these ever-evolving processes may be met with adaptive solutions that are responsive to their changing environments. Our analysis concentrated on uncovering the change processes of a particularly successful ICT4D implementation over time. Based on these findings, we developed a process perspective of bricolage-driven change in ICT4D in which bricolage practices move through 3 different stages we identify to be 'opportunity based', 'locally owned' and 'locally driven' in nature. These insights are aimed at aiding researchers as well as practitioners in the ICT4D domain in the implementation of long term ICT4D solutions.

Keywords: ICT4D · Bricolage · Sustainability · Change

1 Introduction

While the field of ICT4D has been occupied with making ICT solutions work in the most challenging contexts for over two decades, it continues to grapple with making ICTs sustainable in these environments [1]. Accordingly, the sustainability of ICT4D solutions has been the subject of a significant amount of research and a whole spectrum and combination of factors have emerged that explain either failure or success.

Success in ICT4D projects is generally associated with a situation in which '*stakeholders attain their goals and do not experience significant undesirable outcome*' [2, p. 102]. As pointed out by Sanner and Sæbø [3], failure may be attributed to factors such as lack of alignment of interests and responsibilities among stakeholders [4], the often limited duration of donors' financial support and technical bias of projects [5] and a "pilot project" orientation [6, 7]. In addition, Kimaro and Nhampossa [4] perceive the main challenge to be the (often lacking) development of local capacity to adapt to changing technologies and needs.

While insightful, such accounts of success (and by extension its antonym, failure) in studies are often problematic in understanding how to create sustainable solutions. Due to the implication, success and failure can be measured in a series of (predefined) factors in relation to the outcome [8]. In this regard, Nijhia and Merali [9] note that initiatives may be judged prematurely as having failed (or succeeded) in the absence of a longitudinal understanding of change processes which may be required for the 'right' confluence of conditions and pressures. Andreassen [8] has a similar perspective of the

K. Krauss et al. (Eds.): IDIA 2018, CCIS 933, pp. 171–185, 2019.
https://doi.org/10.1007/978-3-030-11235-6_12

organic nature of ICT4D processes, arguing that, in some ways, any effects and achievements that could be labelled failures or successes, are side-effects. In addition, Walton and Heeks [10] advocate process approaches that avoid using 'successes' and 'failures' as single, cross-sectional, final judgements, but rather treat them as multiple, contingent and passing in nature, and as a basis for learning. However, ICT4D projects are rarely equipped to anticipate the longitudinal and organic nature of ICT4D processes that was previously outlined. As noted by Meyer et al. [11], ICT4D projects tend to be especially thin on describing methods of achieving 'embeddedness' and focusing on the developing of local capacity to integrate ICT4D solutions into the environment where it should reside [11].

This paper contributes to the previous knowledge gap by proposing how organic processes may be met with organic solutions, both of which evolve and mature alongside each other as time passes on and circumstances change. This way, side-effects can nevertheless be nurtured, manipulated, grown and deflected, based on adaptive, reflexive and interactive intervention. To achieve this, we expand on the role of local developer teams as 'bricoleurs' (as coined by Ciborra [12]) in planning for changing ICT4D projects. We propose the seeding of bricoleurs as part of ICT4D projects in the form of stable agencies that nest in between ICT4D solutions and their environment, upon which they act and react over time as solutions and environmental factors change. We perceive these bricoleurs, while in some ways entangled with the solution's (potentially hostile) environment, to become essential points of reference for development intervention.

Empirically, we draw on experiences of local developers in Tanzania, in the development and implementation of a health information system called 'District Health Information System' (DHIS). DHIS is developed as part of the Health Information Systems Programme (HISP) under the coordination of the Department of Informatics at the University of Oslo (UiO), and in collaboration with a vast global network of local developer teams, consultants and development partners.

2 Related Literature

Planning for change processes is perhaps one of the most difficult challenges both researchers and practitioners are faced with, in developing ICT solutions that are sustainable and appropriate in the complex context of developing countries as part of development strategies. While the ICT4D field would benefit from understanding change processes in ICT4D [13], to require flexible and long-term endeavors in a changing context [10], Andreassen reminds us that while any design may be an interpretation of an intentional future, development is a 'world in the making' and that anticipating outcomes for interventions as dynamic as those found under the ICT4D label is 'extremely difficult if not impossible' [8, p. 251].

When we understand ICT4D projects to be side-effect-driven and 'worlds-in-the-making' [5, 8], sustainability becomes a moving target. The previous image strokes with a metaphor used by Star and Ruhleder [14, p. 112], compare scaling IS solutions in general with *'building a boat you're on while designing the navigation system and being in a highly competitive boat race with a constantly shifting finish line'*. This would imply that we should not plan to install ICT4D solutions, but to breed and raise living organisms: responsive constellations that can interact with changing resources, capacity, infrastructure and politics, if we are to have any realistic expectations about their maturing. Is this truly an impossible mission? Taking on the previous quest, this study started with the following research question:

What design approaches may enable the long-term, organic and evolutionary development of ICT4D projects?

The closest we have come to identifying an approach that attempts at 'building the boat while sailing' is known as *bricolage*. Ciborra [12] introduced this concept in response to his search for the development of 'true' information systems that avoid 'easy imitation'. With a focus on creating sustainable competitive advantage, Ciborra conceptualized bricolage as a grassroot approach, in which IS emerged from the grassroots of the organization. Ciborra's preferred English translation of the French word 'bricolage' was 'tinkering', to contrast the importance of strategy and expert roles with the importance of improvisation in dealing with challenging designs. This approach builds on the perspective that limitation is a driving force behind success [15].

The same way ICT4D researchers question that success or failure can be measured from setting goals in advance, Ciborra questioned the managerial habit of engaging in purely cognitive processes of strategy formulation in planning the implementation of IS. Instead, he argued that strategy formulation should follow the continuous acquisition of knowledge in various forms. Especially in volatile environments, Ciborra perceived effective solutions needed to be embedded in everyday practices which formed the 'petri dish for tinkering' [12, p. 288]. This furthermore required environments that allow for serendipity, open experimentation, unskilled learning, recognizing failures as the stepping-stones for success, being receptive to 'raw material for innovation' being produced, and that enable collaborations on unfamiliar territory – or even involving competitors, in order to 'learn by intrusion' [16]. Ciborra [12, p. 289] referred to the previous principles as the oxymorons that could represent a new "systematic" approach *'precisely because they are paradoxical [could] unfreeze existing routines, cognitive frames and behaviors'*, guided by traditional, managerial forms of strategic framing responsible for project failure.

Strangely, however, the role assigned to the bricoleur in ICT4D literature so far has been somewhat disappointing. While bricolage is cited occasionally to refer to the importance of local fixes and creative grassroot solutions [17], these practices are seldom linked to the long-term ability of projects to adapt to changing conditions, let alone leading to discussions on the embedding, and even institutionalizing, of bricoleurs in ICT4D project environments. Ali and Bailur [5] take a rare stance in arguing that bricolage could, in fact, be an answer to the development of sustainable ICT4D; however, they also question the likelihood that implementing agencies for ICT for development projects would allow for bricolage. In contrast, Da Silva and Fernandez [18, p. 3] argue that the bricolage approach of Ciborra is *'likely to be less relevant for [the sustainability of] ICT4D initiatives, due to the more problematic context of developing countries'*.

Like Ali and Bailur [5], we see in the bricolage approach apotential to provide the systematic and yet organic process approach ICT4D researchers have been looking for in designing for 'worlds in the making' that ICT4D projects are perceived to be. To us, the low-resourced context of developing countries makes an understanding of how a bricolage could be applied systematically in ICT4D, all the more relevant. In line with notions from Ciborra [12], we understand bricolage to concern a grassroot process of 'tinkering' and improvisation by developers, based on resources available that thrive in serendipitous, over-controlled environments. Importantly, we do not approach bricolage as an individualistic undertaking, but as a mode of operation that can include teams and external stakeholders (the same way more traditional project management approaches are not the strategy of a single manager).

3 Methodology

This case was developed as part of an ongoing research effort to study the networked innovation around DHIS2 as part of the Health Information System Program. The authors are both researchers involved in studying various aspects of this networked innovation, and bundled their knowledge to understand how organic and changing ICT4D processes can be made more sustainable. As a result of their individual engagement with practices within the HISP Network, they developed a particular interest in the role of local developer teams that are also informally referred to in the network as 'HISP nodes'.

The first author, in the role of a researcher, has been extensively exposed to various perspectives from different HISP nodes over a period of 3 years. The second author had been exposed to the practices within the HISP network over a period of 10 years before joining the research community, while participating in various strategies deployed by one HISP node at the University of Dar es Salaam (UDSM) (from here onwards referred to as the UDSM TZ node).

What makes the Tanzanian case particularly valuable is the way it is generally considered a best-practice example by others in the HISP network. First, the deployment of DHIS2 is one of the oldest in the network, and its successful national scale-up continues to be well embedded. Second, the team has developed a strong relationship with the Ministry of Health (MoH) and its stakeholders in its role as sole provider of technical support as stipulated in the national health strategic plan. Third, the UDSM TZ team stands out because of the way it has been actively extending DHIS2 with innovative 'work arounds' in addressing needs emerging from local use cases that the 'core' of the system failed to facilitate in time. While such work arounds are typical for the practices of (most) other nodes in the network, UDSM TZ is, at present for instance, the leading HISP node that is contributing to the 'DHIS2 app store' in creating generic apps that can be used elsewhere in the network. The following study is the result of a shared interest in understanding how the UDSM TZ node came to be where it is now, and what we can learn from these efforts about the long-term sustaining of ICT4D projects in general.

3.1 Data Collection

Data collection was done during a 3-week field visit to the UDSM TZ node in February 2018. During the visit, the study met with strong support from the rest of the team, which resulted in a team effort to map out all the projects that the node had been engaged with over time, identification of the stakeholders it had worked with, and reflection on the outcomes of the projects, as well as lessons learned. This was done over an intensive 2-day exercise which involved four senior members of the team and combined workshop elements (recalling the various projects and listing them) with focus group discussions (recalling project progress related aspects and the linkages among them). The second author was part of these discussions, as part of it was a team-effort; however, he was engaged as little as possible, in order to keep interference with the data collection process at a minimum, and give the other team members space to present their perspective of events.

A total of 11 interviews were conducted (an overview is provided in Table 1, Appendix 1). One interview had been conducted with the second author prior to the visit in February 2015, regarding his role as a Senior Implementer at UDSM TZ. Although data from this interview proved an important point of departure for the study, and the creation of an initial timeline when the authors began their collaboration on this study in late 2017, additional interviews were structured around open questions designed to allow the surfacing of contrasting views.

Interviewees were selected, based on their knowledge of specific periods as well as various aspects of the organization's processes. For one of these interviews, the first author conducted a one-day field visit to one of the first pilot sites, Kibaha district in Pwani region. Both authors furthermore attended a (1-hour) presentation at MoHSW on how the malaria program currently used a DHIS2 interactive dashboard application. Documents analyzed included MESI documentation, the MoU, an evaluation report by the MoH reflecting on 5 years of DHIS2, and various theses and research publications that emerged from UDSM TZ activities at various points in time.

3.2 Data Analysis

The analysis process featured a grounded theory approach [19], as adapted by Charmaz [20, 21]. This approach emphasizes the examining of processes, making the study of action central, and creating abstract interpretive understandings of the data, in order to move from data to a contextualized theory. Central to the previous process was the creation of a timeline in which progress and challenges in the implementation of DHIS2 were separated from alliances that were formed and formalized. The next step involved the grouping together of instances (events, processes, occurrences) that had central features or characteristics in common. Characteristic for this process was a continuous comparative analysis of the research interests held that motivated the study, a growing body of emerging data, efforts to conceptualize patterns observed, and the creation of various memos and visual displays.

4 Findings

4.1 Promoting a New Health Information System (2002–2010)

This study centers on the story of DHIS development and implementation in Tanzania and what we will refer to as the 'UDSM Tanzania node'[1], a team of DHIS2 developers, instructors, supervisors, and academics hosted by the Department of Computer Science and Engineering (DoCSE) at the University of Dar Es Salaam (UDSM). The early foundations of UDSM TZ can be traced back to the efforts of UDSM staff in 2003, who piloted a health information system co-founded by researcher at the University of Oslo (UiO), then DHIS 1.3. The pilots took place in the Bagamoyo and Kibaha districts in Pwani Region as part of their PhD studies at UiO, and involved implementation of the system, training, conducting research of the data flows, and use at the national and local level.

The pilots aimed to demonstrate the advantages of the system to the MoH, in particularly the Health Management Information System (HMIS) section, in hopes of its nationwide implementation; however, the MoH at the time already had a national system in place, named MTUHA. MTUHA had been implemented by external consultants in 1992, which meant that at present, changes to the system could not be locally accommodated when the consultants were no longer available. This resulted in system crashes and data loss at district levels; however, because it has worked well for a long time, it was known as a success story in the region, and the MoH was reluctant to change it, despite its challenges.

At this point, researchers from UIO graduated, and activities in the mainland were stalled for some time. Nevertheless, the UDSM Tanzania node was involved in another research project in Zanzibar, with support from DANIDA, to implement DHIS 1.4, which had just been developed in South Africa in 2005. During this implementation, attempts to convince the MoH to adopt DHIS 1.4 on the mainland continued. Several lengthy discussions and system demonstrations were held in negotiations between researchers from UiO, the UDSM Tanzania node, and MoH officials in the mainland.

Eventually, DHIS was endorsed by MoH as the standard tool for implementation countrywide in 2007. At this stage, the pilots had demonstrated how DHIS could flexibly manage multiple programs and datasets in an integrated manner, something that was lacking in the MTUHA software.

> *'We could show things, we could demonstrate. You see? Just take these facilities, by 3 clicks; you just move them from here to there. Whenever we wanted to go to a presentation, we would put as much data in the system as possible.'*

Furthermore, the UDSM TZ node had gained experience from the pilots and the Zanzibar project, and could show it had the capacity to customize the software and provide user support locally.

> *'One of the things that gave UDSM Tanzania node an upper hand, was that – we are coming from the University. We are not somebody's pocket, but local team with people who do research... (...) The university is there to stay.'*

[1] This is not the organization's official name.

The adoption of DHIS instigated the signing of a Memorandum of Understanding (MoU) in 2007 between MoH, UDSM and UiO, which included the development of a 5-year national HIS strengthening plan. The initial idea for the HIS strengthening plan was conceived by UDSM TZ with support from UiO, and was first presented to MoH and other stakeholders such as NORAD, the Dutch embassy, and JICA later that year. The plan, however, took a long time to materialize, as it required lengthy negotiations, several revisions of the plan, and the need to include interests and demands from several partners, health programs and donors. While the HMIS section of the MoH was convinced to use DHIS countrywide, persuading the higher management, partners and donors continued to pose challenges. Some partners were not much in favor of the use of DHIS2, with others pushed for their own interests.

While the MoH was pursuing partners and donors to support the HIS strengthening plan, the previous pilots had generated the interest of a number of development partners who requested immediate implementation in their respective sites. For example, in 2008, JICA, supporting the National AIDS Control Programme (NACP), approached UDSM TZ to conduct a similar pilot of DHIS for their programs in Pwani region. During this time, UiO was in the early stages of developing DHIS2, an advanced version of DHIS1, capable of being configured and deployed online, that was developed by researchers in UiO, based on research experiences elsewhere in the network (in countries like India and Sierra Leone). DHIS2 was implemented as part of the JICA pilot (funded by NACP). Around the same time, CHAI and IHI also implemented DHIS2, based on the existing HMIS data collection tools in Mtwara, Lindi and 27 Sentinel Panel of Districts (SPD).

During this time, a Master programme in health informatics was successfully launched at UDSM in 2007, through NOMA funding, and was able to source local capacity for the project (a total of 8 students received scholarships from UiO). The programme was conducted in collaboration with UiO staff to enable knowledge transmission and strengthen the cooperation between UDSM and UiO, and increase capacity within the UDSM team and the MoH. In addition, the programme raised awareness of the activities UDSM was engaged in, supporting the HIS in Tanzania. The university environment also had the advantage that excelling students could be easily picked up by the technical team (UDSM TZ).

4.2 Alignment of Donor Interests (2010–2013)

In 2010, the HIS strengthening plan was endorsed by MOHSW and donors, and renamed the "M&E strengthening initiative" (or MESI). The formulation of MESI was a cornerstone that paved the way for the digitalization of the health system using DHIS2. The MoH worked hard in soliciting funds and aligning donors, and implementing partners in shared outcomes. In 2009, donors had started to pledge support to the MESI initiative as its plans were being finalized; thereafter, in 2010, the first funds from the Dutch embassy were received, later followed by funding from Global Funds. Other support from donors and implementing partners gradually followed over the next 5 years.

The MESI included a consortium of partners, which included the MoH and all relevant development partners and donors. Different committees were formed to foresee and support implementation of various work packages as part of the agreed

MESI. One of the subcommittees in this consortium is the Monitoring and Evaluation (M&E) committee, which is responsible for directly supporting and managing activities related to HMIS. This involved revision and defining of standards for integrated data collection tools and indicators. Importantly, as part of this committee, UDSM Tanzania node became the sole technical support of the MoH in terms of supporting DHIS2, and later also of some other systems such as the Human Resource system (HRHIS).

As agreed to in the formalization of MESI, the rollout of DHIS2 would be preceded by a total 'revamping' of the existing paper tools. This meant that indicators needed to be defined and harmonized across various health programs as much as possible. Pwani was selected again in 2011 as pilot site to test the implementation of DHIS2 with the new HMIS data collection tools. Based on the experiences and the results from the evaluation conducted in Pwani, DHIS2 was scaled to another 6 regions in 2012. Throughout the rollout, UDSM TZ was an important point of contact for DHIS2 users who needed support.

In 2013, the DHIS2 rollout was completed nationwide. This meant all public and private health facilities in the country (around 7000 facilities) were able to report data to the district level where DHIS2 data entry is done. While UDSM TZ had been important in steering the process of the rollout, they were (and still are) cautious to make sure the MoH had ownership throughout the process. Close collaborations between UDSM TZ and the MoH during trainings resulted in the formulation of a national 'DHIS2 implementers' team', which included members from MoH, UDSM and other implementing partners, to provide user support.

4.3 Integrated Information Accessibility (2013 - Onwards)

Overall, the national DHIS2 rollout was considered a vast success. The system could be accessed online (see www.dhis.moh.go.tz), and was capable of capturing and processing all of the nation's routine health aggregate data on a monthly basis. This meant a massive flow of information was pouring in from over 7000 health facilities across the country to a centralized DHIS2 owned by the MoH. In addition, the MoH, in collaboration with UDSM TZ, started efforts to integrate health programs that were not accommodated in the initial national rollout in 2014, such as Tuberculosis and Leprosy (TB&LP), and Human Resource data.

The integration of all major health programs created a staggering demand among development partners to access data in DHIS2, which validated the success of the rollout. This was an important change, because previously this data could only be accessed by approaching health facilities directly, or via the district councils they supported; it also led to an increased interest among development partner programs to use DHIS2 for own use with the support of UDSM. The MoH would have an important role to play in redirecting developing partners toward UDSM TZ. The other way around, the UDSM Tanzania node also became a medium for NGOs and donors to initiate new projects with the support of the MoH.

As a result, the existing user base expanded dramatically. Today, there are over 15,000 users across over 40 programs. For UDSM TZ, facilitating this new 'wave' of users while still handling all previous issues from the initial user base, can be challenging. One of the ways in which UDSM TZ tried to lift pressure on the team was by extending the capacity and size of the national DHIS2 implementer's team by also including members from other MoH sections, development partners and DHIS2 champions.

4.4 Local Capacity Dependency (2015 - Onwards)

The majority of functionalities that were requested by the development partners from the projects that 'mushroomed' out of rollout, were quite advanced, and, to some extent, also very specific to the Tanzanian context; because the team could not completely rely on the core team at UiO to address them for various reasons, this required a lot of 'work arounds'. For instance, when requirements were put on the 'global' DHIS2 roadmap of the core team at UiO, they would be pushed forward endlessly because they were too specific, and not needed in many other countries at the time. In addition, the nature of these projects would often be very short and surrounded by financial insecurities, as explained by one interviewee:

> *'They [donors] need to show results (...) they have maybe a 5 year project but there are some deliverables they have to produce to sustain it. So if they give you a long term project and you don't deliver you kill that project. So they want to monitor you: give you 6 months project, good results? Let me extend one year. Good results? Ok, then we can commit.'*

What makes things more challenging is that many requirements would come in an ad hoc fashion, and always with priority status, while at the same time, the client himself would not always fully grasp the complexity of what they request and how much time and money is required to deliver. In addition, support from UDSM TZ to the MoH would continue even during funding gaps:

> *'Between one contract to another there is always a gap, maybe 6 months maybe a year, but what do you do, how do you sustain? (...) We [assistant director within the ministry] were talking one day and he was telling me: you know what? I think we have a marriage between the ministry and the University of Dar Es Salaam, and once you are married, off course you are not supposed to break up that marriage... for better or worse.'*

> *'That is the beauty and burden of the University of Dar es Salaam, (...) Sometimes you just have to take one for the team.'*

The previous situation required a lot of additional 'in house' investment on the side of UDSM TZ, that would never be contracted. In order to deliver quickly, and in the face of extremely limited resources, UDSM TZ developed an innovation strategy that attempted the re-use of innovations as much as possible. This was not only due to the experience that requests would often be similar in nature across projects, but also because there was a need to re-use the capacities and skills of a limited team. Despite the growing demand for support, expanding the team at times of high demand was risky, given its unpredictable nature. An interviewee explains:

> *'Instead of waiting for international support that may never come, we proactively start to do something and then people can see 'ah we can do that' and then we continue chipping away at it. (...) So sometimes you compromise and say 'ok, lets first deliver this, then come back and redraft it to make sure that going forward most of the code and the initiative can be re-used.'*

Being able to deliver is also important for UDSM TZ, to build relationships with development partners. For instance, in 2009 the team was contracted by JICA again for 6 months to create a workaround for a dysfunctional HR system in order to preserve the data while the delivery of a new solution, developed by another company, faced delays. Rather than to create a temporary fix, the team saw the opportunity to create a more durable solution by rebuilding a completely new HRHIS system. Fortunately, because UDSM TZ had showed all this could be done in 6 months, JICA decided to go forward with this solution instead, and the team still finds themselves supporting this system 8 years later. Based on these experiences, JICA reached out to the team again in 2014 to develop a web based portal for the Ministry of Agriculture, and again, the team took on the challenge and delivered. In this case, they build on applications developed during earlier projects, and by making radical adjustments were able to meet the client's demands in timely fashion.

Expanding activities to different sectors and ministries (presently health, agriculture, water, aggregation, sanitation and social welfare) meant exposure to a high variety of requirements. This continues to force the team to push the boundaries in developing generic 'cross-cutting' applications. Pushing these boundaries is important, because a large user base is needed to make sure others have a stake in the upkeep, ongoing development and maintenance of applications, and are willing to contribute.

> *'What people don't fully understand is how open source works. Most people are tied to money, and it doesn't usually work when you say:' we have done this, it has taken us a lot of time, resources, energy and research to do it, you can have it for free but can you pay something back?' So you try to work around that (..) You give it to them but you know demand is always expanding and they will reach the limit of what you give them. It is not enough but we believe in the long term perspective [this approach] will eventually become sustainable, it will break even in the far future.'*

In an effort to make generic applications sustainable, the team also tries to communicate with the core team at UiO for support. Presently an estimated 20% of the DHIS2 application developed by UDSM TZ has been absorbed in the 'global' DHIS2.

5 Analysis

The previous case describes a grassroot process that started with a single pilot, limited funds and capacity, and resulted in a sustainable, nationwide solution that could be adapted to changing local requirements over time in the presence of local technical support. In the previous low-resourced environment, creating local capacity to sustain the initial pilot was not planned for in advance. Rather, it followed a chain reaction of opportunities, both created and identified, that were successfully solidified into either achievements or alliances that would pave the way for increased levels of adhesion. Here, alliances either followed from previous achievements, put them into motion and/or were strengthened by them.

During this process, the role of the local developers changed. At first, they were able to somewhat lift along with a series of opportunities and circumstances in a highly improvised manner. The pilots, enabled by PhD scholarships, offered an important opportunity for learning (both on the mainland as well as offshore), while technical advancements elsewhere contributed to an attractive solution that proved to be customizable to the local context. Here, a basis was created for a series of achievements and alliances that gave way to a more systematic approach.

Initially, this approach was about rooting the local development team and solidifying its relationships with the MoH, its development partners and users at different levels of the health system. Investing in a lengthy participatory process bought the team the time to deliver during the rollout. The previous process had the result that not only a single actor (the MoH), but a wide range of stakeholders, had a stake in the rollout. As a result, its success triggered a much broader demand for innovations among partners that could fan out of the nationwide implementation.

This increase in demand was important for the team to remain a functional and reliable support to the MoH amid funding gaps; however, it also exerted new pressure on the team's limited capacity. The team responded to this challenge with a generic innovation strategy through which technological features could be re-used. This approach leveraged on strong ties with the MoH and various partners, which increased exposure to a diverse range of user requirements, and enabled UDSM TZ to actively sew demand for new innovations.

As a result, the team could keep support of previous activities ongoing, while affording itself the ability to every now and then bite off a bit more than it could chew. This enabled the developers at UDSM TZ to break with a somewhat passive dependency on ad hoc funding opportunities, and to proactively start cultivating a serendipitous environment instead. The previous process was illustrated in Fig. 1. In the following section, these developments are theorized as three different stages of 'bricolage', which emerge as a result of the stepwise accumulation of achievements, and the expansion and strengthening of stakeholder alliances discussed.

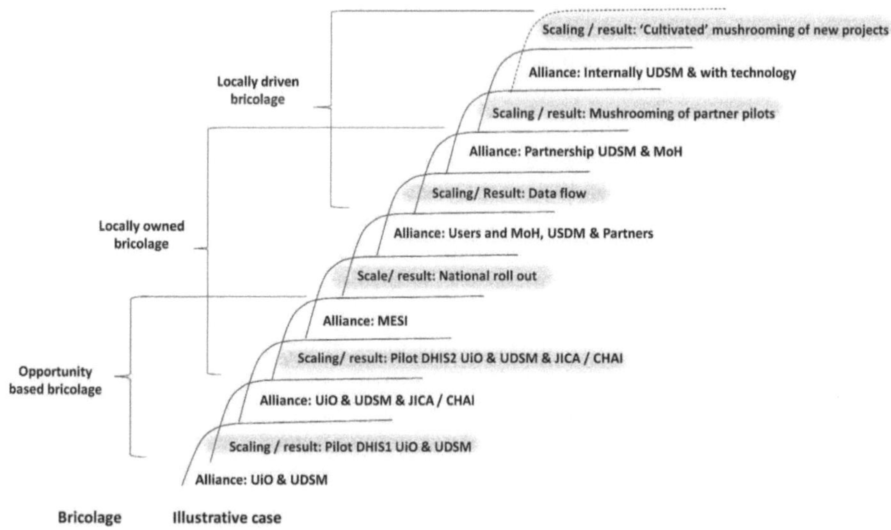

Fig. 1. Analysis

6 Bricolage-Driven Change in ICT4D

The UDSM TZ case illustrates that the role of local developers in ICT4D environment matches that of a 'bricoleur': action-oriented improvisers who, operating in the midst of scarcity and chaos with limited resources, are pushed to draw on their own creativity, move boundaries, and develop strategic collaborations with others. Doing so, they pave the way for an evolution of their mode of operation which becomes connected with their ability to sustain the previous processes. Based on the previous findings, the bricolage process can be segmented out into three stages.

Bricolage begins with '*opportunity based bricolage'* which may be externally driven. During this stage, the role of the bricoleur is external; new, fresh alliances need to be forged, and while potential solutions may be shipped in from elsewhere, they need to be 'piloted' locally and customized along the way. This stage also comes with a risk that bricolage is not nested in follow-up phases. When bricoleurs tinker with a rather short-term goal in mind, this may keep them from forging needed alliances, or recognizing their importance for the next stage in the bricolage process that will secure the first one which is still fragile at this point.

The next stage involves '*locally owned bricolage'*. During this stage, bricoleurs will have to both nurture and nourish the previous process in traditional bricolage fashion, that requires workarounds and improvisation. While the bricolage process is still opportunity based, the role of the bricoleur is nested in existing routines and practices. During this phase, these alliances need to involve (or be handed over to) local bricoleurs, and extended to (new) stakeholders that occupy spaces in which initiatives can grow. Words like "nurturing" and "nourishing" don't do justice to the volatile nature of this process, in which bricoleurs are pushed to their limit. This stage is all about survival for the bricoleurs, as well as that of previous achievements.

Finally, a stage of '*locally driven bricolage'* is entered when efforts from the previous processes start to pay off. At this point, bricoleurs are able to turn workarounds created as they tinkered their way through unpredictable forces into opportunities that make the bricolage process itself easier. When done successfully, bricolage is no longer based on ad hoc improvisation in response to limitations encountered; the bricoleur has made the limitations of his environment his own, and is now able to proactively manipulate it to make it more harmonious and cooperative. Nevertheless, this stage does not represent a final destination; the bricoleurs are likely to shapeshift further in an attempt to settle processes initiated in the most recent stage that are simply not known yet. It is through the accumulation of alliances in which the actors embed themselves, that it becomes easier to adapt to new roles and forms of bricolage, as well as accelerate its process.

Alliances act somewhat like intervertebral discs in the backbone of the previous bricolage process, that give it the flexibility necessary for its own evolution, needed to adapt to a changing system and environment. Achievements are then the bones that carry the process forward. In addition, we borrow from Actor Network Theory [22], the idea that *alliances can include technology*, in the sense that achieving locally driven bricolage relies on the ability of bricoleurs to get the technology on their side. The ability to tinker, hack, improvise, and work around in a way that is not responsive and reactive, but orchestrated, and, where possible, strategic, and requires a certain level of mastery, creativity, capacity and skills.

Our case illustrates how developing alliances with technology needed for more systematic forms of (locally driven) bricolage, can be a difficult and risky undertaking. It reveals the true nature of bricolage, which comes with the major limitation that it happens outside of project agreements, and is excluded from funding arrangements which can (at times stubbornly as well as ignorantly) rely on the engineers in their traditional 'expert' roles. In contrast to other alliances, which rely on the commitment of other stakeholders, generic innovation strategies of locally driven bricoleurs are, to a large extent, developed separately from other alliances. The next key ally at this stage of the process is the technology, which needs to be tamed and mastered with the right set of skills and dedication.

This will often involve hefty innovation processes that are started without knowing where they will lead, or if they will lead anywhere, based on the mere intuition of the bricoleur that innovations tend to come back across projects, and especially across contexts, and, therefore, the hope that the investment made will save the bricoleurs time in the future, and provide a lifeline when faced with unrealistic project deliverables. Other times, the bricoleurs will have to wait patiently, develop a short-term fix, and return to it later when more time and resources are freed up.

These findings generate insights into the generation of a serendipitous environment that allows bricoleurs to 'climb' from opportunity based to more systematic, locally driven bricolage. It is only at this stage that we can begin to discuss the local sustainability of ICT4D. Importantly, these findings imply that bricolage in ICT4D should be recognized as a social process as much as a technical one, in which piecing together alliances in adapting volatile environments is crucial for the ability to be creative, innovative and novel. In reflecting upon this process, we found ourselves imagining this aspect of bricolage to relate to the way a spider builds a web – but then within an ICT4D environment that is designed to count the flies it catches. We perceive the dominant focus on visible achievements to be as much a risk factor to the sustainability of ICT4D projects as the individual factors that can be analyzed to contribute to their momentary successes and failures (this includes an emphasis on these aspects in the literature). In this regard, this study identifies an important role for universities in hosting bricoleurs, and counterbalancing the previous risks, given their climates can be more facilitative of timely processes as a result of their learning-oriented objectives.

7 Conclusion

This paper has illustrated how bricolage, as an approach to creating novel innovations with limited resources, may benefit the sustainability of ICT4D solutions in the face of numerous challenges in relation to unaligned stakeholder interests, funding limitations, pilot orientations, technical biases and limited local capacity. The paper argues that ICT4D projects become more sustainable as the ability of the bricoleur increases to shape their environment in ways that enable bricolage to thrive. In explaining these achievements, a three-stage process of bricolage-driven change is formulated that expands our current understanding of bricolage and the role of local bricoleurs in

ICT4D projects. Practically, these findings offer practitioners insights into the significant role of bricolage in sustaining changing ICT4D solutions. Theoretically, they generate novel insights into the nature of bricolage and its role in the sustainability of ICT4D projects.

Acknowledgements. We wish to express our appreciation to the UDSM TZ team for their support and cooperation during the data collection period. We hope this paper will highlight their tremendous efforts in managing and maintaining the national system, and offer a source of inspiration for other HISP groups in the DHIS2 community.

Appendix 1

Table 1. Interviews

Participant	Organisation	Duration	Location	Recorded
Senior implementer	UDSM	1 h	Oslo	Yes
Head of department of computer science	UDSM	1,5 h	UDSM	Yes
Lead developer at UDSM TZ	UDSM	2,5 h	UDSM	Yes
Head of RCH	MoHSW	1,5 h	UDSM	Yes
Head of Malaria program and M&E officers	MoHSW	40 min	MOHSW	Yes
Head of the TB and Leprosy program and two M&E officers	TB and Leprosy program	1 h	TB and Leprosy program	Yes
M&E Director, Assistant directors and head of HMIS	MoHSW	1 h	MoHSW	No (on request)
District health management information system coordinator	Kibaha Health Centre, Pwani Region	1 h	UDSM	Yes
Senior implementer at UDSM TZ	UDSM	1 h	UDSM	Yes
Researcher 1 UiO Involved in TZ case from 2003 onwards	UiO	20 min	UiO	No
Researcher 2 UiO Involved in TZ case from 2007 onwards	UiO	20 min	UiO	No

References

1. Walsham, G., Sahay, S.: Research on information systems in developing countries: current landscape and future prospects. Inf. Technol. Develop. **12**(1), 7–24 (2006)
2. Heeks, R.: Information systems and developing countries: failure, success, and local improvisation. Inf. Soc. **18**(2), 101–112 (2002)
3. Sanner, T.A., Sæbø, J.I.: Paying per diems for ICT4D project participation: a sustainability challenge. Inf. Technol. Int. Develop. **10**(2), 33 (2014)
4. Kimaro, H., Nhampossa, J.: Analyzing the problem of unsustainable health information systems in less-developed economies: case studies from Tanzania and Mozambique. Inf. Technol. Develop. **11**(3), 273–298 (2005)
5. Ali, M., Bailur, S.: The challenge of "sustainability" in Ict4D – is bricolage the answer? In: Proceedings of the 9th International Conference on Social Implications of Computers in Developing Countries, pp. 54–60 (2007)
6. Lucas, H.: Information and communications technology for future health systems in developing countries. Soc. Sci. Med. **66**(10), 2122–2132 (2008)
7. Sanner, T., Roland, L., Braa, K.: From pilot to scale: towards an mHealth typology for low-resource contexts. Health Policy Technol. **1**(3), 155–164 (2012)
8. Andreasson, K.: Digital Divides: The New Challenges and Opportunities of e-Inclusion. CRC Press, Boca Raton (2015)
9. Njihia, J., Merali, Y.: The Broader Context for ICT4D Projects: A Morphogenetic Analysis. MIS Q. **37**(3), 881–905 (2013)
10. Walton, M., Heeks, R.: Can a Process Approach Improve ICT4D Project Success? Working Paper Series, vol. 47, pp. 1–32. Manchester Centre for Development Informatics (2011)
11. Meyer, I., Marais, M., Ford, M., Dlamini, S.: An exploration of the integration challenges inherent in the adoption of ICT in an education system. In: Choudrie, J., Islam, M.S., Wahid, F., Bass, J.M., Priyatma, J.E. (eds.) ICT4D 2017. IAICT, vol. 504, pp. 463–474. Springer, Cham (2017). https://doi.org/10.1007/978-3-319-59111-7_38
12. Ciborra, C.U.: From thinking to tinkering: the grassroots of strategic information systems. In: ICIS 1991 Proceedings, vol. 30 (1991)
13. Walsham, G., Robey, D., Sahay, S.: Foreword: special issue on information systems in developing countries. MIS Q. **31**(2), 317–326 (2007)
14. Star, S., Ruhleder, K.: Steps toward an ecology of infrastructure: design and access for large information spaces. Inf. Syst. Res. **7**(1), 111–134 (1996)
15. Rosenberg, N.: Inside the Black Box: Technology and Economics. Cambridge University Press, Cambridge (1982)
16. Nanoka, I.: Toward middle-up-down management: accelerating information creation. Sloan Manage. Rev. **29**(3), 9–18 (1988)
17. Matavire, R., Chidawanyika, H., Braa, J., Nyika, P., Katiyo, J.: Shaping the evolution of the health information infrastructure in Zimbabwe. J. Health Inform. Africa **1**(1), 83–90 (2013)
18. Da Silva, A., Fernandez, W.: Beyond free lunch: building sustainable ICT4D. In: Proceedings of the 21st European Conference on Information Systems, p. 85 (2013)
19. Glaser, B., Strauss, A.: Discovery of Grounded Theory: Strategies for Qualitative Research. Routledge, Abingdon (2017)
20. Charmaz, K.: Grounded theory: objectivist and constructivist methods. In: Denzin, N.K., Lincoln, Y. (eds.) The Handbook of Qualitative Research. Sage Publications, London (2000)
21. Charmaz, K.: Constructing Grounded Theory: A Practical Guide Through Qualitative Analysis. Sage Publications, London (2006)
22. Latour, B.: Reassembling the Social: An Introduction to Actor-Network-Theory. Oxford University Press, Oxford (2005)

References

Design

Building Empathy for Design Thinking in e-Health: A Zimbabwean Case Study

Masiya Alex Marufu(✉) and Alta van der Merwe

Informatics Department, University of Pretoria,
Lynnwood Road, Pretoria, South Africa
alexmarufu@gmail.com, alta@up.ac.za

Abstract. The challenges of healthcare delivery in Africa are well documented. Advances in technology present an opportunity to address some of these challenges in a cost-effective manner. Notwithstanding these advances, many initiatives fail to deliver the desired benefits, with a lack of citizen engagement cited as one of the reasons for this failure. Design thinking is an approach to innovation that places human needs at the centre of design by gaining empathy with those for whom the designs are initiated. This paper reports on the empathy building conducted in trying to understand the needs of mothers seeking post-natal care in a low-income neighbourhood in Zimbabwe. Through interviews, observations, journals, and using service-dominant logic theory to analyse the output, a picture emerges of the lives of the mothers and babies, and their interaction with the healthcare system. Working in teams with mobile application developers and nurses, the mothers participate in a workshop that produces points of view that define problems the teams would like addressed, using technology in a design thinking exercise.

This paper reports on the work of hospital midwives, and chronicles the lives of several mothers in the eight weeks after giving birth. It also sets out four design challenges based on the points of view derived from the design thinking workshops.

Keywords: Design thinking · e-Health · Service dominant logic Zimbabwe

1 Introduction

The challenges of healthcare delivery are rooted in inadequate funding [1], often in the face of growing demand due to population growth [2] and, in Africa especially, the spread of disease. challenge for healthcare providers [3]. The growing availability of low-cost ICT resources makes the use of ICT in healthcare an attractive proposition [4]; despite the resources being thrown into these eHealth initiatives, however, many of them fail to deliver meaningful results, due to poor citizen engagement [5–7].

Design thinking is a tool that can be used to improve healthcare [5]. Implementation of design thinking is still novel in Africa, and its use is mainly restricted to the design industry [6], yet its usefulness extends beyond the areas that have previously been closely associated with design [7]. Cases of design thinking, in both healthcare

K. Krauss et al. (Eds.): IDIA 2018, CCIS 933, pp. 189–205, 2019.
https://doi.org/10.1007/978-3-030-11235-6_13

and ICT, are numerous within the academic literature [8]. Design thinking processes are anchored on empathy building, a process through which designers find out the needs and wants of those they design for, by engaging in their lives. The application of design thinking in low-resource environments, such as those encountered in many African countries, requires the attention of researchers, in order to encourage the future uptake of such methods in practice.

This study approaches the subject by focusing on the provision of post-natal care in a low-resource environment, by addressing the following three research questions:

Main research question (MRQ): How can design teams incorporate the needs and wants of service beneficiaries in their designs?
Sub-research question 1(SRQ1): What are the circumstances of those offering and receiving post-natal care services?
Sub-research question 2 (SRQ2): What design challenges can help designers build better systems for the provision of post-natal care?

Working with Chitungwiza Hospital, a provincial hospital in the low-income neighbourhood of Chitungwiza in Harare, Zimbabwe, the researchers sought to find ways of improving post-natal care services using ICT design thinking. The team studied the lives of new mothers and their babies in the eight weeks after giving birth, and building a rich understanding of their lives and their expectations from the healthcare system. The information collected from engagement with the mothers as well as the healthcare system, formed the basis of empathy input that was used in a design thinking exercise aimed at improving post-natal care. This study adds to the academic awareness of the process of engaging consumers of services, by means of interviews, observations, journals, and the use of storytelling as a mechanism for transmitting the information gathered.

Section 2 of this paper provides a brief survey of the literature related to the key ideas explored in this study. Section 3 describes the methodology followed in setting up the study, while Sect. 4 reports on the results, focusing on answering the two sub-research questions. Section 5 reports on observations and conclusions from the study, and proposes an answer to the main research question.

2 Literature Review

This study explores the use of design thinking methods in improving the applicability of ICT in healthcare, by gaining an improved understanding of the circumstances of those for whom designs are being made. This section reviews the literature on design thinking, and how ICT is being used in health, as well as the opportunities for research in this e-Health.

2.1 Design Thinking

Design thinking is a human-centred approach to problem solving that moves beyond the rational and analytic, but looks to utilise intuitive and pattern-recognition abilities to suggest functional products and services that appeal to their users emotionally [9]. Products and services built on assumptions about user preferences fail to fulfil the needs of those they are designed for. Proponents of design thinking argue that the perspective of end users of products and services are brought to the fore, and, when used together with rapid prototyping, more effective solutions are quickly found [9]. While arguing that users' ideas are often difficult to convert into commercial services, Magnusson et al. [10] concede that users do make a positive contribution if their role is properly managed.

Brown and Wyatt [9] describe design thinking as being "optimistic, constructive, and experiential", offering a pragmatic approach for building solutions that the end users value. Brown [11] describes a design thinking exercise as consisting of three phases: inspiration, ideation and implementation. An alternative is proposed by the Stanford D. School [12], whose design thinking process is made up of five working spaces or modes which a design team traverse in their journey to a final solution. The empathy mode allows designers to understand people, and people's needs and wants, by talking to them, listening to them, and observing their lives within the context of a design challenge. The definition mode tries to bring clarity to the area of interest within the design challenge, with the goal of coming up with a meaningful and actionable problem statement or "point of view" (POV). The idea generation mode looks for possible solutions to problems before zeroing in on the most viable, feasible and desirable solutions for prototyping, testing, and possible implementation. The activities within each of these spaces are not necessarily sequential, but may be recursive in nature, allowing design teams to revisit prior spaces to seek clarification or enhance their understanding.

Empathy lies at the heart of design thinking [15–17]. Empathy is about stepping into the lives of those for whom designs are targeted, so that the designs are relevant not only to their circumstances, but also to their lives in general [13]. Empathy entails knowing what others feel and value [14]. Gaining empathy requires that designers understand others' point of view, their beliefs, concerns and, ultimately, their needs [15]. Building empathy involves the following [15, 16, 21]:

- Observing the world in minute detail
- Noticing things that others do or not do
- Probing
- Watching
- Listening
- Collecting stories
- Caring about other people's lives

According to the Stanford D. School [12], empathy gathering helps designers uncover unmet needs, guides innovation, identifies the correct people to design for, and helps discover the emotions that guide the behaviour of those whom the designs are intended for. Liedtka [16] concludes that empathy building in design thinking helps reduce the cognitive biases that typically afflict design projects. These biases include projection bias, egocentric empathy gap, focusing illusion, hot/cold gap, say/do gap, planning fallacy, hypothesis confirmation bias, endowment effect, and availability bias. Failure to manage these biases in design may result in designers ignoring novel, value-creating, and diverse ideas. Designers may also undervalue or overvalue designs, based on their own values, if they do not take into account the perspective of those for whom they are designing.

The ideas behind design thinking resonate with the core tenets of service-dominant logic [17]. Vargo and Lusch [18] have developed, over the last twenty-five years, a set of ideas that now form the basis of service-dominant logic theory. In their 2017 [18] paper, their ideas have been reduced to a set of five axioms that define all economic exchange as being based on service. These axioms are summarised in Table 1, and used in this study as a basis for understanding the ecosystem around service offering [19]:

Table 1. The axioms of service-dominant logic [18]

$Axiom_1$	**Service** is the fundamental basis of exchange
$Axiom_2$	Value is co-created by multiple **actors**, always including the beneficiary
$Axiom_3$	All social and economic actors are resource integrators **{service network}**
$Axiom_4$	Value is always uniquely and phenomenologically determined by the **beneficiary**
$Axiom_5$	Value co-creation is coordinated through actor-generated **institutions** and institutional arrangements

This study exploits the axioms of service-dominant logic to guide the collection and analysis of empathy data.

2.2 ICT in Healthcare: e-Health

Chandrasekhar and Ghosh [4] point to three ways in which ICTs can drive service innovation in the healthcare sector, a field that has come to be known as e-Health. Firstly, ICTs can be used to inform and train healthcare workers on the latest advances in the field, providing them with access to techniques, information on drugs, as well as diseases and their cures. Secondly, dissemination of information on disaster management services to places that are difficult to access, is made easier with the use of ICT. Thirdly, the use of ICT has the capacity to improve transparency and accountability, leading to greater availability and quality of services. Wickramasinghe et al. [20] describe a range of goals of e-Health, cautioning that e-Health is more than just the use of the Internet in medicine, a position that is in sync with that taken for this paper. e-Health drives efficiency through improved communication, while increasing quality of service. e-Health has the capacity to empower consumers and patients, while providing a platform to educate healthcare providers. e-Health redefines the geographical scope of service delivery, while also redefining the relationship between patients and service providers.

The full potential of e-Health is yet to be reached [20, 21], as both developed and developing countries stand to benefit from improvements that e-Health can bring [20]. Ricciardi et al. [22] argue that while the full potential of e-Health may not be understood, advances in ICT, increased adoption of ICT, and improvements in health policy, all driven by social changes, as well as consumer expectations, are driving e-Health forward. ICT will play a pervasive role as a stimulus for change and support for the healthcare system and individual practitioners [23]. Westbrook and Braithwaite [21] advocate a shift from simple automation of processes to innovation – a move from evolutionary changes to disruptive approaches, in order to harness the full potential of e-Health.

Mettler and Raptis [24] point out three areas as warranting attention with regard to ICT in healthcare, on which research should be focused. Personal health and independent living systems are concerned with care outside traditional medical facilities, while e-Health and clinical systems are concerned with medical processes and treatments. The third area relates to cross-sectional topics, such as the impact of ICT in healthcare on education, society, the economy and behaviour. In the area of personal health and independent living systems, Mettler and Raptis [24] advocate the investment of research effort in home care and chronic diseases, patient safety, interoperability of consumer and clinical systems, ICT for personalised inclusion, consumer health informatics, and personal guidance systems for people with impairments. In the area of e-health and clinical systems, they advocate research into patient-centred systems, clinical support systems, medical knowledge and decision support systems, bioinformatics, ICT for public health, and interoperability of medical and administrative systems. Cross-sectional topics are concerned with the social implications of human-computer interaction, standardisation and conformity, education, training and dissemination, security issues in health networks, and the value of ICT in healthcare.

3 Methodology

The main objective of this study was to explore empathy building in a design thinking exercise aimed at improving healthcare, using ICT. The researchers sought to collect empathy input whose focus was on the improvement of post-natal care in a hospital in a low-income neighbourhood. The study adopted a pragmatic, philosophical stance, and collection of data was guided by the ideas behind the theory of service-dominant logic and, in particular, the five axioms of service delivery [18].

This work was guided by the recommendations of the Committee for Research Ethics and Integrity of the Faculty of Engineering, Built Environment and Information Technology at the University of Pretoria, whose approval was sought at the start of the project. The Faculty of Health Sciences granted further ethical approval to conduct research in the healthcare sector. Local approval was granted by the Chief Executive of Chitungwiza Hospital on behalf of the Medical Research Council of Zimbabwe. All the participants in the study were requested to sign consent forms after receiving an explanation either in English, or in Shona. All interviews and journals referenced only code names, with an index to actual names only available to the main researcher, and stored in a safe in Harare.

An initial interview, conducted with the head of Chitungwiza hospital and his deputy, resulted in the decision to focus on the improvement of post-natal care. The interview aimed at gaining a broad understanding of the institutional perspective of offering care, with the objective of providing a broad scope for the design thinking work. Using a semi-structured interview format, questions were asked regarding the service that the hospital offers, and challenges faced in providing this service. The interview also looked at who the key players in service provision are and the roles they play. The two medical officers were questioned about their contact with patients after discharge, and the tools they use in the discharge of their duties as a central hospital. This meeting also served as an introduction to the hospital environment, with several follow-up meetings arranged with key personnel because of the recommendations from this meeting. The information collected formed a basis for understanding the dynamics of service provision in the hospital and the ecosystem around it.

An advertisement was placed in local newspapers for midwives to participate in a research study. Twenty midwives responded to the advertisement, of whom thirteen arrived. After explaining the nature and purpose of the research work, 10 midwives agreed to participate in the study, and they signed the consent forms. Midwives who participated in the interviews ranged in experience level from a few years to over 30 years in the case of one of the midwives. Their experience was a combination of both private and public sector experience.

The interviews with the midwives focused on their roles in providing post-natal care. The nurses were encouraged to go into detail regarding the processes they follow, with a special focus on how they manage their work and its flow. The weaknesses in service offering, and challenges faced, were investigated. The researcher questioned the midwives on their interaction with new mothers and their babies, both within the hospital and after discharge. The interviews also explored their experience with mothers as they return to the healthcare system for immunisation of their babies. The handling of information was of particular interest, and the midwives were asked to explain their experience.

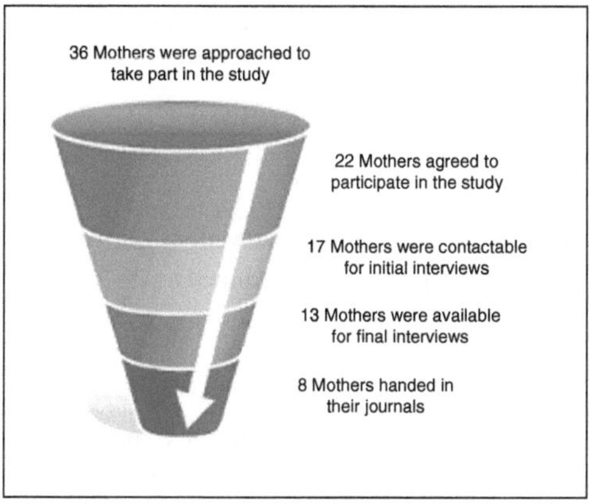

Fig. 1. Participation of mothers in the study

Twenty-two mothers who had just given birth were identified for participation in this study, as illustrated in Fig. 1, with the help of the hospital head. The cross-section of mothers included first-time mothers, as well as those who had given birth before. The group included mothers who had given birth normally, as well those who had had caesarean sections. The sample of twenty-two came out of a total population of thirty-six mothers who were presented to the researcher by the hospital, as potential participants, in groups of twelve per day over three days. At a selection session on each of the three mornings, the researcher and a midwife assistant explained the purpose of the study, and went through the informed consent considerations in both English and Shona. We explained to the mothers that our interest was in mothers who were able to maintain a journal over a six-week period, had no privacy issues at home, and had no religious concerns. On the first and second days, seven mothers apiece volunteered to continue with the study, while five mothers were released. On the final day, eight mothers came forward to bring the total to twenty-two. Figure 1, above, illustrates the outcome of the mother selection process.

Mothers were asked to write about their experiences on a day-to-day basis, detailing the common things that they went through in their lives, starting from their discharge from hospital. A week later, home follow-ups were conducted to ensure that the mothers were comfortable with the journal experience and to conduct an initial interview. At this stage, seventeen mothers were contactable, with five having become untraceable. It became apparent from talking to the other mothers that it was common practice to give false contact information to the hospital, as those with outstanding bills did not want to be found. After six weeks, a final interview was conducted, and the journals collected from the mothers. We were able to contact thirteen of the seventeen mothers who had been contacted in the first round of interviews. Of these thirteen mothers, eight had faithfully completed their journals and these were collected by the researcher (Table 2).

Table 2. Field data collection sample sizes

Purpose	Instrument		Number
Define problem area	Hospital head interview (CEO + CNO)	Interview	1
Building empathy	Midwife interviews	Interviews	10
	Initial interviews	Interviews	17
	Follow up interviews/Observations	Interviews	13
	Patient diaries/journals (returned)	Journals	8
Definition	Workshop/Focus group		24

The results of the various data collection techniques employed were analysed, and collated into a presentation that was given to a design group consisting of mobile application designers and developers, midwives, and some of the mothers. The group split into four teams at the end of the presentation, and each team was asked, using the concepts behind service-dominant logic to aid in further analysis, to come up with a point of view [POV] along the lines of the following:

"We would like to help X by providing a service Y that allow them to be a better Z"

Where X was a beneficiary of their choice, Y was a service or set of services, and Z was an outcome that they felt would be desirable for X.

The results of the data collection, as well as the resulting points of view, are presented in the next section.

4 Findings

These findings focus on the two sub-research questions, helping to understand the circumstances of those offering and receiving post-natal care (SRQ1), and, in the process, helping to define design challenges for use in designing potential solutions for improving post-natal care (SRQ2).

Midwives' Perspective: Content analysis was used to analyse interviews conducted with midwives on their role, their interaction with mothers, how they handled information, and the challenges they faced. Midwives reported that their role was to look after the mother and baby soon after birth, as well as provide education to mothers. Their interaction was intensive before the mothers' discharge; then followed a programme, recommended by the World Health Organisation, of a three-day, ten-day, and six-week visit for baby monitoring and immunisation (Table 3).

Table 3. The role of the midwife in post-natal care (Sample Analysis output) psychological support (Midwife responses)

Midwife 02	We also check on the mental health of the mother to see how they are coping after birth
Midwife 02	We are concerned about psychosis after birth
Midwife 07	So I might get a first time mother; or a mother who wanted a girl and she gets a boy, someone may want four babies, but they have method failure or the husband may not be so supportive
Midwife 07	There are psychological issues associated with the father as well and these need to be taken into account. The father may have wanted a boy and got a girl
Midwife 07	There are lots of issues to consider. As a midwife, I try and bring them together (as a family)
Midwife 08	In private hospitals, the hospital may allow the father to be present during birth, so I allow the three of them to bond
Midwife 08	So I place emphasis on the psychological aspects, congratulating them on the baby, and you will see from the facial expressions if there are any hidden concerns. So someone may start sobbing, or crying, or smiling, and I take it from there
Midwife 10	In the post-natal wards, you also have to access the mental contents of the mother. Some can develop people psychosis, and then you should monitor if they are not in that condition

Their information system was largely manual, based on registers and cards that the mothers carried. Major challenges in delivering health centred on the shortage of resources, the inability to follow-up on mothers who had given birth, and a subsequent lack of contact. Poor coordination of the healthcare delivery system was also given as a major challenge for the nurses (Table 4).

Table 4. Summary findings from the midwives

Role of the midwife	• Baby care • Mothers' physiological support • Mothers' psychological support • Education
Interaction	• Intensive while in hospital • Three-day visit • Ten-day visit (also referred to a 7-day visit after the 3-day visit) • Six-week visit • Follow-up visits managed by clinics except in exceptional cases
Information system	• Manual system built around register and patient cards
Challenges	• Lack of resources • Inability to follow up • Availability of information • Lack of coordination in healthcare

Mother's Perspective: The interviews with the mothers focused on the health support network around them, the challenges they faced, and their suggestions for improvement. Mothers felt that hospitals were difficult to access, and they relied heavily on friends and relatives. The church, local pharmacies, books, and the Internet were also seen as valuable sources of information. While mothers agreed with the midwives' version of the frequency of interaction, they regarded hospitals as the last port of call, and only to be visited in critical circumstances outside the pre-agreed immunisation visits. Resources were a major constraint, affecting their ability to access the hospital, drugs and even food. The quality of service from the hospital was also of major concern (Table 5).

Table 5. Summary findings from the mothers' perspective

Sources of information	• Hospitals and clinics difficult to access • Friends, neighbours and relatives a major source of information • Churches are influential • Pharmacies play an important role • Books • The Internet
Healthcare system interaction	• In hospital services • Three-day check-up • Seven-day check-up • Six-week check-up • Generally mothers do not engage the healthcare system unless critical
Challenges faced	• Difficulties in accessing healthcare • Finances/Lack of resources – For transport to get to the hospital – For drugs – For food • Family influence • Quality of services
Suggestions for improvement	• Healthcare system should understand their circumstances • More effort should go into educating mothers • Home follow-ups are necessary • Healthcare should be easier to access • Timeous service delivery • Available remote service (by phone/Internet) • Better scheduling of visits • Services should be more affordable

Mothers' Stories: The most compelling evidence that came out of the interaction with the mothers came out of the journals, which the mothers completed on a daily basis. The information from the journals was triangulated, and complemented with the researchers' own notes from visits undertaken to the mothers in their homes in the presence of a registered nurse/midwife. The journals were analysed, and three representative stories extracted. The first one tells the story of a mother who lives a humble but happy life with her husband and children. The second tells the story of a woman living a more challenging life, but is very representative of the lives of many of the women we met. The final story is the story of an outlier whose experience led to a tragic ending.

Table 6. Anna's story: a happy mother

Anna is the mother of four children. She gives birth to her fourth child at Chitungwiza hospital on the 11th of May 2017. Anna is happy with her child, and the nurses treat her with respect. Despite having two other boys, her husband is disappointed that she gave birth to a girl, but he is happy and supportive all the same. He comes to see her in hospital and takes her home when she is discharged the day after giving birth. Anna lives in a cottage at the back of a large house that she and her husband are building. The husband has a steady job, and she runs a profitable mushroom growing business at home. Anna lives with her husband and children and at the start of the project has no household help. Her cousin comes to visit and gives her hints and tips on looking after the child, even though she has had three other children. Anna's mother-in-law is less pleased with her child and refuses to hold the child, claiming that she has been called a witch in the past. This causes Anna much pain, and she is often left in tears after speaking to her mother-in-law. Despite this, Anna spends a week in the rural areas with her mother-in-law, to allow her to bond with the newborn while the husband returns to town to look after the other children. Anna's mother-in-law notices that Anna writes a journal and tries, unsuccessfully, to locate it so that she can see what Anna writes in it. Anna uses public transport to return from the week in Mutoko, as her husband is busy at work. Back home, Anna's days are filled with cooking, cleaning, looking after her children, along with tending to her mushroom crop. Having given birth normally, she recovers quickly despite heavy bleeding the days following her delivery. Anna keeps a copy of the book "Where There Is No Doctor: A Village Health Care Handbook", [25] by her bedside to help guide her in looking after her children. She keeps no formal records of her interaction with the hospital, other than the health card given to her by the hospital. Other than having had to return to the hospital where her youngest baby was born to collect a birth record, she has no further contact with them. Anna is lucky to live close to a clinic, which she visits for the regular check-ups as advised at the hospital. Anna is generally happy with the health system, her only complaints being that the linen at the hospital was inadequate and not in the cleanest state, and that the clinic keeps no records of the care they give; relying only on evidence produced by the mother when she visits.

Anna's story (Table 6) stands out as an exception, rather than the norm.

Vimbai's story (Table 7) mirrors the stories of many other women whose diaries we saw. Trina's story, presented in Table 8, represents a powerful outlier, which had a strong impact on the design teams that participated in the first workshop.

Table 7. Vimbai's story: a struggling mother

Vimbai gives birth on the 9th of May 2017 to her only child. She is discharged from hospital on the morning of the 10th, but is unable to settle the bill, so she is only able to leave the hospital after 5pm. Having been discharged in the morning, she does not get food from the hospital, so she is tired and hungry when she finally makes her way home. Frustrated, with a baby in her hands, she boards the wrong public taxi to take her home and is dropped off a long way from the correct route. She then walks to get the correct taxi home, arriving to welcoming neighbours and friends. Her husband cooks a meal of sadza and fish for her, and she goes to bed happy.

Home is a routine of housework and looking after the baby. The baby hardly sleeps at night, which keeps her and her husband up most nights, and leaves her very tired during the day. Her husband is a faithful provider but occasionally scolds her for sloppiness, which makes her unhappy. She has a small circle of friends who come to visit, and she receives presents for her baby, which pleases her. She regularly goes to church for prayers, and when she is unable to go to church she watches church services on TV. Her mother lives close by, and she occasionally takes the baby to visit her. She also takes time to visit friends that live in the neighbourhood.

Food is occasionally in short supply in Vimbai's home. Her diet consists of sadza[a], mainly with fresh or dried fish, and occasionally chicken and beef when they can afford it. When there is little money in the house, Vimbai cooks sadza with vegetables or beans. Her breakfast is generally rice and tea. Occasionally her husband or a friend brings her some fruit. On many days, she goes to sleep hungry, and she thinks her hunger leads to headaches and the tiredness she frequently feels.

During the early days after giving birth, Vimbai suffered from severe back pain and pain in her stomach. She is frequently tired and suffers from headaches, and she attributes this to her poor diet. She takes no medication for her pain, and the only medication in the house is the methylated spirit that she uses on her baby's umbilical cord, which falls off after three days. She occasionally feels lonely, and when her husband leaves her to visit his mother in the rural areas one weekend, she is left in tears. Despite not being in the best of health and on no medication, she soldiers on to look after her baby, and finds time to visit her mother who is also unwell. Although the baby is supposed to go back to the hospital for a check-up after ten days, Vimbai does not return to the hospital, as she has no funds to do so.

Two weeks after giving birth, she begins to feel better, and finds time to attend church services with her baby, carrying her on her back on the way there and back. She resumes her business of making and selling ice-lollies. She is unhappy with her husband one morning when he, fumbling in the dark while preparing to leave for work, kicks a bucket containing syrup she was preparing to freeze to make ice-lollies. Not only does she have extra cleaning up to do, but also the loss of raw material is a setback for her business. Her husband does not apologise for the mistake, and this leaves her feeling depressed.

Month end is particularly stressful, as rent is due and there is no money in the house. The landlord threatens to evict the family, and when she packs up to go to visit her sister, she is stopped by the landlord, who promises to have the family's belongings in the street when they return. The stress takes its toll on Vimbai, and her headache and back pain becomes unbearable, yet she cannot afford to visit the hospital. She asks a neighbour to look after her child so that she can get a few hours of much needed sleep.

A month after the birth of her baby, Vimbai goes to the hospital to collect her daughter's birth record. This visit is with much trepidation, as the thought of the outstanding bill is on Vimbai's mind. She is much relieved when it turns out there is no mention of money and, in fact, no payment is required for the birth record itself. A few days later, she wakes up early and takes the long walk (she has no money for bus fare) to the local administrator's office to collect a formal birth certificate. She is informed that the birth certificate will be ready by the end of that day, and with nothing to do, she walks back home to eat lunch before she goes back to collect the birth certificate. She returns to collect the birth certificate and she finds that it has errors on it, so she is asked to come back the next day to collect the corrected certificate.

Forty-four days after her baby is born, Vimbai wakes up early to walk to the clinic to have her baby attended to as part of the six-week check advised by the hospital. She arrives at 7am but by mid-morning she has not been attended to, so she walks back home to find something to eat. She walks back to the clinic and is finally attended to after lunch, and then she walks back home. The baby cries all the way home because of the immunisation injection she received.

[a] *Sadza is a staple food in many countries in Southern Africa. It is a thick porridge made with maize meal. It is also know as pap (South Africa), nsima (Zambia/Malawi), ugali (Tanzania/Kenya).*

Table 8. Trina's story: a tragic story

Trina gives birth to a baby boy on the 7th of May 2017. A mother of two other children, the birth is a caesarean birth. She is discharged on the 10th of May at 10:00am, but having no money to settle the final bill, she calls her husband to inform him of the $192 bill that has to be paid before dis charge. She negotiates to pay the $50 that she has on her and the hospital confiscates her National Identification Card, and allows her to leave. Four hours later the husband comes to find her and the child restless and tired. The outstanding bill is paid, but as she leaves, she is told that a BCG injection must be given to the child, although a nurse expresses reservations about the injection, as the child's temperature is high at 37.8 °Celsius. At home, she notices her child's temperature continues to be very high, but thinks it will eventually normalise.

She struggles to feed the child, as she is not producing enough milk. Her child is continually groaning and has hiccups. A visiting aunt on the 12th expresses concern at the child's groaning. She asks to examine the baby's stool, which she says is not normal. A suggestion is made to purchase Gripe water[a]* for the child since the child is not sucking. The child continues to groan for a few more days until the aunt insists on taking mother and child to the local clinic on the 14th. At the clinic, they wait for thirty minutes for a nurse to attend to them. When she does arrive, she sends them to the hospital, as the case appears beyond her. They wait in a queue at the hospital until a relative, who is also staff at the hospital, comes and attends to them. Mother and child are admitted, and the child is placed in a nursery.

The hospital asks for payment for blood testing and medication, but she is unable to pay. Eventually the medication is bought, and the child is placed on a drip. According to the doctor who attends to her, the child is dehydrated. The drip is discontinued after the first day, but when the doctor returns the next day, he is angry with the nurses for having discontinued the drip, noting the child is severely dehydrated. The baby's head has started to sink in from the top, commonly kn own in Shona as "kudona nhova", a sunken fontanelle, and a known sign of dehydration, and the parents are asked to buy another drip, which is procured. Meanwhile, the child's condition continues to decline.

On the 23rd of May 2017, a week after admission into hospital, the child dies. The father chooses that the baby be cremated, and the mother returns home. The mother is in pain from the complications of the caesarean birth, as the wound on her stomach stubbornly refuses to heal. She consults friends and relatives, and all are surprised that she was only given one set of tablets, each one thinking that there should be more. She continues to treat her wound with methylated spirit, and taking the medication provided from hospital. After a few more days, she decides to go to the pharmacy and she is offered a painkiller, the first time she has received a painkiller since the birth of her child.

Trina's relationship with her husband becomes strained as the days after the child's death become weeks. The husband and his relatives visit traditional healers to establish the cause of the child's death, and they are told that the mother sacrificed the child. This causes tremendous tension in the household. Despite not having fully recovered, Trina decides to go back to work to take her mind away from her predicament.

Trina meets with the interviewer during her lunch break from work. What was meant to be a routine interview, turns into a counselling session as the young mother bares her soul for over an hour, frequently sobbing, and breaking down at some points. Between the interviewer and the accompanying midwife, we try to console, and provide words of encouragement. At the end, she stands up, wipes her tears, and thanks us. It is the first time I have told my story to a nyone, she says as she departs.

[a] *Gripe water is a non-prescription product sold in many countries around the world to relieve colic and other gastrointestinal ailments and discomforts of infants.*

Defining a Point of View [POV]: A point of view serves as a design challenge, and helps focus the efforts of a design team. In this exercise, the feedback from interviews, as well as the stories, were presented to a design group consisting of mobile application designers and developers, midwives, and some of the mothers who were split into four teams. Further analysis of the findings was modelled around the five constructs of service-dominant logic [18, 19]:

- services on offer or those required
- actors involved in the delivery of these services
- network that influences how they consume service
- institutions and institutional arrangements that impact delivery of these services
- beneficiaries of the services

A complete analysis of this service ecosystem became the backbone of the empathy input, analysis of which was used to identify a suitable point of view to address in the rest of the design thinking exercise. The POV derived by the four design teams are summarised in Table 9, below:

Table 9. Points of view [19]

Team 1: A-team	Team 2: Med-Innov
We would like to provide Chipo with information on nutrition for both herself and baby so that she feels responsible, happy, and caring as a responsible mother, and raises her healthy self-esteem	We would like to provide Anna with information on the importance of breast-feeding, so that she feels she is a responsible mother. Healthy baby = happy mother
Team 3: Tech-Health	Team 4: Technovators
We would like to provide Janet with information on post-natal care so that she feels wanted, cared for, valued, and bonds with her baby	We would like to provide Trish with health education, to make her feel proud of being a responsible good mother and a good wife

5 Discussion and Conclusions

The aim of this study was to explore how design teams could incorporate the needs and wants of those for whom systems are being designed. In getting to this understanding, the study sought to understand the circumstances of those providing services, and those receiving services. This input was analysed, and presented to a design group that included some of the participants in the service process, as well as designers. This empathy input was then used by the design group, divided into four teams to come up with four points of view, which were then later used to guide the development of systems for use in improving post-natal care.

Three types of instruments were used to gain an understanding of the circumstances of the potential consumers of systems. The interview with the hospital head and his assistant allowed the researchers to focus on the area of post-natal care; it also gave the researcher an understanding of the key players, and some of the constraints related to offering service. Interviews with the midwives gave an insight into the services they offer and the constraints they face. Interviews were also used to understand the circumstances faced by mothers as they seek service from the healthcare system, their challenges, and to seek ideas for improvements. Observations of mothers in their homes provided useful information that proved invaluable in triangulating the mothers' own stories, as told in the journals. The journals themselves gave a depth of information, which would otherwise not have been unearthed by the semi-structured interviews that had been used before.

The stories about the mothers, narrated by the researcher to a design group consisting of mobile application designers and developers, midwives and mothers, served as a powerful means of communicating information that had been gleaned from the mothers' journals. The stories were of such a moving nature that the bulk of the room was left in tears, with mothers empathising with one another, and midwives appearing shocked at the reality that their patients face after discharge. The weight placed upon the occupants of that room appeared to give added impetus to wanting to find a solution to how service could be improved. This study reinforces literature on storytelling that positions it as an illustrative, symbolic tool for sharing concepts in a way that creates emotional bonds with the audience [7].

The analysis of the interviews with mothers and nurses, together with the stories told, lend themselves to understanding the circumstances of those offering and receiving care (MRQ1). The points of view [POVs] that resulted from the design workshops served as design challenges (MRQ2) that the design teams employed as a starting point in the design of mobile-based applications – an exercise that was outside the scope of this paper.

This study was built on trying to understand how design teams can incorporate the needs and wants of service beneficiaries in their designs (MRQ). Three practical answers to this question arise from this study:

- Seeking a deep understanding of the circumstances of those for whom systems are being designed
- Framing design challenges, or points of view, around the stakeholders and their circumstances
- Engaging the systems' stakeholders in the design process.

While this study has built a useful understanding of the circumstances surrounding the lives of those seeking and offering post-natal services, its real contribution lies in the experience of using the various instruments in building empathy for use in design thinking work.

This work will be of interest to practitioners of design thinking – not only in healthcare, but in any industry that may require service innovation.

References

1. Dixon, A., Figueras, J., Kutzin, J.: Funding Health Care: Options for Europe. McGraw Hill, New York (2002)
2. Di Pasquale, D., Padula, M., Scala, P.L., Biocca, L., Paraciani, D.: Advancements in ICT for healthcare and wellbeing: towards Horizon 2020. In: Proceedings of the Fifth International Conference on Management of Emergent Digital EcoSystems (2013)

3. Jahan, S., Chowdhury, M.M.H.: Assessment of present health status in Bangladesh and the applicability of e-health in healthcare services. World J. Comput. Appl. Technol. **1**(6), 121–124 (2014)
4. Chandrasekhar, C.P., Ghosh, J.: Information and communication technologies and health in low income countries: the potential and the constraints. Bull. World Health Organ. **79**(9), 850–855 (2001)
5. Brown, T.: Change by Design. HarperBusiness, New York (2009)
6. le Roux, E.: Design thinking in South Africa: An exploratory study among Johannesburg design agencies using force field analysis. The Independent Institute of Education, Creative Brand Leadership (2018)
7. Tschimmel, K.: Design thinking as an effective toolkit for innovation. In: The XXIII ISPIM Conference – Action for Innovation: Innovating from Experience. ISPIM, Barcelona (2012)
8. Plattner, H., Meinel, C., Leifer, L.: Understanding Innovation Design Thinking Research: Studying Co-creation in Practice. Springer, Berlin (2012). https://doi.org/10.1007/978-3-642-21643-5
9. Brown, T., Wyatt, J.: Design thinking for social innovation. Stanford Soc. Innov. Rev. **8**(1), 30–35 (2010)
10. Magnusson, P.R., Matthing, J., Kristen, P.: Managing user involvement in service innovation : experiments with innovating end users. J. Serv. Res. **6**(2), 111–124 (2003)
11. Brown, T.: Design Thinking. Harvard Business Review, Massachusetts, June 2008
12. D. School. (D. School, Producer), 19 February 2016. http://dschool.stanford.edu/. Accessed 19 Feb 2016
13. The Field Guide to Human-Centered Design. IDEO, Canada (2015). www.IDEO.Org
14. Wagner, B.: Motivation, leadership and emotional intelligence in the hospitality industry. In: Proceedings of the QUIS13 International Research Symposium on Service Excellence in Management, Karlstad, Sweden (2013)
15. Vianna, M., Vianna, Y., Adler, I.K., Lucena, B., Russo, B.: Design Thinking : Business Innovation. MJV Tecnologia ltda, Rio de Janeiro (2012)
16. Liedtka, J.: Perspective: linking design thinking with innovation outcomes through cognitive bias reduction. J. Prod. Innov. Manage. **32**(6), 925–938 (2014)
17. Edman, K.W.: Exploring overlaps and differences in service dominant logic and design thinking. In: DeThinking Service; ReThinking Design, vol. 59, pp. 201–212. Linköping University Electronic Press (2009)
18. Vargo, S.L., Lusch, R.F.: Service-dominant logic 2025. Int. J. Res. Mark. **34**(1), 46–67 (2017)
19. Marufu M.A., van der Merwe A.: Using service-dominant logic to build empathy for design thinking in a health service delivery environment. In: Yang, X.S., Sherratt, S., Dey, N., Joshi, A. (eds.) Third International Congress on Information and Communication Technology. Advances in Intelligent Systems and Computing, vol. 797. Springer, Singapore (2019). https://doi.org/10.1007/978-981-13-1165-9_46
20. Wickramasinghe, N.S., Fadalla, A.M.A., Geislet, E., Schaffer, J.L.: A framework for assessing e-health preparedness. J. Electron. Healthc. **1**(3), 316–334 (2005)
21. Westbrook, J.I., Braithwaite, J.: Will information and communication technology disrupt the health system and deliver on its promise? MJA **193**(7), 399 (2010)
22. Ricciardi, L., Mostashari, F., Murphy, J., Daniel, J.G., Siminerio, E.P.: A national action plan to support consumer engagement via e-health. Health Aff. **32**(2), 376–384 (2013)
23. Georgiou, A.: Data, information and knowledge: the health informatics model and its role in evidence based medicine. J. Eval. Clin. Pract. **8**(2), 127–130 (2002)

24. Mettler, T., Raptis, D.A.: What constitutes the field of health information systems? Fostering a systematic framework and rescarch agenda. Health Inform. J. **18**(2), 147–156 (2012)
25. Werner, D., Thurman, C., Maxwell, J.: Handbook, Where There Is No Doctor: A Village Health Care. Hesperien Health Guides (1973)

Coming to Terms with Telemetry: A Scoping Review

Martin Weiss[1(✉)], Adele Botha[2(✉)], and Marlien Herselman[2]

[1] Jembi Health Systems NPC, and SAMRC, Cape Town, South Africa
[2] School of Computing, CSIR Meraka & UNISA, Pretoria, South Africa
ABotha@csir.co.za

Abstract. mHealth solutions, in resource constrained public healthcare settings, are often an extension of the reach of the government health system. As such, mHealth is subjected to demands resulting from not only restrictions due to constrained health service offerings, but technically constrained limitations inherent in the provisioning of said services as well. Telemetry may be able to offer a workable strategy in mitigating some of these technical constraints. Telemetry, in various guises, has been in use since 1912. The term is used in Information Systems to refer to a conceptual understanding of remote monitoring and control. The concept morphs from its initial concept of Supervisory, Control, and Data Acquisition (SCADA), to often become synonymous with more evolving trends such as machine-to-machine (M2M) and the Internet of Things (IoT). Where there is a clearer understanding of the domain differences between the latter two, Telemetry, in contrast, is poorly expanded on and is predominantly used to denote the features in and of a system. As such, the agreement of what constitutes the components of a telemetry system, or a telemetry framework, is implicitly referred to from within reports and case studies. It follows that the notion of a telemetry framework or, telemetry perspective, is inferred by its context, and changes as its conceptual application changes. This paper aims to articulate the components for a Telemetry implementation from literature, and to suggest design criteria that could be considered for an mHealth telemetry implementation.

Keywords: Telemetry · SCADA · IoT · M2M · mHealth
Resource constrained

1 Introduction

The use of mobile technology has found numerous applications, but nowhere has its effect on society been as great as in developing contexts. The rapid escalation of devices in the hands of ordinary people, facilitated by an equally swift investment in infrastructure, has grown a significant user base, and paved the way for application in various domains. One of these applications has been the use of mobile technology in healthcare, commonly referred to as mHealth. Utilising the opportunities offered by a near ubiquitous communication medium, pilot projects have mushroomed to the extent that some described the situation as mHealth having *pilotitis*. *Pilotitis* is a term used to describe a "scenario where many NGOs are funded for relatively similar, but isolated,

K. Krauss et al. (Eds.): IDIA 2018, CCIS 933, pp. 206–222, 2019.
https://doi.org/10.1007/978-3-030-11235-6_14

pilot projects, resulting in no resources left for scaling them up" [1, 2]. Between 2008 and 2009, Uganda, for example, had over 23 large-scale mHealth initiatives that were not sustained, and ceased as funding dried up. The fragmentation, duplication and brevity of the initiatives led to the Uganda Minister of Health to issue a moratorium on all mHealth projects in 2012 [3]. The pilotitis trend is in no ways unique to Uganda, as similar trends are evidenced in South Africa [4].

The utilisation of mHealth in the South African Public Healthcare is characterised by a number of commonalities. The following are noted: applications are, more often than not, stand-alone, point-to-point implementations that have limited or no access channel interoperability or integration. Initiatives are frequently characterised as quick and dirty, with solutions following a path of least resistance characterised by minimum concern for long-term cost effectiveness and cross-platform integration; the preferred solutions frequently consist of numerous disparate technology platforms, and have multiple network integration points that result in limited reusability [5]. With these limitations in mind, a medium to high level of skill is needed to firstly, integrate or develop extensions, and secondly, to maintain relevance. The highly contextual nature of the solutions results in little or no economies of scale; in addition, there is limited specialisation, scalability or inter-project synergies [5]. McCann [2] further observed that "a system that tracks the entire small-scale NGO graveyard of projects [is needed], because the sum total of the data actually is useful, even if the project itself ultimately wasn't."

It can be argued that the notion of mHealth offers public healthcare many real benefits and opportunities; however, mHealth applications have seemingly failed to live up to their implicit potential [6]. As an inherently parasitic endeavour, it is highly dependent on infrastructure, and subject to business models of Mobile Network Operators (MNO) [4]. The dependency is especially relevant when initiatives are reliant on communication through USSD and SMS to reach the end user. In initiatives where interaction is required, the expenditure escalates as the end user is unwilling or unable to carry the cost of connectivity. In addition, other factors such as the misappropriation of allocated data and software updates, among others, drive the cost of initiatives up even further [7–10]. For large-scale mHealth implementations, to be a viable option in supporting public healthcare, a reconceptualisation of the application of mHealth for public healthcare is called for.

The concept of telemetry can possibly inform these challenges. The application of telemetry has had much more traction from practitioners than from academia. It has been applied in various contexts, but descriptions of its implementation are often inconsistent and ambiguous. Additional nuances are noted, as the term is linked to an aspect of the implementation environment. Examples are found in wireless telemetry [11, 12], medical telemetry [13, 14] and industrial telemetry [15]. No attempt could be found that endeavoured to extract a consensual meaning or outline of telemetry towards a common understanding.

This paper aims to identify the components of a telemetry implementation from literature, towards articulating suggested design criteria to guide an mHealth implementation for public healthcare. In addition, the paper's outcome can contribute towards providing for a common understanding of the notion of telemetry. Such an understanding will be able to facilitate debate on systems built utilising this perspective.

2 Method

Schueffel [16], in a similar quest, takes his departure point from Copi, Cohen and McMahon [17]. In evaluating meaningfulness in terms of formal logic, they hold that characterisations need to be broad enough to capture essential qualities, and at the same time specific enough to be distinctive [16]. In identifying components, a similar methodology is followed as suggested, towards articulating a useful taxonomy [18–20]. A taxonomy would consist of various unique categories, and as that aligns with the aim of this paper, is adapted, and within the context of its application. Three views to conceptualising categories are evident from literature. Firstly, there is an empirical approach following deductive reasoning. This approach starts from literature, and derives classification using clustering analysis or thematic clustering. This approach is referred to as *phenetic* in biology [19, 21]. Secondly, there is the inductive approach, referred to as *constructed categories* [22]. Thirdly, there is classification constructed through abductive reasoning [23]. Abduction can be understood as inference to the best explanation [24]. A full treatment that would do justice to the underpinning and conversations around the philosophic grounding is beyond the scope of this paper, but is acknowledged.

Nickerson et al. [20] suggests an approach to taxonomy development in IS, based on the work of Bailey [21]. The approach adapted for this study consists of three stages, of which only the first is relevant for this paper: firstly, a deductive stage that aims to identify general distinguishing components as a first version of the eventual taxonomy; the second stage entails a scrutiny of the taxonomy to identify additional components that might not have been identified, or been present in the original data set; and thirdly, the taxonomy is applied to practice to gauge its utility. After each stage, revision might be needed to add additional components. The scope of this paper is limited to the first stage of the taxonomy construction applied to the identification of components of a telemetry implementation. It is operationalised through a scoping review, to identify relevant components from literature that will be used to suggest design criteria for a telemetry system application in mHealth in a resource-constrained environment.

Brien, Lorenzetti, Lewis, Kennedy and Ghali [25], with reference to the work of Arksey and O'Malley [26], argues that scoping reviews are novel research strategies to overview domain literature. Scoping reviews are similar to systematic reviews in some respects, providing a way to interrogate a body of literature; however, systematic reviews tend to be more focused in nature, and predominantly endeavour to answer a clearly defined question, using explicit methodologies. Scoping reviews are geared towards examining the extent, range and nature of research in a particular field, the focus being on the outcome of the review. As such, the selection primarily on the quality of the selected literature, is an ancillary concern. Scoping reviews include work in progress, practitioner reports, credible websites and case studies, sometime referred to as grey literature [26, 27]. This is especially relevant to telemetry, due to the dearth in formal engagement available in academic literature.

As a scoping review essentially follows the same methodological steps as systematic reviews, its result can potentially be considered reliable and replicable. Ellis and Levy [28] affirm that such a review, conducted with sufficient scientific rigour, can provide a solid foundation for grounding research.

This scoping review was performed by adapting the frameworks of Arksey and O'Malley [26] for a scoping review, and Okoli and Schabram [29] for a systematic review respectively. They offer the following flow: (i) identify the purpose, scope, goal and research questions; (ii) develop a protocol with specific steps and procedures to be followed; (iii) search and identify relevant studies; (iv) eliminate studies that do not address the research questions and do not meet a defined set of inclusion criteria; (v) charting the data; and (vi) collate, summarise and report the results.

2.1 Search Strategy

To identify relevant papers for consideration, the search and extraction strategies included the following databases: ACM digital library, IEEE Xplore, Scopus and ScienceDirect. Relevant papers were considered those that did not only implement telemetry, but also engaged in discussion around the identification of telemetry frameworks, models, categories or components. In addition, Harzing's Publish or Perish software was used to identify and include highly cited studies which might have been missed in the database search. Relevant patents were included. To supplement these papers, a manual search was conducted, using Google, to include business and industry discussions of sufficient quality from publications on the web. Corporate white papers, case studies and websites were included where architecture discussions were relevant. The search period had no data limit.

2.2 Inclusion and Exclusion Criteria

The search criteria included search terms: ('telemetry' AND ('framework' OR 'model')) OR ('components' AND 'telemetry'). An initial search was done, limiting records to only items sited more than once and the term *Supervisory, Control and Data Acquisition* (SCADA) was significantly used in relation to telemetry-type solutions (over 170). As a result, the search terms were extended to included (('SCADA' AND ('framework' OR 'model')) OR ('components' AND 'SCADA') AND 'telemetry').

This *SCADA*-related search, in addition to the *telemetry* search provided 1080 relevant, unique papers describing telemetry-type solutions, detailed predominantly from an implementation perspective.

Google searches of relevant grey literature identified an additional 23 relevant papers, which were included. Table 1 outlines the record eligibility assessment grid used for the screening of records. The screening process excluded 145 foreign language articles. Further filtering of heading and abstract text related to cybercrime and bespoke solutions (crime, cybersecurity, attack, network vulnerabilities, integrity attacks, security threats, hack, forensic, power, electric, weather, sub-station and energy) was done with reference to the grid provided in Table 1:

Table 1. Eligibility assessment questions for inclusion

	Eligibility assessment question	Response
1	Is the study written in English?	☐Yes (Include) ☐No
2	Does the study discuss or include a discussion on telemetry?	☐Yes (Include) ☐No
3	Does the study examine security-based concerns or is it a commercial offering?	☐Yes (Include) ☐No
4	Is the record relevant in the domain (does it have an acceptable H Score)	☐Yes (Include) ☐No
5	Does the title of the article suggest relevancy to the research?	☐Yes (Include) ☐No
6	Is the article relevant with reference to the abstract?	☐Yes (Include) ☐No

This screening process identified 184 remaining records. The fulltext records were read, and some were excluded based on either the focus of the paper or the relevance of the application domain. Subsequent to the screening process and eligibility evaluation, 24 records were selected. Figure 1 illustrates the identification, screening and eligibility searching and filtering process followed, based on the PRISMA statement for reporting systematic reviews [30].

Some researcher bias is acknowledged, as the researchers were required to make judgment calls as to the relevancy of the selected papers for inclusion. In addition, the search presents a snapshot in time, and it is acknowledged that further publications could influence later searches. Having outlined the methodology used to identify the remaining records that would be considered in this review, the following section provides insights that were gained.

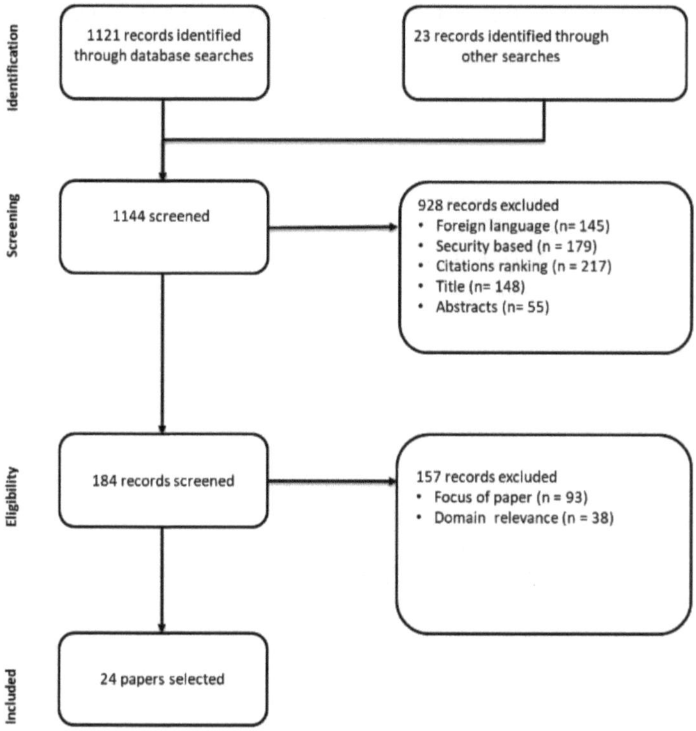

Fig. 1. Record selection process. Adapted from [30]

3 Conceptualisation of Telemetry

Telemetry is conceptualised through a narrative that evolves alongside technology affordances and, as a result of various specific focuses, is to be found in the discussions of SCADA, M2M and IoT. Table 2 provides a summary of the selected 24 articles, with reference to each article's focus within this narrative.

SCADA systems generally made use of simple wired networks, as well as dial-up networks (point to point) that connected Main Terminal Units (MTU) to Remote Terminal Units (RTU) as early as 1912. It enabled the monitoring and/or measuring of the environmental and other variables. Additionally, SCADA included the ability to remotely control relays, valves, actuators, etc., as well as monitor their status [56]. As Ethernet technology became prevalent in industrial settings circa the 1970s, SCADA solutions migrated to make use of this fixed wire Local Area Network (LAN) technology, to provide the next channel for connecting MTUs to RTUs [49, 50]. In these closed networks, data security and data compression was of no real concern, as these were physical, private networks with little chance of data being compromised, or malicious control of equipment being attempted from outside the factory walls [38, 47]. In these closed networks, data security and data compression was not a priority, as it

Table 2. Selected articles with reference to their telemetry focus.

	Article	Focus			
		SCADA	M2M	IoT	Telemetry
1	Alaya, Banouar, Monteil, Chassot and Drira [31]		x		
2	Borgia [32]			x	
3	Botta, de Donato, Persico and Pescapé [33]			x	
4	Castro, Jara and Skarmeta [34]		x		
5	Chen, Wan, González-Valenzuela, Liao and Leung [35]				
6	Davidson, McArthur, McDonald, Cumming and Watt [36]	x			
7	Dayarathna [37]				
8	Dhande [38]	x			
9	Fan, Haines and Kulkarni [39]		x		
10	Gabbai [40]			x	
11	King [41]	x			
12	Kwasnick, Karayacoubian, Polasam, Wang, Biswas, Tayeb, Mattani and Arbab [42]				x
13	Mineraud, Mazhelis, Su and Tarkoma [43]			x	
14	Pereira and Aguiar [44]		x		
15	ptc.com [45]			x	
16	Queiroz, Mahmood and Tari [46]	x			
17	Rezai, Keshavarzi and Moravej [47]	x			
18	Sajid, Abbas and Saleem [48]			x	
19	Shahzad, Musa, Aborujilah and Irfan [49]	x			
20	Shahzad, Musa, Aborujilah and Irfan [50]	x			
21	Shakya [51]			x	
22	[52]		x		
23	Wireless [53]			x	
24	Wireless [54]			x	
25	Wu, Talwar, Johnsson, Himayat and Johnson [55]			x	

comprised physical private networks. As a result, data being compromised, or malicious control of equipment being attempted from outside the factory walls, was secondary [38, 47].

The emergence of the Internet in the 1980s provided the possibility of a pervasive network, and was followed by the evolution of protocols, such as Transmission Control Protocol (TCP) and Internet Protocol (IP). The interoperability of machines became a necessary for SCADA systems taking advantage of the developments for remote monitoring and control. Key issues such as device (or asset) identification, security and legacy point-to-point architectures had to be re-examined with the Internet inherently being subject to a new level of vulnerability in SCADA solutions [49, 50].

This ability to now provide SCADA services across the Internet led to a new paradigm in telemetry, namely Machine to Machine communications (or M2M) – and refers to the ability of machines to communicate with other machines across the

Internet [34, 39, 44, 48], without having to deploy any fixed network, wiring or infrastructure; these infrastructural needs were met by Internet Service Providers (ISP).

Besides being able to present information remotely in the form of dashboards on terminals and computer screens, pervasive, commercial human interaction with these machines had not yet become commonplace. M2M can be considered as niche solutions for companies expanding their centralised control to extramural assets such as hot-water boilers, air conditioners, water meters, alarm and fire sensors, etc. as a means of reducing operational costs [35]. Due to the technology cost of the monitoring equipment, however, these devices are mostly constrained in terms of communication, processing power and energy efficiencies. As a result, communications techniques and protocols are optimised to ensure unit costs can be kept as low as possible without compromising functionality [46, 52].

With worldwide GSM (Global System for Mobile communications) adoptions' exponential growth in the mid-1990s, SCADA solution providers were able to capitalise on new GSM networks affordances, and acquired an additional channel for communicating to remote assets. This was supported by mobile network operators promoting their technology, not only for voice and Short Message Service (SMS), but also for data communications (initially called 2G networks). At first, GSM voice channels were used for communications between machines using Dual Tone Multi Frequency (DTMF) techniques, as well as SMS messages to relay text-based commands [51–54].

M2M solutions based on GSM data channels, however, were not as reliable as protocols designed for Ethernet and fixed wire. These M2M solutions were not considered robust, and early 2G and 3G GSM networks, being pseudo-packet switched data, introduced a multiplicity of issues not foreseen by the SCADA communities [51–54]. Only with the advent of true packet switched GSM data technologies did issues around the robustness of the protocols get resolved (4G onwards). Commercial GSM modems and chip sets, however, were still not yet pervasive, and only select large corporates such as luxury car and truck manufacturers could integrate telemetry modules into their solutions as early adopters. The eventual uptake in GSM modules resulted in mass production of mobile telemetry components and led to the eventual commercialisation of products (cost effective GSM M2M chips and miniaturised embedded GSM modems, etc.) that today form the base of connected monitoring devices found in electricity meters, traffic light controllers, etc. [45, 53].

As mobile handsets became pervasive, and the cost of GSM modems continued dropping, the concept of a *connected world* began to include the human as part of the connected ecosystem, and the term *Internet of Things* (coined much earlier on in 1999) was used to describe the interactions that were not just between machine to machine, but included the interaction with humans [40]. Mobile handsets became both the Remote Terminal Unit – used to monitor physiological variables such as, for example, heart rate – as well as the Main Terminal Unit – the dashboard to view, analyse and control *things* across the Internet. Where possible, IOT service providers developed clouded platforms to reduce operational costs and provide online integrated information services through batch and predictive analytics, producing information used by corporates to engage with their clients [32, 33, 37, 43].

Numerous building blocks in back-end services, as well as electronic components and hosted service offerings, are currently available. Development, integration and deployment of scalable IoT solutions are now not only practical, but able to manage large bases of remote assets cost effectively [31, 53].

More recently, M2M service providers are exposing Application Program Interface (API) integration points that allow even wider interaction of devices across solutions in an attempt to harmonise common services, and reuse existing information and solutions. Commercial clouded M2M and IOT platforms (such as those offered by Amazon, Microsoft, IBM, Google, PTC, Sierra Wireless, Huawei, Telit and others) are now available through the Internet for third parties to develop solutions or provide additional services [31, 54],

Kwasnick et al. [42], describing a contemporary Telemetry implementation propose that telemetry software should enable the desired measurement date, meet privacy and security requirements, have minimal impact on users systems and network performance, and include a capability for transmitting the acquired data.

Figure 2 depicts how original SCADA functionality has been adopted by M2M services, and how these M2M services are being integrated through APIs to form IOT platforms. It is thus argued that telemetry, as a concept, incorporates SCADA, Machine to Machine as well as Internet of Things solutions. These all have features that allow them to be *identified as telemetry solutions,* but differ in their *application and scope* of application. Telemetry can then be considered as presenting an overarching perspective, whereas –

- SCADA is more specific and focuses on industrial or commercial machine monitoring;

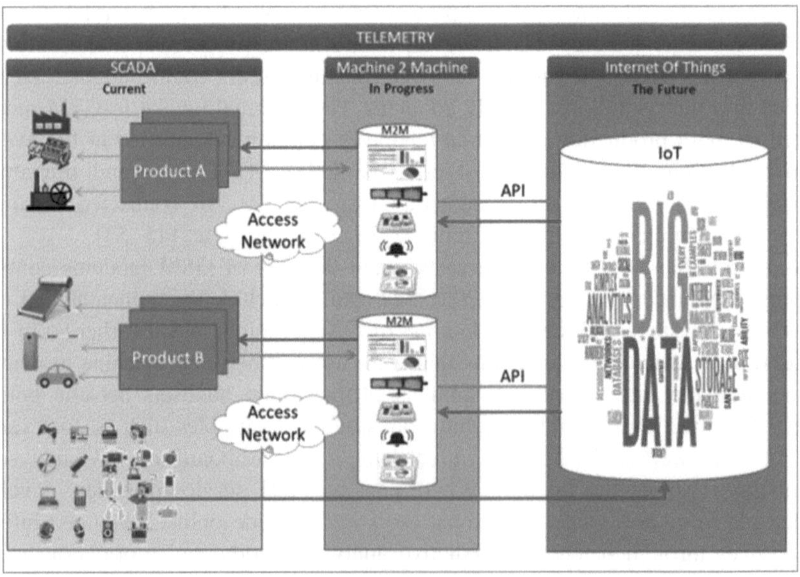

Fig. 2. Graphical representation of a telemetry conceptualisation.

- M2M is more specific and aimed at solutions that make use of wireless connectivity such as GSM, and would include applications such as vehicle tracking, fire monitoring, etc.; and
- IoT is more specific and extends to the aggregation of M2M platforms to mine information not normally available in a single M2M solution. For example, IoT solutions would include the ability of a boiler to determine autonomously when the most cost-effective period would be to heat water, based on the electricity consumption of the household.

This view is further used towards identifying the components of a telemetry system. Telemetry is outlined as an automated communications process by which measurements and other data are collected at remote or inaccessible points and transmitted to receiving equipment for monitoring.

4 Components of Telemetry

In conceptualising telemetry, it is contended that it would be an amalgamation of the affordances of each of the described perspectives. This idea is furthered to identify the components of a telemetry system through the examination of the components of SCADA, Machine to Machine, as well as Internet of Things solutions.

Through examining the literature, five (5) categories were identified as relevant:

- *Data Analytics* – whereby the collected data is analysed, presented, and in some cases triggers another event.
- *Communication* – that entails the communication process from a centralised point to remote or removed locations.
- *Data Management* – that is described by remote collection of measurements and other data, and the transmission of this data to a central point. In addition, it implies –
- *Asset Management* – that outlines the remote managing and control of assets, and
- *Socio-Technical* issues – that are related to the human engagement in the interaction.

With relevance to these, the selected literature was revisited to further unpack the components to identify the constituent elements of each component.

4.1 Data Analytics

Advanced analytics offer current information and insights on the state of systems such as water treatment. The availability of up-to-date dynamics of system use and implementation is set to become a key integrator in the future [43]. In addition to analytics, the emerging predictive capacity of such a system offers an additional value add, and reduces operating costs [53, 54]. Dayarathna [37] surmises that intelligent analysis of data contributes real-time, predictive and interactive analytics potentially on both the device and on the platform. The identified elements are analytics at the edge, with batch data analytics, predictive analytics and real-time data analytics.

4.2 Communication

Remote communication enables networked devices and services to exchange information and perform actions [44]. Various communication channels and protocols are identified between different machine and human actors. Dhande [38] provides descriptions for input channels utilised for sensing and/or metering, and output channels for control, indication or alarms and communications. He argues that "[o]ne of the prevailing features of SCADA architectures is variety, present at different intensities of granularity; this consists of devices such as intelligent sensors and network links", allowing for communication flexibility, the complexity of which is not experienced by the user, but facilitated through various interfaces [44]. The need to accommodate devices with different varieties and functionalities is additionally noted, as well as a requirement to act within an environment that provides limited system resources [56]. As such, lightweight communications protocols are employed to enable low energy and low bandwidth resource use that includes application, payload container, messaging and legacy protocols [37, 56]. Elements of this component are noted as Ethernet, wireless, dial-up network, point-to-point, point-to-multi-point, secure protocols and lightweight protocols.

4.3 Data Management

Dayarathna [37] describes data management structures as incorporating information security, and the verification of devices and edge analytics. Castro et al. [34] extends this to include standardisation. Data management provides for strong end-to-end encryption in an open access network to safeguard, among other things, private information. Data security measures need to be in place to ensure data integrity [32, 41]. Software and firmware that is centrally loaded onto a remote device needs to ensure the integrity of the firmware by verifying the source of the firmware; additionally, verification of the device will ensure that a device is who it claims it is. This is necessary to ensure data is mapped to ae correct site [37]. Data compression can effectively reduce the amount of data necessary to be transmitted [32, 56]. The other approach is edge analytics, which can reduce the amount of raw data transmitted to the IoT server [37]. In a further effort to reduce processing power and decrease latency in the system, remote devices can be programmed to only transmit data exceptions, and not the repetitive data; for example, in temperature measurement there is no value in continuously transmitting the temperature of a fridge if the temperature has not changed [37].

This component identifies the following elements: out-of-order data, security, remote measurement, and data compression.

4.4 Asset Management

Asset management includes having an inventory of devices and being able to track operational status [32]. This feature is also acknowledged as the most important, by most of the sited papers that investigate M2M and IoT platforms. As distributed devices need to be managed, it might become necessary to take control of an asset when it becomes a vulnerability [34, 53]. The ability to centrally apply new firmware versions to remote devices, as well as maintaining firmware version control where not all devices require the same firmware, is highlighted as desirable [31].

A software library or application that resides on the remote device and performs services on behalf of the central service and has the ability to collate remote statistics of a single device or asset at the point of acquisition, is outlined by Dayarathna [37]. The component 'asset management' then is seen to have device authentication, remote control, device management and device verification as elements.

4.5 Socio-Technical

As a socio-technical system, issues other than technology related are noted. As such, Dayarathna [37] highlights ethics as it relates to data integrity, sharing of private data, and confidentiality of data. This component concerns the element 'ethics'.

Table 3 maps the components and their elements, outlined above, to the publications reviewed. Having identified the components and their elements, they are applied to a mHealth implantation.

5 mHealth Application

Relating the identified components and elements to mHealth in South Africa, a public health strategy of deploying community health workers in rural settings would need very similar management tools in order to optimise services, as well as make informed decisions based on acquired data. In the case of mHealth, however, the assets are a combination of the health worker, their mobile device and the patient. In accepting this concept, the *asset* now forms part of a management process that allows central control and monitoring of a multitude of variables – through which a health department is able to extract or mine information to make informed decisions. As such, a design decision suggests viewing the healthcare worker and their mobile device as a remote asset through a telemetry perspective.

The telemetry perspective would provide the tools needed for an mHealth platform to remotely manage mobile cellular devices' firmware, security and access to data, and aggregate real-time data for informed decision-making. The vulnerability associated with the mobility of access is addressed through device and person identity and enables the remote revoking of access. With data management ensuring frugal use of available limited bandwidth, the cost of financing a variety of services with different data needs can be predicted, better anticipated, and also save costs.

Table 3. Components and elements mapped to selected publications

Papers X = discussed as a requirement for telemetry in the article Blank = not discussed as a requirement for telemetry in the article / = Not applicable in the article	Dimensions																		
	Data analytics				Communication							Data management				Asset management				Socio technical
	Analytics at the edge	Batch data analytics	Predictive analytics	Real time data analytics	Ethernet	Wireless	Dial up network	Point to point	Point to multipoint	Secure protocols	Lightweight protocols	Out of order data	Security	Remote measurement	Data compression	Device authentication	Remote control	Device management	Device verification	Ethics
Alaya et al. [31]	/	x	x	x	x	x		x	x	x	x	x	x	X	x	x	x	x	x	
Borgia [32]	x	x	x	x	x	x		x	x	x	x	x	x	x	x	x	x	x	x	x
Botta et al. [33]	x	x	x	x	x	x		x	x	x	x	x	x	x	x	x	x	x	x	x
Castro et al. [34]	x	x	x	x	x	x		x	x	x	x	x	x	x	x	x	x	x	x	x
Chen et al. [35]	x	x	x	x	x	x		x	x	x	x	x	x	x	x	x	x	x	x	x
Davidson et al. [36]	x	x			x		x	x			x	x		x			x	x		
Dayarathna [37]	x	x	x	x	x	x		x	x	x	x	x	x	x	x	x	x	x	x	x
Dhande [38]		x	/		x	/		y	y					x			x	x	x	
Fan et al. [39]	x	x	x	x	x	x		x	x	x	x	x	x		x	x	x	x	x	x
Gabbai [40]	x	x	x	x	/	/	/	/	/	x	x	/	x	x	/	x	x	/	x	x
King [41]		x			x		x	x	x	x			x	x		x	x	x	x	
Mineraud et al. [43]	x	x	x	x	x	x		x	x	x	x	x	x		x	x	x	x	x	x
Pereira and Aguiar [44]	x	x	x	x	x	x		x	x	x	x	x	x		x	x	x	x	x	x
ptc.com [45]	x	x	x	x	x	x		/	/	x	x	x	x	x	x		x	x	x	x

(continued)

Table 3. *(continued)*

Papers X = discussed as a requirement for telemetry in the article Blank = not discussed as a requirement for telemetry in the article / = Not applicable in the article	Dimensions																			
	Data analytics				Communication							Data management				Asset management				Socio technical
	Analytics at the edge	Batch data analytics	Predictive analytics	Real time data analytics	Ethernet	Wireless	Dial up network	Point to point	Point to multipoint	Secure protocols	Lightweight protocols	Out of order data	Security	Remote measurement	Data compression	Device authentication	Remote control	Device management	Device verification	Ethics
Queiroz et al. [46]					y	/		x	x	x			/	x			x	x	x	
Rezai et al. [47]	/	/	/	/	x	x		x	x	x	x	x	x	/	x	x	/	/	x	x
Sajid et al. [48]	x	x	x	x	x	x		/	/	x	/	/	x	/		x	/	/	x	x
Shahzad et al. [49]	/	/	/	/	x	x		/	/	x	x	x	x	/	x	x	x	x	x	x
Shahzad et al. [50]	x	/	/	/	x	x		/	/	x	x	x	x	/	x	x		x	x	x
Shakya [51]	/	/	/	/	x	x		x	x	x	x	x	x	/	x	x	/	/	x	x
[52]	x	x	x	x	x	x		x	x	x	x	x	x	x	x	x	x	x	x	/
Wireless [53]	x	x	x	x	x	x		/	/	x	x	x	x	x	x		x	x	x	x
Wireless [54]	x	x	x	x	x	x		x	x	x	x	x	x		x	x	x	x	x	x
Wu et al. [55]	x	x	x	x	x	x		x	x	x	x	x	x	x	x	x	x	x	x	x

6 Conclusion

The aim of this paper was to identify components for an mHealth solution that could be built on the strategies, experiences and resources inherent in the notion of telemetry. Towards this aim, a scoping review was done to identify the categories of a telemetry solution. Telemetry is defined as an automated communications process by which measurements and other data are collected at remote or inaccessible points, and transmitted to receiving equipment for monitoring. It was identified as having components related to SCADA, M2M and IoT as data analytics, communication, data management, asset management, and related socio-technical aspects.

Just by the nature of the telemetry features, it is evident that telemetry solutions provide the mechanisms to manage, monitor and control remote assets. The features defined across SCADA, M2M and IOT provide a unique suite of management tools to ensure the smooth operation of remote assets, as well as the ability to make informed decisions based on acquired data from remote assets.

References

1. AID LEAP. https://aidleap.org/2014/11/20/is-there-too-much-innovation-in-development/
2. ICTworks. https://www.ictworks.org/ugandan-mhealth-moratorium-good-thing/#.Wr4NpC5uZEY
3. Otto, K., Shekar, M., Herbst, C.H., Mohammed, R.: Information and communication technologies for health systems strengthening: opportunities, criteria for success, and innovation for Africa and beyond. Discussion Paper. World Bank Group (2015)
4. Botha, A., Booi, T.C.: The current state of mHealth intervention strategies and implementation in South Africa. IST AFrica, Durban, South Africa (2016)
5. Botha, A., Makitla, I., Fogwill, T., Tolmay, J.: Channel agnostic access for providing services to the masses. In: ZA-WWW, 2011 Conference (2011)
6. NDoH: eHealth Strategy for South Africa 2012–2017. South African National Department of Health, Pretoria (2012)
7. Mehl, G., et al.: Harnessing mHealth in low-resource settings to overcome health system constraints and achieve universal access to healthcare. In: Behavioral Healthcare and Technology: Using Science-Based Innovations to Transform Practice, p. 239 (2014)
8. Fischer, G.: A conceptual framework for computer-supported collaborative learning at work. In: Goggins, S.P., Jahnke, I., Wulf, V. (eds.) Computer-Supported Collaborative Learning at the Workplace, pp. 23–42. Springer, New York (2013). https://doi.org/10.1007/978-1-4614-1740-8
9. Chib, A., van Velthoven, M.H., Car, J.: mHealth adoption in low-resource environments: a review of the use of mobile healthcare in developing countries. J. Health Commun. **20**, 4–34 (2015)
10. Chib, A.: The promise and peril of mHealth in developing countries. Mobile Media Commun. **1**, 69–75 (2013)
11. Harrison, R.R., Watkins, P.T., Kier, R.J., Lovejoy, R.O., Black, D.J., Solzbacher, F.: A low-power integrated circuit for a wireless 100-electrode neural recording system. IEEE J. Solid State Circ. **42**, 123–133 (2007)
12. Fonseca, M., English, J., Arx, M.V., Allen, M.G.: Wireless micromachined ceramic pressure sensor for high-temperature applications. J. Microelectromech. Syst. **11**, 337–343 (2002)

13. Shi, E., Chan, H., Rieffel, E., Chow, R., Song, D.: Privacy-preserving aggregation of time-series data. In: Annual Network & Distributed System Security Symposium (NDSS). Internet Societ (2011)
14. Malan, D., Fulford-Jones, T., Welsh, M., Moulton, S.: CodeBlue: an ad hoc sensor network infrastructure for emergency medical care. In: International Workshop on Wearable and Implantable Body Sensor Networks, vol. 5 (2004). icawww.epfl.ch
15. Kopp, B.: Industrial telemetry. In: Carden, F., Jedlicka, R.P., Henry, R. (eds.) Telemetry Systems Engineering. Artech House, Norwood (2002)
16. Schueffel, P.: Taming the beast: a scientific definition of fintech. J. Innov. Manag. **4**, 32 (2016)
17. Copi, I.M., Cohen, C., McMahon, K.: Introduction to Logic. Routledge, New York (2016)
18. Nickerson, R.C., Varshney, U., Muntermann, J.: A method for taxonomy development and its application in information systems. Eur. J. Inf. Syst. **22**, 336–359 (2013)
19. Nickerson, R., Varshney, U., Muntermann, J., Isaac, H.: Towards a taxonomy of mobile applications. In: AMCIS 2007 Proceedings, p. 338 (2007)
20. Nickerson, R., Muntermann, J., Varshney, U., Isaac, H.: Taxonomy development in information systems: developing a taxonomy of mobile applications. In: European Conference in Information Systems (2009)
21. Bailey, K.D.: Typologies and Taxonomies: An Introduction to Classification Techniques. Sage, Thousand Oaks (1994)
22. McKinney, J.C.: Constructive Typology and Social Theory. Ardent Media, New York (1966)
23. Aliseda, A.: Abductive Reasoning. Springer, Dordrecht (2006). https://doi.org/10.1007/1-4020-3907-7
24. Sober, E.: Core Questions in Philosophy: A Text with Readings. Prentice Hall, Upper Saddle River (2001)
25. Brien, S.E., Lorenzetti, D.L., Lewis, S., Kennedy, J., Ghali, W.A.: Overview of a formal scoping review on health system report cards. Implement. Sci. **5**, 2 (2010)
26. Arksey, H., O'Malley, L.: Scoping studies: towards a methodological framework. Int. J. Soc. Res. Methodol. **8**, 19–32 (2005)
27. Sandelowski, M., Docherty, S., Emden, C.: Qualitative metasynthesis: issues and techniques. Res. Nurs. Health **20**, 365–371 (1997)
28. Ellis, T.J., Levy, Y.: A guide for novice researchers: design and development research methods. In: Proceedings of Informing Science & IT Education Conference, InSITE. Citeseer (2010)
29. Okoli, C., Schabram, K.: A guide to conducting a systematic literature review of information systems research. Sprouts: Working Papers on Information Systems, vol. 10 (2010)
30. Liberati, A., et al.: The PRISMA statement for reporting systematic reviews and meta-analyses of studies that evaluate health care interventions: explanation and elaboration. PLoS Med. **6**, e1000100 (2009)
31. Alaya, M.B., Banouar, Y., Monteil, T., Chassot, C., Drira, K.: OM2M: extensible ETSI-compliant M2M service platform with self-configuration capability. Procedia Comput. Sci. **32**, 1079–1086 (2014)
32. Borgia, E.: The Internet of Things vision: key features, applications and open issues. Comput. Commun. **54**, 1–31 (2014)
33. Botta, A., de Donato, W., Persico, V., Pescapé, A.: Integration of Cloud computing and Internet of Things: a survey. Futur. Gener. Comput. Syst. **56**, 684–700 (2016)

34. Castro, M., Jara, A.J., Skarmeta, A.F.: An analysis of M2M platforms: challenges and opportunities for the Internet of Things. In: 2012 Sixth International Conference on Innovative Mobile and Internet Services in Ubiquitous Computing (IMIS), pp. 757–762. IEEE (2012)
35. Chen, M., Wan, J., González-Valenzuela, S., Liao, X., Leung, V.C.: A survey of recent developments in home M2M networks. IEEE Commun. Surv. Tutor. **16**, 98–114 (2014)
36. Davidson, E.M., McArthur, S.D., McDonald, J.R., Cumming, T., Watt, I.: Applying multi-agent system technology in practice: automated management and analysis of SCADA and digital fault recorder data. IEEE Trans. Power Syst. **21**, 559–567 (2006)
37. DZone.com. https://dzone.com/articles/iot-software-platform-comparison
38. Dhande, N.S.: Review On SCADA: Virtual Instrument Management
39. Fan, Z., Haines, R., Kulkarni, P.: M2M communications for E-health and smart grid: an industry and standard perspective. IEEE Wirel. Commun. **21**, 62–69 (2014)
40. Gabbai, A.: Kevin Ashton Describes "the Internet of Things". Smithsonian Magazine (2015)
41. King, P.: SCADA systems–looking ahead. Control Microsystems Whitepaper, p. 83 (2005)
42. Kwasnick, R., et al.: Telemetry for reliability. In: 2017 IEEE International Reliability Physics Symposium (IRPS), pp. 6C-2.1–6C-2.6. IEEE (2017)
43. Mineraud, J., Mazhelis, O., Su, X., Tarkoma, S.: A gap analysis of Internet-of-Things platforms. Comput. Commun. **89**, 5–16 (2016)
44. Pereira, C., Aguiar, A.: Towards efficient mobile M2M communications: survey and open challenges. Sensors **14**, 19582 (2014)
45. https://www.ptc.com/en/products/iot
46. Queiroz, C., Mahmood, A., Tari, Z.: An analytical framework for evaluating survivability of SCADA systems. In: 2010 IEEE 10th International Conference on Computer and Information Technology (CIT), pp. 877–881. IEEE (2010)
47. Rezai, A., Keshavarzi, P., Moravej, Z.: Key management issue in SCADA networks: a review. Eng. Sci. Technol. Int. J. **20**, 354–363 (2017)
48. Sajid, A., Abbas, H., Saleem, K.: Cloud-Assisted IoT-Based SCADA systems security: a review of the state of the art and future challenges. IEEE Access **4**, 1375–1384 (2016)
49. Shahzad, A., Musa, S., Aborujilah, A., Irfan, M.: The SCADA review: system components, architecture, protocols and future security trends. Am. J. Appl. Sci. **11**, 1418 (2014)
50. Shahzad, A., Musa, S., Aborujilah, A., Irfan, M.: A review: industrial control system (ICS) and their secuity issues. Am. J. Appl. Sci. **11**, 1398–1404 (2014)
51. dzone.com. http://thinkpalm.com/blogs/lets-get-mqtt-rolling/
52. Wan, J., Li, D., Zou, C., Zhou, K.: M2M communications for smart city: an event-based architecture. In: 2012 IEEE 12th International Conference on Computer and Information Technology, pp. 895–900 (2012)
53. https://www.sierrawireless.com/resources/#/q=Case%2520Study%7CAirVantage%2520IoT%2520Platform&p=0
54. Wireless, S.: Planning a longterm wireless strategy. Sireea Wireless (2018)
55. Wu, G., Talwar, S., Johnsson, K., Himayat, N., Johnson, K.D.: M2M: from mobile to embedded internet. IEEE Commun. Mag. **49**, 36–43 (2011)
56. Ahmed, I., Obermeier, S., Naedele, M., Richard III, G.G.: SCADA systems: challenges for forensic investigators. Computer **45**, 44–51 (2012)

Towards a Provisional Workplace E-learning Acceptance Framework for Developing Countries

McDonald van der Merwe(✉) and Gavin Armitage

Department of Information Systems, University of South Africa,
Corner of Christiaan de Wet Road and Pioneer Avenue, Florida, South Africa
vdmertm@unisa.ac.za, gavin.a.armitage@gmail.com

Abstract. Using the available literature and existing critical success factors models and frameworks as bases, this paper proposes a provisional workplace e-learning acceptance framework for developing countries. The intended outcome was to evaluate whether or not the framework appropriates employee acceptance of current e-learning initiatives. The study was conducted by means of a survey questionnaire that was distributed to three South African organisations that already make use of e-learning. Categories User characteristics, Technology influence and Instructor influence returned an average median that reflected a general agreement with positive statements about e-learning initiatives offered. Respondents were, however, less enthusiastic about the category Support influence, which returned a lower average median. Whereas several individual tensions were identified across categories, these did not have a pronounced impact on the category Overall acceptance of e-learning. The latter finding provided preliminary evidence that the proposed framework, at minimum, established priorities that may in time contribute to the establishment of a validated framework for developing countries.

Keywords: Workplace e-learning · Acceptance framework
Critical success factors · Technology Acceptance Model

1 Introduction

In an increasingly competitive global economy, human capital is viewed as an important enterprise resource that nurtures innovation and renewal while enhancing competitiveness [4]. In addition, the shift from a product-based to a knowledge-based economy means that knowledge workers are in increased demand [24]. For this reason, it is important that companies bring their workforce to a mature competitive level in a relatively short period. Here, workplace e-learning has been used to train and upskill employees on a relatively affordable and widespread platform [4].

Although workplace e-learning has been utilised in developed countries for many years with satisfying results, it remains a relatively new concept in developing countries. Whereas the goal of e-learning in a developed country is to provide a higher level of education, the goal in a developing country would be to develop an effective knowledge economy and enhance lifelong education [2]. This distinction is largely

K. Krauss et al. (Eds.): IDIA 2018, CCIS 933, pp. 223–242, 2019.
https://doi.org/10.1007/978-3-030-11235-6_15

grounded in the reality that developing countries tend to be more abundant in unskilled and semi-skilled labour [16], with the character of their reform dependent on a variety of specific and situational factors. In a developing country like South Africa, for example, only 25% of the employed workforce are skilled, with 46% semi-skilled and 25% low-skilled [34]. Whereas there exists a distinct need for upskilling, an additional factor that promotes reform in this particular setting is that of employment equity legislation. For example, employee skills development is one of five measured elements inherent in the Broad-Based Black Economic Empowerment Act 53 of 2003, to which companies who deal with the government or parastatals need to adhere. Other Acts, such as The Skills Development Act 97 of 1998 and the Skills Development Levies Act 9 of 1999, were specifically established by the local Department of Labour in an attempt to encourage learning in the workplace, with employers allowed to claim back portions of a skills levy they pay to government if they train their staff [39]. Yet, whereas there exists sufficient impetus for upskilling of employees, and while 81% of executives of South African companies surveyed in 2016 recognised the importance of continuous learning, 58% were not ready for workplace learning, with only 16% helping employees grow and navigate careers within the company [11].

A term that becomes particularly relevant in such settings, and which has been widely adopted in technology-focused research in both developed and developing countries, is critical success factors (CSF). CSFs within an organisation are those things that must be done if a company is to be successful [15], and in the context of workplace e-learning initiatives, must be considered if such initiatives are to be accepted by employees. However, research literature that addresses employee acceptance of e-learning systems in organisational contexts is scarce [22]. Where technology acceptance research has been conducted in wider settings, the Technology Acceptance Model (TAM) and its derivatives, TAM2 and UTAUT, have mainly been used as the underlying theoretical model for many empirical studies [22]. However, as posited more than a decade ago and an assessment which appears still valid today, the applicability of existing parameters of the TAM are insufficient to fully reflect end-users' acceptance of e-learning initiatives within organisations [24]. Furthermore, there are perceived limitations to the applicability of TAM models in developing countries [38]. The net result is that a different set of parameters and CSFs are required.

To facilitate workplace e-learning acceptance, and increase the possibility of success in developing countries, it is therefore necessary to pay attention to CSFs from both the business and individual perspectives. This requires a systematic approach to identify CSFs that affect both adoption and the ongoing acceptance of e-learning within organisations situated in low-resources or low-income regions.

Following on from the above, the broad purposes of this paper are threefold: (i) to identify, from literature, categories and characteristics of CSFs relevant to workplace e-learning initiatives in developing countries; (ii) to propose a provisional workplace e-learning acceptance framework applicable to a developing country setting; and (iii) to apply the framework by surveying employees who have had exposure to workplace e-learning initiatives. The intended outcome is to evaluate if the proposed framework appropriates employees' acceptance of current e-learning initiatives. This study does not make an attempt to validate the proposed framework, but, as an exploratory study, is intended to establish priorities and to assist with the identification of provisional

CSFs that may, in time, contribute to a validated framework that can be used to direct and evaluate purposeful workplace e-learning.

The rest of this paper is structured as follows: The next section introduces e-learning, and how e-learning is used within the workplace, and also identifies CSFs from the e-learning literature as they relate to the business context.

2 Literature

2.1 Benefits of E-learning in the Workplace

E-learning in the workplace has become widely recognised as an effective way to acquire knowledge and skills for competency development, and to increase organisational effectiveness [12]. Workplace learning has been summarised as the means, process and activities in the workplace by which employees learn basic skills to high-end technologies and management tactics that are immediately beneficial to their jobs and organisational roles [6]. There are also a few key trends that are driving organisations to capitalise on e-learning: a knowledge-based economy; the notion that people are a competitive advantage; that there is an increasing shift to skilled labour; a shortage of skills; a competitive global economy; and, the speed of technological change [20].

Several direct benefits when making use of e-learning to train up a workforce have been identified: time and location flexibility, cost and time saving, self-paced and collaborative learning, better access to instructors, unlimited access and usage of content, and multimedia-based learning [27]. Not surprisingly then, e-learning has been recognised as a supportive practice for learning at work [6]. Any organisation, however, will go through different stages while adopting e-learning [3]. The first phase is when an organisation offers e-learning from different departments. The second phase is when the learning is disciplined, and now delivered from a nominated department, with learning now expected to meet the organisation's goals. The final phase is where an organisation's strategy is linked to e-learning, which allows it to implement change and affect culture.

Given such benefits, organisations that have invested in infrastructure can easily make use of e-learning to justify the expense of that infrastructure [20, 23]. Conversely, underutilisation of an e-learning system is a key issue that needs to be considered [22]. CSFs such as user perception and effective use of the system then become factors that need consideration.

2.2 CSFs Factors for E-learning

Most of the research on user acceptance research focused on the role of CSFs in Higher Education Institutions (HEIs); however, many similarities exist between corporate and HEI requirements as it relates to e-learning challenges. The benefits of e-learning in both HEIs and corporations, for example, can only be realised if the technology is adopted, and is useful and easy to use [7, 22, 45]. Likewise, HEIs have invested in e-learning to meet three business goals, namely increasing or sustaining the quality of education, improving access to learning opportunities, and, finally, to reduce costs [13]. For such reasons, the extant literature on e-learning in HEIs is considered useful for the purposes of the current study.

Several contextual elements, as items which would deem e-learning a success at an HEI, have been identified, including a conducive environment, technical and subject matter skills, learning support, appropriate learning content, and instructor knowledge and support [8]. Likewise, individuals with low computer self-efficacy tend not to recognise the benefits of e-learning, whereas a higher self-efficacy appears to be a significant determinant of perceived usefulness, perceived ease of use and perceived creditability [7]. One of the lesser known attractive features of e-learning is that it raises curiosity, which provides a "teachable" moment [14]. While there is a mix of conditions or CSFs for e-learning initiatives related to institutional support, technology, developers, teachers, and student learning and experience, the relative importance for continuation is not known [26]. In comparing successful and unsuccessful initiatives reported from the literature, the following factors are identified as important: financial support, the maturity/stability of technology used, the time and training available to teachers and developers, and support as part of the developer's job description.

As with local organisations, South African HEI's have faced numerous changes in external and internal environments, and have had to continually respond to developments in ICTs [1]. Successful implementation of e-learning within local HEIs has therefore required a strategy that was designed to meet the learners and business goals of the institution, and a need for recognition of the e-learning team within the core business of HEIs [13, 36]. A study completed at three of South Africans HEIs showed that students are more motivated, receptive, engaged, and more likely to learn, if they play a larger role in pushing the use of technology [19]. Likewise, knowledge of instructional web tools allowed lecturers to successfully develop and teach courses. E-learning also needs to cater for a diverse set of requirements with students from economics, industrial psychology, money and banking and library science concerned about module exposure and enjoyment, while the engineering faculties were concerned about facts and rote learning [30]. Support staff skill sets and cost, and the support base of the LMS, were identified as other important factors to consider when deploying e-learning. For a learning institute to successfully integrate with ICT, note has to be taken of good teaching and learning practices, fostering a supportive institutional environment and providing the necessary technological teaching and learning tools [41]. Additional imperative factors reported were obtaining buy-in from the shareholders, consulting as widely as possible, and providing a stable infrastructure, a very good training system and a support system.

As noted in the introduction, CSF studies on workplace e-learning in developing countries are scarce. One notable study [2] reported six critical dimensions to consider when implementing e-learning. These dimensions include learner characteristics, infrastructure and system quality, institution and service quality, instructor characteristics, course and information quality, and extrinsic motivation (perceived usefulness and ease of use - see [21]). The study concluded that the most important dimension was that of the learner characteristics, while infrastructure and system quality were a high dimension for the organisation implementing the e-learning system. Other user benefits identified are better content delivery, personalised instructions, and increased accessibility to information, content standardisation, accountability, interactivity, confidence and increased convenience [12]. Key CSFs identified within a South African workplace context were the following: dealing with change management, integration of business and e-learning strategies, adequacy of resources, bringing planning down to earth, focusing on strategic issues, sponsorship of implementation, and a stable and conducive hardware and software environment [9]. One other key CSF identified was that of an organisation aligning the e-learning with an employee's job competency [6]. Furthermore, students who have enrolled for courses to cater for their work commitments, view distance learning as a technology to facilitate their need to acquire new skills. This has also benefited companies which have been able to gain increased skills based on institutions being able to provide these technologies for teaching and learning [35].

It is readily apparent that there exists a complex pattern of both interrelated and standalone CSFs that act or could act as determinants of the successful implementation of workplace e-learning. Constructing an appropriate workplace e-learning acceptance framework for a developing country therefore remains a significant challenge.

3 Theoretical Research Framework

Within all organisations, CSFs can be weighted differently, due to different requirements of e-learning based on infrastructure limitations. For example, whereas a smaller organisation may not have the infrastructure to run heavy, rich media content, a larger organisation has the infrastructure to allow for this type of learning. As each organisation's e-learning offerings mature, certain CSF's may therefore become less or more relevant. For this reason, it is proposed that the evaluation of an e-learning system should make use of a hierarchical framework with a fuzzy logic step approach and analytical network process to develop an evaluation approach to weight measures [40]. This will allow one to determine the dependence between these measures and to prioritise their weighting. The hierarchical structure is based on five aspects containing twenty-one criteria. The aspects are determined as follows: learner attractiveness (example of criteria: provide an appropriate learning scenario), quality of system (example of criteria: ease of access to learning material), instructor attitudes (example of criteria: responsiveness to learner inquiries), service quality (example of criteria: ease of contact to instructors), and supportive issues (example of criteria: enough support is provided to enable the user to learn remotely).

Several other studies have proposed frameworks for evaluating CSFs. One is an e-learning framework that includes intellectual property, suitability of the course, building the e-course, course maintenance, the platform, and measuring the success of the content within an organisation [29]. Another prerequisite framework for a successful e-learning implementation consists of seven benchmark items, namely institutional support, teaching and learning, faculty support, student support, course development, and course structure, evaluation and assessment [18]. Within the proposed framework, the purpose of e-learning is to achieve the learning objective. The attainment of these objectives can be measured in the following categories: environmental, technological, student related and instructor related. A confirmatory model research paper conducted at an HEI, and widely conceived as a seminal study, categorised the abovementioned CSFs as student-, information technology-, instructor- and university support [31].

The Technology Acceptance Model (TAM, [10]) has been widely used to assess learner satisfaction, acceptance and usage of e-learning tools [44]. TAM2 [43] introduced social influence processes (subjective norm, voluntarily and image), and cognitive instrumental processes (output quality, job relevance, result demonstrability) affected both perceived usefulness and intention to use. Since ease of use can easily influence perceived usefulness, other major external factors that influence perceived ease of use, which in turn influences both perceived usefulness and behavioral intent, have been proposed in TAM3 [42]. These external factors include the anchor's computer self-efficacy, perception of external control, computer anxiety and computer playfulness. In addition to these anchors, perceived enjoyment and objective usability have been added as further adjustments to influence perceived ease of use (Fig. 1).

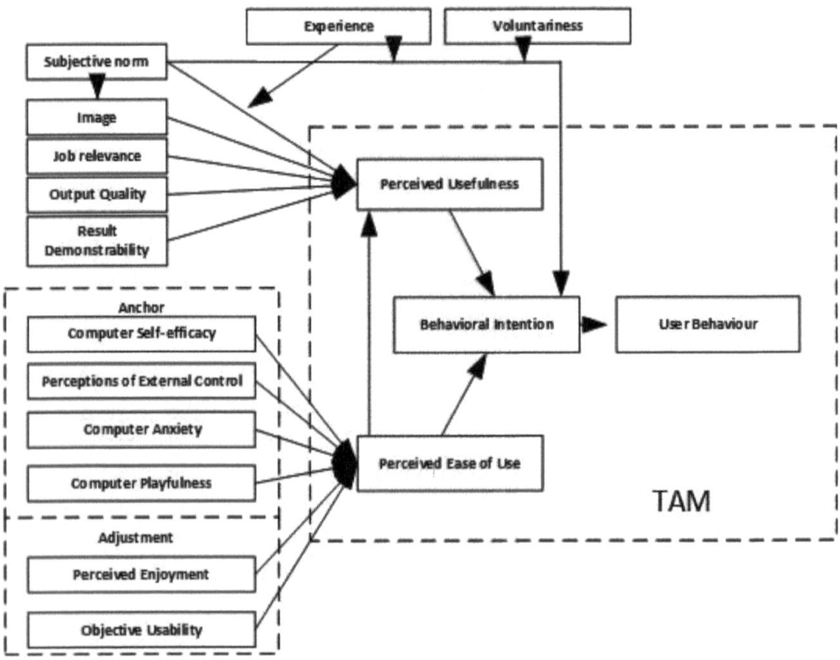

Fig. 1. Extended TAM3, inclusive of external factors [42]

TAM 3, however accurate it appears on face value and/or supported by research, is not necessarily reflective of a developing country context. Throughout the literature, the broad CSF categories, identified earlier [31], appear pervasive: user characteristics, instructor influence, technology influence and support influence. In mapping these categories onto an adapted version of the extended TAM3, a provisional workplace e-learning acceptance framework for developing countries is offered in Fig. 2.

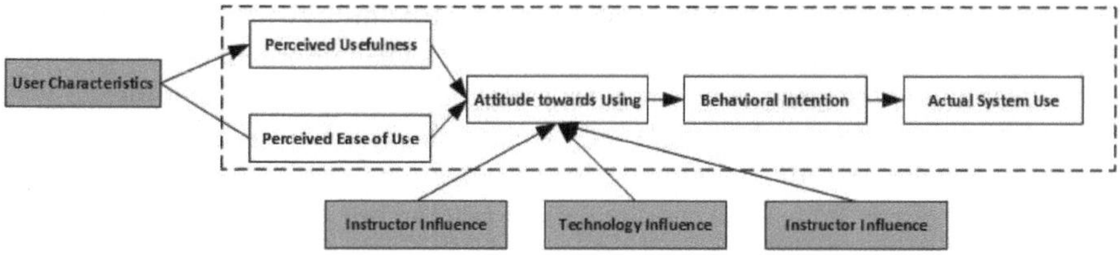

Fig. 2. Proposed workplace e-learning acceptance framework for developing countries (authors)

In measuring the categories, the following broad characteristics within each of these categories were identified [31]: User characteristics - computer competency, interactive collaboration and e-learning content design; Technology characteristics - access to technology and infrastructure; Support characteristics - support access and response; and, Instructor characteristics - attitude towards and control of the technology, teaching style. Following on these measurements, and with the proposed workplace e-learning acceptance framework and the literature as foundation, the following specific workplace e-learning acceptance measures (**category** (*characteristic):* measure/s) are forwarded:

- **User Characteristic** (*perceived usefulness*): Motivation to make use of e-learning technology; user competency; and general mindset about e-learning
- **User Characteristic** (*perceived usefulness*): Collaboration capabilities of workplace e-learning
- **User Characteristic** (*perceived ease of use*): E-learning content and design of the learning content provided
- **User Characteristic** (*perceived usefulness*): E-learning benefits job performance
- **Technology Influence** (*attitude towards using*): User attitude towards using e-learning with regard to their Internet access, browsing speeds, website ease of use and user interface efficiency
- **Technology Influence** (*attitude towards using*): Technology to deliver the service and IT infrastructure to support e-learning
- **Support Influence** (*attitude towards using*): Support to improve user access to support and relevance of support response
- **Instructor Influence** (*attitude towards using*): The impact of instructor attitude towards technology
- **Instructor Influence** (*attitude towards using*): Instructor teaching style

With the above measures in place, the research design is presented next.

4 Research Design and Methodology

For each measure identified, a series of appropriate survey questions [31], presented in the results section tables, were employed. Using a case study approach, users within three random South African organisations with mandated and established e-learning management systems (LMS) in place, were requested to complete the survey.

The LMSs, accessible via multiple devices, were SABA (http://www.saba.com), which delivers personal learning experiences making use of social, informal, micro, video and mobile learning approaches, and Oracle OLM (http://oracle.com), which offers a wide range of functions, from catalog and online class management to learner enrolments and learning paths, and collaboration via forums, chats and web conferencing. Whereas specifics may differ, both allow for individualised and constructive variations in the management, delivery and tracking of the learning process.

Purposive sampling, where e-learning end-users were recommended by the administrators of such e-learning systems, was employed. A total of 36 subjects were identified and provided with the questionnaire. A five-point Likert scale ranging from Strongly Disagree (=1) to Strongly Agree (=5), was employed. At the end of each section, participants were provided with an opportunity to add any further information that they felt was important as it related to that section. To evaluate the effectiveness of the proposed framework in measuring user acceptance, a closing measure included was **User Characteristic** (*actual system use*): Acceptance of e- Learning by the end-users within the organisation. Finally, to remove ambiguity in the statements and ensure reliability, a small pilot study was completed with 4 individuals.

Given the small study population, simple descriptive statistical analysis techniques were employed to count how many times certain behaviours occurred (quantitative method), coupled with participant narratives (qualitative method) where appropriate. The intention was to identify patterns that will explain employees' acceptance or non-acceptance of current workplace e-learning initiatives, the latter presented as "tensions" that prevent acceptance.

5 Results

5.1 Demographic Profile

The survey response rate achieved was 78%. The majority of respondents (71%) had between 2 and 10 years' experience with e-learning initiatives, with 17% having more than 10 years' experience. Nearly 90% of the respondents were employed at professional to senior manager level within their organisation. Close to 86% of respondents were older than 33 years of age, with an equal number of male/female respondents.

The following sections provide an analysis of the questionnaire data sets.

5.2 User Characteristics (Perceived Usefulness): Motivation to Make Use of E-learning Technology; User Competency; and General Mindset About E-learning

Table 1 lists responses to questions posed to determine respondents' motivation to use, their competency and their general mindset.

All questions posed, and presented in the top row of each table, were stated in the positive. To assist the reader in interpreting the results, shaded cells are employed to visually represent the general direction of the majority of responses – i.e. oriented towards strongly disagree (a weak category) or strongly agree (a strong category). A difference of 6% and less is used for cell inclusion.

Table 1. User characteristics: motivation, competency and mindset

	Q1 E-learning encourages me to search for more facts than traditional learning	Q2 E-learning encourages me to participate more actively in discussions than traditional methods	Q3 I enjoy using personal computers	Q4 I use the personal computers for work and play	Q5 I was comfortable with using the PC and software applications before I took up the e-learning based courses
	%	%	%	%	%
1 Strongly Disagree	0	7	4	0	0
2 Disagree	18	29	0	7	0
3 Neutral	25	7	11	4	4
4 Agree	39	39	36	39	36
5 Strongly Agree	18	18	50	50	61
Median	4	4	4	4	5
Mode	4	4	5	5	5
Range	4	5	5	5	3
Inter-quartile Range	3-4(1)	2-4(2)	4-5(1)	4-5(1)	4-5(1)

	Q6 My previous experience in using PC and software applications assisted me in the e-learning based courses.	Q7 I am not intimidated by e-learning courses	Q8 I learn best by absorption	Q9 I learn best by construction (by participation and contribution)	Q10 I learn better by construction than absorption
	%	%	%	%	%
1 Strongly Disagree	0	0	0	0	0
2 Disagree	0	4	18	4	7
3 Neutral	7	0	29	14	11
4 Agree	50	43	43	54	50
5 Strongly Agree	43	54	11	29	32
Median	4	5	4	4	4
Mode	4	5	4	4	4
Range	3	4	4	4	4
Inter-quartile Range	4-5(1)	4-5(1)	3-4(1)	4-5(1)	4-5(1)

With two exceptions, the shaded cells in Table 1 show most respondents to agree or strongly agree with the questions posed. Questions 1, 2, 7, 8, 9 and 10 dealt specifically with user motivation, and revealed respondents willing and encouraged to make use of e-learning within the workplace. This positivity is evident in user comments:

"I have seen a lot of benefit with using e-learning, it has made it easy to access content whenever I have some free time to learn. Overall I would say that I have had satisfactory results from e-learning."

"E learning is a wonderful avenue to study however you may need to practice or test yourself on progress via the construction avenue. This will help to measure your understanding of the subject and progress. I am learning a language via e learning."

Table 2. User characteristics: extent of collaboration

	Q11 I only read messages posted in discussions	Q12 I read messages as well as participate in discussion group	Q13 The instructor initiated most of the discussions	Q14 Students initiated most of the discussions	Q15 The instructor participated actively in discussions
	%	%	%	%	%
1 Strongly Disagree	0	15	7	7	14
2 Disagree	33	15	21	18	7
3 Neutral	37	19	39	46	39
4 Agree	30	52	29	29	36
5 Strongly Agree	0	15	8	7	14
Median	3	4	3	3	3
Mode	3	4	3	3	3
Range	3	5	5	5	5
Inter-quartile Range	2-4(2)	2-4(2)	2-4(2)	2-4(2)	3-4(1)

5.3 User Characteristics (Perceived Usefulness): Collaboration Capabilities of Workplace E-learning

A second set of questions gauged the extent of collaborative activities that take place (Table 2).

Q11 and Q12 focused on passive and active use of discussion groups. The split between participants who either read, do not read, or sometimes read posts are more or less even (30% vs 33% vs 37%), while the majority (71%) are active participants. Q13–15 focused on the collaborative role of the instructor. The consistent medians and ranges of 3 show respondents to be of the opinion that instructors could contribute more to discussions taking place, and for this reason a tension is identified: **T1:** *Inadequate instructor collaboration.*

5.4 User Characteristics (Perceived Ease of Use): E-learning Content and Design

The next set of questions focused on participants' perceptions of the ease of use of system components as it relates to content and design aspects.

Table 3. User characteristics: e-learning design and content

	Q16 I found the instructions on using the e-learning components to be sufficiently clear	Q17 I found the course content sufficient and related to the subject	Q18 It was easy to understand the structure of the e-learning components	Q19 It was easy to navigate through the course	Q20 The e-learning components were available all the time	Q21 The course materials were placed online in a timely manner	Q22 I perceive the design of the e-learning components to be good
	%	%	%	%	%	%	%
1 Strongly Disagree	4	0	4	4	0	0	4
2 Disagree	7	0	0	4	11	4	4
3 Neutral	18	22	15	18	0	21	4
4 Agree	50	63	63	54	59	46	64
5 Strongly Agree	21	15	19	21	30	29	25
Median	4	4	4	4	4	4	4
Mode	4	4	4	4	4	4	4
Range	5	3	5	5	4	4	5
Inter-quartile Range	3-4(1)	4-4(0)	4-4(0)	3-4(1)	4-5(1)	3-5(2)	4-4(0)

Table 3 reveals positive responses throughout, with medians and modes of 4, and 71–89% of respondents agreeing or strongly agreeing to a high presentation standard. Some users, as is evident in the first 4 columns, are neutral, possibly leaning towards specific content and design requirements that other respondents felt were not met:

> *"An important aspect of e-learning to me is that you should be able to access any element of the content within a maximum of 3 mouse clicks."*

> *"E-learning should be made easier to navigate, it is difficult to follow the steps provided. E-learning is a great tool and if made more user friendly will make a big impact on the way we learn going forward."*

> *"A frustration that presents itself from time to time is the situation where I've lost the progress made or it was not stored regularly enough. This is perhaps more a problem with the way the e-learning content was designed than the actual supporting system. Content creators should consider putting in enough checkpoints to limit the amount of re-work required should the internet connection be disconnected or the student abruptly stop the course."*

> *"Most Instructional Designers are not up to speed with the latest e-learning trends"*

> *"My observation from a design point of view is that most online course designers tend to neglect the fundamental step in the information gathering process of understanding what is required by your end user. They develop these elaborate courses and at times the learning experience is overshadowed by animations and clicks every so often."*

Combined, these user responses are noted as a tension: **T2:** *Instructional design shortcomings*.

5.5 User Characteristics (Perceived Usefulness): E-learning Benefits Job Performance

Q23 and Q24 attempted to gauge the extent to which respondents' e-learning played a role in enhancing their job performance (Table 4).

Table 4. User characteristics: job relevance

	Q23 I feel that the content has helped me perform my job better	Q24 The content was applicable to the role that I perform in my organisation
	%	%
1 Strongly Disagree	0	4
2 Disagree	12	7
3 Neutral	19	14
4 Agree	46	46
5 Strongly Agree	23	29
Median	4	4
Mode	4	4
Range	4	5
Inter-quartile Range	3-5(2)	3-5(2)

For both questions, a majority (69% and greater) indicated that they experience a direct benefit from e-learning as it relates to their job performance. Thirty-one percent and 21% of users, however, expressed a neutral stance or disagreeing to the two questions, resulting in comments that point at content being mismatched at various levels:

"Generally, e-learning within the organisations that I have been employed at had very simplistic course material and subjects. Things like Office or how to use a computer. My job requires advanced computer knowledge and usage and these types of e-learning courses are way below my expectations of learning material."

"I would like to see more content available and not just regulatory type learning."

"The content was not very efficient for my level of expertise. I would like to be able to provide feedback on the content so that they can improve the content. The content can sometimes be especially long and time consuming."

"No job specific e-learning programs have been delivered to staff in my department. As such we have only been exposed to compliance related e-learning programs as well as e-learning that is not job related."

Content that has no job relevance serves no purpose, hence **T3:** *Mismatched content* is identified.

5.6 Technology Influence (Attitude Towards Using): Technology to Deliver the Service and IT Infrastructure to Support E-learning

The next set of questions measured the extent to which technology impacted on respondents' attitude towards workplace e-learning. Of interest are Internet access, browsing speeds, website ease of use and user interface efficiency.

A positive technology impact was recorded from Q25–Q30 (97%, 75%, 79%, 79%, 79% and 70%, respectively), with respondents reporting adequate access to, and use of, technology. One user, in a comment about Internet speed, highlights the fact that workplace e-learning may happen outside an organisation's network, which can be problematic (Table 5).

Table 5. Technology influence: access to technology and infrastructure

	Q25 I have easy access to the Internet	Q26 I did not experience problems while browsing	Q27 Browsing speed was satisfactory	Q28 Overall, the website was easy to use	Q29 Information was well structured and presented	Q30 I found the screen design pleasant
	%	%	%	%	%	%
1 Strongly Disagree	0	0	0	0	0	0
2 Disagree	0	7	7	7	4	7
3 Neutral	4	18	14	14	18	22
4 Agree	36	39	39	43	54	48
5 Strongly Agree	61	36	39	36	25	22
Median	5	4	4	4	4	4
Mode	5	4	4	4	4	4
Range	3	4	4	4	4	4
Inter-quartile Range	4-5(1)	3-5(2)	4-5(1)	4-5(1)	4-4(0)	3-4(1)

"As mentioned above bandwidth speeds with wi-fi at home is slower than at the office and frustrating. SAs average bandwith speed of 2.0 mbs is lower than the global average (3.0 mbs). The top 10 countries in the world reaches speeds of up to 12–13 mbs."

The above comment, however, is an exception to the pattern noted.

5.7 Technology Influence (Attitude Towards Using): Technology to Deliver the Service and IT Infrastructure to Support E-learning

A second set of technology influence questions covered technology available to deliver and support workplace e-learning (Table 6).

Table 6. Technology influence: delivery of service and infrastructure

	Q31 I can rely on the computer network	Q32 Overall, the information technology infrastructure is efficient
	%	%
1 Strongly Disagre	0	0
2 Disagree	12	4
3 Neutral	11	18
4 Agree	50	57
5 Strongly Agree	27	21
Median	4	4
Mode	4	4
Range	4	4
Inter-quartile Ran	4-5(1)	4-4(0)

As with the previous section on technology, responses to Q31 (77%) and Q32 (79%) show most respondents to be satisfied with the infrastructure in place. For a percentage of users (33% and 22%) this is, however, not the case. One plausible reason, and as highlighted in the previous section, is that some users are reliant on technology outside the workplace.

The next section deals with the influence support has on respondents' attitude towards workplace e-learning.

5.8 Support Influence (Attitude Towards Using): Technical Support to Improve User Access and Relevance of Support Response

Access to technology and support with such technology impact on user attitude towards using e-learning, and Table 7 list responses to questions that evaluated the extent of support available.

A consistent spread of positive responses across Q33 and Q35–36 indicates adequate access support for a large percentage of users, although not all respondents are equally enthusiastic about access to hardware and the level of support available from technicians; hence, two respondents noted:

"It has been quite difficult to receive and support and have not made the learning experience pleasant".

Table 7. Support influence: support access and response

	Q33 I can access the central repository and search for materials	Q34 I can request technical support from technicians	Q35 There are enough computers to use and practise	Q36 I can print assignments and materials easily
	%	%	%	%
1 Strongly Disagree	0	7	4	8
2 Disagree	4	11	4	4
3 Neutral	22	26	22	23
4 Agree	44	41	48	46
5 Strongly Agree	30	15	22	19
Median	4	4	4	4
Mode	4	4	4	4
Range	4	5	5	5
Inter-quartile Range	3-5(2)	3-4(1)	3-4(1)	3-4(1)

"The support is not sufficient and the process for gaining support is time consuming and frustrating."

T4: *Low levels of technician support* is identified as a tension.

5.9 Instructor Influence (Attitude Towards Using): Impact of Instructor Attitude

Instructor attitude can influence user attitude towards workplace e-learning in a number of ways, with questions constructed around these ways (Table 8).

Table 8. Instructor influence: impact of instructor attitude

	Q37 The instructor is enthusiastic about teaching the class	Q39 The instructor's style of presentation holds my interest	Q39 The instructor is friendly towards individual learners	Q40 Learners felt welcome in seeking advice/help	Q41 The instructor encourages learner interaction
	%	%	%	%	%
1 Strongly Disagree	4	4	4	7	4
2 Disagree	4	0	4	0	0
3 Neutral	39	43	39	36	39
4 Agree	39	36	43	46	43
5 Strongly Agree	14	18	11	11	14
Median	4	4	4	4	4
Mode	3	3	4	4	4
Range	5	5	5	5	5
Inter-quartile Range	3-4(1)	3-4(1)	3-4(1)	3-4(1)	3-4(1)

	Q42 The instructor handles the e-learning units effectively	Q43 The instructor explains how to use the e-learning components	Q44 I feel the instructor is keen that we use the e-learning based units	Q45 We were invited to ask questions /receive answers	Q46 We were encouraged to participate in class
	%	%	%	%	%
1 Strongly Disagree	4	4	0	0	4
2 Disagree	0	11	0	7	4
3 Neutral	54	48	57	44	36
4 Agree	36	30	25	30	39
5 Strongly Agree	7	7	18	19	18
Median	3	3	3	3	4
Mode	3	3	3	3	4
Range	5	5	3	4	5
Inter-quartile Range	3-4(1)	3-4(1)	3-4(1)	3-4(1)	3-4(1)

An even spread across the "Agree" and "Neutral" categories, with the latter more prominent, suggests that (current) instructors are not active promoters of workplace e-learning. The impression gained is that there is a focus on technology-replacing-the-instructor, with the instructor not recognising the need for differentiated instruction outside the use of technology:

"I would like to see the instructor make more use of e-learning and encourage users to make use of e-learning before and after classes."

"Blended learning delivery methods are very new to my organisation and we are still working on changing my organisation's learning culture. Being a corporate institution, this is taking time."

".. the instructional design process is fundamentally flawed because it does not incorporate the Blended Learning approach. We want our users to embrace online learning yet we do not create the appropriate support platforms and also do not consider that while other end users will take to this kind of learning like fish to water, there are quite a number of users who are still drawn to the traditional learning ways of instructor led sessions."

Given the above, a further tension is identified: **T5:** *No differentiated instruction.*

5.10 Instructor Influence (Attitude Towards Using): Instructor Teaching Style

A final set of instructor influence questions attempted to gauge how the teaching style of instructors impacted on the attitude of the user to make use of e-learning (Table 9).

Table 9. Instructor influence: teaching style

	Q47 **The instructor encourages and motivates me to use e-learning**	**Q48** **The instructor is active in teaching me the course subjects via e-learning**
	%	%
1 Strongly Disagree	0	3.7
2 Disagree	7.1	3.7
3 Neutral	50	52
4 Agree	32	30
5 Strongly Agree	11	11
Median	3	3
Mode	3	3
Range	4	5
Inter-quartile Range	3-4(1)	3-4(1)

Both questions resulted in a largely neutral (50% and 52%) stance, which is possibly related to **T5** identified in the previous section.

5.11 User Characteristic (Actual System Use): Acceptance of E-Learning by the Users Within the Organisation

The closing question provided insight into respondents' overall perception of e-learning within their organisation (Table 10).

Table 10. User characteristics: overall acceptance

	Q52 E-learning approaches are accepted within our organisation
	%
1 Strongly Disagree	0
2 Disagree	4
3 Neutral	39
4 Agree	43
5 Strongly Agree	14
Median	4
Mode	3
Range	5
Inter-quartile Range	3-4(1)

With 82% of the responses evenly spread between "Neutral" and "Agree", the perception gained is that e-learning approaches are accepted, but not necessarily embraced. A possible reason for this view is that full acceptance is related to the way e-learning is approached and offered:

> *"I have not seen the actual benefit of the learning within my organisation. I think that the e-learning needs to be centrally controlled and promoted in my organisation to make a success, currently there are no champions that are willing to make this a success."*

> *"In general, I would say that the implementation has been successful. The system could be promoted more and extra attention given on how to get assistance when using the system."*

> *"Overall the idea of e-learning is a good one. It is easier to complete and less intrusive than structured class room based training. With it being e-learning, self-paced learning, many employees did not complete the courses within the provided timeframes. There must be a commitment just as with classroom based training, that time will be made available for an employee to complete the course."*

One respondent provided insight into the benefits associated with e-learning if it is correctly implemented:

> *"e-learning has been successfully implemented within our organisation and provided us with a number of benefits. Overall cost of learning has been reduced primarily through the reduction in printing and dispatch costs. Learners find the courseware useful in that this is available as and when needed. In addition, we have been successful in providing our employees with the skills needed for the implementation of new systems within a very short time frame. For example, we trained 7500 front line employees within 2 months using e-learning - this feat could not have been achieved through traditional classroom training."*

T6: *Reserved e-learning acceptance* is identified as a tension.

6 Discussion

To gain a better understanding of the results, the average median of each CSF category, as well as the overall user e-learning acceptance, was mapped onto a bar chart. Figure 3 reveals most respondents to agree, with a median of 4, with categories User Characteristics, Technology Influence and Support Influence, which is reflected in the Overall Acceptance category. The category Instructor Influence, and specifically User

Characteristics (perceived usefulness): collaboration capabilities of workplace e-learning, returned a lower weighted median of 3, which resulted in a specific tension, **T1:** *Inadequate instructor collaboration.* Whereas instructor collaboration presents a single aspect of instructor influence, it nevertheless confirms reporting of the importance of facilitation of collaborative learning [28]. Contributing to the lower median was **T5:** *No differentiated instruction,* identified under the category Instructor Influence (*attitude towards using*): impact of instructor attitude. Differentiated instruction is typically embodied in blended learning approaches, the effectiveness of which has long been recognised [17, 32]. Given the presence of two tensions within the same category, it is evident that in the current case, instructor influence is an existing limitation to workplace e-learning acceptance, when they should make use of and promote e-learning within their organisations [30].

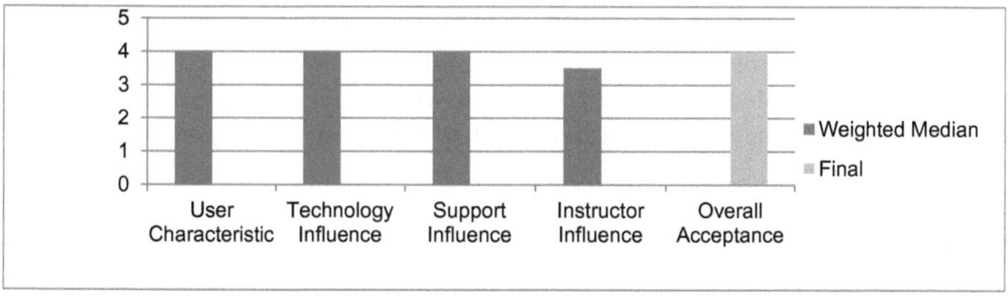

Fig. 3. Association of weighted medians

Next, and despite an average positive median of 4 reported for the category User Characteristics, the two tensions **T2:** *Instructional design shortcomings,* and **T3:** *Mismatched content,* as identified in characteristics-measures *Perceived ease of use*: e-learning content and design, and *Perceived usefulness*: e-learning benefits job performance, respectively underscore the importance and influence of two CSFs: instructional design as an ergonomic dimension that drives successful e-learning [25, 37], and the importance of aligning the e-learning with an employee's job competency [5, 29]. Here it is noted that depending on the technical level of the sampling population, this measure is likely to change in other settings.

The overall median of 4 achieved for the technology category shows that the current organisations have sufficient infrastructure and bandwidth to support the current e-learning environment. This characteristic is supportive of the research that shows conducive hardware and software environments as a key CSF [9]. Whereas the support influence category retuned an average positive median of 4, the tension identified, **T4:** *Low levels of technician support,* was not entirely unexpected. Many studies in e-learning (e.g. [33]) have found technical support to be lacking.

Having discussed key category–characteristic-measure/s, the category Overall Acceptance (median of 4) of e-learning within the current organisations mirrored 3 of the 4 categories. As such, it provides preliminary evidence that the proposed framework is reliable; however, there was evidence that for some employees, the specific e-learning initiatives implemented have shortcomings. With 3 organisations surveyed, it is possible that **T6**: *Reserved e-learning acceptance* was constrained within a single organisation's offering.

7 Conclusion

Using the available literature and existing CSF frameworks and models as bases, this paper proposed, and surveyed, a provisional workplace e-learning acceptance framework for a developing country. The intended outcome was to evaluate if the proposed framework appropriates employees' acceptance of current e-learning initiatives. The present study represented the first phase of the development of a suitable framework, and in our opinion the results are encouraging. That stated, research advances the way we think about almost everything, and for this reason the establishment and validation of a workplace e-learning framework for developing countries should not be rushed, but approached with rigorous care. A next logical step would be to repeat the current research with more robust statistical procedures, with the aim to refine and validate the framework for both the South African as well as broader developing country settings.

References

1. Alexander, S.: E-learning developments and experiences. Educ. Train. **43**, 240–248 (2001)
2. Bhuasiri, W., Xaymoungkhoun, O., Zo, H., Rho, J.J., Ciganek, A.P.: Critical success factors for e-learning in developing countries: a comparative analysis between ICT experts and faculty. Comput. Educ. **58**(2), 843–855 (2012)
3. Berge, Z.I., Schreiber, D.A.: Distance training. How innovative organizations are using technology to maximize learning and business objectives. Josey-Bass, San Franciso (1998)
4. Chen, H.J.: Linking employees' e-learning system use to their overall job outcomes: an empirical study based on the IS success model. Comput. Educ. **55**(4), 1628–1639 (2010)
5. Cheng, B., Wang, M., Yang, S.J.H., Kinshuk, D., Peng, J.: Acceptance of competency-based workplace e-learning systems: effects of individual and peer learning support. Comput. Educ. **57**(1), 1317–1333 (2011)
6. Cheng, B., Wang, M., Moormann, J., Olaniran, B.A., Chen, N.S.: The effects of organisational learning environment factors on e-learning acceptance. Comput. Educ. **58** (3), 885–899 (2012)
7. Chigona, A., Dagada, R.: Adoption and use of E-learning at tertiary level in South Africa: a qualitative analysis. In: Barton, S., et al. (ed.) Proceedings of Global Learning 2011, pp. 93–101 (2011)
8. Cowley, J., et al.: Preparing students for E-learning. Creative Commons License (2002)
9. Dagada, R., Jakovljevic, M., Stoltenkamp, J.: Factors that impede the successful implementation of e-learning strategy. In: Cantoni, L., McLoughlin, C. (eds.) Proceedings of World Conference on Educational Multimedia, Hypermedia and Telecommunications 2004, pp. 2850–2857 (2004)
10. Davis, F.D., Bagozzi, R.P., Warshaw, P.R.: User acceptance of computer technology: a comparison of two theoretical models. Manag. Sci. **35**(8), 982–1003 (1989)

11. Deloitte. Rewriting the rules for the digital age. Global Human Capital Trends Report for South Africa (2017). https://www2.deloitte.com/content/dam/Deloitte/za/Documents/human-capital/za_2017-Human-capital-trends_7_13%20March2017.pdf. Last Accessed 12 Feb 2018
12. Doornbos, A.J., Simons, R.J., Denessen, E.: Relations between characteristics of workplace practices and types of informal work-related learning: a survey study among Dutch police. Hum. Resour. Dev. Q. **19**(2), 129–151 (2008)
13. Engelbrecht, E.: A look at e-learning models: investigating their value for developing an e-learning strategy. Progressio **25**(2), 38–47 (2003)
14. Fletcher, J.D., Tobias, S., Wisher, R.A.: Learning anytime, anywhere: advanced distributed learning and the changing face of education. Educ. Res. **36**(2), 96–102 (2007)
15. Freund, Y.P.: Critical success factors. Plan. Rev. **16**(4), 20–25 (1988)
16. Fu, X., Peitrobelli, C., Soete, L.: The Role of Foreign Technology and Indigenous Innovation in Emerging Economies: Technological Change and Catching Up. Inter-American Development Bank, Technical Notes (2010)
17. Garrison, D.R., Kanuka, H.: Blended learning: uncovering its transformative potential in higher education. Internet High. Educ. **7**, 95–105 (2004)
18. Govindasamy, T.: Successful implementation of e-learning; pedagogical considerations. Internet High. Educ. **4**(3–4), 287–299 (2002)
19. Kinuthia, W., Dagada, R.: E-learning incorporation: an exploratory study of three South African higher education institutions. Int. J. E-Learn. **7**, 623–639 (2008)
20. Kosarzycki, M., Salas, E., DeRouin, R., Fiore, S.M.: Distance Learning in Organizations: A Review and Future Needs. JAI Press, Greenwich (2003)
21. Lee, M.K.O., Cheung, C.M.K., Chen, Z.: Acceptance of Internet-based learning medium: the role of extrinsic and intrinsic motivation. Inf. Manag. **42**(8), 1095–1104 (2005)
22. Lee, Y.H., Hsieh, Y.C., Ma, C.Y.: A model of organisational employees' e-learning systems acceptance. Knowl. Based Syst. **24**(3), 5–366 (2011)
23. Levy, Y.: Assessing the Value of e-Learning Systems. Information Science Publishing, Hershey (2006)
24. Ong, C., Lay, J., Wang, Y.: Factors affecting engineers' acceptance of asynchronous e-learning systems in high-tech companies. Inf. Manag. **41**(6), 795–804 (2004)
25. Menchaca, M.P., Bekele, T.A.: Learner and instructor identified success factors in distance education. Distance **29**(3), 231–252 (2008)
26. McGill, T.J., Klobas, J.E., Renzi, S.: Critical success factors for the continuation of e-learning initiatives. Internet High. Educ. **22**, 24–36 (2014)
27. Nunamaker, J.F., Zhang, D.: Powering E-learning in the new millennium: an overview of e-learning and enabling technology. Inf. Syst. Front. **5**(2), 207–218 (2003)
28. Paecther, M., Maier, B., Macher, D.: Students' expectations of, and experiences in e-learning: their relation to learning achievements and course satisfaction. Comput. Educ. **54**, 222–229 (2010)
29. Papp, R.: Critical success factors for distance learning. Paper presented at the americas conference on information systems, Long Beach, CA, USA (2000)
30. Pienaar, A.: Evaluating institutional readiness for implementation of an educational technology system. University of the Free State, South Africa (2010)
31. Selim, H.M.: Critical success factors for e-learning acceptance: confirmatory factor models. Comput. Educ. **49**(2), 396–413 (2007)
32. Singh, H.: Building effective blended learning programs. Educ. Technol. **43**, 51–54 (2003)

33. Ssekakubo, G., Suleman, H., Marsden, G.: Issues of adoption: have e-learning management systems fulfilled their potential in developing countries? In: Brown, I., et al. (ed.) Proceedings of the South African Institute of Computer Scientists and Information Technologists Conference on Knowledge, Innovation and Leadership in a Diverse, Multidisciplinary Environment, pp. 231–238 (2011)
34. Statistics South Africa: Employment, unemployment, skills and economic growth. An exploration of household survey evidence on skills development and unemployment between 1994 and 2014. Statistics South Africa (2014)
35. Stoltenkamp, J., Mapuva, J.: An integrated e-learning model: indications of a changing organisational culture at the University of the Western Cape (UWC). In: Global Learn, 28 March 2011, Melbourne, Australia. Association for the Advancement of Computing in Education (AACE) (2010). ISBN 978-1-880094-85-3
36. Stoltenkamp, J., Kasuto, O.A.: E-learning change management and communication strategies within a HEI in a developing country: Institutional organisational cultural change. Educ. Inf. Technol. **16**, 41–54 (2011)
37. Sun, P., Tsai, R.J., Finger, G., Chen, Y., Yeh, D.: What drives a successful e-Learning? An empirical investigation of the critical factors influencing learner satisfaction. Comput. Educ. (2008). https://doi.org/10.1016/j.compedu.2006.11.007
38. Tarhini, A., Hone, K., Liu, X., Tarhini, T.: Examining the moderating effect of individual-level cultural values on users' acceptance of E-learning in developing countries: a structural equation modeling of an extended technology acceptance model. Interact. Learn. Environ. **25**(3), 306–328 (2016)
39. Terblanche, T.E.: Technical and vocational education and training (TVET) Colleges in South Africa: a Framework for leading curriculum change. Dissertation presented for the degree of Doctor in Philosophy in the Faculty of Education at Stellenbosch University (2017)
40. Tseng, M.L., Lin, R.J., Chen, H.P.: Evaluating the effectiveness of e-learning system in uncertainty. Ind. Manag. Data Syst. **111**(6), 869–889 (2011)
41. van der Merwe, A.: Evaluating the integration of ICTs into teaching and learning activities at a South African higher education institution. Ph.D. thesis, Stellenbosch University (2004)
42. Venkatesh, V., Bala, H.: TAM 3: Advancing the technology acceptance model with a focus on interventions. Unpublished manuscript (2010)
43. Venkatesh, V., Davis, F.D.: A theoretical extension of the technology acceptance model: four longitudinal field studies. Manag. Sci. **46**, 186–204 (2000)
44. Wang, Y.S.: Assessment of learner satisfaction with asynchronous electronic learning systems. Inf. Manag. **41**(1), 75–86 (2003)
45. Wang, Y.-S., Wang, H.-Y., Shee, D.Y.: Measuring e-learning systems success in an organisational context: scale development and validation. Comput. Hum. Behav. **23**(4), 1792–1808 (2007)

Localize-It: Co-designing a Community-Owned Platform

Maria Rosa Lorini[1(✉)], Melissa Densmore[1], David Johnson[1], Senka Hadzic[1], Hafeni Mthoko[1], Ganief Manuel[2], Marius Waries[2], and André van Zyl[2]

[1] University of Cape Town, Rondebosch, 7701 Cape Town, South Africa
mariarosalorini@gmail.com
[2] Ocean View Community Representative, Ocean View, 4052 Cape Town, South Africa

Abstract. One of the most difficult, yet undocumented, aspects of information and communications technologies and development (ICTD) projects is that of establishing partnerships around which researchers' interventions will develop, be tested and grow. Constraints on timing and funding usually lead to short-term projects, in which benefits are biased towards researchers rather than the partner community. In order to avoid empty and unethical promises and to increase the potential benefit for the community, we consider the process of developing participatory partnerships in ICTD projects. The objective is to make the project community owned, allowing the participants to develop what they value as important. Using the case of a township-based wireless community content sharing network, we describe the potential and some of the challenges with this approach. The paper highlights building blocks, such as ethical behaviour and trust, to avoid recreating the dichotomy between research and practice, and building a constructive collaboration.

Keywords: ICTD · Partnership · Community wireless · Ownership

1 Introduction

There is no clear formula for how to make an information and communications technology and development (ICTD) project successful, despite the many theories around why they fail. Many emphasise the importance of project champions and community intermediaries [1] to help facilitate connections and translate local knowledge, but this leaves projects vulnerable to a single point of failure [2] when a project champion seeks opportunities elsewhere. Toyama [3] suggests that technologies are an amplifier – that they fail because they cannot replace gaps in existing institutional and human capacity, but, rather, can multiply both negative and positive capacities where they already exist. Design-reality gaps [4] suggest the problem lies in the technologists – that they are designing without an understanding of reality. Others suggest that participation is the key; it helps eliminate design-reality gaps through efforts done with the stakeholders, rather than merely for them, and factors in existing institutional and human resources [5]. Given all of this advice, how should ICTD

K. Krauss et al. (Eds.): IDIA 2018, CCIS 933, pp. 243–257, 2019.
https://doi.org/10.1007/978-3-030-11235-6_16

researchers go about establishing the partnerships around which we can engage with communities in the use of information and communications technologies to address their needs?

The norm for much ICTD research is for researchers based in another country to find a collaborating organisation or community in a target country, and to fly there for short periods to do data gathering and deployments [2]. In these cases, immersion can be prohibitively expensive, and relationships are built over many relatively short visits, or worse, not built at all (a.k.a. bungee research). However, as researchers based in Cape Town, working in a township in the same city, we have the opportunity to develop deeper relationships over a longer period with our collaborators. In this paper we reflect on this type of participatory partnership, and the ways in which we are working together with two communities to realise shared objectives. The iNethi project is an effort to co-design a community-owned wireless network to support local content sharing and services, and to lower the cost of using the Internet. Because of the many challenges present in participatory design approaches, such as sustainability and the risk to deploy 'white elephant' projects [5] that are abandoned soon after their creation, we tried to co-design a project in a different way – in particular, trying to avoid the dichotomy research-practice. While pursuing this aim through the creation of a fruitful partnership, during the initial phase of the project we created the conditions for what we believe is a more ethical approach. In this approach we value local ownership and local service and content creation in our co-design, in order to foster sustainability. Since we are still at the beginning of the project, there are many open questions. We use this case to outline some of the key principles to keep in mind while developing long-term collaborative ICTD projects, and to discuss some of the associated challenges entailed.

Section 2 provides background information about community networks and their objectives. Section 3 presents the methodology used. Section 4 outlines our activities so far, and in Sect. 5 we discuss these activities with respect to theory. The conclusion highlights the potential offered by relationship building for research and practice in ICTD.

2 Background

2.1 Community Wireless

Community wireless networks are bottom-up projects in which communities use affordable wireless networks such as WiFi-based mesh and other technologies to set up communications infrastructures for themselves, often in locations where mobile coverage is lacking, or costs are prohibitively high. Community networks can support the building of local economies, and open up new possibilities for underserved areas [6].

In the context of developing countries, there are several fully operational community networks in deep rural areas of South Africa (Zenzeleni, [7]), in Zambia (Macha) and in Mexico (Rhizomatica). Most community networks currently focus on provisioning for phone calls and global Internet access; however, by virtue of their proximity to the end-users, community networks also offer an ideal platform for sharing content within the community, whether through caching of commonly accessed global content, or distribution of content they have created themselves. Each of these projects were affected by a series of embedded community connections and relationships, and achieved results because specific goals of the project were met. Macha lowered barriers to Internet access [8]; Zenzeleni tried to solve the affordability issue; and, Rhizomatica brought coverage where it was not available, and reduced communication costs for the population.

For the iNethi project, communications technology is not just about connecting to the rest of the world, but a service that communities can use to connect community members, as well as nearby communities. While affordability of Internet access is a recognised problem, the team of researchers and community representatives highlighted, as a priority, to build up infrastructure to support community-based services and content sharing.

2.2 Local Content Creation

Studies of existing use bolster our argument for using communications infrastructure to support local content creation. Phokeer and colleagues have done a preliminary study of mobile data usage in the communities where the iNethi project is based, finding not only constrained usage of mobile data, but that much of the interaction and content sharing was between people within the community [9]. Yet for the most popular applications, including WhatsApp and Facebook, messages destined for neighbours across the street must first travel the world over expensive and constrained data links. iNethi reduces costs by offering community-based services and content sharing of music, video, voice and images that remain locally based.

In addition to studies related to the local use of the network interaction, an increasing volume of literature is interested in the type of content shared. Due to globalisation, local economies and cultures are under threat, and this is amplified by modern communications technologies. This has resulted in increased attention to local cultures, and their distinctiveness is emerging in academic literature. In particular, in the once so-called developing world, attention is turning towards the use of ICT to preserve indigenous knowledge (IK) - the unique, traditional and local knowledge existing within and developed around the specific conditions of women and men indigenous to a particular geographic area [10]. IK is embedded in the community and is unique to a given culture, location or society [11].

Management of local and indigenous knowledge, especially culturally sensitive and unique knowledge, implies a need for gathering existing information, resources, and processes to store and distribute the collected data. On the one hand, preservation of indigenous and traditional knowledge involves discussion about its access and stakeholders' intellectual property rights. On the other hand, protection of property rights should not prevent the community from sharing and partaking in local knowledge generation and protection of local values. ICT can support knowledge management: both the preservation of local traditions and the potential amplification of local culture, for the benefit of the community and beyond. ICT in both scenarios can assist in gathering, storing and sharing local content and knowledge, as well as creation of new content and knowledge. Attention would be required in dealing with the ethical principles and in consideration of the technological deterministic risk [12].

2.3 Ocean View and Masiphumelele

Despite tremendous growth in Internet-capable mobile device adoption, Internet usage and access to data is limited in South Africa by prohibitive costs and unequal coverage. The research is based on a project which developed in two under-resourced communities in Cape Town: Masiphumelele (a.k.a. Masi) and Ocean View.

The two areas differ in their composition. In particular, as presented in the 2011 Cape Town census, the Ocean View population is predominantly Coloured (91%) (multiracial ethnic group native to Southern Africa); 48% of households have a monthly income of R3, 200 or less (slightly more than $200 per month); 84% of households live in formal dwellings (leaving a significant percentage of the population in informal buildings – shacks) [13].

The key results emerging from the 2011 census for the suburb of Masi highlight a population that is predominantly Black African (91%), and where the percentage of people living behind the poverty line of R3, 200 per month is higher than in Ocean View, reaching 82% of households. A limited 27% of households live in formal dwellings. An elevated presence of non-governmental organisations (NGOs) characterises the community environment where the civil society recognises their capacity to meet their daily needs [14].

Initial research results for the two communities show that Internet access is not affordable for most users, due to the high costs of cellular network data packages. The alternatives to access the web at affordable prices are limited, considering the reduced presence of public Wi-Fi and the non-availability of the services offered by the public schools at night and during the weekends.

2.4 Overview of the iNethi Approach

The iNethi Network provides wireless backhaul over a television white spaces (TVWS) and WiFi mesh network and an access network to user devices using WiFi access points. Mesh networks are used as they provide a simple set-up (self-forming) and repair process (self-healing) when radios in the network fail or lose power.

The platform allows users in the community to communicate, share information and to generate new local content. To this end, the project is building mini data centres called "cloudlets". The cloudlet currently hosts different services running on individual containers. The current proposed services are (i) Diaspora: a Decentralized Social Network; (ii) OwnCloud: a file sharing application; and (iii) RocketChat: an instant messaging service. The services are running in docker containers on a main host connected to a wireless Access Point (AP). The AP serves as an entry point for end-users who connect to the iNethi SSID. Once the users are connected, the devices can connect to the different services running locally on the cloudlet. The iNethi cloudlets are able to synchronise to other available iNethi cloudlets via a wireless network and/or via a global cloudlet server using an Internet link.

3 Methodology

Key to our framing of this research is to take a participatory co-design approach, working with the community to establish needs, norms and other project aspects.

Authors on this paper include both academic researchers and community members from the Ocean View township. We are an inter-disciplinary group, with expertise in networking, information systems, human-computer interaction, education and community development. Our authors from Ocean View have additional expertise in contextualising the work, connecting us to other people in the community, but, more importantly, helping us to define parameters for our partnership.

Thus, for this paper, we have all been engaged in participant observation – noting and reflecting on our activities. As themes have emerged, we have discussed aspects that we considered to be most important, always working to ensure that the community voice is given prominence.

The participatory and reflective methodology was maintained along the project, facing the upcoming challenges. The description of the activities in Sect. 4 covers the most important moments. These events, discussions and decisions taken represent the turning points in the development of a project that was not pre-designed before the deployment. The initial encounters took place with community representatives to verify the possibility to collaborate after a researcher noticed a commonality of intentions with some activists. The initial phase saw the involvement of more people interested in participating from both the community and the university. Several workshops followed, as well as the eventual establishment of a governing board for the project. The ethical issues, such as usage policies and privacy, required the researchers to explore temporary and long-term solutions while ongoing community engagement was taking place. In the short term, the team decided to deploy an iNethi server and WiFi hotspot at the school, while discussing its potential to test the people's interest, capacities and commitment.

While developing the activities, the mixed team could reflect over the approach, test this against the needs of the people, and adjust the platform where needed. The main result of this process is expressed by the philosophy adopted by the local and external participants.

4 Activities

In this section, we detail the partnership development activities entailed in setting up the iNethi project. As stated previously, we are still in the very early stages of this project, having taken almost two years to establish partnerships, and to understand the needs and dynamics of the Ocean View and Masi communities.

4.1 Initial Community Engagement

A number of non-governmental organisations (NGOs) based in Masi represented the entry point for the researchers into the community. The choice to work with NGOs and community-based organisations (CBOs) was maintained while developing the relationships with several community representatives. The community leaders started attending the meetings of brainstorming around the possibility to deploy a wireless community network. After reaching an agreement over the various activities to be carried on in the locations, the mixed team decided to officially introduce the project to some potential local partners.

In particular, a one-day workshop took place in May 2017 involving representatives of the students, of the teachers and some community leaders. The conclusion of the brainstorming with all the possible participants, resources and areas of intervention, was summarised in a poster and placed in a visible space, in order to maintain visibility and awareness of the project. In September 2017, a three-day workshop was prepared by a team composed by researchers and leaders of the two communities. The team elaborated on the programme, and discussed who could be invited and how. The community representatives spread the news over social media and during community events, distributing a flyer co-designed during the preparatory meetings. To involve potential stakeholders, the programme was presented and critically discussed with local NGOs.

Community representatives of the two townships attended the workshop. The workshop 'House Rules' were discussed at the beginning, and reflected the principles of participatory design values: respect for one another, a collaborative spirit, and a peer-to-peer approach where everybody should feel free to ask as well as answer. The peer-to-peer learning methodologies [15, 16] were used during the different phases of presentations, activities, games and discussions. The group activities were essential to give a voice to everybody, to be at ease, active and creative, and to start using the new services. Furthermore, the group activities allowed the different participants to focus their attention on the fields they felt more passionate about: community services, education, news or entertainment.

During the following months, a series of activities took place to maintain and strengthen the relationship with the community. In particular, an application to create, record and share music was developed by some university students and community representatives, in order to target younger musicians with limited technological devices and connectivity. At the end of 2017, a music festival was organised in Ocean View and this gave the team an opportunity to introduce and test iNethi in the community. The festival offered the space to deploy the technology, present the work done, experiment new uses (such as record and upload of music), connect services, and involve new artists and community members. To attract people and discuss opportunities for the community, a free local voice calls application was tested, and a presentation of Internet of Things was done.

4.2 Establishing a Governing Board

Apart from special events and the development of iNethi services and content, regular weekly meetings are taking place, involving the community leaders, several specialised researchers and, depending on the occasion, new stakeholders which can support the project. The challenges related to its establishment and growth, and potential to reach out for more beneficiaries, are connected with the capabilities to engage the community at large. At present, the main participants are activists and artists. The involvement of the schools and religious institution representatives, as well as that of the local government, is seen as a necessary further step.

The team started the discussion over the creation of a governing board which will be responsible for the regulation of the use of the platform. The governing board might be a decentralised structure, possibly with a body section in Ocean View and one in Masi. From the discussions, the importance of diversity in the governing board emerged, such as the inclusion of women, elders, artists, activists and youth. Over time, the board will decide what services and content will be allowed on the iNethi platform by community members, and ensure that any modification of the platform is for the benefit of their community.

This decision will mark a strong distinction from the existing rules and implemented systems of the large Internet service providers, where general rules are settled without community involvement, and limited space is available for negotiation of individual and specific cases. As stated by one of the community members: "Often, applications and service providers, due to the number of users and quantity of contents shared, manage the resolution of controversies using electronic systems, globally" (John, a community activist).

The community representatives that form part of the future governing board will register the company as an NPO, to allow the community network to access specific funds to support their activities. An NPO can also generate profit that can be channelled back into project activities, such as salaries and other revenues necessary to maintain the network. The constitution of the NPO will allow the network and platform to apply for licences to operate the network (for the backhaul mesh network and access points and to supply localised services such as chat, voice, and file sharing over the network). A licence exemption, that allows the network to be operated without paying any licence fees, due to its not-for-profit status, will also be applied for.

In addition to registering an NPO, a co-operative will also be applied for, in order to support the duplication of the iNethi concept in other neighbouring communities, and to allow resources to be pooled (e.g. training workshops for multiple communities to be held, or common global cloud storage to be used among multiple communities).

4.3 Acceptable Use Policy

The governing board started operating after discussing the users' policy, and the draft of an Acceptable Use Policy (AUP) had been shared between the participants to clarify some essential decisions taken and to guide the work to come. The iNethi AUP is a framework which offers guidelines for the use of the wireless network and its services. These guidelines are solely to protect the usefulness and enjoyment of the wireless network and the users – in this instance, members of the community. The promulgated guidelines, as such, are not punitive in nature, even though there are certain consequences should these guidelines be breached.

The underlying intention is focused on community ownership, whereby the community set up and use guidelines that are acceptable to that community, and collectively agreed upon through a process of consultation and deliberation. These communities will then be solely responsible for the implementation and administration of the AUP through the governing board, which is representative of each community.

The AUP draft is designed to encompass the values, cultures, traditions and beliefs of the community to be inclusive of the cross-section of the community. The purpose of the AUP is underpinned by a legal framework, in order for users to take steps to avoid or refrain from any activity that affects the accessibility, legality and security of the wireless network. Also, the AUP ensures respecting the rights of other users, the integrity of the physical facilities, and all pertinent licence and contractual agreements. Furthermore, users are expected to behave in a responsible, ethical and legal manner.

4.4 Building Wireless Infrastructure

In the two communities, the team started building the wireless infrastructure required to support the community network. The process undertaken to involve the community to build out the mesh network faced a series of challenges related to inclusiveness and infrastructure. To ensure the coverage of the community, and disclose the potentiality of the wireless community network, the community representatives and the university colleagues discussed details about specific structures and organisations that would form ideal mounting points for the mesh radios. The team decided to install the initial AP and mesh on critical points from two perspectives. The choice was dependent on the height of the structures, the ability to reach other targeted sites, and covering as many buildings (people) as possible with a limited number of mesh radios. In addition, the decision needed to involve the owners of the building. The installation of an AP in a strategic community centre or a religious building, for instance, would open up new opportunities to start a relationship and collaboration with the stakeholders involved.

The community representatives started a mapping exercise supported by technical advice from university researchers. The initial APs were selected on the basis of the maximisation of the coverage of each community and minimisation of infrastructural issues related to power availability and vandalisation. Points of alignment with the first AP were searched for, as well as higher points in the communities. One of the community representatives, and member of the governing board, said: "I have a neighbour as well, whom already gave permission to put up an antenna as well. Line of sight to school." One of his colleague echoed him by saying: "I also spoke to the elders in the mountain on where we can install the antenna."

The meetings and encounters with the stakeholders became a skill transfer opportunity for everybody to learn how to install, orient the antennas, and set up channels to avoid interference from existing Wi-Fi. An initial presentation on mesh building was done during the introductory workshop, together with a discussion on its cost and maintenance. Every new installation became an active workshop.

The community representatives will expand the mesh network from existing radio sites. If they install mesh radios in areas where good coverage and good quality mesh links are ensured, they will quickly demonstrate the potentiality of the network to new community members, and new partnerships might develop.

4.5 Developing Local Services

Local servers have been installed in Ocean View and Masi to provide iNethi services. A portable iNethi server is also available for festivals and other community events. The servers are running several open source services, including social networking (Diaspora), chat (RocketChat), file-sharing (OwnCloud), and web authoring (WikiFundi). Concerning these existing services, during the workshop several ideas emerged on their potential utility for the community.

RocketChat could be used to (i) report and provide crime alerts or general alerts about community events; (ii) create dedicated groups for safety and emergencies; (iii) share links to update journalists in the neighbouring communities with the latest information, in order to connect and update each other; and (iv) create groups for teachers to communicate.

OwnCloud can be used by community members to (i) upload activities that happen in the community, such as a cultural festival; (ii) upload DIY community services (i.e. tutorials on how to fix dripping taps and leaking taps); (iii) upload videos of news and events such as taxi strikes; and (iv) upload study materials.

Diaspora could be used as a platform for (i) advertisements; (ii) job opportunity hubs to offer and search vacancies in the area; and (iii) uploading of photos and links of current issues. Another local service is real-time voice communication, also already available and installed in the platform allowing the use of voice, chat and video sharing locally, among people registered on iNethi.

The Cloudlet platform will support new services designed for and by the community. The locally hosted applications and services will be co-designed, and eventually chosen by, the community. The community at large might also be encouraged to create local innovative services, inspire communities to create content for both local and global consumption, and the creation of Wiki content. The community owning the project will make decisions on the licensing of content, the availability of content at a local or global level, and the level of privacy attached to the content.

4.6 iNethi Philosophy

The phase of encounter, discussion, negotiation of rules and approaches, events and tests, supported the development of the iNethi philosophy: people taking control over the creation, construction, management and costs of a wireless network. The idea was generated contemporarily in the academia and NGO sector of Masi, as well as among a few activists in Ocean View. It concretised through the encounter between these stakeholders, which transformed the idea into a community project where technology is used as an amplifier of what people are doing and believing in.

The design and conceptualisation of the platform were elaborated on by some community leaders, supported by researchers who chose to collaborate to develop an initial phase to be shown and proposed to the community at large. The visualisation of the potential of the community network was considered essential, in order to present the idea, sponsor it among interested people, and gather support to expand the project. The conceptualisation of the network, nevertheless, implies the possibility for the community to refine the idea and become the driver and owner of the project.

The choice to give space to different types of expressions and ecologies, and the possibility "to develop an internet culture", as expressed by one of the activists, are among the guiding principles of the participants. iNethi represents an opportunity to create a critical mass in the community and to develop internal creativity. Concerning the decentralised content distribution, iNethi Cloudlets encourage content generation and local innovation for local content use, storage and sharing (through a credit process of the content, and localised/permissive licences based upon participants' decisions).

iNethi will not serve only the local needs for internal communication. The workshop highlighted the interest of the participants to also pre-populate the server with global content – such as free educational media. In this way, the goal to create a critical mass of community knowledge could be amplified, showing the potential to influence global information distribution through participation in the entire process of knowledge creation. With the increase of the critical mass of local content and knowledge, the network can work towards its inclusion in the global community. Over time, the services offered will expand and amplify the capabilities of the community to connect, co-produce, and share knowledge with external communities and eventually the web at large. The iNethi co-operative will coordinate the community-co-designed, -managed and -owned network.

5 Discussion

The activities described represent the initial phase of an ICTD project, from the formalisation of the idea among some representatives to the decision to structure the idea at different levels (the community network, the governing body and licenses, the infrastructures). Reflecting over the process, the involved people recognised a series of building blocks that allowed participants to get involved, and to the project to start and develop focusing on the community needs and desires, and create the conditions for community ownership and potential sustainability. The participation principles are highlighted with reference to literature on ICTD projects.

5.1 Building Relationships

An initial slow start is required in ICTD projects in order to familiarise the involved community and meet potential participants. Suchman [17] reminds us about the social relations that can be formed only over time. The phase of cognisance of the community represents the ethnographic phase of a study [18], where researchers are behaving mainly as observant participants and are evaluating the conditions of the community, the resources, and possible discussion points to start a collaboration. As Krauss [19] highlights, the community entry phase requires a series of steps to be taken over time, such as 'collaborative needs or situation analysis' and 'appropriate alignment with local leadership' [19, p. 25]. Attention to power relations and 'appropriate and culturally sensitive community engagement' are further issues to be considered when initiating collaboration in a cross-cultural setting, with developmental proposals (idem).

Acknowledging the limitations of results derived from a rapid ethnographic initial phase, Brereton and colleagues [20] suggest moving 'beyond ethnography' to strengthen the value of reciprocity and mutual learning between researchers and local participants. A collaborative environment based on shared knowledge and desire to mutually benefit, creates a foundation for the design novelty to fit into the local culture and for the participants to improve their practices.

In our project, the relationship developed slowly over several months. It is based on open dialogue, confrontation, and regular encounters organised both in the community and at the university. It was built over a long time, to (i) ensure the clarity of intentions of every participant; (ii) build trust among the local and external participants; (iii) evaluate the ethical issues; (iv) verify the potential of the collaboration, (v) involve more stakeholders; (vi) become inclusive; and (vii) build towards sustainability. From the researchers' side, there was availability to organise workshops, discuss new proposals, and evaluate the best solutions for the deployment of the technology. From the community representatives' side, there was the intention to involve more people, to support the mapping and analysis of the data collected, and to be the engine of the process by registering their organisation in order to achieve a common goal.

5.2 Engaging Community Stakeholders

Working within communities is not a straightforward task, and requires researchers and local participants to come together to accomplish a common goal. Such a process of engagement is often met with challenges which hinder the successful implementation of ICTD projects. The engagement process is one whereby roles, expectations and benefits of the research being undertaken need to be negotiated on a continuous basis [5, 21]. Project expectations and roles are prone to evolve, given the complex and changing environment in which ICTD projects find themselves. Therefore, continuous interaction with local participants is required to further ensure that learning (by allowing the project to adapt and be flexible to context) and inclusiveness, is occurring [5, 21]. This would then mean involving communities from the project's initiation stage and throughout its lifecycle [21, 22]. This includes all project planning, including sustainability and scalability concerns that arise.

Working with local participants throughout the project lifecycle further aids in uncovering joint benefits, which need to be clearly demonstrated to local participants to foster further engagement [5, 22]. Demonstrating the research benefits to local participants builds from a clear understanding of the context in which the desired engagement is being developed [22, 23]. The desire then is to become more people centred (rather than task oriented) and embedded within their way of life [24]. For example, allowing the community to be the ones to decide how best to engage is a means of being people centred [21]. Through that contextual understanding, researchers are in a better position to develop strategies for engagement, which Balestrini and colleagues [22] highlight as important; therefore, it should be clearly outlined what community outcome is being desired through the partnership being developed [23]. Moreover, demonstrating a clear understanding of the context further shows that researchers do value the community [22]. Stakeholders need to feel valued and recognise that they too have a role to play within a project. Excluding local participants or engaging them in a haphazard fashion only demonstrates a lack of trust; however, trust is important when building relationships, and needs to be built over time [21–23]. This necessitates a shift in mindset from the "us" (researchers) as all-knowing and "them" (the community) as lacking [24].

5.3 Ethics and Trust

'…As outsiders in complex social situations it is often difficult to identify the potential harms that might arise from our actions. This problem is compounded by the extreme imbalance in financial and social power of typical ICTD researchers and the people that they (we) work with' [25, p. 46]. Ethical guidelines, including universities' ethical clearance, consent forms, and signed agreements about the use of images and words of participants, are sometimes not 'enough' [26] to avoid harming the people involved in a research project. The risks associated with the balance of power between researchers and local participants cannot always be counterbalanced with the compliance with basic rules to protect vulnerable people. ICTD projects, in particular, deal with environments and conditions substantially different in economic, academic, social and political points of view, where there is often much heterogeneity present among the community members. In cases related to ICT, the researchers often deal, as well, with a quantity of data not received directly from the participants, but mediated by project technology [27].

The ethical standards expected of researchers and practitioners are nevertheless the foundation of a collaboration based on mutual respect. Ethical behaviours support, as well, the climate of trust that needs to be built into a project's roadmap, and cannot be taken for granted. In fact, over time, several projects experienced withdrawal of participants because of unethical behaviour and cultural insensitivity perceived by the people involved [28]. Sometimes, the collaboration is halted because of the discrepancy between expectations raised by the researchers and the limited practical results caused by insufficient funds or interest to develop a project. In those cases, the relationship is interrupted, and trust is at risk due to the breakdown of confidence.

In order to defuse that crisis and continue working towards the negotiation of community ownership, inclusion of the community members, and sustainability of the wireless network, relationships and trust are built incrementally. Relationships established over time in the communities of Ocean View and Masi, respected ethical research principles and guidelines. Further, research approaches were transparent, as were budgets for funds and resources. Establishment of roles and activities to be carried out over time were also important, to clarify the responsibilities and ethical attitudes expected from both sides – researchers and local participants.

5.4 Negotiating Ownership

Sustainability of any ICTD initiative, including community networks, depends on local ownership. According to Pade [29], the sense of local ownership has to be stimulated at the early stage of an ICTD initiative. For each project, the ownership is dynamic and highly dependent on the cultural, social and socio-economic context. Banda [30] suggests community engagement from the early stage of a telecentre project in Malawi, while external stakeholders need to withdraw slowly and empower communities to take the lead, as this will result in a sense of ownership.

Gram Marg Rural Broadband project at IIT Bombay, India has been working on a cost-effective technology solution with a sustainable business model for their community network, through field trials and test bed deployments [31]. They suggested a community-owned network that will enable them to 'own the Internet'. This partnership enables the network to be community owned for effective decision-making, and to prioritise services based on village needs. Zenzeleni adopted a co-op model. The community in rural South Africa co-created the network together with researchers, and now owns its own telephone and Internet "company". A not-for-profit co-operative was formed, and successfully applied for a licence exemption to operate the network infrastructure and offer services. Revenue used to sustain the network can also be used for other community needs [32]. Rhizomatica [33] is a community network in rural Mexico, where communities have become both network owners and operators. Sustainability is ensured by combining regulatory reforms, community involvement, training, and maintenance of network equipment. Heimerl and colleagues [34] provide an analysis of locally owned cellular networks deployed using a bottom-up approach. They evaluated this model by building and deploying a for-profit community cellular network in rural Papua, Indonesia, in partnership with two local NGOs.

In the case of iNethi, the community opted for a co-op business model similar to the one of Zenzeleni. The involved members, to be as inclusive as possible, choose three interim committee members until the first annual general meeting of the newly created NPO gets an opportunity to elect its formal committee. One temporary member of the governing board, concerning the further steps to be taken, highlighted some suggestions showing its competency and readiness to move forward: "I recommend that once the NGO is approved, immediate application to issue certificates before any transaction takes place; it speeds up approval process".

6 Conclusions and Future Work Discussion

Qureshi, referring to several publications concerning research and practice, highlights how "few researchers engage in advancing policy positions or contributing to practice" [35, p. 512]. The dichotomy between research and practice continues being an issue of relevance when approaching ethical claims and disclosing the intentions of stakeholders participating in an ICTD project.

Building genuine community-based projects is not trivial. Efforts and engagements in research and practice activities require constructive collaboration. The relationship between research and practice is based on trust and ethical behaviour, as is the relationship between local and external participants. The ethical stance, based on justice and care principles brings benefits for communities – which will become project owners. Researchers benefit by intensifying collaboration with communities, mutual learning and knowledge sharing and creation.

The iNethi project is developing, and new ideas are constantly emerging because of the potential offered by providing a community-owned and -driven network following a participatory design approach.

References

1. Blake, E.H., Tucker, W.D.: User interfaces for communication bridges across the digital divide. AI Soc. **20**(2), 232–242 (2006)
2. Brewer, E., et al.: The case for technology in developing regions. Computer **38**(6), 25–38 (2005)
3. Toyama, K.: Geek Heresy: Rescuing Social Change from the Cult of Technology. Public Affairs, New York (2015)
4. Heeks, R.: Health information systems: failure, success and improvisation. Int. J. Med. Inf. **75**(2), 125–137 (2006)
5. Winschiers-Theophilus, H., Zaman, T., Yeo, A.: Reducing white elephant ICT4D projects: a community-researcher engagement. In: Proceedings of the 7th International Conference on Communities and Technologies, pp. 99–107. ACM, New York (2015)
6. Rey-Moreno, C., Miliza, J., Mweetwa, F., van Stam, G., Johnson, D.: Community networks in the African context: opportunities and barriers. In: Proceedings of the First African Conference on Human Computer Interaction, pp. 237–241. ACM, New York (2016)
7. Rey-Moreno, C., Roro, Z., Siya, M.J., Simo-Reigadas, J., Bidwell, N.J., Tucker, W.D.: Towards a sustainable business model for rural telephony. In: 3rd International Workshop on Research on ICT for Human Development, pp. 208–220. Telkom (2012)
8. Johnson, D.L., Belding, E.M., Almeroth, K., van Stam, G.: Internet usage and performance analysis of a rural wireless network in Macha, Zambia. In: Proceedings of the 4th ACM Workshop on Networked Systems for Developing Regions, no. 7. ACM, New York (2010)
9. Phokeer, A., Densmore, M., Johnson, D., Feamster, N.: A First look at mobile internet use in township communities in South Africa. In: Proceedings 7th ACM Symposium on Computing and Development, no. 15. ACM, New York (2016)
10. Grenier, L.: Working with Indigenous Knowledge: A Guide for Researchers. IDRC, Ottawa (1998)
11. Chikonzo, A.: The potential of information and communication technologies in collecting, preserving and disseminating indigenous knowledge in Africa. Int. Inf. Libr. Rev. **38**(3), 132–138 (2006)
12. Roman, R., Colle, R.D.: Content creation for ICT development projects: integrating normative approaches and community demand. Inf. Technol. Dev. **10**(2), 85–94 (2003)
13. City of Cape Town. https://www.capetown.gov.za/en/stats/Pages/-Census-Suburb-Profiles-land.aspx. Accessed 06 Apr 2018
14. Alexander, S.: Masiphumelele library: a holistic service to youth and children in the community. Paper presented at IFLA WLIC 2015 - Cape Town, South Africa in Session 162 - Libraries for Children and Young Adults (2015)
15. O'Donnell, A.M., King, A.: Cognitive Perspectives on Peer Learning, eBook edn. Routledge, New York (2014)
16. Keppell, M., Au, E., Ma, A., Chan, C.: Peer learning and learning-oriented assessment in technology-enhanced environments. Assess. Eval. High. Educ. **31**(4), 453–464 (2006)
17. Suchman, L.A.: Practice-based design of information systems: notes from the hyperdeveloped world. Inf. Soc. **18**(2), 139–144 (2002)
18. Lorini, M.R., Van Zyl, I., Chigona, W.: ICTs for inclusive communities: a critical discourse analysis. In: Proceedings 8th International Development Informatics Association Conference, Port Elizabeth, South Africa, pp. 78–94 (2014)
19. Krauss, K.E.: A confessional account of the community entry phases of a critical ethnography: doing emancipatory ICT4D work in a deep rural community in South Africa. In: Proceedings of the 7th Annual SIG GlobDev, no. 9, Auckland, New Zealand (2014)

20. Brereton, M., Roe, P., Schroeter, R., Lee Hong, A.: Beyond ethnography: engagement and reciprocity as foundations for design research out here. In: Proceedings of the SIGCHI Conference on Human Factors in Computing Systems, pp. 1183–1186. ACM, New York (2014)
21. Chamberlain, A., Crabtree, A., Davies, M.: Community engagement for research: contextual design in rural CSCW system development. In: Proceedings of the 6th International Conference on Communities and Technologies, pp. 131–139. ACM, New York (2013)
22. Balestrini, M., Bird, J., Marshall, P., Zaro, A., Rogers, Y.: Understanding sustained community engagement: a case study in heritage preservation in rural Argentina. In: Proceedings of the SIGCHI, Conference on Human Factors in Computing Systems, pp. 2675–2684. ACM, New York (2016)
23. Geldof, M., Grimshaw, D. J., Kleine, D., Unwin, T.: What are the key lessons of ICT4D partnerships for poverty reduction? Systematic Review Report, pp. 1–89. Prepared for the UK Department for International Development (2011)
24. Krauss, K.: Towards self-emancipation in ICT for development research: narratives about respect, traditional leadership and building networks of friendships in rural South Africa. Afr. J. Inf. Syst. **4**(2), 46–60 (2012)
25. Dearden, A.: See no evil? Ethics in an interventionist ICTD. In: Proceedings of the Fifth International Conference on Information and Communication Technologies and Development, pp. 46–55. ACM, New York (2012)
26. Sherman, M., Berrang-Ford, L., Ford, J., Lardeau, M.P., Hofmeijer, I., Cortijo, C.Z.: Balancing indigenous principles and institutional research guidelines for informed consent: a case study from the Peruvian Amazon. AJOB Prim. Res. **3**(4), 53–68 (2012)
27. Stahl, B.C., Eden, G., Jirotka, M.: Responsible research and innovation in information and communication technology: identifying and engaging with the ethical implications of ICTs. In: Owen, R., Heintz, M., Bessant, J. (eds.) Responsible Innovation, pp. 199–218. Wiley, Chichester (2013)
28. Israel, M.: Research Ethics and Integrity for socIal Scientists: Beyond Regulatory Compliance. Sage, London (2014)
29. Pade, C., Mallinson, B., Sewry, D.: An elaboration of critical success factors for rural ICT project sustainability in developing countries: exploring the Dwesa case. J. Inf. Technol. Case Appl. **10**(4), 32–55 (2008)
30. Banda, C., Chigona, W.: The impact of stakeholder management on the sense of ownership in telecenter projects: the case of Malawi. In: Choudrie, J., Islam, M., Wahid, F., Bass, J., Priyatma, J. (eds.) ICT4D 2017. IFIP Advances in Information and Communication Technology, vol. 504, Springer, Cham (2017). https://doi.org/10.1007/978-3-319-59111-7_36
31. Gram Marg. http://grammarg.in/. Accessed 12 June 2018
32. Rey-Moreno, C., Sabiescu, A.G., Siya, M.J., Tucker, W.D.: Local ownership, exercise of ownership and moving from passive to active entitlement: a practice-led inquiry on a rural community network. J. Commun. Inf. **11**(2), 1–16 (2015)
33. Rhizomatica. http://www.rhizomatica.org. Accessed 02 Apr 2018
34. Heimerl, K., Hasan, S., Ali, K., Parikh, T., Brewer, E.: A longitudinal study of local, sustainable, small-scale cellular networks. Inf. Technol. Int. Dev. **11**(1), 1–19 (2015). [ICTD2013 Special Issue]
35. Qureshi, S.: Are we making a better world with information and communication technology for development (ICT4D) research? Findings from the field and theory building. Inf. Technol. Dev. **21**(4), 511–522 (2015)

Innovation and Maturity

The Role of the Marginalized and Unusual Suspects in the Production of Digital Innovations: Models of Innovation in an African Context

Paul Mungai[1], Andrea Jimenez[2], Dorothea Kleine[2], and Jean-Paul Van Belle[1](✉)

[1] University of Cape Town, Cape Town, South Africa
jean-paul.vanbelle@uct.ac.za
[2] University of Sheffield, Sheffield, UK
d.j.kleine@sheffield.ac.uk

Abstract. The rapid proliferation of innovation concepts addressing experiences in the Global South raises crucial questions about the relevance of this phenomenon for development. In an effort to bring conceptual clarity, this paper reviews several related understandings of innovation and related approaches to, firstly, map overlaps and differences, and secondly, understand how they are situated within the development discourse. This study uses a literature review and applies thematic analysis in identifying the various innovation concepts, and the extent to which they include the marginalized in their framing and operationalization. In particular, this study evaluates whether these innovation concepts are framing innovation as something developed outside of poor communities but on behalf of them, whether innovation is designed alongside poor communities, or whether it is designed by and within poor communities. The findings of this study revealed that in most cases, these concepts are pro-poor, with very few exceptions of innovations done in collaboration with the poor, in a per-poor process.

Keywords: Innovation models · Digital innovation · Development Marginalized · Africa

1 Introduction

For the past 10 years, international organizations have been promoting an innovation for development agenda in Africa. Bold claims include, for instance, that there is a "[…] need for bold leadership by developing country leaders […] to move subsistence agriculture to a knowledge intensive sector" [1] or, viewing innovation as a tool for achieving "a prosperous Africa based on inclusive growth and sustainable development" [2] as in the formulation of the African Union's Commission Agenda 2063. Further, Sustainable Development Goal nine focuses on building resilient infrastructure, promoting inclusive and sustainable industrialization, and fostering innovation

K. Krauss et al. (Eds.): IDIA 2018, CCIS 933, pp. 261–278, 2019.
https://doi.org/10.1007/978-3-030-11235-6_17

[3]. In all these, innovation is regarded as a key driver of new income and employment opportunities, aimed at the socioeconomic and political development of society [4, 5].

Some recognize that an excessive focus on innovation for economic growth has enhanced the already existing inequalities in the world [6], and thus new concepts have emerged in the literature to describe the experiences of the Global South[1] and more specifically, the marginalized [7]. Although innovation is widely studied across different disciplines and contexts, we are mainly interested in concepts which position innovation in relation to development [8]. We came together as a multi-disciplinary, multi-country working group, with colleagues from both the Global South and Global North, under the umbrella of the Global Challenges Research Fund Strategic Network on Digital Development[2], and sought to develop a research agenda on innovation which cut through the modish rhetoric and examined what value concepts and practices of innovation might hold for development.

In this respect, terms like 'frugal innovation, 'pro-poor innovation', 'Bottom of the Pyramid (BOP) innovation', 'grassroots innovation' and 'inclusive innovation' are most popular in the literature [9–14]. Although these concepts, which we will review, have expanded our understanding of innovation by focusing on the marginalized in society, they have also added complexity and confusion. In the first instance, they share a similar (philosophical) view: enhancing innovation capacity is an important element of development [14]; however, they differ in their approach and how they conceptualize the marginalized. For instance, the context of frugal innovation [15] frames the concept as an umbrella term for 'inclusive innovation', 'disruptive innovation', 'pro-poor innovation' and 'grassroots innovation'; furthermore, they differ in how they include the marginalized into their framing.

In an effort to bring conceptual clarity, this paper reviews several of these concepts to map overlaps and differences and understand how they are situated within the development discourse. Our framework is informed by the extent to which these concepts include the marginalized in their framing and operationalization. More specifically, using a classification proposed by Heeks, we will evaluate whether these innovation concepts are framing innovation as something developed outside of poor communities but on behalf of them (pro-poor), whether innovation is designed alongside poor communities (para-poor), or whether it is designed by and within poor communities (per-poor) [16].

Our argument is that these distinctions matter in a conversation around development. If innovation includes the marginalized only, in the end-goal as beneficiaries, how much are we enhancing sustainability and empowerment? To what extent are we really co-constructing a more equal future in partnership with those at the sharp end of inter-country and intra-country inequality? We do not intend to provide answers to these questions, as they go beyond the scope of this paper. However, they motivate us to evaluate these concepts on how they conceptualize the marginalized.

---

[1] The Global South is a term used to denote the "interconnected histories of colonialism, neo-imperialism, and differential economic and social change through which large inequalities in living standards, life expectancy, and access to resources are maintained" (Dados and Connell 2012).

[2] Funding was provided by the UK Economic and Social Sciences Research Council, Grant Number ES/P006582/1.

This paper is organized as follows: the first section will attempt a working definition of who the marginalized are, to situate the literature in reference to how this group is framed. This is followed by the methodology of this paper, which focuses on the selection of key articles. The next section will introduce the innovation concepts, providing insights and examples stemming from the African context. We then provide an analysis of such concepts, illustrating the similarities and overlaps, and evaluate them for the extent in which they include the marginalized. We conclude this paper with proposed directions for future research.

2 Who Are the Marginalized?

Different ways to conceptualize the marginalized exist in the literature. For instance, we might argue that resources (for instance, in Kleine's list, material, financial, natural, geographical, social, educational, psychological, cultural, health, time, information) are unevenly distributed, and structural factors such as laws, social norms and policies may reinforce or address inequalities [17]. Easier access to formal education, material equipment, financial resources, relevant social resources (social capital with investors), self-controlled time and better access to information all make the relatively more privileged groups more likely innovators if a conventional view of innovation is taken. This picture is refracted differently in the formal and the informal sector. For instance, in the African context, significant work has demonstrated that innovation activity is very active in the informal sector [18], yet mainstream innovation literature fails to grasp these realities. Furthermore, innovation policy aims are often framed as an 'imperative to catch-up with or keep-up with an apparently universal techno-economic frontier' [19]. This view does not recognize other activities or modes of thinking, of which there are many in the Global South. Long years of fieldwork experience have demonstrated to us that less privileged, more marginalized individuals and groups are often highly inventive, despite and particularly in the face of, challenges and resource constraints. Yet, the innovation literature tends to focus on mainstream innovations by mainstream or privileged innovators. By contrast, we suggest that the 'marginalized' are also the "unsung", and, in that sense, "unusual suspects" of innovation. For this, we examine the literature for the traces of the marginalized as unusual suspects in the production of innovations, especially regarding digital innovation.

Similar to the more holistic conceptualization presented above, the literature suggests that marginalization takes many forms [20]. For the purposes of this paper, we focus on the economically marginalized and socially marginalized, although we recognize that individuals could be subject to both forms of marginalization and indeed many more.

Economically Marginalized: Economic challenges are indicated by static, highly variable or declining real incomes, often simplistically expressed as, for instance, less than $1.90 per person per day.[3] As an effect of low income, there may also be uneven

[3] http://documents.worldbank.org/curated/en/360021468187787070/A-global-count-of-the-extreme-poor-in-2012-data-issues-methodology-and-initial-results.

access to state resources and weak redistributive policies [21]. Economically marginalized groups lack access to supporting infrastructure [22]. An almost negligible counter-trend is that established private companies often allocate some limited budgets to support the poor in entrepreneurship as part of their CSR programmes [21]. Some of the much needed infrastructure includes electricity and telephone-line or cable connections, which are frequently also a challenge to maintain in low-income communities or regions, due to lack of indigenous/local technicians [22]. Some of the common issues affecting economic inequality include mobility, intra-household decision-making and responsibilities, intra-household time use, laws on inheritance and land ownership, and access to education and training [23, 24].

Socially Marginalized: When we refer to social inequality and marginalization, we include also values, attitudes and gender roles [25]. In this respect, the socially marginalized are those who are socially disadvantaged. This frequently includes women, youth, the disabled, the unemployed, people with low education levels, the elderly, migrants and ethnic minorities/indigenous people [23, 26].

With the possible exception of youth, representatives of the above groups have been less likely to be the poster-children of digital innovations, whether for Silicon Valley or for digital innovation milieu in Africa. A clear example of social marginalization around gender is the under-representation of women in science, technology, engineering and math (STEM) jobs and university qualifications, and differential pay compared to their male counterparts with the same credentials [24]. Innovation can also be framed as a gendered experience; for instance, the example of some women, who were also mothers, applying unorthodox management strategies modelled around their experiences as mothers, to successfully run their enterprises [27]. However, despite their reported success in women-owned or -managed businesses, these strategies are not considered to be management oriented, which is another form of marginalization [28]. This example illustrates both the power of breaking with dominant narratives of the usually male "hero innovator" and the risk of essentialist notions of women (here: women's deeper insights deriving from their role as mothers) being positioned as a counter-discourse.

3 Research Methodology

A systematic literature review approach was applied for this study. This approach is systematic and reproducible, and assisted in identifying, evaluating and synthesizing the existing body of research [29]. A description of the planning, selection, extraction and execution process is provided below.

Planning: The main aim of this study is to trace the recognition, role and framing of the marginalized in innovation by reviewing the extent to which innovation concepts focus on the marginalized. The previous section provided a detailed description of who the marginalized are, and a literature review on innovation concepts, with a focus on the marginalized, will be provided in the following section.

Selection: This study focused on research journals and key conference proceedings. The following search terms were used: 'digital innovation by communities in Africa, inclusive innovation in Africa, indigenous digital innovation in Africa, below-the-radar technological innovation in Africa, pro-poor innovation in Africa, grassroots innovation in Africa.' The first author undertook the search, selecting the most pertinent 100 articles from Google Scholar using these search terms. Relevant articles were included in an annotated bibliography comprising a reference and a short description of each article and grouped based on the themes emerging from the data.

The exclusion criteria were based on one of the following considerations: (1) duplicate studies where content was published in a research journal or conference proceeding and grey literature without additional findings; (2) sources with unclear research design or methodology; or (3) sources that were not written in English. The decision to focus on English-speaking literature was taken for pragmatic reasons, but immediately raises the need for further research reviewing literature in other languages.

Extraction and Execution: Thematic analysis was applied [30]. The search terms were used as codes, and additional codes arose during the reading of the literature. This resulted in several themes emerging from the data [29]. These themes were identified through a systematic analysis guided by the following questions focused on each literature item: (1) What is the authors' definition of innovation? (2) In their methodology, have they created action research initiatives to support marginalized groups? (3) If so, what are the methodologies used to allow the marginalized to participate? We applied Heeks's [16] classification of pro-poor, para-poor and per-poor innovation, recognizing both the strength and the weaknesses of this classification. One of the weaknesses is that it seems to apply a universal preference for more in-depth involvement when there are important exceptions, and when this approach is less appropriate – for instance, when a more light-tough engagement would lower the time costs to engagement and make it more inclusive. Where possible, we also asked (4) how sustainable any reported project was, with regard to people's willingness to continue engaging in the project, and (5) if the literature item included mention of the project's limitations.

The data extracts from literature were sorted according to these themes. The researcher conducted a deeper review of the identified themes. to determine whether there was need for further refinement, after which the analysis was transformed into an academic summary.

4 Innovation Concepts Focused on the Marginalized

Innovation has been given different names, depending on the emphasis of the strategy [7]. In this paper, we review the concepts of frugal innovation, Bottom of the Pyramid (BoP) innovation, grassroots innovation and inclusive innovation.

4.1 Frugal/Jugaad Innovation

Frugal innovation has been defined by the ability 'to do better with less resources for more people' [31]. The origin of this term 'frugal/jugaad' innovation has been traced to India, where systematic attempts have been made to strip off some of the features of products requiring high-intensity technological investment [11]. From this perspective, innovation is also a matter of redesigning products and processes to cut costs [31]. In this respect, authors establish connections between Jugaad and frugal innovation [31].

Jugaad is a common term in India, and is used to symbolise the 'quick fixes' often observed in the activities of the informal sector, ranging from solving an emergent problem to resource constraint. Jugaad innovation is characterised by lower prices, capital, skills and use of local material. Jugaad targets communities or individuals who are not served by the mainstream formal sector market; thus, initiatives by multinationals such as the Nano car by Tata, do not qualify as Jugaad innovation [32], but are a good fit for frugal innovation.

The concept of frugal innovation operates within the notion of shared value and efficiency [31]. Scholars using this concept are concerned with quantity, cost and the resources needed to produce a particular innovation. As a result, some consider that given the low cost involved, it may have low quality and limited functionality [32]. This is also driven by the need to modify some of the implicit components, which include designer assumptions about the values or knowledge of local users [33]. A very small group of scholars have suggested that frugal innovation is an empowerment mechanism for low-income populations [33].

Frugal innovation therefore refers to the process of reducing the resources, costs and complexity of a product, with the aim of addressing the specific needs and welfare of a marginalized community [5]. The end products are still "good enough", since they are able to meet the basic needs of the economically more marginalized resource-constrained consumers. A good example in this case is the Tata Nano, the world's cheapest car [32, 34].

Firms in the Global North have started to engage in frugal innovation, mainly through their Research and Development (R&D) subsidiaries in the Global South. This is motivated by the difficulty to penetrate the emerging markets due to the unaffordable pricing. The strategy then is to only include must-have features to make the product affordable, while remaining profitable [32].

This innovation is mainly pro-poor, as it is mainly undertaken to meet the (monetizable) needs outside the poor community, without involvement during the design of the product/service [16]. Thus, they are described mainly as potential consumers and beneficiaries of innovation.

4.2 Bottom of the Pyramid Innovation (BoP)

Innovation at the BoP gathers a number of studies that focus on below-the-radar innovations, with particular attention to innovations that seek to alleviate poverty [13]. BoP innovation is profit-centred, and is carried out by existing for-profit business enterprises, which seek to tap opportunities at the BoP.

This innovation faces four main challenges, including management of large numbers of low-margin products, working with informal markets, legacy and overhead costs that may undercut profit, longer time to generate sustainable returns, and an organizational culture that may stifle innovation [34]. Innovations are conceived as products and processes that could be done with very little cost, resembling the aforementioned frugal discourse. Accordingly, the poor are targeted as a new and unsaturated markets, while BoP products seek to create profit and deliver social value simultaneously [13].

BoP is evolving, moving from seeing the role of the economically marginalized as merely consumers, and products designed outside marginalized communities, to products being designed alongside poor communities, using a participative and user-centred design approach [16]. Pansera refers to this new perspective of BoP as BoP2, distinguishing it from the original BoP1, which did not engage the community during design, and did not consider the role of institutions in the process [13].

We present three examples of BoP innovations to illustrate how the concept frames the marginalized. The first is BRCK – "a rugged, self-powered, cloud enabled Wi-Fi hotspot router with built in fail-overs". This innovation, developed by a company in Nairobi, can be used by intermediaries or entrepreneurs to provide Wi-Fi access to the marginalized at a much-subsidized fee, especially in remote areas where no other affordable alternative is available [35, 36].

Another BoP innovation is M-Kilimo, a farmer help-line service company that started operations in 2009 [37]. It was developed by Kenya's largest business process outsourcing company, KenCall, with support from the Rockefeller Foundation. It had reached an average of over 20,000 users one year after its launch. Farmers – 43% of whom were women, were able to speak to a consultant for agricultural expertise and advice [37]. This was a new process and mobile-enabled network, which was said to be increasing the efficiency and scalability of the agriculture value chain. Its success suggests that M-Kilimo had made the right partnerships and earned the trust of its customers, investors, and top management at KenCall, which are necessary factors in achieving success in innovation. By 2011, due to high operational costs and lack of renewed funding, M-Kilimo had to wind down operations [38, 39]. This is an example of an innovation targeted at the BoP, which was reported as being successful initially, but failed to break even, leading to its closure. Furthermore, it is an example of a pro-poor innovation, and thus a BoP1 innovation, since the farmers were not engaged during the design and implementation process [16].

The final example of BoP innovation is mFarm, an SMS-based application that helps farmers in eliminating the middlemen, by connecting them directly with buyers/markets [40]. It was founded in 2010 by a female entrepreneur who was motivated after reading that farmers often had to rely on middlemen to find markets for their products [41]. As a result, a mobile application was designed, with up-to-date market information for farmers [42]. This resulted in price transparency [41]. mFarm is funded by the World Bank under the infoDev project [40, 43], and Tech for Trade, a UK charity that provided the first seed funding of $100,000 in 2010 [41]. The mobile app is based on the Unstructured Supplementary Service Data (USSD) technology, since not all farmers have access to smartphones.

mFarm provides daily updates of more than forty-two crops sold in five major markets; however, after the mobile solution was rolled out and interacting with farmers, it was noted that information was only part of the problem. Given that farmers produced in low volumes, it was not profitable for them to seek potential buyers, due to transport costs [41]. As a result, mFarm introduced communal storage facilities or designated collection facilities where farmers would bring their produce – often in low quantities, and invite buyers once they had sizeable stock. This called for an extension of the mFarm app to allow farmers to track their farm product deliveries to the designated collection points. In addition, mFarm extended the mobile application with the group buying feature, to farmers, to pool resources and negotiate better prices for farm requirements like fertilizer. mFarm reported more than 7,000 users of their platform in 2012. One of the ways that mFarm has adapted to ensure sustainability is the introduction of a transaction fee for SMS transactions, and sale of its data to research organizations focusing on consumer behavior or food scarcity. The interaction with farmers is characteristic of a user-centred design approach that seeks to understand user needs within their community, which then qualifies mFarm as a BoP innovation [16] with a para-poor approach.

The examples provided here suggest that both BOP1 and BOP2 overlap in several ways with frugal innovation, in terms of the resources and cost. However, the distinction is that in BOP1, innovations are designed by poor people but without their participation (pro-poor); in BOP2, they are engaged in the process.

4.3 Grassroots Innovation

Grassroots innovation has been defined as "bottom-up solutions for sustainable development; solutions that respond to the local situation and the interests and values of the communities involved" [44]. More specifically, grassroots innovation is mainly associated with innovation that emerges from poor communities [45]. It takes a long-term approach to solving local problems, with the use of locally available or even recycled resources [46]. In this respect, the marginalized are brought to the fore of the product design and development process [45]. This is characteristic of per-poor innovation, which involves undertaking innovation within and by the marginalized in their communities [16]. As such, it is identified as a way of addressing inequality, since it is driven by the lower-income group themselves [21]. It aims at exploiting and further enhancing their capabilities to innovate [45].

It is often also frugal in nature – not just in terms of the cost of the output, but also with regard to its skills and infrastructure resource requirements [40]. For instance, farmers involved in the Honey Bee Network (HNB) in India, which profiles farmers with their own innovations, were inspired when they saw people like them innovating their processes, especially because they could identify with them. This also brought pride to the communities where profiled farmers come from. The profiled farmers would go along with the HNB team, to allow for further conversations with the target community where the content was displayed. The strategy of profiling farmers created "the demand for being scouted, catalogued, and recognized", which is necessary in extending the goals of HBN and people's willingness to continue engaging [47].

However, [48] warns that in cases where participation is through community representatives, there are chances that they will not legitimately represent the interests and concerns of the community, especially when that role is taken up by elites or competing interest groups. The socially marginalized are frequently ill-served by local "community representatives" [49]. The HBN profiling approach does skew representation to the socially more self-confident. Further, [50] notes that grassroots innovations seldom scale up, which results in very limited dissemination and use. This is mainly attributed to difficulty in obtaining finance to scale up, limited knowledge and skills, and lack of information on the needs of the poor. One way of overcoming knowledge and skills challenges is to localize content. For instance, the Honey Bee Network (HNB) adopted multimedia and multi-language technology in an effort to overcome language, literacy and preference challenges in the rural communities [51]. The same approach was later applied by the Africa Rice Center (ARC), which facilitated the development and translation of eleven videos on rice quality and integrated rice management into more than thirty African languages between 2005 and 2009. The videos dealt with issues like seed sorting, flotation, drying, storage, soil fertility management, and more. It has been reported that the videos improved the capacities of hundreds of thousands of farmers and more than five hundred organizations, which, if substantiated, is very large scale. There were also instances where these videos were used for national agricultural programmes, as was the case in Gambia, Uganda and Nigeria [49]. This HNB approach to innovation helps in demonstrating that some grassroots innovations can indeed scale up, depending on the nature of the innovation.

Grassroots innovation can help in resolving agricultural sustainability challenges, by forming alliances between crop breeders and farmers, and combining scientific and indigenous farmers' knowledge in selecting and developing more appropriate crops and seed varieties [52]. This approach was put to the test in Kenya, and some of the benefits from the observations include sustainability of smallholder livelihoods [52]. Another approach is the integrated rural learning approach, detailed above, which was pioneered by the Honey Bee Network (HBN) and adopted by other organizations such as the Africa Rice Center (ARC) [47, 49].

Grassroots innovation at times informs mainstream Science and Technology Innovation (STI) institutions in pursuit of their goals. [51] for instance, consider that engineers and designers may engage with grassroots innovation as long as they include the grassroots in innovation processes from the outset, and 'put local knowledge and communities in the lead in the framing of a collaborative innovation activity'.

This creates the need to negotiate on joint policy models for inclusive innovation, noting that there is diversity in the interpretations and framings in relation to what and who gets included or excluded [19]. In addition, policy-makers need to ensure coherence among the various development policies within a country or region [53]. The major challenge with this recommendation is the level of diversity among rural places, which makes it difficult to design national policies that factor in specific needs of the rural communities [54], so a balance needs to be struck between national support and locally diverse implementation. There is also a need to ensure that these policies involve all stakeholders, with the aim of ensuring that the interests of the more marginalized, such as women, youth and budding entrepreneurs, are adequately considered [53]. Lead stakeholders such as government policy-makers at national, regional and local level, need to ensure that inclusive innovation is factored in within government strategies and policies, making it easier to innovate [55].

4.4 Inclusive Innovation

Inclusive innovation has been defined in many ways, e.g. '[..] the inclusion within some aspect of innovation, of groups who are currently marginalized' [7]. For [6], inclusive innovation refers to 'the development and implementation of new ideas which aspire to create opportunities that enhance social and economic wellbeing for disenfranchised members of society'. The aforementioned definitions share a focus on particular groups which are marginalized. This suggests that instead of focusing necessarily on the products or processes, inclusive innovation focuses on people; however, when it comes to proponents of inclusive innovation explaining who they mean by "the marginalized", we found limited information.

For [9], 'innovation needs to be "inclusive" in at least two ways: inclusive in terms of the process by which it is achieved and inclusive in terms of the problems and the solutions it is related to'. [56] suggest that inclusive innovation should include those new ways of doing things – including technologies, institutions, and other things – that may improve lives of the 'most needy'. The "most needy" in this definition is left deliberately vague because who this represents is supposed to be answered on a study-by-study basis.

Perhaps one of the most explicit works on how to define the marginalized in relation to innovation could come from Heeks et al.'s [44] work on inclusive innovation. These authors propose a multi-level approach coined as 'the ladder of inclusive innovation' which proposes different aspects of inclusivity. This mirrors to some degree Arnstein's ladder of citizen participation, though it omits the perceptive critique of non-participation and tokenism in Arnstein's model [57]. The first steps are the means by which new goods and services are developed with some aspect of inclusion of the marginalized, either to address a specific problem of the poor on their behalf (pro-poor innovation), involve the poor in the development process (para-poor or grassroots innovation), or aim at benefiting the livelihoods of the poor (pro-poor) [7]. Inclusive innovation usually results from tensions within the socio-technical systems, which can either be caused by social or economic factors. This ladder, based on Arnstein's model [57], can to a degree assist in studying the level of inclusivity in the relationships between stakeholder involvement, institutional structures, and the resulting outcomes as suggested by [56]. The ladder comprises six levels, which are illustrated in Fig. 1.

Inclusion of Intention refers to innovations that seeks to integrate the intentions and needs of the marginalized. Inclusion of Consumption refers to innovations that are adopted and used by the marginalized. Inclusion of Impact refers to innovations that have a positive impact on the livelihoods of the marginalized (there is some overlap with the previous rung). Inclusion of Process refers to innovation that involves the marginalized during design and development [44], which calls for dialogue, conflict-solving procedures, trust, and a strong motivation to interact [9]. Inclusion of Structure refers to innovation that is created within an inclusive structure. Post-structural inclusion refers to innovation that is created within an inclusive frame of knowledge

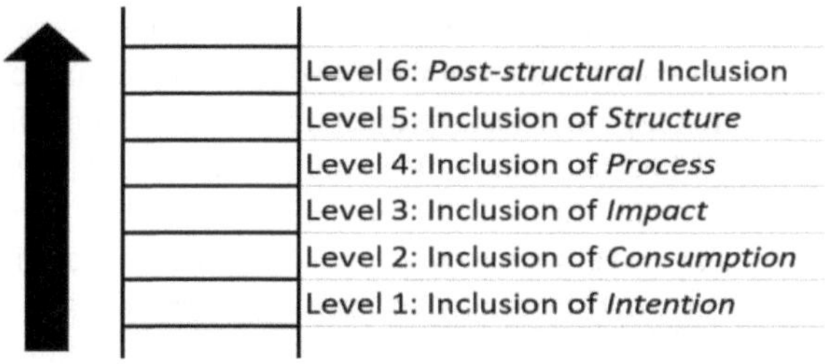

Fig. 1. Levels of inclusive innovation [33]

and discourse [44]. The model offers a useful classification in many ways, while insufficiently distinguishing between meaningful and tokenistic inclusion, and also suggesting a linear set of steps when these are parallel and systemic processes:

Inclusivity therefore entails active consultation, participation and engagement with the marginalized at various stages of the innovation process. For instance, living labs are founded on a common methodology that endeavours to create innovation environments within real-life user communities, frequently through the formation of so-called public-private-people-partnerships [58], but they are likely to vary in the level of inclusivity. This is mainly because of contextual variations and normative implications with regard to the dynamics between actors [56, 59], based on demand and embedded in the context [60].

This could be illustrated through the example of Siyakhula Living Lab (SLL), which was established by the Meraka Institute, following a directive by the South African Department of Science and Technology (DST). SSL is located in Dweca-Cwebe, a so-called "deep rural" area in the Wild Coast area of the Eastern Cape province of South Africa. Until 2009, a majority of the households in Dweca-Cwebe did not have direct access to electricity and running water, and the road infrastructure within the region was limited. SSL began operations in 2005, guided by the user-driven approach in understanding local requirements and constraints in ICT. The multi-disciplinary nature of the team or researchers working with the community, which consisted of researchers from anthropology and computer science departments, collaborated with community members to identify the social-technical challenges and opportunities for innovation [61]. SLL focused on ICT training at the initial phase of the project. This followed the train-the-trainer/champion model, where volunteer teachers and community members were trained by university-based researchers. The champions then used the acquired knowledge and skills to teach, using their own language, which resulted in increased uptake from the community. SSL helped in providing access to Internet and computer hardware by setting up a facility within the community. This enabled members of the community, who now had more access to the Internet, to not only make use of information available on the Internet, but to also produce content. This platform also assists government in testing ICT infrastructure within a rural context, such as Dweca-Cwebe [61]. Inclusive innovation requires consultation with the necessary stakeholders, prior to tackling a problem that may be of mutual concern and interest [61].

In the case of SLL, trust and social resources (social capital) were cornerstones for success in engaging with community members [4]. Normative implications as described by [56] are also at play, since the project relies on funding from a particular sponsor (the major fixed-line telecommunications provider) and thus the project can only maneuver within the boundaries of the objectives set by this sponsor. In the case of SLL, the South African government came in as a regulator, claiming to defend the interests of the community, and facilitator in terms of approvals and goodwill. Social capital and trust between the researchers and community members was already established at the beginning, since the anthropology department researchers had previously engaged with the community on other research initiatives [61]. The train-the-trainer model helped in building confidence and buy-in, as the community members could relate more with one of their own. Local community members were also trained on how to maintain the infrastructure [61] which was necessary in securing ownership and sustainability of the initiative. This description places SSL, at least in its aspiration, at level 4 - "inclusion of process" of [44] 's ladder of inclusive innovation, since community members are involved in developing and maintaining the initiative.

Inclusive innovation can also be pro-poor – for example, with the case of Lumkani, an early fire detection warning system that seeks to reduce the destruction caused by fires in urban informal settlements. The system creates a 60-m radius network of the detectors, which would become activated simultaneously in case of a fire, and thus enables the community to respond before the fire becomes uncontrollable [62]. It was designed by an engineering honours student from the University of Cape Town, taking input from the community during the design and testing phases of the proposed solution. They took a frugal approach in building the fire detector, by using affordable components and local manufacturers, for the most part. This is an example of a pro-poor inclusive innovation with aspects of frugal, and which was inclusive in the process of getting input from the community.

5 Similarities and Differences Between the Innovation Concepts

Describing the various innovation concepts reveals an overlap in meanings or objectives, some of which are still evolving. For instance, BoP innovation has since rebranded and updated from the "poor-as-consumers" perspective, following criticisms and experience, to the perspective of the poor as "co-innovators" [13]. In an attempt to illustrate the overlaps further, Table 1 highlights the key differences, and illustrates the similarities, between the innovation models which were highlighted.

BoP1 and frugal innovation are both pro-poor, since they are undertaken outside the poor communities, but on their behalf. Inclusive innovation and BoP2 are para-poor, since they are undertaken alongside poor communities, and involves them in the design and/or development of the product/service [44]. BoP1, BoP2 and frugal innovation are similar, since they are all frugal in nature.

Table 1. Key differences and overlaps between various innovation models

Innovation Model	Definition Primary Focus	Role of the 'poor' (as per Heeks, 2008)	Overlap with other innovation models?				
			Grass roots Innovation	BoP1 Innovation	BoP2 Innovation	Frugal / Jugaad Innovation	Inclusive Innovation
Grassroots Innovation	Innovator = marginalized people	Per-poor					
BoP1 Innovation	Target = the poor (often services)	(usually) pro-poor					
BoP2 Innovation	Target = the poor (often services) Community engagement	(usually) para-poor					
Frugal / Jugaad Innovation	Affordability of design or final product/service	(usually) pro-poor					
Inclusive Innovation	Poor/marginalized are included in problem definition and/or design	Para-poor					

6 Discussion

In this paper, we suggested that mainstream innovation literature failed to grasp some of the innovation activity taken by the marginalized in the Global South. As such, we notice that the marginalized are frequently the "unsung" and "unusual suspects" of innovation. A first observation is that all the innovation concepts discussed here are relevant to the paper's focus on these in the production of innovation in an African context, albeit to varying degrees.

Frugal innovation focuses again more on the quality of the product and the potential for those marginalized to benefit from it. BOP1 and BOP2 frame the marginalized based on their economic capacity, and focus on innovation that will be successful in the market. Grassroots innovation is the only one that focuses on innovation made by marginalized and for the marginalized. Inclusive innovation attempts to focus on the inclusion of those marginalized, yet it suggests that if they are "lightly" included then that is still good. Not all will need to be involved to the level of level 4 "inclusion in process", and there are good reasons to, in some cases, trade off time savings and lower barriers to participation in exchange for more in-depth inclusion. These trade-offs are hard to visualise within the metaphor of the "ladder". This was illustrated by the example of M-Kilimo, which was described under BoP innovation. Despite being developed outside the marginalized farmers' communities, it still gained significant traction based on the number of callers, which implies that it had a positive impact on the agriculture value chain. Whether designing in closer collaboration with the farmers would have made it more likely that a sustainable business model could have been found when funding ended, is an open question.

The second observation is that most of the innovations discussed here are either funded by development donors, large corporations, NGOs, or venture capitalists, which are mainly from the Global North. This suggests that most of the concepts are framed as pro-poor innovation. This implies that digital inclusive innovation requires access to these financial networks. This, in turn, requires innovators to pitch their proposal or product in a particular format. This requires skills, access to resources, including the right habitus (as part of cultural resources in the *Kleine* sense) resources that allow one to engage with these networks. Lack of access and exposure to these networks can result in a new form of marginalization.

The third observation is that most literature focuses more on products, less on processes, and even less on people. It is more about the innovation, and less about who is innovating. For instance, it was difficult to determine whether there was engagement with the marginalized/farming communities in Kenya, and what role they played in the design of the farmer help-line service. The literature describes the features of the service, the reaction of the learners after using it, and the frugality of the product, but nothing about the design process, or who was involved in this process. We therefore are invited to assume that this innovation was carried out outside the marginalized community, and only introduced as a complete product for them to use 'as is'. This would then be typical of off-the-shelf products which cannot be customized. More generally, we will only progress in our understanding of innovation processes with marginalized community members, if we start documenting and discussing these processes.

A fourth observation is that just like in early participation literature, "the community" becomes discursively constructed in the literature as some form of homogenous and conflict-free group of co-creators, when in reality members of the community operate with very varied resource portfolios, are positioned differently in the social structures and experience different forms and degrees of marginalization [63, 64]. It is rarely the most marginalized who are asked to represent "the community".

A final observation is that most of the digital innovations documented in the literature, including some of those that were highlighted here, are frequently founded by tech-savvy men, and those who are either from the Global North or have personal experience visiting or living in the Global North. This raises the question of whether women are innovating in the digital space, and whether they have had the same opportunities as their male counterparts. Further, it raises the question whether links to the Global North are conducive to, or even a precondition for, such innovation, and further research should be undertaken into the nature and function of such links.

We have provided an explanation of these concepts with the objective of showing to what extent and in what ways they include the marginalized. The reasoning behind this is to provide conceptual clarity. Our review leads us to see that even though these concepts have expanded our understanding of what impact innovation may have on development, they frequently fall short in exploring the agency of the marginalized themselves.

By evaluating these concepts from a perspective of the marginalized, we are arguing that innovation in development should focus on people [8]. For this to happen, it will be necessary to move away from seeing communities as homogenous, towards further distinguishing between the positionality of individuals and groups and their relative marginalization.

7 Conclusion

There has been much discussion in the literature around the role of innovation for socioeconomic development. This has resulted in the proliferation of concepts which aim to describe and understand innovation in the Global South, often either targeting or benefitting the marginalized.

This paper has attempted to analyse what is meant by 'the marginalized' in innovation concepts. Drawing on both theoretical literature and concrete examples, it has reviewed the extent to which innovation concepts that address development impact focus on the marginalized. It has evaluated how existing innovation concepts are responding to the question of including the marginalized, through an analysis of whether innovations are designed on behalf of the poor, with the poor, or by the poor.

This paper has contributed to the literature around innovation concepts by illustrating how little it includes people in the analysis, let alone a more sophisticated examination of which of the actors is economically and socially marginalized. Moving forward, we thus aim to broaden the innovation for development agenda to include the marginalized in the conceptualization and practice, widening our understanding of innovation from products and processes to one that includes people, and specifically people experiencing different kinds of marginalization.

References

1. Kraemer-Mbula, E., Wamae, W.: Innovation and the development agenda. OECD Publishing, Ottowa (2010)
2. African Union Commission: Agenda 2063 - The Africa We Want. Addis Ababa, Ethiopia (2014)
3. UNIDO: Industrial Development Report 2016: The Role of Technology and Innovation in Inclusive and Sustainable Industrial Development. Vienna (2015)
4. Guth, M.: Innovation, social inclusion and coherent regional development: a new diamond for a socially inclusive innovation policy in regions. Eur. Plann. Stud. **13**(2), 333–348 (2005)
5. Papaioannou, T.: How inclusive can innovation and development be in the twenty-first century? Innov. Dev. **4**(2), 187–202 (2014)
6. George, G., Mcgahan, A.M., Prabhu, J.: Innovation for inclusive growth: towards a theoretical framework and a research agenda. J. Manage. Stud. **49**(4), 661–683 (2012)
7. Foster, C., Heeks, R.: Conceptualising inclusive innovation: modifying systems of innovation frameworks to understand diffusion of new technology to low-income consumers. Eur. J. Dev. Res. **25**(3), 333–355 (2013)
8. Jiménez, A., Yingqin, Z.: Tech hubs, innovation and development. Inf. Technol. Dev. **24**(1), 95–118 (2018)
9. Cozzens, S., Sutz, J.: Innovation in informal settings: a research agenda. Ottawa, Canada (2012)
10. Ramani, S.V., SadreGhazi, S., Duysters, G.: On the diffusion of toilets as bottom of the pyramid innovation: lessons from sanitation entrepreneurs. Technol. Forecast. Soc. Change **29**(4), 676–687 (2012)
11. Chataway, J., Hanlin, R., Kaplinsky, R.: Inclusive innovation: an architecture for policy development. Innov. Dev. **4**(1), 33–54 (2014)

12. Levidow, L., Papaioannou, T.: Which inclusive innovation? Competing normative assumptions around social justice. Innov. Dev. 1–18 (2017)
13. Pansera, M.: Discourses of Innovation and Development: Insights from Ethnographic case studies in Bangladesh and India. University of Exeter (2014)
14. Pansera, M., Owen, R.: Framing inclusive innovation within the discourse of development: insights from case studies in India. Res. Policy **47**(1), 23–34 (2018)
15. Meagher, K.: Cannibalizing the informal economy: frugal innovation and economic inclusion in Africa. Eur. J. Dev. Res. 1–17 (2018)
16. Heeks, R.: ICT4D 2.0: the next phase of applying ICT for international development. IEEE Comput. Soc. **41**(6), 26–33 (2008)
17. Kleine, D.: Technologies of Choice? ICTs, Development, and the Capabilities Approach. MIT Press, Cambridge (2013)
18. Kraemer-Mbula, E., Wunch-Vincent, E. (eds.): The Informal Economy in Develop-ing Nations: Hidden Engine of Innovation? New Economic Insights and Policies. Cambridge University Press, Cambridge (2016)
19. Fressoli, M., Arond, E., Abrol, D., Smith, A., Ely, A., Dias, R.: When grassroots innovation movements encounter mainstream institutions: implications for models of inclusive innovation. Innov. Dev. **4**(2), 277–292 (2014)
20. Mowat, J.G.: Towards a new conceptualisation of marginalisation. Eur. Educ. Res. J. **14**(5), 454–476 (2015)
21. OECD: Innovation and Inclusive Development: a discussion of the main policy issues. OECD Science, Technology & Industry working paper 2013/1. OECD Publishing (2013)
22. Blake, M.K., Hanson, S.: Rethinking innovation: context and gender. Environ. Plan. **37**(4), 681–701 (2005)
23. Codagnone, C. (ed.): Vienna Study on Inclusive Innovation for Growth and Cohesion. European Commission, Brussels (2009)
24. Vossenberg, S.: Gender-aware women's entrepreneurship development for inclusive development in sub-Saharan Africa. J. Chem. Inf. Model. **53**, 1689–1699 (2016)
25. Beede, D., Julian, T., Langdon, D., McKittrick, G., Khan, B., Doms, M.: Women in STEM: A Gender Gap to Innovation, Economics and Statistics Administration Issue Brief 04–11, U. S. Dept of Commerce, Washington, DC (2011)
26. Gefen, D., Straub, D.W.: Gender differences in use of e-mail: an extension to the technology acceptance model. MIS Q. **21**(4), 389–400 (1997)
27. Bhatti, Y., Ventresca, M.: How can 'frugal innovation' be conceptualized?. Soc. Sci. Res. Netw. (2013)
28. Altenburg, T., Lundvall, B.: Building inclusive innovation systems in developing countries: challenges for IS research. Handb. Innov. Syst. Dev. Ctries. Build. Domest. Capab. Glob. Setting 33–56 (2009)
29. Braun, V., Clarke, V.: Using thematic analysis in psychology. Qual. Res. Psychol. **3**(2), 77–101 (2006)
30. Okoli, C., Schabram, K.: A guide to conducting a systematic literature review of information systems research. In: Sprouts: Working Papers on Information Systems, vol. 10 (26) (2010)
31. Zeschky, M., Widenmayer, B., Gassmann, O.: Frugal innovation in emerging markets. Res. Technol. Manag. **54**(4), 38–45 (2011)
32. Prabhu, J.: Frugal innovation: doing more with less for more. Philos. Trans. R Soc. a-Math. Phys. Eng. Sci. **375**(2095), 20160372 (2017)
33. Heeks, R., Foster, C., Nugroho, Y.: New models of inclusive innovation for development. Innov. Dev. **4**(2), 175–185 (2014)
34. Kumar, H., Bhaduri, S.: Jugaad to grassroot innovations: understanding the landscape of the informal sector innovations in India. African J. Sci. Technol. Innov. Dev. **6**(1), 13–22 (2014)

35. Zeschky, M., Widenmayer, M., Gassmann, O.: Frugal innovation in emerging markets. Res. Manag. **54**(4), 38–45 (2011)
36. Kahle, N.H., Dubiel, A., Ernst, H., Prabhu, J.: The democratizing effects of frugal innovation: Implications for inclusive growth and state-building. J. Indian Bus. Res. **5**(4), 220–234 (2013)
37. Heeks, R.: Information systems and developing countries: failure, success, and local improvisations. Inf. Soc. **18**(2), 101–112 (2002)
38. Karamchandani, A., Kubzansky, M., Lalwani, N.: Is the bottom of the pyramid really for you? Harv. Bus. Rev. **89**(3), 107–111 (2011)
39. BRCK: Bridging the digital Divide. brck.org (2016). http://brck.org. Accessed 31 Jan 2018
40. Bright, J.: Kenyan startup BRCK launches SupaBRCK device to solve Africa's internet equation. https://techcrunch.com/2017/03/08/kenyan-startup-brck-launches-supabrck-device-to-solve-africas-internet-equation/. Accessed 31 Jan 2018
41. Narsalay, R., Pongeluppe, L., Light, D.: The Hidden Pitfalls of Inclusive Innovation. Stanford Soc. Innov. Rev. 48–53 (2015)
42. Duncombe, R.: Facilitating change in agricultural value chains with app services. ICT Update, pp. 6–7 (2017)
43. Solon, O.: MFarm empowers Kenya's farmers with price transparency and market access. http://www.wired.co.uk/article/mfarm. Accessed 31 Jan 2018
44. Kedja, S.: Four building stones for a vibrant ICT environment. ICT Update, pp. 8–9 (2017)
45. Manfre, C., Rubin, D., Allen, A., Summerfield, G., Colverson, K., Akeredolu, M.: Reducing the Gender Gap in Agricultural Extension and Advisory Services: How to Find the Best Fit for Men and Women Farmers. MEAS Brief # 2. MEAS, Urbana (2013)
46. Heeks, R.: IT innovation for the bottom of the pyramid. Commun. ACM **55**(12), 24 (2012)
47. Ngoasong, M., Korda, A., Paton, R.: Impact Investing and Inclusive Business Development in Africa: A research agenda. The Open University, Milton Keynes (2015)
48. Seyfang, G., Haxeltine, A.: Growing grassroots innovations: exploring the role of community-based initiatives in governing sustainable energy transitions. Environ. Plan. C Polit. Sp. **30**(3), 381–400 (2012)
49. Paunov, C.: Innovation and inclusive development: a discussion of the main policy issues. Cape Town, South Africa (2013)
50. Kenny, C.: Could Solar Lighting Be the Next Mobile Phone? Center for Global Development (2012). https://www.cgdev.org/blog/could-solar-lighting-be-next-mobile-phone. Accessed 31 Jan 2018
51. Burger, R.: What we have learnt from post-1994 innovations in pro-poor service delivery in South Africa: a case study-based analysis. Dev. South. Afr. **22**(4), 483–500 (2005)
52. Van Mele, P., Wanvoeke, J., Zossou, E.: Enhancing rural learning, linkages, and institutions: the rice videos in Africa. Dev. Pract. **20**(3), 414–421 (2010)
53. Dahlman, C.J.: Innovation Policy for Inclusive Development. OECD Global Forum, Paris (2014)
54. Smith, A., Fressoli, M., Thomas, H.: Grassroots innovation movements: Challenges and contributions. J. Clean. Prod. **63**, 114–124 (2014)
55. Leach, M. et al.: Transforming Innovation for Sustainability. Ecol. Soc. **17**(2) (2012)
56. Bryden, J., Gezelius, S.S., Refsgaard, K., Sutz, J.: Inclusive innovation in the bioeconomy: concepts and directions for research. Innov. Dev. **7**(1), 1–16 (2017)
57. Arnstein, S.R.: A ladder of citizen participation. J. Am. Inst. Plann. **35**(4), 216–224 (1969)
58. Atkinson, D.: Regional development, innovation and pro-poor development: missing links in the South African planning system. In: Conference on Overcoming Structural Poverty and Inequality in South Africa, pp. 1–26 (2010)

59. Kapuire, G.K., Winschiers-Theophilus, H., Chivuno-Kuria, S., Bidwell, N.J., Blake, E.: A revolution in ICT, the last hope for African Rural Communities' technology appropriation. In: International Development Informatics Association Conference (2010)
60. UNCTAD: Pro-poor technology, innovation and entrepreneurship policies. In: United Nations Conference on Trade and Development (2012)
61. Gumbo, S., Thinyane, H., Thinyane, M., Terzoli, A., Hansen, S.: Living Lab Methodology as an Approach to Innovation in ICT4D: The Siyakhula Living Lab Experience. In: IST-Africa (2012)
62. Viviers, A.: A fire detection system for shacks. designindaba.com,.http://www.designindaba.com/articles/creative-work/fire-detection-system-shacks. Accessed 31 Jan 2018
63. Dearden, A., Rizvi, H.: Adapting participatory and agile software methods to participatory rural development. In: 10th Conference on Participatory Design, pp. 221–225 (2008)
64. Fendler, L.: Others and the problem of community. Curric. Inq. **36**(3), 303–326 (2006)

Investigating Business Intelligence (BI) Maturity in an African Developing Country: A Mozambican Study

Sunet Eybers[1(✉)], Marie J. Hattingh[1], and Osvaldo M. P. Zandamela[2]

[1] University of Pretoria, Private Bag X20, Hatfield 0028, South Africa
{sunet.eybers,marie.hattingh}@up.ac.za
[2] University of South Africa, P.O. Box 392, Unisa, Pretoria 0003, South Africa
Osvaldo.Zandamela@south32.net

Abstract. The term 'Big Data' has placed renewed focus on the untapped value of data in organizations. Despite the hype of Big Data and the obvious benefits associated with it, organizations often battle with dealing with 'normal' transactional data, obtained from various information systems to make vital business decisions. The objective of this qualitative study was to investigate the extent to which Business Intelligence System (BIS) were implemented in a developing country such as Mozambique through the lens of organizational maturity. Maturity assessment is a popular method for assessing the readiness of organizations by means of processes, people and data toward the adoption of a particular approach. In this instance, the Business Intelligence maturity model (biMM) developed by Dinter [1] was adopted to establish the BI maturity in the Mozambican organizations for the purpose of comparing results. The study found that high maturity levels were achieved in the integration between technological production and development infrastructure and the availability of BIS in organizations; however, huge challenges were faced in the area of metadata management, master data management, low level access, and support of analytical information to operational business processes.

The findings make an important contribution towards understanding the BIS maturity level of Mozambican organizations for the purpose of future data related technological adoptions.

Keywords: Business Intelligence Systems (BIS) · BIS maturity
Developing country

1 Introduction

The need to work with large, complex data sets have introduced numerous management challenges in analyzing data computationally with one of the main objectives of discovering patterns and trends. For example: the managerial challenges include an adjustment of leadership, talent management, technology, decision making, and company culture [2]. The unique data sets, also referred to as 'Big Data' sets can, when successfully analyzed, provide deeper insight into consumer behavior and product

K. Krauss et al. (Eds.): IDIA 2018, CCIS 933, pp. 279–294, 2019.
https://doi.org/10.1007/978-3-030-11235-6_18

basket analysis (to name a few) [2]; however, despite the managerial challenges and obvious benefits of successfully introducing Big Data capabilities in organizations, some organizations are still having difficulties implementing solutions to cater for structured data from their transactional and operational processing systems [3]. In fact, research has shown that the majority of these projects, also referred to as Business Intelligence Systems (BIS) often fail. The IT Research firm Gartner (2011), as cited by Marin-Ortega et al. [4], indicates that the failure rate of BI projects are estimated to be between 70% to 80%. The findings are supported by several academic researchers such as Chuah and Wong [5], Olszak and Ziemba [3], Cidrin and Adamala [6] and Hawking [7]. These statistics are alarming when considering that key business decisions are based on the availability of the right information at the right time, often provided by BIS.

As with many IT projects, there is no crystal ball for predicting BIS implementation success [8]; however, research by Williams [9] has shown that organizations are more likely to implement BIS successfully if the organization is ready for the adoption of a new technology. Readiness assessments, also referred to as maturity assessments using maturity models, propose certain measurements to establish the degree to which people, processes, and technologies are implemented and capable of proper service delivery [9]. Maturity models provide organizations with a roadmap for reaching higher maturity and, therefore, higher business effectiveness [10–12]. Additionally, an organization's maturity assessment provides an overview of the benefits such an organization would reap should it pursue higher maturity levels [13, 14]. Having an overview of these benefits would motivate organizations to adopt initiatives for reaching higher maturity levels.

The objective of this study is to investigate the maturity level of BIS focusing on the top Mozambican manufacturing companies (described later in the study). The research question is "*what is the level of BIS maturity reached by manufacturing companies in a developing country such as Mozambique*?" Manufacturing companies can use the findings in this study to improve their current BI maturity level, and hence, increase their competitiveness in the market [13, 14]. It can also serve as a business case for organizations in developing countries wishing to adopt BIS prior to the adoption of Big Data Solutions.

The paper starts with a brief introduction to various BI maturity models as well as a short description of the theoretical framework adopted (biMM), followed by examples of studies focusing on BIS maturity in developing countries. The methodology section provides insight into the research approach followed by a description and discussion of the results of the study. A conclusion section concludes the paper.

2 Maturity Models

The concept of a maturity model has its origin in the field of total quality management (TQM) [15]. Talib [16] defines TQM as a framework which is "intended to promote continuous and sustained improvement in quality and performance, and develops an attitude of quality culture". Improvement is achieved by the enhancement of quality of work and employee satisfaction through participation. One of the means of achieving participation is by involving the employee in all decision-making concerning this employee's work, or working area [16]. Talib [16] argues that when organizations adopt TQM, these organizations encourage each collaborator to contribute with suggestions which enable the organizations to enhance the quality of their processes. Improvements in the processes' quality prevent the production of defective products. Consequently, these improvements reduce the amount of rework and flawed products. As a result, organizations will potentially reduce their production costs and increase their competitive advantages [17, 18].

Humphrey and his colleagues at IBM, while studying software quality, noticed that the software quality was directly related to the quality of the process on which the software was produced [19]. This analysis resulted in the conception of the maturity model, adapted from Crosby's quality management [19–21]. Since then, subject-specific maturity models have been developed in many disciplines such as systems engineering, software engineering, and integrated product and process development [5] and finally BIS.

2.1 Current BI Maturity Models

BI maturity models are an example of a capability maturity model developed for assessing the BIS capability of an organization focusing on BI [5].

There are a number of maturity models developed by both industry practitioners, and industry practitioners in collaboration with academics. An extensive review of all the models was not the objective of the paper and constitutes a research paper on its own; therefore only some of the more popular models will be briefly discussed. Table 1 provides a summary of additional BI maturity models found in literature.

Table 1. Summary of BI maturity models

Maturity model	Author(s)	Focus
Business Intelligence Development Model (BIDM)	Sacu and Spruit [22]	Integration of existing BI development stages of various maturity models to propose a framework for holistic BI maturity assessment
Enterprise Business Intelligence Maturity Model (EBI2M)	Chuah and Wong [5]	BI maturity model considering a staged representation and continuous representation considering five evolutionary maturity levels (Initial, Managed, Defined, Quantitatively managed and Optimized)
Gartner maturity model	Hostmann and Hagerty [23]	Five levels of maturity, namely Unaware, Initial, Standards, Enterprise and Transformative
The Data Warehousing Institute's (TDWI) maturity model	TDWI [24]	Six maturity stages, namely Prenatal, Infant, Child, Teenager, Adult and Sage across eight dimensions, namely: Scope, Sponsorship, Funding, Value, Architecture, Data, Development, and Delivery

(*continued*)

Table 1. (*continued*)

Maturity model	Author(s)	Focus
Data warehouse stages of growth	Watson et al. [25]	Three stages of growth, namely Initiation, Growth and Maturity
Data warehouse process maturity model	Sen, Ramamurthy and Sinha [26]	Focus on the failure of data warehouse initiatives proposing that data warehouse processes could mitigate large-scale failures
The ladder of business intelligence (LOBI)	Cates, Gill and Zeituny [27]	Six maturity levels (Facts, Data, Information, Knowledge, Understanding and Enabled Intuition) considering organizational business strategy and the people, processes, and technology
The three levels of analytic capability model	Lavalle et al. [28]	Evaluate three levels of analytic capability: Aspirational, Experienced and Transformative
biMM	Dinter [1]	Focus on three perspectives namely Functionality, Technology and Organization with sub dimensions

In order to provide the research with a proper theoretical foundation one maturity model had to be selected. The selection process was based on a method of comparative analysis after considering the most prevalent BI maturity models (as described above). The selection method followed a successive elimination approach.

The EBI2M, BIDM and LOBI were the first models to be eliminated due to a lack of documentation. Without clear documentation on how to use these models, it becomes complex to conduct an assessment using these BI maturity models whilst increasing the risk of using the wrong implementation approach. The Gartner BI Maturity Model was eliminated, although extensively documented; implementation documentation is only available to Gartner's clients at a cost. Furthermore, some models only focus on particular aspects of BI such as the technical aspects (Data Warehousing Institute's BI Maturity Model), limited components of BI implementations (three levels of analytic capability model excluding BI governance, reporting and architecture) or data warehousing (data warehouse stages of growth and the data warehouse process maturity model).

The biMM model has been extensively tested by industry practitioners and continuous iterations were made. In addition, the model has been extensively documented for implementation and therefore seemed suitable for the purpose of this study. The model is described in more detail below.

2.2 Theoretical Model: The BI Maturity Model (biMM)

The biMM evaluate BI maturity using three perspectives; namely a functionality perspective, technology perspective and organization perspective. For each of the perspectives, sub dimensions have been identified: Functionality perspective (scope, data architecture and penetration level); Technology perspectives (technical architecture, data management and information design); and Organization perspective (organization structure, processes, profitability and strategy). Each of these perspectives and the dimensions are evaluated amongst five maturity levels (for the functionality perspective) and five stages (for the technology and organization perspective) [1, 29]. Tables 2, 3 and 4 illustrate the layout of the biMM.

3 Previous Studies Focusing on BI Maturity Assessments in Developing Countries

The importance of BI maturity in developing countries is evident in the research conducted in countries such as Brazil, Pakistan and South Africa. Each of the studies is briefly described.

3.1 The Role of BI in Developing Countries: A Brazilian Study

Petrini and Pozzebon [30] assessed BI maturity focusing on Brazil. The study had the objective of identifying the types of BI projects implemented by Brazilian companies and their subsequent perceived value to gain a competitive advantage. The findings indicated that, besides the increasing interest in BI systems, only few BI projects were implemented; therefore, Petrini and Pozzebon [30] claim that the benefits of investing in BI remain to be proved.

3.2 A Case of BI Adoption in Pakistan

Shah [31] conducted a study to assess the adoption of BI in Pakistan with the objective of: (1) Identify the key driving forces for adopting BI; (2) to determine the benefits and challenges faced when adopting BI; and (3) to investigate the current BI maturity level. The findings of the study identified:

- The key drivers of BI adoption namely: (1) The need to increase competitiveness; (2) The need for efficient and quick decision-making; (3) Efficiency and availability of data according to management needs; (4) Management of data contained in third-party software and data centralization.
- The benefits of BI adoption: (1) Better resource management, (2) Better view of current progress and future projection, (3) Summarized group level information with different perspectives and information clarity;
- BI adoption challenges: (1) Low personnel acceptance of changes, (2) Low personnel cooperation in adopting new technological environment, (3) Lack of understanding of the management objectives;
- BI adoption maturity level: Based on the framework from Lavalle et al. [28] (see Table 1) the findings suggested that organizations are on the Experiented level of BI adoption.

3.3 Studies Focusing on a South African Context

In 2011, Ponelis and Britz [32] conducted an exploratory study focusing on BI in knowledge-based South African small and medium enterprises (SME) to get insights into BI usage. The objective of the study was threefold: (1) to understand how organizational information is used in SMEs (small and medium enterprises); (2) to describe BI in the context of SMEs; and (3) determine why some SMEs are not using BI. The key findings of the study were:

- ICT is perceived as a means to achieve business objectives and inexpensive, flexible solutions that are easy to implement;
- All owner-managers in the SMEs are well-educated domain experts but not necessarily educated in the management and administration of the business;
- All firms use information from internal and external data sources for decision-making and would like to see improved access to existing and additional data sources as key asset in their enterprises;
- Data integration, manipulation, and analysis are predominantly manual using internally developed and/or custom-developed spreadsheets provided by external parties;
- Half of the SMEs need to share data with their clients to ensure healthy relationships and prompt payment;
- External assistance from trusted parties is sometimes required to assist with data analysis, although decision makers prefer no intervention from external parties.

In a similar study conducted by Lautenbach et al. [40] the authors adopted a Technology-Organization-Environment (TOE) framework to understand the utilization of BI in organizations. It was argued that, if organizations understand the utilization of BI, efforts can be channeled to increase the motivation for the adoption of these technologies. The findings of the study suggested that at least one factor from each of the elements of the TOE framework had a significant impact on the utilization of BI.

The likelihood of successful BI implementations were under investigation in a study by Dawson and van Belle [41] and Eybers and Hattingh [42] which focused on the identification of Critical Success Factors (CSF). Both authors proposed a number of factors that can contribute to the success of BI implementations of which a strong business case and the involvement of a business champion were the most popular.

4 Methodology

The research is aimed at assessing the maturity level of top Mozambican manufacturing companies in terms of their BI implementations. The objective was to determine the current level of BI maturity using the biMM [1] as a reference model.

The top Mozambican organizations were selected using the top 100 manufacturing company ranking systems by KPMG [35]. This ranking mechanism has been used in several academic studies [33, 34].

The KPMG list of the top 100 companies in Mozambique only contains fourteen manufacturing companies, nine of which are located in Maputo [35]. These nine companies were selected to participate in the study, using a convenience sampling methodology [36]. This sample of nine companies contains a good representation of the main types of industries in Mozambique (1 from metallurgy, 6 FMCG, 2 construction), although only seven organizations agree to participate in the research.

A semi-structure interview template was used as guideline during the individual one-on-one private on-site interviews with IT managers, or senior IT members responsible for BI implementations in the organization. The template was based on the BI maturity level assessment model selected for this research namely, biMM [1]. The template consisted of three sections: Section A focused on functionality related implementation topics; Section B on BI implementation maturity from a technology perspective; and Section C on BI implementation maturity from an organizational perspective. The interview template was tested in a pilot study prior to the actual interviews. The three hour long interview sessions took place during a period of three months.

5 Data Analysis

Phase one of the data analysis started with a process of coding-unique identifiers (IDs) were allocated to each of the participative organizations. The IDs ranged from A to G, in alphabetical order. After the coding process, the data from the interviews were analyzed qualitatively, using thematic analysis approach with the main objective of identifying themes [37, 38]. The themes obtained from the first phase of analysis were coded into dimensions, categories and objects, which express the existing commonalities and diversity of characteristics [38].

In Phase two, the resulting data from Phase one was analyzed against the key BI maturity level indicators of the biMM maturity model to establish the extent to which the maturity level was reached.

6 Findings

The findings of the study are grouped according to the three sections of the biMM adopted for the purpose of the study, namely the maturity with regards to the functionality perspective, the technology perspective and the organizational perspective.

6.1 Functionality Maturity Perspective

The functionality maturity perspective focused on issues of BI scope, data architecture and penetration level [1]. Sub themes include the extent to which BI is used by users, and the degree of integration of the analytical information provided to support the decision-making process [1]. Each of these sub-themes will be briefly discussed below.

Scope: The scope consists of (1) BI systems usage in the organization and (2) the BI system coverage. Four of the seven participant organizations indicated that BI systems are used only by some organizational units. Three out of the seven surveyed organizations reported that the BI system is available to every employee within the organization. One of these three organizations indicated that both the BI and Enterprise Resource Planning (ERP) systems are available to employees, but that users don't use the ERP system's reporting functionality regularly. In general, results indicated that the organizational BI systems are not used across the organization. In some instances the limited usage resulted from a belief that users don't need access to BI systems due to the nature of their work. With regards to BI systems coverage, six of the participant organizations reported that their BI systems only cover some relevant business activities. One of the participant organizations indicated that their BI systems provide an enterprise-wide view of business activities. The majority of participant organizations acknowledges the importance and value of access to data from various data sources, and therefore plans to gradually increase their BI systems coverage. As a result manual activities are being progressively replaced by automated processes.

Data Architecture: The data architecture consists of business semantics and the ability to process poly-structured data. With regards to the former, the key roles of master data management include maintaining information quality and semantic consistency across an enterprise (i.e. the meaning of key business related terminology) [39]. While investigating master data management, the researcher also explored the extent to which data is consolidated in their BI systems, i.e. providing the users with "a single version of the truth". Feedback from participants indicated that, BI systems were characterized by silos and therefore lacks consolidation from various business functions. With regards to the latter, all the surveyed organizations reported that their BI systems only support the storage and retrieval of poly-structured data. All the organizations indicated that an example of poly-structured data currently stored in their BI systems include Adobe files, which are attached as complementary documentation for transactional type of operations. All the participant organizations indicated that that their BI systems do not support the extraction and processing of information contained in these types of files for the purpose of analysis and reporting.

Penetration Level: The penetration level consists of the (1) level of support of the analytical systems (analyzing historical events), to the operational business process (real-time processes), and (2) BI as the foundation of all decisions. With regards to the former, six of the participants indicated that event related data from operational business processes are not captured, and therefore not available in analytical systems; however, one of the respondents indicated that their analytical systems contain some operational business process data and therefore perceived the level of support between these two systems as 'medium'. In general the implementation of BI systems does not provide access to analytical information during the execution of business process. With regards to the latter, all the surveyed organizations indicated that BI is not used as a foundation for all decision-making processes; however, participants indicated that data from their BI systems were used as the foundation for making critical business process decisions part of the strategic decision making process.

Summary: Based on the findings contained in the discussion section (Sect. 5), the results were consolidated to establish the maturity level on each of the three perspectives; namely functionality, technology and organizational dimensions. Table 2 provides a summary of the functionality maturity dimension as crosses.

Table 2. Summary of functionality maturity dimension

Design object	Overall maturity level				
	One	Two	Three	Four	Five
Scope					
Use			x		
Diffusion in application areas and business processes			x		
Data architecture					
Content consolidation	x				
Business data management	x				
Penetration level					
Impact of BI		x			
Use of synergies	x	x			

6.2 Technology Maturity Perspective

The technological perspective focuses on aspects such as BI systems design, data management, and reporting. Sub-themes include an understanding of the BI Architecture, metadata management, master data management, and agile analytics systems. Each of these sub-themes will be briefly discussed below.

Technical Architecture: Technical architecture consist of (1) integration of data marts used for analysis and reporting, (2) type of integration of the data marks, (3) BI resources composition in the organization, (4) support for dedicated real-time warehousing, (5) BI redundancies and consistency, and (6) the link between the production and the development infrastructure. Firstly, two organizations reported that they make use of geographically decentralized unintegrated data marts for the purpose of analysis and reporting using independent toolsets. For each of the organizational units, the production marts are separate entities from the Enterprise Resources Planning (ERP) systems. One out of the organizations pointed out that they perform analysis and reporting based on the single enterprise-wide data warehouse. The data warehouse includes data from all the ERP processes and the majority of production operations. Four of the organizations indicated that they are using multiple enterprise-wide BI applications based on an integrated group of data marts (dedicated data warehouses). Based on the responses it can be argued that the majority of the organizations (except two) have integrated data marts. The level of integration varies from application-wide data marts integration to single enterprise-wide data warehouse integration. Secondly, two out of the organizations surveyed indicated that there was no integration between the various data marts available in the organization for the purpose of analysis and reporting. The other five organizations reported that data mart integration is possible within the organizations. These integrations were on a logical rather than physical level, as contained in the data warehouse structure. Thirdly, the participant organizations indicated a lack of integration between production and enterprise management systems. In addition, organizations have many standalone systems from various different vendors. The environment is therefore characterized by heterogeneous data sources and various technical toolsets. Only one organization indicated that their organization's BI resources consists of consolidated and integrated tools as part of an infrastructure portfolio. Fourthly, five of the participant organizations reported that their data warehouse contains real-time events based on organizational processes. Two of the seven organizations furthermore indicated that the real-time information is made available to other business units; however, in instances where participant organizations were geographically separated (two of the seven), no physical nor logical integration existed between the sharing of data (let alone real-time data). Fifthly, all of the surveyed organizations indicated that their BI system was large, with complex data and application redundancies. Adding to the challenge is that the majority of the redundancies were not identified nor documented. Finally, all the participant organizations expressed that there was no link between the production and the development infrastructure. Both infrastructures and systems development were developed and maintained by external companies.

Data Management: Data management consists of (1) quality management within the organizations, (2) Metadata repositories architecture in participant organizations and (3) Master data management. Firstly, four organizations indicated that they did not implement or enforce any data quality management procedures, whilst the other three organizations automated procedures to ensure data quality. This was not surprising as the BI data storage entities were developed and maintained by external vendors whilst the transactional database management systems (DBMS) tables are maintained by BI system developers. This does not mean that data management procedures do not exist, but only that they are not involved in enforcing such procedures. Secondly, the majority of the participant organizations reported that they did not have access to any ERP metadata documentation. Four participant organizations have access to the Production Management System (PMS) metadata documentation but did not have access to the ERP metadata documentation. Two of these organizations have no access to any metadata documentation. One of the participant organizations had access to the metadata documentation but did not use it. Thirdly, none of the participants had any Master Data Management mechanisms in place; however, documentation was available pertaining to products and consumables used in their production and/or operational environment.

Information Design: Information design consists of (1) analysis and reporting in the organization, (2) online analytical processing tools and agile analytics, (3) report generation, and (4) access to analytical information. Firstly, participants were asked about the process followed to perform analysis and reporting. All of the participant organizations reported that they analyzed historical information to gain insight regarding the performance of the organization. These insights include knowledge ranging from the performance of specific organizational units up to the enterprise-wide operations performance. Secondly, none of the participants used any form of Online Analytical Processing Tools; however agile analytical requirements are performed using a group of spreadsheets and customized databases (ex: Microsoft Access). Furthermore, participants indicated that their BI systems offer certain agile analytic capabilities. Unfortunately, these agile analytic capabilities are not used by the majority of BI users due to their perceived complexity. Thus, BI users prefer alternative tools for agile analytic requirements. Thirdly, all the participant organizations indicated that the majority of data management and provision processes are typically automated and standardized. This means that the majority of reports are automatically generated, and in some instances, published, to mobile devices (such as mobile phones). In some instances, where specific reports are requested not part of the automated report batches, a manually process can be used to generate it. Fourthly, out of the seven surveyed organizations, five indicated that analytical information is only shared between the analyst and a small, undefined community of users (focusing on managerial level such as engineers, analysts and operational supervisors). Two of the participant organizations reported that analytical information is provided centrally for the entire organization.

Summary: Table 3 shows that the number of participant organizations maturity characteristics distributed between levels one to three, indicated as crosses. Dinter [1] does not elucidate the weight of each design object in overall BI maturity level due to the fact that overall/average maturity levels for organizations are not considered; however, for the purpose of the study – to get a general overall indication of maturity levels – it was assumed that all the design objects have the same weight in overall BI maturity; therefore, on average, the participant organizations are between BI maturity levels one to three, when correlated with biMM. Table 3 provides a summary of the technology maturity dimension.

Table 3. Summary of technology maturity dimension

Design object	Overall maturity level				
	One	Two	Three	Four	Five
Technical architecture					
Architecture			x		
Utilization of tools		x			
Integration of/with operational process			x		
Data management					
Data integration	x				
Technical data management	x				
Information design					
Analysis functionality		x			
Reporting		x			
Information channels			x		

6.3 Organizational Maturity Perspective

The organizational maturity perspective is defined as focusing on getting insights from the organizational perspective regarding BI system management, data governance, and availability. This section also includes BI profitability and other relevant aspects of BI from the organizational perspective.

BI System Management: BI system management consists of (1) BI governance, and (2) Data governance. Firstly, five of the participant organizations indicated that they have implemented BI systems governance as part of the IT organizational structure including defined responsibilities. BI systems, in general, follow IT organizational structure strategies and BI processes. Two of the participant organizations reported that BI systems governance is handled by the IT department (also responsible for the ERP system) and the production department (handling the PMS). Secondly, the researcher explored how data domains and metrics are handled by participant organizations. All the participants indicated that they have data stewards across the organization. These data stewards have assigned mandatory rights and duties enforced as part of IT governance procedures. Unfortunately data owners do not focus on data domain metrics; such as metadata management, data quality and maintenance of business semantics (which refers to the business meaning of data elements).

Processes: The processes item consist of (1) Standards for BI implementation and (2) BI availability. Firstly, the objective of this item was to determine whether organizations follow certain IS/IT standards. Only one organization indicated that both IT personnel and contractors follow international standards for implementing BI projects, namely the Technology Infrastructure Library (ITIL). The remainder of participates indicated that they do not follow specific internationally established standards. Secondly, one of the participant organizations reported that their organization have control over the availability of BI products; however, the organization also indicated that they have occasional, short BI availability interruptions, with no big impact on the overall business activities. This participant organization further indicated that interruptions are more common in ERP applications due to cloud hosting unavailability. The remainder of the organizations indicated high BI systems availability.

Profitability: Profitability consists of (1) BI cost and benefits and (2) BI project assignments. Firstly, all of the participant organizations indicated that the software and service delivery costs pertaining to BI are purchased according to fixed prices and Service Level Agreements (SLAs). Six of the participant organizations indicated that they have a well-defined IT supplier portfolio. Their BI products are tendered and acquired from organizations which are part of this portfolio; however, one organization indicated that BI suppliers are selected based on best-fit sourcing using open tenders. The best proposal is selected based on costs versus benefits. Secondly, all the participants indicated that their BI solutions are outsourced to external vendors. Whilst one organization purchased an off-the-shelf BI system, the rest of the organizations opted for customized BI systems.

BI Strategy: All of the participant organizations indicated that although they have a clear BI strategy that forms part of the overall IT strategy; however, the execution of the BI strategy is often challenging, and not often implemented.

Summary: Based on the discussion above it can be concluded that the majority of the characteristics presented by the participant organizations are classified as level two and three characteristics, when correlated with biMM. This is indicated in Table 4 with crosses. Therefore, it can be said that as regards technology dimension, participant organizations are between level two and level three of BI maturity. The majority of the characteristics presented by the participant organizations are classified as level three characteristics, when correlated with biMM, whilst the majority of organizations achieved a level five maturity level for system availability. Overall it can be concluded that organizations achieved a maturity level on the organizational dimension between level three to five. Table 4 contains a summary of the organization maturity dimension.

Table 4. Summary of organization maturity dimension

Design object	Overall maturity level				
	One	Two	Three	Four	Five
Organizational structure					
BI Governance			x		
BI organizational structure		x			
Data ownership			x	x	
Processes					
Processes			x		
(System) Availability				x	x
Profitability					
Profitability calculations				x	
Sourcing			x		
Projects assignment			x		
Strategy					
BI Strategy			x		

7 Discussion and Conclusion

Although current studies focusing on investigating the maturity level of organizations in developing countries as described in the studies in Brazil [31], Pakistan [32] and South Africa [33, 41] do not attempt to identify specific maturity levels (apart from the study conducted in Pakistan), some comparisons between the findings of this study could be made: Although the study conducted in Brazil investigating focusing on SMEs that the adoption rate is low but growing, BI is nevertheless used in instances where it was implemented. This is similar to the findings of this study where, although the adoption rate was higher (this can be due to the sample population selected) it was extensively used.

The study focusing on Pakistan concluded that the BI adoption maturity level of the organizations is on an experienced level; this means that the vast majority of the organizations successfully adopted BI. This is slightly better than the organizational maturity dimension of a level three, with one item scoring a level five (level five is highest level for BI system availability). Similar to the study conducted in SMEs in South Africa, parties agree that data is an important asset in their organization; however, role players would like to have increased access to additional, integrated data sources to base key decisions which can only be achieved if a higher maturity level is reached. This was also confirmed by the study conducted by [41].

Results from this study indicated that Mozambican organizations reached a very low level of maturity on both the functional and technology maturity level (level one to three), but that higher levels of maturity were reached on the organizational level (level three to five). The rationale is that, should Mozambican organizations focus on improving the functionality and technological levels, more benefits will be achieved from their BI investments. Future work can possibly expand the study to include more organizations in the context of Mozambique with possible guidelines to improve current maturity levels. It will also be interesting to compare the results of this qualitative study with results from a quantitative approach.

References

1. Dinter, B.: The maturing of a business intelligence maturity model. In: 18th Proceedings on Americas Conference on Information Systems Proceedings, Seattle, USA, pp. 1–10 (2012)
2. McAfee, A., Brynjolfsson, E.: Big Data: The Management Revolution. Harvard Bus. Rev. **90**, 60–69 (2012)
3. Olszak, C.M., Ziemba, E.: Critical success factors for implementing business intelligence systems in small and medium enterprises on the example of Upper Silesia, Poland. Interdiscip. J. Inf. Knowl. Manag. **7**, 129–150 (2012)
4. Marín-Ortega, P.M., Dmitriyev, V., Abilov, M., Gómez, J.M.: ELTA: new approach in designing business intelligence solutions in Era of big data. Procedia Technol. **16**(1), 667–674 (2014)
5. Chuah, M., Wong, K.: Construct an enterprise business intelligence maturity model (EBI2 M) using an integration approach: a conceptual framework. In: Business Intelligence - Solution for Business Development, pp. 1–15 (2012)
6. Cidrin, L., Adamala, S.: Key success factors in business intelligence. J. Intell. Stud. Bus. **1**, 107–127 (2011)
7. Hawking, P.: Business intelligence excellence: a company's journey to business intelligence maturity. In: Proceedings of the Americas Conference of Information Systems (AMCIS), Detroit (2011)
8. Lönnqvist, A., Pirttimäki, V.: The measurement of business intelligence. Inf. Syst. Manag. **23**, 32–40 (2006)
9. Williams, S.: The business value of business intelligence. Bus. Intell. **8**(301), 30–39 (2003)
10. Forrester Research, Continuous Delivery: A Maturity Assessment Model, Forrester Research Consulting. https://www.scribd.com/document/145896458/Continuous-Delivery-A-Maturity-Assessment-ModelFINAL-pdf. Accessed 4 Aug 2018
11. Newman, D., Logan, D.: Gartner Introduces the EIM Maturity Model. Gartner Research ID Number, 1–8 December (2008)
12. Spanyi, A.: Beyond Process Maturity to Process Competence. BPTrends, pp. 1–5 (2004)
13. Jaklic, J., Popovic, A., Coelho, P.S.: Information quality improvement as a measure of business intelligence system benefits. WSEAS Trans. Bus. Econ. **6**(9), 502–512 (2009)
14. Namvar, M., Cybulski, J.: BI-based organizations: a sense making perspective. In: Proceedings of 35th International Conference on Information Systems, Strenger, Auckland, pp. 1–17 (2014)
15. Brookes, N., Clark, R.: Using maturity models to improve project management practice. In: Proceedings of POMS 20th Annual Conference, Orlando, pp. 1–12 (2009)

16. Talib, F.: An overview of total quality management: understanding the fundamentals in service organization. Int. J. Adv. Qual. Manage. **1**(1), 1–20 (2013)
17. Arunagiri, P., Babu, A.G.: Review on reduction of delay in manufacturing process using lean six sigma (LSS) systems. Int. J. Sci. Res. Publ. **3**(2), 1–4 (2013)
18. Taher, G., Alam, J.: Improving quality and productivity in manufacturing process by using quality control chart and statistical process control including sampling and six sigma. Global J. Res. Eng. **14**(3), 9–13 (2014)
19. Curtis, S., Tobergte, D.R.: People capability maturity model (P-CMM). J. Chem. Inf. Model. **53**(9), 1689–1699 (2013)
20. Aljedaibi, W., Alsulami, A.A.: Capability maturity model integration for beginners. Int. J. Adv. Res. Comput. Sci. Software Eng. **7**(6), 81–88 (2017)
21. Marcineková, K., Sujová, A.: The influence of the process control level on the enterprises' ROE. Procedia Econ. Finan. **34**(15), 290–295 (2015)
22. Sacu, C., Spruit, M.: BIDM - the business intelligence development model. In: Proceedings of the 12th International Conference on Enterprise Information Systems, DISI, Funchal, Madeira (2010)
23. Hostmann, B., Hagerty, J.: IT score for business intelligence and performance management. Gartner IT Leaders Research Note, September, pp. 1–5 (2010)
24. Serra, J.: Business Intelligence Maturity Assessment. http://www.jamesserra.com/archive/2013/06/business-intelligence-maturity-assessment/. Accessed 4 Aug 2018
25. Watson, H., Ariyachandra, T., Matyska, R.J.: Data warehousing stages of growth. Inf. Syst. Manage. **18**(3), 42–50 (2001)
26. Sen, A., Ramamurthy, K., Sinha, A.P.: A model of data warehousing process maturity. IEEE Trans. Software Eng. **38**(2), 336–353 (2012)
27. Cates, J., Gill, S., Zeituny, N.: The Ladder of Business Intelligence (LOBI): a framework for enterprise IT planning and architecture. Int. J. Bus. Inf. Syst. **1**(2), 220–238 (2005)
28. Lavalle, S., Lesser, E., Shockley, R., Hopkins, M.S., Kruschwitz, N.: Big data, analytics and the path from insights to value. MIT Sloan Manage. Rev. **52**(2), 21–32 (2011)
29. Dittmar, C., Ossendoth, V., Schulze, K.-D.: Business intelligence: are european companies ready for big data? European biMA Survey 2012/13 (2013)
30. Petrini, M., Pozzebon, M.: What role is "business intelligence" playing in developing countries? A picture of Brazilian companies. In: Current Issues and Trends in E-Government Research, January, pp. 269–288 (2008)
31. Shah, S.S.A.: A Case of BI Adoption in Pakistan: Drivers, Benefits & Challenges. http://www.diva-portal.org/smash/get/diva2:603014/FULLTEXT01.pdf. Accessed 4 Aug 2018
32. Ponelis, S.R., Britz, J.J.: An exploratory study of business intelligence in knowledge-based South African SMEs. In: Procceedings of GlobDev 2011 Pre-AMCIS Workshop: ICT in Global Development, Detroit, MI, 4 August 2011
33. The African Development Bank Group, Republic of Mozambique. https://www.afdb.org/fileadmin/uploads/afdb/Documents/Policy-Documents/Mozambique%20-%202011-15%20CSP.pdf. Accessed 4 Aug 2018
34. World Bank: Diagnostic Review of Consumer Protection and Financial Literacy Volume II Comparison with Good Practices. http://responsiblefinance.worldbank.org/~/media/GIAWB/FL/Documents/Diagnostic-Reviews/Mozambique-CPFL-DiagReview-2015-Volume-II-FINAL.pdf. Accessed 4 Aug 2018
35. KPMG: KPMG Top 100 Companies. https://home.kpmg.com/mz/en/home/insights.html. Accessed 4 Aug 2018
36. Etikan, I.: Comparison of convenience sampling and purposive sampling. Am. J. Theor. Appl. Stat. **5**(1), 1–4 (2016)

37. Clarke, V., Braun, V.: Teaching thematic analysis: overcoming challenges and developing strategies for effective learning. Psychologist **26**(2), 120–123 (2013)
38. Jansen, H.: The logic of qualitative survey research and its position in the field of social research methods. Qual. Surv. Forum: Qual. Soc. Res. **11**(2), 1–21 (2010)
39. O'Kane, B., Palanca, T., Moran, M.: Magic Quadrant for Master Data Management Solutions, Informatica. https://www.informatica.com/magic-quadrant-MDM.html#fbid=aaJu3RcRHgx. Accessed 4 Aug 2018
40. Lautenbach, P., Johnston, K., Adeniran-Ogundipe, T.: Factors influencing business intelligence and analytics usage extent in South African organisations. S. Afr. J. Bus. Manage. **48**(3), 23–33 (2017)
41. Dawson, L., Van Belle, J.-P.: Critical success factors for business intelligence in the South African financial services sector. SA J. Inf. Manage. **15**(1), 1–12 (2013)
42. Eybers, M., Hattingh, M.J.: Critical success factor categories for big data: a preliminary analysis of the current academic landscape. In: IST-Africa 2017 Conference Proceedings, Namibia, IIMC International Information Management Corporation, Windhoek (2017)

The Project Management Information System as Enabler for ICT4D Achievement at Capability Maturity Level 2 and Above

Mark Jonathan Corrigan[1(✉)], John Andrew van der Poll[2], and Emmanuel Samuel Mtsweni[3]

[1] School of Computing, University of South Africa, Phapha Building, 2nd Floor Science Campus, Cnr Christiaan de Wet & Pioneer Streets Florida, Johannesburg, South Africa
4151690@mylife.unisa.ac.za

[2] Graduate School of Business Leadership, University of South Africa, Cnr Janadel and Alexandra Avenues, Midrand, South Africa
vdpolja@unisa.ac.za

[3] School of Computing, University of South Africa, G J Grewel Building, 3rd Floor Science Campus, Cnr Christiaan de Wet & Pioneer Streets Florida, Johannesburg, South Africa
mtswees@unisa.ac.za

Abstract. Current trends in project management promote Agile as a solution for challenges around project delivery, focusing more on individuals and interactions than on processes and tools. This paper postulates that any project method, especially agile, if undertaken with limited process focus below Capability Maturity (CM) Level 2, may well result in project delivery failures, despite best intentions from the project team. With dynamic Internet growth in developing countries, and advancements in virtual collaboration, projects ought to involve tailoring jointly-agreed project management processes at Capability Maturity level 2 and above. In addition, the utilisation of a Project Management Information System (PMIS) emplacement is essential for project management success. The use of a PMIS is in line with a process-driven approach to ICT4D, and will facilitate the ICT value proposition for a developing economy. Following a comprehensive literature review, the paper asserts that Capability Maturity Level 2 will remain relatively unattainable, unless the PMIS emplacement becomes a strategic driver for success. To this end, we propose a PMIS CM Improvement Framework to the PMBOK Process Group and Knowledge Area matrix, and establish the value proposition for ICT4D.

Keywords: ICT4D · Agile · Capability maturity levels · Chaos Productivity · Theory of Constraints · Project management Process management · Project Management Information System Software engineering · Earned value management · Value proposition

K. Krauss et al. (Eds.): IDIA 2018, CCIS 933, pp. 295–310, 2019.
https://doi.org/10.1007/978-3-030-11235-6_19

1 Introduction

The recent dynamic growth of the Internet in developing countries unlocks the numerous benefits of a Project Management Information System (PMIS) emplacement, accessible in real time by a collaborating team. To this end, ICTs have the potential to initiate new developments (cf. ICT4D) in project management professionalism and expertise. Coupled with these, the well-intentioned use of Agile undertaken at CM Level 1 could result in inferior project products from a software engineering quality perspective. Consequently, our premise is that both Traditional and Agile Project Management methods may benefit from a PMIS emplacement, thereby enhancing ICT4D for South Africa as a developing country.

Unlike Business as Usual, the sixth (6th) edition of the Project Management Body of Knowledge Guide (PMBOK®) defines a project as "a temporary endeavour undertaken to create a unique product, service, or result" [1].

The 49 processes of the PMBOK sixth edition are collated in a matrix that combines five Process Groups across ten Knowledge Areas (including one Integration area) down the side. Supporting each process are Inputs; Tools and Techniques; and Outputs. The PMBOK Process Group and Knowledge Area matrix in Fig. 5, below, forms an overview of a project management lifecycle and its constraints [1] (p. 25). This matrix is often simplified to the concept of the Iron Triangle which focuses on Time (Schedule), Cost and Scope processes as the essential managed constraints for the achievement of a project management goal.

The Standish Chaos Reports [2] and Agile Manifesto [3] question the value of processes, tools and, especially, the Iron Triangle, stating that Traditional Project Management with its Waterfall Approach has no agility, and will continue to fail to deliver successful projects. Proponents of these ideas advocate an agile approach as the way forward. Yet, as argued in this paper, the use of a PMIS may go a long way in facilitating increased ICT capability, enhancing a more mature ICT4D approach and ultimately improving the value proposition for developing economies.

Edwards W. Deming, prime mover of the Capability Maturity model estimated that in his experience, "most troubles and most possibilities for improvement add up to the proportions something like this: 94% belongs to the system (responsibility of management) and 6% special" [4] (p. 248); Therefore, once the trouble has hit the floor, the worker level, the workers will have little ability and control to improve anything. Consequently, managerial insistence on a "Just Do IT" agility, if expended at CM Level 1, would imply that effort expended by underpowered or underskilled project personnel, despite their best efforts, would not have the desired effect, and may well lead to project failure. This is especially relevant in the South African context, often suffering from a lack of resources and skilled personnel.

The PMIS emplacement, utilising the strengths of virtual team collaboration, and facilitating focus on the "peopled task" in an environment based on game theory (the Developed Schedule as playing field within the PMIS), could be the solution needed to galvanise project management improvements in capability, maturity and professionalism, for success. In this context, the concept of the "peopled task, project tasking or time asking" is essentially who on the project team agrees to do what, with what and by when. The project playing field, typically a Gantt chart, in planning is populated by the project team tasks comprising professional estimates for project goal achievement. Measured in hours of work, in project execution, task slippage, illustrated graphically in the chart with a slip line, or as a variance against an agreed baseline, would be cause for team concern.

The layout of the rest of the paper is as follows: Our research questions are given in Sect. 1.1. An overview of project management aspects follows in Sect. 2, 3, 4, 5, and 6 These include Project Management being challenged, the Methodology and Agility dimension, the Capability Maturity dimension, the People-Process-Technology triad dimension and the role of the PMIS, especially in the local (SA) context. The main contribution of our work – the development of a PMIS CM Improvement Framework, is presented in Sect. 7. Conclusions and future work, followed by a list of references, conclude the paper.

1.1 Research Questions

Our above discussion leads to three research questions:

- What is the interplay between Agile and traditional project management methodologies (**RQ1**)?
- To what extent may the use of a PMIS (Project Management Information System) facilitate Capability Maturity (CM) Level 2 development, thereby enhancing the ICT value proposition for a developing economy (**RQ2**)?
- How may the PMBOK Process Group and Knowledge Area matrix be enhanced to cater for sustainable Capability and Maturity improvements (**RQ3**)?

2 Literature Review

2.1 Project Management Being Challenged

Since the release of the original Chaos Reports, these have received global attention. Some criticise the reports on statistical inaccuracies and a lack of research process transparency [5]. Most of the reports, however, illustrate a fundamental and deep concern at the inability to control high project costs, often failing to deliver the (ICT) value that has been promised to stakeholders and the community.

The original Standish Group Chaos Report [2] (p. 9) identifies that software development companies often experience numerous project challenges and impaired factors which include, among others, limited support from the Executive Management, a lack of clarity of objectives, an inability to plan correctly, and unrealistic expectations.

Schach identifies managerial challenges as a main result of the Chaos Reports findings. They found that only 35% of projects were successfully completed, and 19% were either cancelled before completion, were over budget, late, had fewer features and functionality than initially specified, or were never implemented. In fact, “just over one in three software development projects was successful and almost half the projects displayed one or more symptoms of the software crisis” [6] (p. 5).

According to Guess [7] (p. 25), the reasons why software development projects failed or where challenged, are attributed to poor user inputs, vague requirements, poor cost and schedule estimates, failure to plan, and late or ignored failure warning signals.

Despite criticisms, the Chaos Reports have caused many organisations to question their approach to project management. There appears to be agreement that renewed focus has caused project management (PM) maturity to rise in certain areas [8] (p. 6), but Capability Maturity (CM) Level 2 ought to be a clear starting point if productivity and quality, and not risk, rework and waste, are the goals stakeholders are aiming for. Agile, while well intentioned as a panacea, if undertaken at (CM) Level 1, could be fallacious; therefore, the strategic use of a PMIS in a software project management (SPM) methodology to achieve Level 2 maturity, holds much promise to alleviate the said challenges and increase the ICT value proposition.

3 Methodology and Agility as a Horizontal Dimension

The PMBOK is often disregarded as 'Traditional Project Management' utilising the 'Waterfall' approach, yet this is not correct. In fact, the latest version of the PMBOK embraces Traditional, *Agile*, *Iterative* and *Adaptive* environments. While the PMBOK is primarily a Body of Knowledge, it is also a method that can accommodate full project lifecycles or project phases (Process Groups) as its 'Close Project or Phase' (process #4.7 – Fig. 5) elucidates. In addition, PMBOK processes can be configured in size, complexity and speed; and process flows can be made to iterate with outputs leading back to prior processes, if needed [1, 9].

Numerous other project management methodologies exist. In this paper, PRINCE2 Agile [10], formerly PRINCE2 [11], Dynamic Systems Development Method (DSDM) [12], SCRUM [13] and Extreme programming (XP) [14] are considered.

Project methodologies are often assessed in terms of their agility. The **PR**ojects **IN** **C**ontrolled **E**nvironments method (**PRINCE**) [11] is tightly process-driven, while its latest edition, PRINCE2 Agile [10], fully embraces Agile, albeit within the Board control and tight governance of the original method. The Dynamic Systems Development (DSDM) [12], SCRUM [13] and Extreme programming (XP) [14] methods conform more closely to pure Agile as defined by the Agile Consortium Manifesto [3].

The Agile Manifesto embodies the prioritisation of individuals and interactions on the left over processes and tools on the right, working software over comprehensive documentation, customer collaboration over contract negotiation, and responding to change over following a plan [3]. Boehm [15] tells us to "get ready for agile methods, with care." Steven Rakitin [16] voiced his concern that "in his experience, the items on the right are essential," and by following those on the left, the Agile Manifesto "served only as easy excuses not to do the difficult work" and with "hacker interpretations" there would be no understanding of, or adherence to, generally accepted and essential engineering disciplines. According to Rakitin, the essence of following the items on the left means, "Great! Now I have a reason to avoid planning and to just code up whatever comes next." Schach believes that Agile will be unable to handle complex software projects – "Anyone can successfully hammer together a few planks to build a doghouse, but it would be foolhardy to build a three-bedroom home without detailed plans." [17] (p. 61).

The concepts of Big Design Up Front (BDUF), Enough Design (EDUF) and No Design (NDUF) can further assist with an understanding of Agile. It is possible to map BDUF, EDUF and NDUF in a right-to-left continuum against the four core values of the Agile Manifesto. While Traditional Project Management on the right utilises detailed documentation and design up front, Agile, with SCRUM and Extreme programming (XP) to the left of the continuum, uses limited to no detail. The Dynamic Systems Development Method (DSDM) towards the middle of the continuum, being a compromise between the two, utilises what could be considered by some as the nebulous concept of just enough detail before moving a project into execution. A challenge with the traditional approach is that projects can be delayed while creating the big design – the territory is often unclear until the project is under way. The challenge with Agile is that if the required detail for a complex project is not available, this can be a serious risk. In addition, a project budget commitment is often established up front without fully understanding the detail, and, once pre-allocated, a rigid managerial mindset may not be flexible if additional budget is required. In a resource-scarce economy, an additional budget to sustain project development may simply not be available [18] (p. 11).

Wysocki's [19] (p. 59) project type selection matrix in Fig. 1 advocates that 'up front selection' of the best method for the type of project being run is essential for project success:

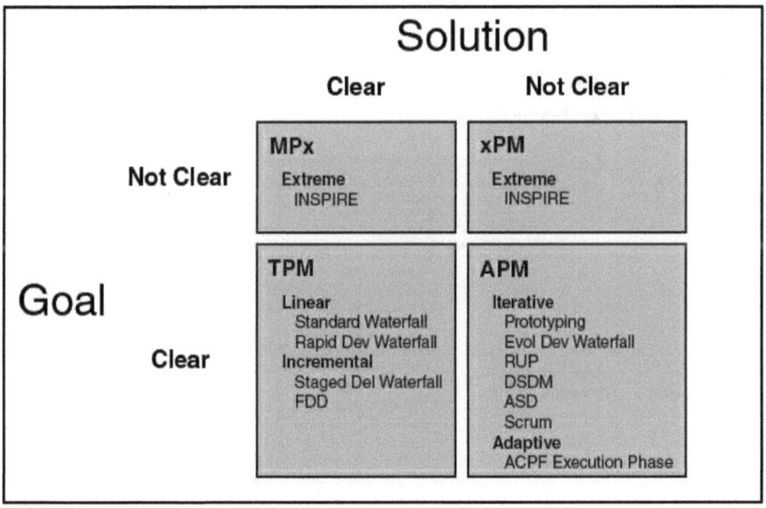

Fig. 1. The project type selection matrix [19]

While project methods constantly improve, a unique approach could be a combination of methods. For example, PRINCE 2 Agile method could be followed as a recipe under Board Supervision (Board Executive as Head Chef), while PMBOK could be followed to select the best project processes as 'ingredients to be added' [20]. The PMIS, implementing stage gates, can assist to reinforce project quality throughout a project lifecycle. If agility is required without the planning overhead, task slippage on the PMIS Schedule (baselined in the PMBOK Execution Process Group in Fig. 5, below), will quickly show whether agile activity is delivering value for the business and its stakeholders, or not.

4 Capability Maturity Levels as a Vertical Dimension

The Capability Maturity Model integrated (CMMi) [21] (p. 52) depicted in Fig. 2, below, is a recognised process improvement model from the Software Engineering Institute at Carnegie Mellon University in the U.S. As it is difficult to achieve Capability Maturity (CM) Level 2, companies need to address and conquer process improvement challenges to do this. Hirsch [8], discussing the PMI (Project Management Institute's) Pulse of the profession found a positive correlation between higher maturity levels, and on time and on budget delivery of projects. Naturally, the ability to run projects that deliver value on time and on budget can have significant benefits for resource-strained industries in the South African economy.

Capability Maturity Model – Integrated

Level	Focus	Process Areas	Result
5 Optimizing	*Continuous process improvement*	Organizational Innovation & Deployment Causal Analysis and Resolution	Productivity & Quality
4 Quantitatively Managed	*Quantitative management*	Organizational Process Performance Quantitative Project Management	
3 Defined	*Process standardization*	Requirements Development Technical Solution Product Integration Verification Validation Organizational Process Focus Organizational Process Definition Organizational Training Integrated Project Management Risk Management Decision Analysis and Resolution	
2 Managed	*Basic project management*	Requirements Management Project Planning Project Monitoring & Control Supplier Agreement Management Measurement and Analysis Process & Product Quality Assurance Configuration Management	
1 Initial	*Competent people and heroics*		Risk & Waste

Fig. 2. Capability Maturity Model integrated (adapted from [21])

A starting point for CM Level 2 is the Project Planning (PP) and Project Monitoring and Control (PMC) processes. PP and PMC processes also reside on either side of the PMBOK Execute Process group, to strengthen it. The crucial importance of PMBOK planning is emphasised by the fact that just under half the total of 49 PMBOK processes fall within the planning process group. Consequently, it can be argued that with limited or no planning, and a lack of good monitoring and control processes in place, projects are operating at CM Level 1 (initial phase) and would exhibit high levels of risk, rework and waste.

Deming's 14 Observations for Management, Red Bead Experiment, and Plan, Do, Check, Act (PDCA) cycle, among other contributions, clearly showed that without planning, and monitoring and control in place to guide and improve execution, quality delivery via streamlined production processes will remain the elusive silver bullet [22], hence ICT4D, with respect to SPM value delivery, if undertaken heroically at CM Level 1, would be ineffective and would remain a pipe dream.

In support of the above, the Dunning and Kruger effect [23] (p. 1) states that "people tend to hold overly favourable views of their abilities in many social and intellectual domains." The Dunning-Kruger effect has implications for the project management profession, as illustrated in Fig. 3, below. Project process stability at CM Level 2, for both traditional and agile project management, can be viewed as the start of a move up the slope of enlightenment, towards the goal sustainability of ICT projects.

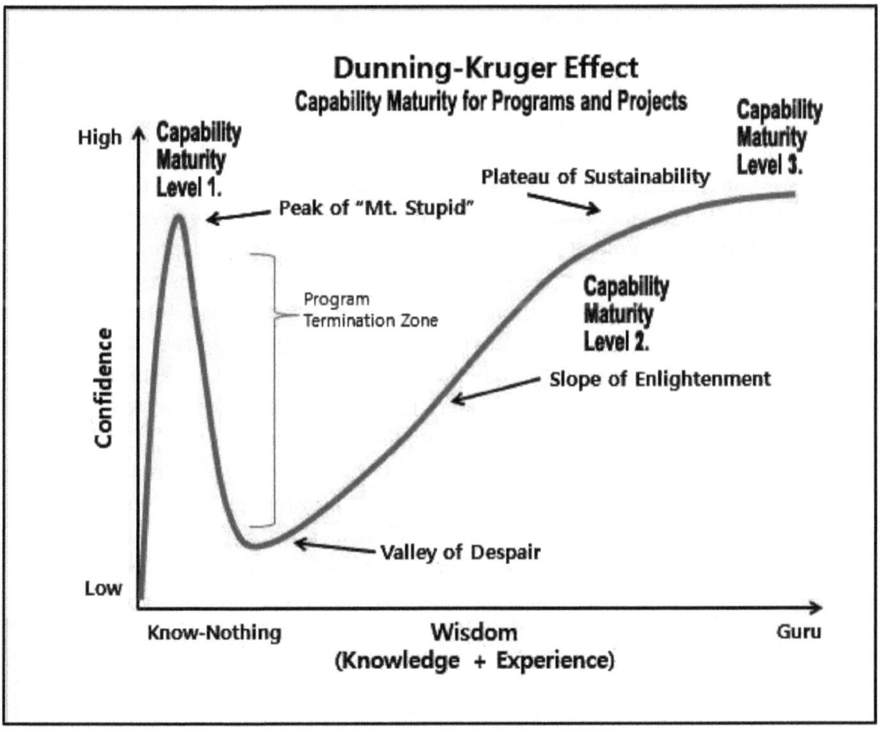

Fig. 3. Dunning-Kruger effect on projects and programs (adapted from [24])

The Dunning-Kruger effect, when applied to complex projects, implies a lack of experience and unrealistic expectations, and may set a project up for failure. CM Level 2, which is essentially a base project management process set, ought to be the starting point to facilitate project success and stakeholder satisfaction. Consequently, a complex, Agile-driven project at CM Level 1 runs the risk of being severely challenged, thereby compromising good ICT4D intentions.

5 The People-Process-Technology Triad Dimension

According to Deming, "the supposition is prevalent the world over that there would be no problems in production or service if only our production workers would do their jobs in the way that they were taught. Pleasant dreams. The workers are handicapped by the system, and the system belongs to the management." [4] (p. 121). Also, "it is not enough that management commit themselves to quality and productivity, they must know what it is they must do. Such a responsibility cannot be delegated" [4] (p. 8); in addition, "people are already doing their best. The problem is with the system. Only management can change the system." [4] (p. 8). Chrissis *et al.*, on the Capability Maturity Model integrated (CMMi), further elucidates Deming's wisdom: "while process is often described as a node of the people-process-technology triad, it can also be considered the 'glue' that ties the triad together" [21] (p. 4). Essentially, while everyone realises the importance of having a quality and motivated workforce, even the most talented staff might not perform at their best if the process (system) is not clearly understood, or is operating non-optimally (cf. slow or inoperative systems, compromising the value ICT brings to a developing economy).

In addition, software design and development, and deployment of technology, are complex undertakings and, according to Brooks, "can be regarded as being one of the most difficult undertakings" [26, 27] (p. 5). In Brooks' Anniversary Edition [27], some 20 years after the original publication of the *Essays on Software Engineering*, he again emphasised project complexity and why software development projects to create 'programming systems products' can, if not carefully managed, often become mired in ever-increasing difficulties he referred to as the "tar pit" of failed software projects. Brooks' description is of ancient lumbering beasts of old ensnared, yet "the fiercer the struggle, the more entangling the tar, and no beast is so strong or so skillful but that he ultimately sinks. Large-system programming has, over the past decade, been such a tar pit, and many great and powerful beasts have thrashed violently in it" [27] (p. 4).

In terms of answering the research questions, when projects are complex, especially if software engineering projects are involved, many CM model processes can be used to make the arduous journey safer. The correct balance of people-process-technology within the triad should always be an important consideration for business success.

Conclusion: The preceding discussions provide an answer to our 1st research question, **RQ1,** in the sense that a CM Level 2 is much needed, and may not necessarily be provided by following pure Agile, if naively undertaken at Level 1. Note that some groundwork towards ICT4D addressed in **RQ2** has also been established.

6 The Project Management Information System (PMIS)

Bočková [28] (p. 712) explains that game theory can be used to position each project as a game to “maximize gains and minimize losses,” focusing the team towards the achievement of success. Team visibility via a PMIS of the Developed Schedule (process #6.5 baselined and moved into Execution) implies that all share a jointly-agreed playing field where teams and individuals can excel. The goal of utilising a PMIS ought to be, as Braglia and Frosolini [29] (p. 1) put it “to boost efficiency by making the development cycle more visible.” As mentioned before, a task with a slip line would be cause for concern; however, if the Deming wisdom is understood, then this project task should also be correctly allocated, fully resourced and agreed by the task owner that it is achievable at worker level, before a commitment baseline is installed on the Developed Schedule.

The PMI [8] (p. 7) found that the number of Project Management Offices (PMOs) was on the increase. A PMO with a PMIS can automate various components of the project management process, including automating the schedule, work authorisation, resource management, risks and issues management, and team collaboration. In addition, the PMIS (built on a database or, more generally, a data warehouse) can capture and disseminate information and report on key performance indicators (KPIs), baselined against actuals and many other metrics. Meredith and Mantel [30] (p. 462) discuss how a PMIS is beneficial where project complexity is an issue. They recommend choosing an application that offers “functions of friendliness” (User Experience – UX) which includes calendars, budgets, graphics, charts, reports, etc. Ultimately, the PMIS can greatly assist practitioners to detect latent issues before they occur, achieve project milestones, and collaborate more easily and to a greater extent. They conclude that “PMIS makes a significant contribution to project success and should continue to be the object of project management research” [31] (p. 219). The use of qualitative cues, like graphics and charts in a PMIS, instead of natural language text, may work well in South Africa’s multilingual and culturally rich society.

The key benefit of a PMIS is in its ability to facilitate resource allocation. The fact that tasks cannot be created at the same time on different project schedules in a PMIS, means that resource allocation challenges are remedied. Engwall suggests that the resource allocation syndrome might be an effect of “opportunistic project management behaviour within the organizations,” and is a consequence of flawed organisational procedures, rather than poor project management practices [32] (p. 408). Addressing the root cause, Engwall advocates, is for the executive to solve. Ultimately, the resource allocation syndrome of multi-project management is not an issue in itself; “rather it is an expression of many other, more profound, organizational problems of the multi-project setting” [32] (p. 408). Management insistence on heroics, and producing faster with less, will simply exacerbate the problem if they do not grasp how to run projects at CM Level 2 and above.

According to Tromp [33] (p. 213), “the main problem in a multi-project environment is the lack of dedicated teams on one project.” Employees allocated over many projects and demanded simultaneously on these projects have negative consequences for the projects. The Theory of Constraints explains how to isolate the most important limiting factor (or constraint) that stands in the way of achieving a goal. The idea, after identifying the constraint, is to improve it until it is no longer the limiting factor. According to Goldratt [34], challenges common to all projects are bad multitasking; students' syndrome; Parkinson's Law; and dependencies between steps. These can result in budget and time overruns; and compromised content, compromising the ICT value proposition.

A PMIS can also collect and distribute information and report on key performance indicators (KPIs), utilising the baseline plan against actuals. The PMIS also offers summations of complex project status via dashboards using many different visual aids, e.g. Gantt charts, project progress graphs, and task status traffic lights. As before, the SA multilingual society will benefit from these visual cues (Fig. 4).

Fig. 4. The PMIS information stack (synthesized by researchers)

A *process*-based approach to facilitate ICT4D is well established [35]. Apart from the ability to better manage the core CM Level 2 *processes* of Project Planning (PP) and Project Monitoring and Control (PMC), the CM Level 2 process Measurement Analysis (MA) is also derived from the PMIS. The correct installation and use of the PMIS is guided by the PMIS CM Framework in Fig. 6, below, meaning that the CM Level 2 *process* Product and Process Quality Assurance (PPQA) is also installed and streamlined over time.

Documentation saved in the PMIS addresses many of the Project Quality dimensions for good governance. Requirements Management (REQM) and Configuration Management (CM) are pinned down with quality gates on the PMIS, implying that the team can proceed when they are Ready To Do It (cf. acquired sufficient resources, competent skill set, requirements, etc.) and not because of pressure to be heroic and Just Do It. Essentially, this is the difference between going off "half-cocked" on a Developing Schedule in the Planning Process Group, and proceeding correctly off a Developed and Baselined Schedule in the Execution Process Group – as is illustrated in Fig. 5. Risk and Issue Management (RSKM), a CM Level 3 process, is seamlessly accessible in the PMIS to team members. Project challenges are avoided or quickly solved, or escalated to the executive. Ultimately, process improvement projects can be used to install all the Capability Maturity processes up to Level 5. Achieving such maturity would significantly benefit a developing economy often constrained by a lack of resources and a developing workforce. Concerning the people-process-technology triad dimension in Section 5 above, the PMIS (a technology), as a means of installing project management and other important processes (the 'glue'), can facilitate the process whereby project teams (empowered people) can navigate through the tar pit. This should ensure that resources are used optimally, and much needed user-satisfying technology is successfully created.

Finally, working harder is not always the best solution if effort expended is at CM Level 1. Low capability and maturity, and a lack of command and control in project management, must account for many of the problems identified by the Standish Chaos reports. Plausibly, if you cannot readily measure something, you cannot improve it. Arguably, the best way to improve anything must be to start from a known baseline.

Conclusion: The preceding discussions answer our 2nd research question, **RQ2**, namely, how the use of a PMIS may facilitate CM Level 2 development, thereby enhancing the ICT value proposition for a developing economy (**RQ2**).

7 PMIS CM Improvement Framework

The PMIS CM Improvement framework could be a starting point to ensure that the need for the PMIS is more fully understood. It can also be used to guide the installation of PMIS CM Improvement dimensions in a phased and systematic manner. The right-facing arrowheads in Fig. 5, below, have been added by the researchers to identify the PMIS CM Improvement framework scope which has been designed to operate from process #6.5 (the end of project planning) up to process #4.3 (the beginning, after schedule baseline, of project execution). The framework aims to lift CM dimensions from Level 1 to Level 2 compliancy, eliciting the importance of processes to facilitate project success, and contribute to ICTs for development [35].

The PMIS CM Improvement Framework, below, facilitates the creation of a Developed Schedule (resourced and ready for baseline) as an output of the Develop Schedule process #6.5 on the PMIS so that "Now We Are Ready To Do It." This empowers CM Level 2 compliancy at the beginning of the Project Execution Process

Knowledge Areas	Project Management Process Groups				
	Initiating Process Group	Planning Process Group	Executing Process Group	Monitoring and Controlling Process Group	Closing Process Group
4. Project Integration Management	4.1 Develop Project Charter	4.2 Develop Project Management Plan	4.3 Direct and Manage Project Work 4.4 Manage Project Knowledge	4.5 Monitor and Control Project Work 4.6 Perform Integrated Change Control	4.7 Close Project or Phase
5. Project Scope Management		5.1 Plan Scope Management 5.2 Collect Requirements 5.3 Define Scope 5.4 Create WBS		5.5 Validate Scope 5.6 Control Scope	
6. Project Schedule Management		6.1 Plan Schedule Management 6.2 Define Activities 6.3 Sequence Activities 6.4 Estimate Activity Durations 6.5 Develop Schedule		6.6 Control Schedule	
7. Project Cost Management		7.1 Plan Cost Management 7.2 Estimate Costs 7.3 Determine Budget		7.4 Control Costs	
8. Project Quality Management		8.1 Plan Quality Management	8.2 Manage Quality	8.3 Control Quality	
9. Project Resource Management		9.1 Plan Resource Management 9.2 Estimate Activity Resources	9.3 Acquire Resources 9.4 Develop Team 9.5 Manage Team	9.6 Control Resources	
10. Project Communications Management		10.1 Plan Communications Management	10.2 Manage Communications	10.3 Monitor Communications	
11. Project Risk Management		11.1 Plan Risk Management 11.2 Identify Risks 11.3 Perform Qualitative Risk Analysis 11.4 Perform Quantitative Risk Analysis 11.5 Plan Risk Responses	11.6 Implement Risk Responses	11.7 Monitor Risks	
12. Project Procurement Management		12.1 Plan Procurement Management	12.2 Conduct Procurements	12.3 Control Procurements	
13. Project Stakeholder Management	13.1 Identify Stakeholders	13.2 Plan Stakeholder Engagement	13.3 Manage Stakeholder Engagement	13.4 Monitor Stakeholder Engagement	

Fig. 5. PMBOK 6 Process Group & Knowledge Area matrix (adapted from [1] (p. 25))

Group at process #4.3. If an Agile method is used, tasks are built collaboratively (on the fly) by resources, adding their contribution to the schedule on the PMIS, while the project moves into process #4.3 as a next Agile iteration or time box. The PMIS CM Improvement Framework is presented in Fig. 6 below:

12.	The PMIS Resource Pool is a focus of organizational attention towards people and their skills improvement for excellence.	No	Yes (1)
11.	Risk and Issue management on the PMIS is available to any member of the PMIS resource pool with project teams focused on keeping the projects (schedules) healthy and safe.	No	Yes (1)
10.	Earned Value Management Analysis (and other) project status graphics are available on the PMIS.	No	Yes (1)
9.	EPMO / PMIS works off a regular project reporting (actual vs plan / budget) cycle.	No	Yes (1)
8.	Variance tracking of actuals on the PMIS at Task level is available against the baselined project plan / schedule.	No	Yes (1)
7.	PMIS schedule can be represented as a Gantt chart with Task slippage indicator capability.	No	Yes (1)
6.	PMIS offers "virtual Team Collaboration" capability [from anywhere connected to the internet].	No	Yes (1)
5.	Stage / Quality Gates via PMIS Process Group (and other) selectors is available.	No	Yes (1)
4.	The PMIS is a secure repository for all project artifacts (documents etc.) created during a project lifecycle.	No	Yes (1)
3.	EPMO allocates Project Managers to Projects (schedules) on the PMIS.	No	Yes (1)
2.	PMIS has a Resource Management module to facilitate the allocation of skilled resources from the resource pool to attend to Tasks on Project Schedules.	No	Yes (1)
1.	Enterprise Project Management Office (EPMO), driven off a Project Management Information System (PMIS), is in place.	No	Yes (1 Point)

Improvement Dimensions: Using the PMIS for CM Level 2 stability (and above)

Fig. 6. PMIS CM Improvement Framework developed by the researchers

Notes on Fig. 6:

1. The EPMO with PMIS operates with a similar imperative as an Accounting Department underpinned by a financial accounting system.
2. The Resource Allocation Syndrome is prohibited on the PMIS [32].
3. The EPMO has central control of all projects (programs) within the PMIS; out-sourcing Project Management control.
4. Project documents/System Configuration Management documents, etc. are version controlled and accessible on the PMIS by the EPMO/sponsors, managers and teams.
5. Ever mindful of agility; the Process Group selector ensures projects are only moved to a next Process Group when appropriate – i.e. from the perspective of good governance, quality tested, etc.
6. Virtual collaboration is the ability to collaborate with all team members on schedules on the PMIS from anywhere via the Internet – i.e. a secure environment must exist on the PMIS (network/Internet/virtual private network, etc.).
7. Task slip lines typically can be switched on or off. This visual representation facilitates using the project schedule as a playing field from a game theory perspective.
8. Top-level summaries should be available by program (groups of projects on the PMIS) or by a single project and with drill-down capability to task level.

9. Reports typically to Project Boards/Sponsors (and identified stakeholders). As projects become late "a day at a time," reports follow a weekly, week-by-week publication cycle. Reports focus on the Plan, Do, Check, Act cycle.
10. From a PMBOK perspective, EVM includes all project formulas, and especially the "To Complete Performance Index" as "one number" for project health throughout its lifecycle. EVM, built of tasks, is an essential PMIS reporting product facilitating the goal of this paper to use the project schedule as a playing field.
11. Issues are Risks happening. Serious Issues, which a project team are unable to solve, are escalated up to the Project Board Executive/Sponsor who are also members of the PMIS resource pool. Per Deming, "such responsibility cannot be delegated." [4].
12. People excellence is dealt with in People CMM [36]. Excellence can also be measured by CM Focus Area (Development [21], Services, Acquisitions) focusing on process improvement by Category, Process Area and Maturity Level. In addition, the field of Human Resources has much to contribute.

Conclusion: The preceding discussions provide an answer to our 3rd and last research question, namely, how the PMBOK Process Group and Knowledge Area matrix may be enhanced to cater for sustainable CM improvements (**RQ3**). Note the link between the PMBOK *processes*, enabled using a PMIS, and *process*-driven ICT4D. The use of a PMIS as an emplacement and firm base will be a strategic value-generation driver by "focusing effort" in a resource-constrained developing economy.

8 Conclusions and Future Work

Due to project management complexities typically found in software engineering (and other) project types, the main thrust of this research is that without a PMIS, the project team's ability to adequately monitor and control project management processes for CM success at Level 2 (and above) at the task level on a project schedule, would be challenged. The Agile (Scrum) whiteboard with "stickies" will be equally constrained. Consequently, project performance, despite good intentions from a talented team, would, without the PMIS, naturally degrade to Heroic effort at CM Level 1.

The value proposition promised by innovative ICTs for a developing economy – the ICT4D – is pivotal. The way this may be achieved is through process-driven ICT4D, better managed on Developed Schedules (playing fields) on the PMIS. To this end, the use of a PMIS to enhance process maturity in software project management is precisely to promote process-driven ICT4D. Improving process excellence by CM levels promises to optimise scarce resources and improve on a developing skill set such as the South African workforce.

Agile, often viewed as a silver bullet solution [22], if undertaken at CM Level 1 on complex software projects, would often not be able to produce satisfactory results. Therefore, for the attainment of CM Level 2 (Managed), a PMIS is not simply a recommended tool of the 'Direct and Manage Project Work' process #4.3 in Fig. 5, as is stated by the Project Management Institute. Rather, as argued in this paper, it is essential to facilitate project management success for earned value.

Ultimately, within a gradient scale of improvement, a direct relationship appears to exist between the installation (or not) of a PMIS, the way the PMIS is installed within an organisation, and an organisation's ability to achieve stability at CM Level 2 and above.

Future work is this area will be directed at a validation phase of the CM Improvement Framework developed in Fig. 6. This will be undertaken by targeted surveys in selected industries. Such instrument has already been developed, and will be administered in due course, having obtained the necessary ethical clearance and company permission.

Further value to be added by our PMIS in the ICT4D arena needs to be investigated.

References

1. Project Management Institute: A Guide to the Management Body of Knowledge. Project Management Institute, Inc., Atlanta (2017)
2. The Standish Group: The Standish group: the chaos report. Project Smart 16 (2014)
3. Sutherland, J., et al.: Manifesto for Agile Software Development. http://agilemanifesto.org/
4. Deming, W.E.: Out of the crisis. Massachusetts Institute of Technology, Center for Advanced Engineering Study, Cambridge (1986)
5. Eveleens, L.J., Verhoef, C.: The rise and fall of the chaos report figures. IEEE Softw. **27**(1), 30–36(2010). https://doi.org/10.1109/MS.2009.154, ISSN 0740-7459
6. Schach, S.R.: Object-Oriented and Classical Software Engineering. McGraw-Hill, New York (2011)
7. Guess, V.C.: CMII for Business Process Infrastructure. CMII Research Instutite (2006)
8. Hirsch, B.J.a.: PMI's Pulse of the Profession. 2012 PMI Pulse Prof., 1–9 March 2012
9. Vargas, R.: Elaboration of the PMBOK 6 process flow. https://www.youtube.com/watch?v=GC7pN8Mjot8
10. Richards, K., Cooper, L.: PRINCE2 Agile. The Stationery Office, Norwich (2015)
11. Office of Government Commerce: Managing Successful Projects with PRINCE2. TSO, London (2009)
12. DSDM Consortium: Agile PM. Agile Project Management Handbook Version 2. DSDM Consortium (2014)
13. Setpathy, T.: Scrum Body of Knowledge. SCRUMstudy (2016)
14. Extreme Programming Web Site. http://www.extremeprogramming.org/
15. Boehm, B.: Get ready for agile methods, with care. Comput. (Long. Beach. Calif.) **35**, 64–69 (2002)
16. Rakitin, S.: Manifesto elicits cynicism. IEEE Comput. **34**, 4–7 (2001)
17. Schach, S.: Object Orientated and Classical Software Engineering, 8th edn. (2007)
18. Clinning, G., Marnewick, C.: Incorporating sustainability into IT project management. S. Afr. Comput. J. **29**, 1–26 (2017)
19. Wysocki, R.K.: Effective Complext Project Management (2014)
20. LogicalModel.net: Parallels in Delivering Organisational Change as a Bowl Of Soup. http://www.logicalmodel.net/pm_ngt/soop-prince2-and-pmbok-as-a-bowl-of-soup/
21. Chrissis, M.B., Konrad, M., Shrum, S.: CMMI for Development. Addison-Wesley, Upper Saddle River (2011)

22. Brooks, F.P.J.: No silver bullet-essence and accidents of software engineering. In: Proceedings of the IFIP Tenth World Computing Conference, pp. 1069–1076 (1986)
23. Kruger, J., Dunning, D.: Unskilled and unaware of it: how difficulties in recognizing one's own incompetence lead to inflated self-assessments. J. Pers. Soc. Psychol. **77**, 1121–1134 (1999)
24. Dudley, M.: Ladies and gentlemen, here comes the Dunning-Kruger Effect. https://medium.com/@mike.dudkey78/ladies-and-gentlemen-here-comes-the-dunning-kruger-effect-f31b09d52573
25. Scaled Agile: SAFe ® 4.5 Introduction Overview of the Scaled Agile Framework ® for Lean Enterprises. A Scaled Agil. Inc. White Pap. (2017)
26. Brooks, F.P.: No silver bullet: essence and accidences of software engineering. Comput. (Long. Beach. Calif.) **20**, 10–19 (1987)
27. Brooks, F.P.: The Mythical Man - Month. Essays on Software Engineering, Anniversary Edition (1995)
28. Bočková, K.H., Sláviková, G., Gabrhel, J.: Game theory as a tool of project management. Procedia Soc. Behav. Sci. **213**, 709–715 (2015)
29. Braglia, M., Frosolini, M.: An integrated approach to implement Project Management Information Systems within the extended enterprise. Int. J. Proj. Manag. **32**, 18–29 (2014)
30. Meredith, J.R., Mantel, S.J.J.: Project Management: A Managerial Approach (2009)
31. Raymond, L., Bergeron, F.: Project management information systems: an empirical study of their impact on project managers and project success. Int. J. Proj. Manag. **26**, 213–220 (2008)
32. Engwall, M., Jerbrant, A.: The resource allocation syndrome: The prime challenge of multi-project management? Int. J. Proj. Manag. JPMA **21**, 403–409 (2003)
33. Tromp, J.W., Homan, T.: How unplanned changes emerge while implementing a Project Management Information System (PMIS) in a complex multi project R&D environment. Procedia Soc. Behav. Sci. **194**, 211–220 (2015)
34. Goldratt, E.M.: Critical Chain. North River Press, Great Barrington (1997)
35. Walton, M., Heeks, R.: Development Informatics Improve ICT4D Project Success? Development Informatics Group (2011)
36. People Capability Maturity Model (P-CMM) (2009)

Data

Identifying the Constructs and Agile Capabilities of Data Governance and Data Management: A Review of the Literature

Theresa Lillie(✉) and Sunet Eybers(✉)

University of Pretoria, Private Bag X20, Hatfield 0028, South Africa
tessa.lillie@wol.co.za, sunet.eybers@up.ac.za

Abstract. Data has become an invaluable asset to organisations. However, it is evident from the existing literature that despite the increased awareness of the importance of their data assets, many organisations fail to manage and govern these assets with the agility required in a highly competitive and volatile business environment. For data governance to be effective and sustainable in a turbulent, increasingly regulated and competitive organisational environment, all of the elements of data governance should enable and support agility in the organisation's management of its data and information assets. As a result of increased local and global data regulations, a high reliance on technical skills, and economic constraints, organisations in developing countries have experienced challenges with implementing data governance programs. Governance within an organisation comprises the internal processes and policies that enable human capital performance, legal and regulatory compliance, and organisational alignment. There is no single approach to achieving successful data governance, and factors pertaining to the organisation's strategy, structure, business requirements and culture need to be considered. In this study, a systematic review of existing academic literature was conducted to investigate (1) the scope and constructs of data governance and data management, (2) the agile capabilities that are required in data governance and data management for the timeous delivery of useful data to business, and (3) the need for African organisations to establish agile capabilities in their data governance and data management functions. The results of this review should be helpful with assisting organisations in African countries to achieve agility in the governance and management of data, that supports business requirements and organisational agility.

Keywords: Data Governance · Data Management · Organisational agility Agile governance · Complex Adaptive Systems · Agile capabilities

1 Introduction

This study contends that there is an existing requirement for agility in the data governance (DG) and data management (DM) functions of organisations, which stems from a need for the timeous delivery of useful data to business functions, in order to enable and support the execution of business strategy. To be agile is to have the ability

K. Krauss et al. (Eds.): IDIA 2018, CCIS 933, pp. 313–326, 2019.
https://doi.org/10.1007/978-3-030-11235-6_20

to become aware of, acclimatise and respond swiftly and sustainably to environmental changes through a coordinated combination of lean and agile skills, and capabilities with the purpose of delivering greater value to business [1]. It is evident from documented research that, despite increased awareness of the importance of their data assets, many organisations fail to manage and govern these assets with the agility required in a highly competitive and volatile business environment [2, 3]. Effective and efficient DG and DM are required to support risk management and regulatory compliance [4–6], enhance decision-making [7–9], improve customer satisfaction, increase operational efficiency and improve business integration [6, 7].

Varying points of view have emerged in research and industry regarding the scope of DG and the methods that should be used to put sound DG and DM methods into practice [6, 10–12]. A systematic literature review (SLR) was conducted with the objective being to first identify the scope and constructs of DG and DM, and to then identify agile capabilities and how these capabilities apply to DG and DM. Subsequently, the importance of agility in DG and DM was investigated, and the implications of DG and DM for organisations in Africa were considered. In cases where organisations already have successful information technology (IT) governance in place, the need for DG might be questioned, as it is often seen as a function of IT governance. Weill and Ross [13] identify "Information and IT assets", which include digitised data and IT systems, as one of the six key corporate assets that should be governed in support of achieving organisational goals. However, IT governance is more focused on governing the overall IT infrastructure, and ensuring that business value is derived from IT investments [14]. IT governance does not address privacy and security risks related to data flows, and should work in concert with other control frameworks such as the International Organization for Standardization (ISO) and Control Objectives for Information and Related Technologies (COBIT) [14].

There is currently a gap in the research literature regarding how to establish agile capabilities and embed a culture of agility in organisations [15]. Moreover, academic research in DG and DM seems to be in its early stages [16–18]. To sustain growth and competitiveness, organisations need to be agile at both the business and organisational levels. This requires enterprises to establish flexible and adaptable DG functions with responsive governance in place, in order to deliver optimum value to business [1, 19]. This study sets out to first clarify the underlying individual concepts of DG, DM and agility, and to then synthesise these individual components into a comprehensive whole, and propose a novel preliminary framework for the constructs and agile capabilities of DG and DM. Although many of the referenced studies focus on developed countries [20], the challenges associated with DG in these countries are not unique, as they are also relevant to organisations in Africa [21].

2 Methodology

This research followed the systematic literature review (SLR) process as described by Templier and Paré [22]: formulating the problem, searching the literature, screening for inclusion, assessing quality, extracting data, and analysing and synthesising the data. The objective of the SLR in this study was twofold: (1) to identify the constructs of DG and DM, and (2) to identify agile capabilities applicable to DG and DM. The subsequent findings of the SLR were synthesised, in order to develop a research model for agile DG and DM. Thereafter, the model was applied to highlight the need for agility in the governance and management of data in African countries.

The primary search terms used were "data governance" and "data management". The word "agility" was used as a secondary search term. Most of the research considered for this study was conducted from 2008 onwards. The main libraries used in the search were ACM, AISeL, Emerald Insight, IEEE, ProQuest, ScienceDirect and Springerlink. Additional searches were conducted in Google Scholar. The search process posed some challenges. The search term "data management" returned software engineering articles and conference proceedings pertaining to the technical management of data at a hardware/software level, which lies outside the focus of this study. Conference proceedings and journals were included in the searches. Seminal articles were identified by comparing the reference lists of the articles that were closely aligned with the topic of this study. Due to the variation in the definition of the terms "data governance" and "data management", as well as the interchangeability of the terms "data" and "information", refining the initial searches was an important step in eliminating research that was not relevant to this study.

3 Constructs of Data Governance and Data Management

With the growing emphasis on governance in organisations, the application of "good governance" has become crucial to organisational competitiveness [23]. DG specifies a framework that encourages constructive behaviour in data use and management through the specification of accountabilities and decision rights regarding the data [12]. This step in the SLR aimed to answer this study's first research question:

RQ 1: What are the constructs of data governance and data management?

3.1 Findings: Constructs of Data Governance and Data Management

Governance within an organisation comprises the internal processes and policies that enable human capital performance, legal and regulatory compliance, and organisational alignment [24]. Principle 12 of the King IV Report specifies that "[the] governing body should govern technology and information in a way that supports the organization setting and achieving its strategic objectives" [25, p. 62]. DG should, therefore, be seen as a subfunction of corporate governance.

There is no "one-size-fits-all" prescription for how an organisation should implement and optimise the governance and management of data [12]. However, for organisations to remain competitive, and compliant with regulatory requirements, business-critical data must be readily available, accurate and integrated. Most documented research places DG within the context of information technology governance [11]. DG derives concepts from organisational theory and information technology (IT) governance theory. IT governance researchers highlight the importance of aligning IT governance with the strategic and operational business goals of the organisation

[12, 26]. Data quality is highlighted in published research as one of the main components of DG [6, 11, 27, 28].

DG is a socio-technical function that involves all the processes used in the planning, specification, designing, enabling, creation, acquisition, maintenance, use, archiving, securing, retrieval, control and purging of an organisation's data assets [10]. DAMA International (2014) has identified and defined 10 DG knowledge areas: data architecture, data modelling and design, data storage and operations, data security, data integration and interoperability, documents and content, reference and master data, data warehousing and business intelligence (BI), metadata, and data quality.

Governance can be viewed as a socio-technical activity that involves people in a context where technology plays a key role [29]. DG is central to DM, and controls, plans and monitors all DM activities [10, 30]. DG refers to the specific roles of accountability and decision rights pertaining to data assets [11]. By adhering to regulatory compliance requirements, such as those set out by the Basel Committee on Banking Supervision (BCBS 239), organisations can improve their DG practices and develop a data-oriented culture which, in turn, will lead to better governance [5]. DG and DM can therefore be considered interdependent functions of an integrated domain involving people, processes, technologies and interactions at individual, team and organisational levels that span the entire organisation.

4 Agility in Data Governance and Data Management

Existing models for DG and DM do not appear to address the agility requirement that business has of DG and DM. Searches were conducted for academic research on agile capabilities. The relevance of these capabilities for the governance and management of data was considered in order to address this study's second research question:

RQ 2: What capabilities are needed in DG and DM for the agile delivery of data requirements to business?

4.1 Data Governance and Data Management as a Complex Adaptive System

Before exploring the factors that influence agility in DG and DM, the relevance of agility in the governance and management of data should be considered. Complex adaptive systems (CAS) are co-evolving systems that continuously tune themselves towards a point of maximum fitness, producing stability and becoming sustainable [31]. Agents are the semi-autonomous units that form the basic elements of a CAS. Agents evolve over time by continuously seeking to maximise their capability in order to sustain their existence within a changing environment [32]. According to Dooley's nominal definition of a CAS, agents develop mental templates, or schemas, whereby they can define how to interpret reality, and respond appropriately to given stimuli [32]. The phenomena associated with agile governance are positioned in the intersection between chaos and order, where innovation and agile practices emerge and interface with governance best practices [29].

Teams are CASs comprising people as the active agents, and are in themselves agents at a higher composite level, that continuously evolve through self-organisation [33]. DG and DM teams comprise project teams, committees and other collaborative networks of people who are continuously organising and reorganising in an attempt to align with business requirements for data delivery [19, 34]. CAS models provide a way of simplifying complexity, and are characterised by four key elements: agents applying schemata, networks of self-organisation, emergence from the chaordic state (co-evolution at the edge of chaos), and system evolution through recombination [35]. When CAS models are applied to strategic management, an approach unfolds that focuses on building systems that can swiftly evolve effective adaptive solutions [35].

4.2 Findings: Agile Capabilities

The more turbulent the information management environment becomes, the higher the level of agile capabilities required [36]. Agile capabilities, in combination with governance capabilities, enable better management and control of the effects of environmental and moderator factors [1]. Seven agile capabilities which typically coexist with agility, were identified from the literature and are summarised in Table 1.

Table 1. A summary of the seven agile capabilities identified in the literature.

	Agile capability	Description of agile capability
1	Competence	The competency of individuals and teams, which includes their knowledge, skill, expertise and understanding, is a critical factor in successfully accomplishing assignments in an agile manner [37]. An agile team continuously develops its inherent capability, thus its competency, to deal with change [1]. Incorporating a diversity of knowledge, experience and skills in a team improves the team's ability to cope with turbulence and complexity [36]
2	Flexibility	Flexibility, as a capability, is required in governance for agile value delivery to business [29]. Risk data aggregation capabilities require flexibility [5]
3	Leanness	Leanness refers to limiting wastage of resources and striving for simplicity [29], and contributes to overall organizational agility [38]. Smart management, combined with new technology, may enable fewer people to achieve more [39]
4	Reusability	Reusability ensures sustained efficiency, productivity and value for the business [1]. Reuse has a strong influence on speed through repeatability [40]
5	Scalability	Scalability enables the operational environment to quickly add or remove resources without impacting availability or functionality [41]. Scalability in DG and DM plans and provides for future growth, and enables the organisation to quickly scale up to accommodate and service emerging business requirements because the predicted growth is catered for [41]

(*continued*)

Table 1. (*continued*)

	Agile capability	Description of agile capability
6	Speed	The speed offered by agile practices is required for quick delivery [40]. Speed refers to how quickly and effectively raw data can be made available to the business as usable information [42]
7	Responsiveness	The ability to sense, adapt and respond to change is required in governance, for agile value delivery to business [29]. Risk data aggregation capabilities require adaptability, in order to meet risk data aggregation requirements as and when they arise [5]

5 The Need for Agile Data Governance and Data Management in African Organisations

Research conducted by Mann [43] concludes that as digital economies emerge in developing countries, data is becoming increasingly important as a source of power in economic governance. Data for development (D4D) should move away from having a purely humanitarian focus toward a stronger consideration for economic development, whereby African citizens may have opportunities to benefit from their data for power, revenue and knowledge development [43].

DG processes are becoming increasingly complex [5, 6], but, at the same time, DG is of growing importance to organisations worldwide [5, 8, 44, 45]. DG spans the whole enterprise, and should align with business goals [6]. Recent research has found that organisations are having trouble with deriving value from their data initiatives [46]. Access to reliable data is needed for risk management and fulfilling regulatory, compliance and legal requirements, which are of paramount importance to organisations [47]. The proposed need for agility in the governance and management of data was investigated, to answer to this study's third research question:

RQ 3: What is the need for African organisations to establish agile capabilities in data governance and data management?

5.1 Decision-Making

In a competitive world, the business that is ahead of its competition in obtaining the correct data, and is first in gaining insights from high-quality data through analytics, is most likely to sustain its competitive position [7, 8, p. 6]. Businesses require accurate, reliable data to support effective decision-making based on data analysis rather than on intuition [8]. According to Pawelke et al. [48], access to technology and the internet is vital for people living in the remote areas of developing countries, in order for them to benefit from utilising data for improved accountability, transparency, decision-making and public service delivery.

Where there is a lack of trustworthy information, risks and costs increase, and business change and growth are hampered by misguided managerial decisions [49]. The significance of data in decision-making is stressed by Van Schalkwyk et al. [50, p. 6]: "South African university councils need accurate and informative data on the state of their institutions in order to shift the debate from one that is driven by ideology and self-interest to one that is empirically based and in the interest of the performance of the institution". If the data is not reliable, managers revert to using intuition for decision-making and strategy implementation [44]. Accurate data, available at the exact moment that a business needs it, is required for effective, timeous decision-making [28]. A DG capability forms an essential part of data-driven decision-making capability [8].

5.2 Risk Management

When clarifying the role of data as an asset, the regulatory environment's influence on how the business uses data, must be considered [11]. Organisations are at higher risk, given the increased number of regulatory compliance requirements that enforce deadlines for timeous adherence. In most developing countries, frameworks for the protection of personal data are inadequately implemented and governed [48]. The Protection of Personal Information (POPI) Act, which was signed into South African law on 19 November 2013, holds organisations and their employees accountable and responsible for all the personal information that they collect, store, disseminate and destroy during the course of conducting their business. Non-compliance with the POPI Act holds significant criminal and reputational risks for businesses [51].

The Sarbanes-Oxley Act (SOX) was instituted in 2002, and requires Chief Executive Officers (CEOs) and Chief Financial Officers (CFOs) to certify corporate financial reports [13]. In January 2013, the Basel Committee on Banking Supervision (BCBS) published Principles for Effective Risk Data Aggregation and Risk Reporting (BCBS 239). Contained therein are the 14 principles which aim to strengthen the internal risk-reporting and risk-data aggregation capabilities of global, systematically important banks (G-SIB), which includes banks in Africa. The BCBS 239 requires banks to implement robust frameworks for DG [4]. The expected effects from banks that are implementing these principles include enhanced decision-making processes and risk management resulting in an increased ability to cope with crisis and stress situations [5]. Integration and automation of governance, risk and compliance (GRC) are becoming essential, and DG plays a vital part in data aggregation and risk reporting for GRC [47]. Chakravorty [5] explains that banks commonly use two types of reporting for regulatory and compliance requirements. The first type of reporting is run on financial transactional and administration systems. These reports are generally inflexible and inconsistent as a result of manual adjustments being made on the systems. The second type is ad hoc reporting, which usually involves manual, once-off data extracts from source systems, with aggregation performed on the data in spreadsheets. These reporting methods are unreliable, as the "correctness" of the data is often based on the user's opinion [5].

5.3 Data Quality: Operational Efficiency, Integration and Interoperability

Recent research indicates that the management of data quality and its value proposition to business, is posing an increasingly complex challenge to business enterprises [9]. In a study conducted in Ghana, it was found that only 53% of organisations had implemented any form of data quality management [52]. As pointed out by Azumah and Quarshie [52], a data quality initiative can only be successful if it is supported by the organisation's executive management. Improving and maintaining the quality of an organisation's data is viewed as crucial in achieving strategic business goals [6]. DG should promote increased operational efficiency, improve customer satisfaction and support business integration [6]. Missing or incorrect operational data can cause major problems for an organisation. It can prevent sales, upset customers, and cause businesses to lose track of assets [9].

Best data practices focus on preventing data errors at the source by considering both the quality and the accurate business meaning of the data. An organisation can be impacted by bad data quality at both the operational and strategic levels [11]. Redman [28] proposes that the solution to fixing bad data comes in the form of better collaboration between data creators and data users.

Data quality considers four characteristics of data: *accuracy* refers to the data's correctness and its congruence in terms of stored value, actual value and intended use; *timeliness* refers to the right data being available at the right time; *completeness* refers to the required data value being stored to the required breadth and depth; and, *credibility* refers to the trustworthiness of the data source and its data [11]. Even though the specific culture and structure of an organisation need to be considered when designing DG, and the focus of DG might vary from organisation to organization [27, 34], data quality seems to be a requirement common to all organisations [9, 53].

Implementing a data standards layer is important, as it enables automation of data take-on, data quality and data integration processes [42]. Wixom advises that if standardization of data sources is not feasible, a master data management initiative should be considered. Master data management (MDM) refers to a process that is (a) application independent, (b) owns, describes and manages the significant business data entities, and (c) ensures the veracity and consistency of data by using a single set of guidelines. This provides a uniform view of key organisational data, regardless of its storage location [54].

Companies should identify and continuously improve the quality of the data that drives the organisation's profits [28]. Data errors will cause a business to question the reliability and usefulness of the data [52]. However, instead of directing the responsibility for data quality back to the data source for correction, the tendency is for a business to spend time, often repetitively, checking and correcting the data. This creates inefficiencies in business processes, and incorrect data puts a business at perpetual risk of bad decision-making [44].

6 Summary of Findings

The main academic research and practitioner frameworks that underpin this study, are summarised in Table 2.

Table 2. Summary of main theories and frameworks for constructs and agile capabilities

Author	Study or framework name	Contribution to this study
[35]	Complexity theory and organisation science	Considers organisations and teams as CASs
[19]	Data Infrastructures for Asset Management Viewed as Complex Adaptive Systems	Provides research-based evidence that DG and DM could be considered CASs
[37]	Agile software development, the people factor	Emphasises the importance of competence as an agile capability
[10]	DAMA-DMBOK2 Framework	Provides a framework for the definition and function of each of the DM disciplines, including DG
[47]	Governance, risk and compliance (GRC): Conceptual muddle and technological tangle	Highlights the importance of governance, risk management and compliance in organisations
[25]	King IV: Report on Corporate Governance for South Africa, 2016	Provides the locus of and requirement for information governance, including DG, within corporate governance
[8]	The Conceptualization of Data-driven Decision Making Capability	Emphasises the importance of DG and DM for effective decision-making in the organisation
[11]	Designing Data Governance	Provides a framework for understanding the roles and decision rights in the DG domain
[30]	Data Governance: How to design, deploy, and sustain an effective data governance program	Provides definitions, goals and implementation strategy for DG and DM
[1]	Agile Governance Theory: conceptual development	Provides a theory for governance that is based on agile values and principles
[40]	Enablers and inhibitors for speed with reuse	Provides a set of constructs for investigating factors that influence agility (speed and reuse) within manageable areas of the organisation
[9]	Quality and Value of the Data Resource in Large Enterprises	Emphasises the important role of data quality in deriving value from an organisation's data assets
[41]	Scalable SQL	Emphasises the importance of scalability as an agile capability
[34]	Non-invasive Data Governance	Describes an approach to implementing DG that utilises existing organisational structures and roles

7 Discussion

It is apparent, from the available literature, that there is a clear need for DG in organisations to promote effective decision-making [8], risk management [5, 13] and increased operational efficiency and integration [6, 34]. Agile governance is a socio-technical phenomenon, which merges current best practices for governance with innovation and rising practices from agile and lean philosophy [1].

Existing academic and practitioner literature indicates that organisations currently do not have clearly defined and effective methods to establish and maintain agility in their DG and DM functions [2]. Furthermore, it is evident that there is a need for researchers to contribute to the limited body of knowledge relating to the field of DG and DM governance [17, 18].

Research conducted by Otto [6] recognises the need to consider the organisational goals in conjunction with the organisational structure when designing and shaping DG and DM. The substructures within an organisation must serve the organisation's current goals with an increased organisational emphasis on adaptability and participation [39]. Fruehauf et al. [27] conclude that it is vital to gain an in-depth understanding of an organisation, and how its people collaborate with one another in the use of its data when designing an effective DG framework. Challenges are presented to the DG organisation in the form of data silos, politics and data ownership battles where data decisions affect multiple operational business units [34].

There are some variations in the literature concerning what constitutes the exact scope and locus of DG [6, 10, 11], and there is no single, prescribed approach for implementing DG and DM [12]. However, there seems to be consensus that data quality is a common concern and requirement in the realm of DG [7, 9, 24, 27, 34, 44]. The organisation of DG should have representation and involvement at all levels of the business that have an interest in the data being governed [6, 34].

Research conducted in the IT, legal and business fields, respectively, highlights the importance of effective, thorough information and DG [5, 47, 51]. DG must be closely aligned with IT governance in its structure, processes, relationships with IT and business, as well as its goals for creating value for business [11, 45]. Sound DG enables sourcing of good quality data for analytics purposes [8, 28]. The importance of developing and maintaining data standards is also emphasised [42, 44]. DG must support an organisation's decision-making processes [7, 8, 24].

The realm of DG and DM can be viewed as a CAS [19], where agents are the individuals and teams that perform the roles of DG and DM. Agents continuously seek to maximise their capability to sustain their existence within a changing environment [32]. Agile capabilities in organisations lead to higher levels of organisational performance [1, 15, 26, 55]. Agility is viewed as a key element of competitiveness, which better enables the organisation to survive in volatile market conditions [26]. Agile governance capabilities have been hypothesised to increase value delivery to business, resulting in the overall improved performance of the organisation [1]. As shown in Table 1, seven agile capabilities were identified, from the documented research, as aspects that typically coexist with agility. The findings of this study were synthesised, and are presented in Fig. 1.

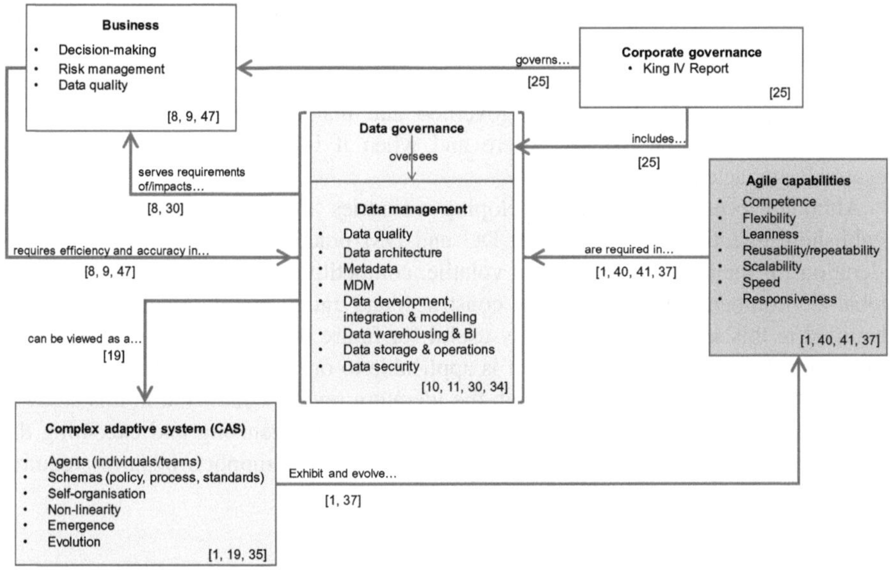

Fig. 1. A preliminary framework for the constructs and agile capabilities of data governance and data management.

8 Conclusion

This research proposed that agility is required in the organisation and execution of DG and DM, in order to deliver value to business and support business agility [15, 26, 29, 36]. The study of DG across entire organisations is of recent interest to researchers [56]. It is worthwhile researching the optimisation of efficiencies in DG and DM, as agility is required at all levels of the DG and DM functions in order to fulfil the business requirements for timeous, useful data for both operational and strategic reasons.

There is currently a limited amount of research available that looks specifically at the phenomenon of agility in the organisation and execution of DG and DM. The agents and schemas of DG and DM operate within a CAS [19]. The non-linear relationships and interactions among the agents and teams of agents within the DG and DM domains, create the chaos within the CAS. Data must survive this chaos to retain its value. The data itself creates complexity, as it passes through many processes, business rules, applications, manual and automated processes, and integration points, which are internal or external to the organisation. The emergence of agile capabilities and innovation occurs at the edge of order and chaos [29, 35].

A limitation of the SLR conducted for this study exists in the possibility that not all the relevant literature was located, and that the types of studies, as well as the methods used in the studies, were not specifically considered [57]. Furthermore, the identified agile capabilities were not empirically tested within the context of DG and DM. Similar research might benefit from a wider investigation of widely-used practitioner frameworks. The focus of research in the domains of technology and business seems to have largely been on agile software development and organisational agility. Data is, however, fundamental to all aspects of organisational activities, from strategy to regulatory compliance. If data is not governed and managed in a way that delivers trustworthy information exactly where and when it is needed, business agility is negatively impacted.

Although organisations in developing countries currently face challenges in establishing effective and responsive DG and DM practices, it is an important consideration for their sustainability in a volatile, competitive, and increasingly regulated global environment [20, 21, 52]. The constructs and agile capabilities of DG and DM identified in this study, are potentially useful for future research looking to develop a framework for agile DG and DM that is applicable to organisations in both developed and developing countries. Even though the literature review conducted in this study is not exhaustive, it served to highlight the importance of organising and executing the governance and management of data in an agile way that supports business requirements and organisational agility.

References

1. Luna, A.J.H.d.O., Kruchten, P., de Moura, H.P.: Agile Governance Theory: conceptual development. In: Conference Proceedings of 12th International Conference on Management of Technology and Information Systems. FEA-USP, São Paulo (2015)
2. DalleMule, L., Davenport, T.H.: What's your data strategy? Harvard Bus. Rev. **95**(3), 112–121 (2017)
3. Ofner, M.H., Huener, K.M., Otto, B.: Dealing with complexity: a method to adapt and implement a maturity model for corporate data quality management. In: AMCIS 2009 Proceedings. AISeL (2009)
4. Bank for International Settlements: Basel Committee on Banking Supervision: Principles for Effective Risk Data Aggregation and Risk Reporting (2013). https://www.bis.org/publ/bcbs239.pdf. Accessed 26 Apr 2018
5. Chakravorty, R.: BCBS239: reasons, impacts, framework and route to compliance. J. Secur. Oper. Custody **8**(1), 65–81 (2015)
6. Otto, B.: A morphology of the organisation of data governance. In: ECIS 2011 Proceedings. AISeL (2011)
7. Davenport, T.H., Harris, J.G., Morrison, R.: Analytics at Work: Smarter Decisions Better Results. Harvard Business School, Massachusetts (2010)
8. Jia, L., Hall, D., Song, J.: The conceptualization of data-driven decision making capability. In: Proceedings of Twenty-first Americas Conference on Information Systems. AISeL (2015)
9. Otto, B.: Quality and value of the data resource in large enterprises. Inf. Syst. Manag. **32**(3), 234–251 (2015)
10. DAMA International: DAMA-DMBOK2 Framework (2014). https://www.dama.org. Accessed 26 Apr 2016
11. Khatri, V., Brown, C.V.: Designing data governance. Commun. ACM **53**(1), 148–152 (2010)
12. Weber, K., Otto, B., Österle, H.: One size does not fit all - a contingency approach to data governance. ACM J. Data Inf. Qual. **1**(1), 1–26 (2009)

13. Weill, P., Ross, J.W.: IT Governance: How Top Performers Manage IT Decision Rights for Superior Results. Harvard Business School Press, Boston (2004)
14. Salido, J.: Data governance for privacy, confidentiality and compliance: a holistic approach. ISACA J. **6**, 1–7 (2010)
15. Appelbaum, S.H., Calla, R., Desautels, D., Hasan, L.: The challenges of organizational agility (part 1). Ind. Commer. Train. **49**(1), 6–14 (2017)
16. Al-Ruithe, M., Benkhelifa, E., Hameed, K.: A systematic literature review of data governance and cloud data governance. Pers. Ubiquitous Comput. 1–21 (2018)
17. Kamioka, T., Luo, X., Tapanainen, T.: An empirical investigation of data governance: the role of accountabilities. In: PACIS 2016 Proceedings. AISeL (2016)
18. Nielsen, O.B.: A comprehensive review of data governance literature. In: Selected Papers of the IRIS, vol. 8, pp. 120–133 (2017)
19. Brous, P., Overtoom, I., Herder, P., Versluis, A., Janssen, M.: Data infrastructures for asset management viewed as complex adaptive systems. Procedia Comput. Sci. **36**, 124–130 (2014)
20. Al Qassimi, N., Rusu, L.: IT governance in a public organization in a developing country: a case study of a governmental organization. Procedia Comput. Sci. **64**, 450–456 (2015)
21. Were, V., Moturi, C.: Toward a data governance model for the Kenya health professional regulatory authorities. TQM J. **29**(4), 579–589 (2017)
22. Templier, M., Paré, G.: A framework for guiding and evaluating literature reviews. Commun. Assoc. Inform. Syst. **37**, 112–137 (2015)
23. UNESCAP: United Nations Economic and Social Commission for Asia and the Pacific (2009). http://www.unescap.org/resources/what-good-governance. Accessed 5 May 2016
24. Avery, A.A., Cheek, K.: Analytics governance: towards a definition and framework. In: Proceedings of Twenty-first Americas Conference on Information Systems, Puerto Rico. AISeL (2015)
25. Institute of Directors in Southern Africa: King IV: Report on Corporate Governance for South Africa 2016, Institute of Directors Southern Africa (2016)
26. Tallon, P.P., Pinsonneault, A.: Competing perspectives on the link between strategic information technology alignment and organizational agility: insights from a mediation model. MIS Q. **35**(2), 463–486 (2011)
27. Fruehauf, J., Al-Khalifa, F., Coniker, J.: Using the Bolman and Deal's four frames in developing a data governance strategy. Issues Inform. Syst. **16**(2), 161–167 (2015)
28. Redman, T.C.: Data Driven, 1st edn. Harvard Business School Publishing, Boston (2008)
29. Luna, A.J.H.d.O., Kruchten, P., do E. Pedrosa, M.L., de Almeida Neto, H.R., de Moura, H. P.: State of the art of agile governance: a systematic review. J. Comput. Sci. Inform. Technol. (IJCSIT) **6**(5), 121–141 (2014)
30. Ladley, J.: Data Governance: How to Design, Deploy, And Sustain An Effective Data Governance Program. Morgan Kaufmann, Waltham (2012)
31. Lewin, R.: Complexity: Life at the Edge of Chaos, 2nd edn. University of Chicago Press, London (2000)
32. Dooley, K.: Complex adaptive systems: a nominal definition. Chaos Netw. **8**(1), 2–3 (1996)
33. Myburgh, B.A.: Complex adaptive responses of organizational teams. Int. J. Comput. Sci. **4**(1), 23–39 (2015)
34. Seiner, R.S.: Non-invasive Data Governance, 1st edn. Technics Publications LLC, New Jersey (2014)
35. Anderson, P.: Complexity theory and organization science. Organ. Sci. **10**(3), 216–232 (1999)

36. Rick, U., Vossen, R., Richert, A., Henning, K.: Designing agile processes in information management. In: Proceedings of the 2nd IEEE International Conference on Information Management and Engineering. IEEE (2010)
37. Cockburn, A., Highsmith, J.: Agile software development, the people factor. Computer **34**(11), 131–133 (2001)
38. Wageeh, N.A.: Organizational agility: the key to organizational success. Int. J. Bus. Manag. **11**(5), 296–309 (2016)
39. Bolman, L.G., Deal, T.E.: Reframing Organizations: Artistry, Choice, and Leadership, 4th edn. Jossey-Bass, San Francisco (2008)
40. Martini, A., Bosch, J., Pareto, L.: Enablers and inhibitors for speed with reuse. In: Proceedings of the 16th International Software Product Line Conference, pp, 116–125. ACM (2012)
41. Rys, M.: Scalable SQL. Commun. ACM **54**(6), 48–53 (2011)
42. Wixom, B.H., Yen, B., Relich, M.: Maximizing value from business analytics. MIS Q. Exec. **12**(2), 111–123 (2013)
43. Mann, L.: Left to other peoples' devices? A political economy perspective on the big data revolution in development. Dev. Change **49**(1), 3–36 (2017)
44. Redman, T.C.: Data's Credibility Problem (2013). https://hbr.org/2013/12/datas-credibility-problem. Accessed 9 Apr 2016
45. Tallon, P.P., Ramirez, R.V., Short, J.E.: The information artifact in IT governance: toward a theory of information governance. J. Manag. Inf. Syst. **30**(3), 141–178 (2013)
46. Nagle, T., Sammon, D.: The data value map: a framework for developing shared understanding on data initiatives. In: Proceedings of the 25th European Conference on Information Systems (ECIS). AISeL (2017)
47. Hardy, C., Leonard, J.: Governance, risk and compliance (GRC): conceptual muddle and technological tangle. In: ACIS Proceedings, Association for Information Systems. AISeL (2011)
48. Pawelke, A., Cañares, M., Hernandez, K., Martin, P.P.: Data for Development: What's Next?. Deutsche Gesellschaft für Internationale Zusammenarbeit (GIZ) GmbH, Bonn and Eschborn (2017)
49. Korhonen, J., Melleri, I., Hiekkanen, K., Helenius, M.: Designing data governance structure: an organizational perspective. GSTF J. Comput. (JoC) **2**(4), 11–17 (2013)
50. Van Schalkwyk, F., Wilmers, M., Czerniewicz, L.: Open Data in the Governance of South African Higher Education. OpenUCT, Cape Town (2014)
51. SAICA: The South African Institute of Chartered Accountants (2016). https://www.saica.co.za/Technical/LegalandGovernance/Legislation/ProtectionofPersonalInformationAct/tabid/3335/language/en-ZA/Default.aspx. Accessed 3 May 2016
52. Azumah, K.K., Quarshie, H.O.: Towards higher quality data: impact of perception of data quality on IT investment – ghana. J. Emerg. Trends Comput. Inform. Sci. **3**(12), 1614–1621 (2012)
53. el Abed, W., Brillant, P., Njonko, F.: Governance of organizational data and information. In: Topi, H., Tucker, A. (eds.) Computing Handbook Third Edition: Information Systems and Information Technology, pp. 1–30. CRC Press, Boca Raton (2014)
54. Smith, H.A., McKeen, J.D.: Developments in practice XXX: master data management: salvation or snake oil? Commun. Assoc. Inform. Syst. **23**(4), 63–72 (2008)
55. Beck, K., et al.: Manifesto for Agile Software Development (2001). http://agilemanifesto.org/. Accessed 26 Feb 2018
56. Otto, B.: Organizing Data Governance: findings from the telecommunications industry and consequences for large service providers. Commun. Assoc. Inform. Syst. **29**(1), 45–66 (2011)
57. Armitage, A., Keeble-Allen, D.: Undertaking a structured literature review or structuring a literature review: tales from the field. Electron. J. Bus. Res. Methods **6**(2), 103–114 (2008)

Author Index

MIX
Papier aus verantwortungsvollen Quellen
Paper from responsible sources
FSC® C105338

If you have any concerns about our products,
you can contact us on
ProductSafety@springernature.com

In case Publisher is established outside the EU,
the EU authorized representative is:
Springer Nature Customer Service Center GmbH
Europaplatz 3, 69115 Heidelberg, Germany

Printed by Libri Plureos GmbH
in Hamburg, Germany